KHAKI-COLLAR CRIME

KHAKI–COLLAR CRIME

Deviant Behavior in the Military Context

Clifton D. Bryant

THE FREE PRESS
A Division of Macmillan Publishing Co., Inc.
NEW YORK

Collier Macmillan Publishers
LONDON

The Free Press
A Division of Macmillan Publishing Co., Inc.
866 Third Avenue, New York, N.Y. 10022

Collier Macmillan Canada, Ltd.

Library of Congress Catalog Card Number: 79-7105

Printed in the United States of America

printing number

1   2   3   4   5   6   7   8   9   10

Library of Congress Cataloging in Publication Data

Bryant, Clifton D.
    Khaki-collar crime.

    Bibliography: p.
    Includes index.
    1. Military offenses.   2. Crime and criminals.
I. Title.
UB780.B79   355.1′33   79-7105
ISBN 0-02-904930-X

Quotations from *The Face of Battle* by John Keegan reprinted by permission of Viking Penguin, Inc. and Julian Bach Literary Agency. Copyright © 1976 by John Keegan.

This volume is affectionately dedicated to my maternal uncles, the late Robert L. Dow and P. Wilson Dow of Jackson, Mississippi, who respectively served in the army and navy in World War II. In sharing their own observations and interpretations of military life with me—almost thirty-five years ago—they gave me the original idea for *Khaki-Collar Crime*.

Contents

Preface

Deviant and criminal behavior is not necessarily "different" or abnormal behavior. For too long social scientists tended to view such behavior as somehow being apart from, or alien to, the mainstream of social life, and thus, a kind of antithesis to more conventional conforming behavior. Deviant behavior does not occur within a social vacuum, however. Rather, it is more appropriately viewed alongside the various institutional normative contexts which it violates. Thus, many configurations of deviant behavior are endemic to, and accordingly, characteristic of, certain major social institutions. What may seem to be normal conforming behavior in one interpretive institutional context may well be labeled as deviant or criminal in another. Deviancy and criminality are, in effect, situational, and, more precisely, institutionally situational.

At one time criminal behavior was thought of essentially as a vocational pursuit, with the pickpocket or burglar simply as an individual with a proclivity for illegal career opportunities. The concept of "white collar" crime, however, sensitized us to the existence of criminal behavioral configurations which were constituent to a larger pattern of middle and upper-class occupational activities which often had a facade of legality, and which were, in effect, not infrequently considered as normative and thus prescribed within the interpretive context of the particular occupational system or work setting. Subsequently, the introduction of additional concepts of occupational deviancy such as "blue-collar," and "blue-coat" crime extended our vistas of insight into other hitherto furtive and obscured modes of occupational deviancy. Additionally, the Watergate scandal afforded even newer and more penetrating perspectives of crime and deviancy, routinized to the point of near normalcy, and conceptualized as appropriate and, which were constituent to yet another institutional system.

Persistent patterns of deviant behavior in the form of varied, clandestine and often elaborate illegal practices are frequently found within the social organization of many legal occupational (and other forms of institutional) pursuits. Because of a unique opportunity structure and work-related subculture, these illegal activities are often endemic or distinctive to a specific occupational specialty and are therefore characteristic of a given work system. The relationship between work (or some other form of institutional activity) is not always immediately apparent because the deviant behavioral configurations are frequently buried beneath the surface of occupational structure.

Many such unique institutionalized forms of normative deviancy exist, as yet, relatively unrecognized, ignored, or neglected, and thus undocumented, by social scientists. Perhaps, among the more neglected of unique patterns of occupational, or other institutionalized, crime and deviancy are those unique patterns of occupational crime and deviancy that are characteristic of, and endemic and constituent to, the military institution—"khaki-collar," as it were. The military entity is a large and complex social system with its own elaborate normative system of social control.

Military justice, as a separate system of social control, additional to that of the larger society is dictated by the particular characteristics of the military population, the nature of the military mission and attendant operations, and the unique logistical requirements of the military as a work system. Violation of military norms constitutes deviant behavior, and such crimes may be subject to severe official sanctions. Thus "fragging" an officer, looting, malingering, going to sleep on duty, insubordination, mistreating prisoners of war, or failing to clean one's weapon, to name but a few among the myriad military offenses, may all constitute varieties of "khaki-collar crime."

Given the magnitude of military crime, and it's not infrequent prominence (especially during the Vietnamese War), it is surprising that it has been largely neglected by sociologists and criminologists, and no effort at systematic review has been attempted.

This volume attempts to develop the thesis that the violation of military norms represents a unique form of criminal behavior. It further will present a conceptual framework for viewing military crime and deviancy, and articulates and develops the various elements of this conceptual framework. The book is concerned primarily with the U. S. military, but takes the position that military crime is characteristic of, and often similar to, the military establishment of any nation or political entity. Thus, the book really addresses the generic concept of "the military," anywhere at any time in history. Our illustrations are, accordingly, drawn from many militaries, many wars, and many periods of history. The discussion is essentially socio-historical, and draws heavily on various biographical and historical accounts of war and the military for documentation. It is also based on other materials and observations made by the author while a military police officer in the U.S. Army, and interviews and notes collected in the interim period.

The genesis of this exposition lies in the "war stories," and tales of life and larceny in the military, which I heard as a youngster during World War II. Many personal accounts of the war, anecdotes, reminiscences, and other military chronicles from friends, relatives, and strangers, provided the germ of an idea which was fueled by the more detailed narratives of military history books, the ersatz reality of the innumerable "war movies" of recent decades, and the humorous and exaggerated, but essentially valid insights afforded by the numerous television series concerning military freebooting such as McHale's Navy, The Sergeant Bilko Show, M*A*S*H, Hogan's Heroes, Baa Baa Black Sheep, and others of this genre. This discussion is only a beginning. There is much to be explored about, and much to be learned from, military crime and deviancy. I hope my paradigm of "khaki-collar crime" will provide a useful and productive framework for the further examination of the parameters of, and the interpretive and precipitating dimensions of, deviant behavior in military context.

Many individuals are to be thanked for their assistance and advice in completing this book. My graduate assistants, Susan Twaddle, Kathy Shiflet, and Debbie Brooks, were invaluable in doing library work and checking out bibliographic sources for me. Dan Dotter and Jane Turner are to be particularly thanked for their excellent indexing efforts for this volume. I am indebted to my colleagues here at VPI&SU, Louis Zurcher, Donald Shoemaker, James Skipper, Charles J. Dudley, and William McWhorter for their helpful reactions and comments on various chapter drafts as the manuscripts developed. A number of my secretaries, Anita Vaughan, Christina Hochstein, Loretta Turpin, Jean Perdue, Cynthia Crawford, Elaine Craig, Diana Muron, and Pat Baker, were involved in typing parts of the book, and their excellent clerical assistance in preparing the manuscript for publication is greatly appreciated.

PART ONE

Military Crime and Punishment

The necessity of Government, Order, and Discipline in an Army is that only which can give these laws a Countenance.
Lord Chief Justice Sir Matthew Hale

CHAPTER ONE

Crime, Deviancy, and Social Control in the Military

Control is unquestionably the most characteristic element of military life. Perhaps no other area of social living is so charged with effective means of social control and regulation. Historians suggest that necessity has been the major factor for the development of military discipline. . . .
Edward C. McDonagh

Sociologists have long demonstrated interest in deviant behavior, examining it in a wide variety of interpretive contexts and institutional settings. In recent years they have shown particular attention to work-related deviancy and crime constituent to various occupational and work systems. Curiously, however, they have largely tended to ignore the unique configurations of crime and deviancy associated with one of the largest work systems in the world, the United States military establishment (or the military establishment of any nation). The U.S. military is an occupational and social system embracing upwards of three and one-half million men and women in the various armed services (and, to some degree, their families as well). The military in this country, and in others, represents formidable populations with the attendant need for appropriate mechanisms of social control. This book articulates a paradigm of crime and deviancy, and the accompanying mechanisms of control and sanction, in a military context, and attempts to document and demonstrate the various components of the typology.

OCCUPATIONAL CRIME AND DEVIANCY

The topic of work and deviant behavior was an early, albeit relatively peripheral, object of sociological interest. The pioneering researchers of the "Chicago School," for example, examined a wide variety of occupational activities that were concomitantly criminal in nature, such as jack-rolling and "professional" thievery, as well as practioners of other deviant pursuits, such as taxi dancers and hobos. In subsequent years the Mayo studies, and later various researchers such as Orvis Collins (1946), Don Roy (1952, 1953, 1954, 1959), Melville Dalton (1948), and Joseph Bensman and Israel Gerver (1963), pointed out the existence of worker-established informal normative systems and the eventuality of individual violation of such norms.

It awaited Edwin H. Sutherland and his sociological concern with "white-collar crime," however, to identify and label a specific pattern of crime characteristic of a given occupational category. In 1939 Sutherland, in the course of an address to the American Sociological Society, defined "white-collar crime" as "crime committed by a person of respectability and high social status in the course of his occupation" (Sutherland 1940). In effect, he suggested the concept of white-collar crime to describe structural criminality in white-collar and commercial work systems. Although Sutherland viewed white-collar crime as usually involving a violation of trust, in recent years the term has been used in a somewhat more general sense to refer to a wide range of illegal activities committed by white-collar persons. Interest in the topic has not abated since Sutherland's initial remarks, and a considerable literature has developed on the subject (Aubert 1952; Hartung 1950; Geis 1962; Quinney 1963; see especially Tompkins 1967; Geis 1968). At the same time, white-collar crime itself has perhaps attained new heights (or depths) of sophistication.[1]

Perhaps as a result of the interest in white-collar crime,

---

[1] Industrial espionage is a highly developed, elaborate, and extensive form of white-collar criminal activity today. A short time back it was reported that a blind man had "broken" a computer code and was stealing from a firm with the aid of its computer by imitating a whistle instruction signal to the computer over the telephone. There have been cases of computer theft that reached $2 billion. Estimates of year-to-year losses from computer theft range from $100 million to $300 million. (For a detailed treatment of computer theft and computer security see National Science Foundation 1978:2–10).

sociologists have more recently identified other forms of occupationally related crime such as "blue-collar crime" (Stoddard 1968; see also Westley 1953; Petersen 1971) and "blue-collar crime" (Horning 1970), referring to illegal activities perpetrated by policemen and nonsalaried industrial operatives, respectively. Such interest centers on the thesis that some occupational social systems and their attendant subcultures provide unique opportunity structures as well as value configurations and norms that permit and promote the commission of specific criminal or other deviant acts.

The contemporary resurgence of ethnomethodological urban studies (reminiscent of the earlier Chicago studies) has focused attention on a number of deviant and sometimes illegal occupational enterprises such as stripping, topless waitresses, faith healers, exploitive carnival concessionaires, and proprietors of underground movie houses and massage parlors. The mass media today have tended to make us more aware of consumer frauds by commercial enterprises, the invasion of legitimate businesses by criminal elements, and the almost endemic nature of political corruption. Similarly, in recent years, as our attention has been focused on social problems involving human addictive behavior, the fact has not escaped us that alcoholism and narcotic usage tend to be more prevalent in some occupational settings than in others.

Deviancy does not occur in a social vacuum; it takes place as part of the ongoing processes attendant to our major social institutions and their behavioral configurations. Such a central institution is that of work. Deviant behavior appears to be related to occupational specialty and concomitant work systems in an elaborate and pervasive fashion (see Bryant 1974). A significant proportion of deviant behavior occurs within, concomitant to, or as a result of work and occupational specialty. Inasmuch as work organization involves both formal and informal normative structure, violations of these work norms, such as "rate busting," quota restriction, the use of forbidden procedures, such as a shortcut technique or covering up mistakes or shoddy workmanship, and unethical professional behavior, are in fact deviant behavior. Because certain kinds of work engender specific routines, pressures, stresses, and problems, some occupational structures and cultures appear to induce, facilitate, and harbor particular kinds of pathological behavior such as alcoholism, narcotic addiction, or homosexuality. Similarly, the structure and culture of some conventionally legal work and occupational systems seem to be conducive to characteristic forms of illegal activities. Such work systems apparently possess singular opportunity structures for crime as well as unique milieus that contribute to the individual motivation for such illicit behavior. Thus the various configurations of work and deviant behavior linkages may be examined from several perspectives, and deviant behavior can be identified and observed in all work systems, including the military.

KHAKI-COLLAR CRIME

The military establishment is a work system and, accordingly, like all occupational and work systems, harbors and sustains unique, endemic, and constituent patterns of deviant behavior and crime. This is true of the military institution of all nations and also appears to be the case historically. The question of crime and deviant behavior in the military context, in our society, in other societies, and historically, has been largely ignored and/or neglected by sociologists and other social scientists. Where it has been addressed, its treatment has been limited and often only peripherally relevant to the larger topic of work-deviancy linkages.

As citizens of the United States (or of any nation), members of the military are theoretically subject to the same full range of civilian legal regulations and contraints as are other citizens, including conventional civilian socio legal codes at federal, state, and local levels. As members of the military, they are also subject to the additional social control imposed by military law, and accountable under supplemental sets of legal constraints governing their occupational behavior, including the U.S. Uniform Code of Military Justice as well as various international treaties. Such constraints are normally enforced and severely sanctioned by the U.S. military establishment. In the event of violation of these prescribed rules of conduct, the offender is subject to military justice and its attendant punishments. In other countries members of the military institution are similarly constrained by their own military law, norms, and tradition, as well as by international treaty and agreement, in addition to the various levels and forms of civilian social control.

In regard to their additional mode of social control, the armed forces postulates three reasons for effecting its own system of law (Department of the Army 1963:4). These are:

a. The Army must have power to punish its own members for the offenses which would be crimes if committed by a civilian, for the Army operates in foreign countries where the systems of law are wholly different from our own, and in places and under conditions where civilian courts are not readily or appropriately available. Thus—just as it must carry its own supplies, equipment, and transportation—the field army must carry its own legal system.

b. Both in time of war and peace, additional rules of conduct—not normal to civiliam life—have been found necessary in the training and operation of a disciplined army. If every soldier had the right to quit the service whenever he saw fit, or to disobey orders whenever he did not like them, it is obvious that the army would be nothing but an uncontrolled mob.

c. Although soldiers are subject to the civilian jurisdiction of Federal and State courts within the United States, and, under the provisions of "Status of Forces" Treaties, in some foreign countries, in time of war this jurisdiction (at least as to State and Foreign Courts) may not be exercised if it interferes with the military functions of the Federal Government. In a case where civilian jurisdiction has been denied effect, however, there must be some method of trying the individual concerned for civilian-type crimes committed.

Thus the specialized nature and mission of the military, and the setting in which it operates, all necessitate a separate and additional system of formalized social control in order to prescribe and regulate appropriate behavior for its members.

In spite of the complex normative system and severe sanctions, violations do routinely occur. Military life is the scene of a wide variety of deviant behavior ranging from excessive use of alcholol and narcotic addiction, to sex crimes, theft, and even mass murder. Much of this behavior may perhaps be attributed to the opportunity structure of the military system and the sociocultural and geographical settings in which the military normally operates, the informal pressures and strains inherent in military culture, as well as the structured subversion of organizational goals frequently component to the military enterprise.

Crime and deviancy in the military must be viewed against the backdrop of the generalized mission of the military, the attitudes and values defining and supporting this mission, the process of occupational selection, the thrust of subcultural socialization, and the posture of the operant formal normative system. The resultant subcultural perspective, linked with the composition of its labor force, combine to produce a uniquely military pattern of deviancy that may perhaps be appropriately labeled as "khaki-collar crime" (Bryant 1972).

This volume briefly examines the range of khaki-collar crime and some of the concomitant elements of military life and milieu that may be contributory to such deviancy, and aid in rationalizing and perpetuating it. It will address itself initially to the varieties of military deviancy and subsequently to some of the operant enabling or facilitative processes and factors, and particularly certain aspects of military training. Accordingly, the vagaries of military deviancy are considerable in terms of both scope and diversity, Traditionally, major categories of civilian crime have included crimes against property and crimes against person. The intense preoccupation of the military with discipline, reflexive action, efficiency, extremely circumspect behavior, and rigidity of role performance, however, argues for an additional major category of military offense—crimes against performance. As suggested by the typological overview detailed in Table 1, khaki-collar crime is conceptualized as being horizontally articulated into three broad categories: (1) crimes against property; (2) crimes against person; and (3) crimes against performance.

The military exists and operates in a number of different social settings. In the first instance it is a social system, in and of itself, and accordingly effects its own social control and equilibrium. It is conceivable that the military might exist in total isolation from other social systems, civilian or military, or sufficiently segregated from other social systems that no interaction would occur. In such an instance, deviant offenses would violate only norms internal to the military itself, thus constituting *intra-occupational military* crime as a model configuration. In effect, this means that perpetrator and victim are always internal to the military system.

In general, however, elements of the military are often located in the midst of, or contiguous to, a civilian social system, with attendant interaction and social activity between members of the military and civilian populations. Where such interaction or behavior on the part of the member of the military encompasses violations of the civilian normative system, abuses of or offenses against civilians or their property, or the social activity between the members is judged to be inappropriate or detrimental to the military or offensive to civilian authorities, the behavior constitutes *extra-occupational military* crime. Here there is a military perpetrator but the victim is component to the civilian system

TABLE 1. Khaki-Collar Crime: A Conceptual Paradigm

Systemic Context of Deviancy	Crimes Against Property	Crimes Against Person	Crimes Against Performance	Source of Formal Sanctions
Intra-occupational (American military system)	Destruction or misappropriation of government property ("moonlight requisitioning") ("scrounging") ("midnight salvaging")	Assaulting or attempting to murder a superior commissioned officer ("fragging"). Cruelty or maltreatment to subordinate ("shaping up the troops") ("bringing smoke")	Malingering, absence without leave and desertion, drunk on duty, misbehavior of sentinel, insubordination, mutiny or sedition, conduct unbecoming an officer and a gentleman. ("goldbricking") ("goofing off")	U. S. Uniform Code of Military Justice and other military regulations
Extra-Occupational (American civilian social system)	Theft, forgery, housebreaking, vandalism, wasting or destroying private property	Assault, rape, murder, etc.	Public uniform violations, public breaches of the peace (fighting, drunk and disorderly). All conduct of a nature to bring discredit upon the armed forces ("letting off steam")	U. S. federal, state, and local legal statutes and regulations (also U.S. Military Law)
(Foreign friendly civilian social	Theft, forgery, etc., as above	Assault, rape, murder, etc. ("kicking the slopeheads around")	Black marketeering, consorting with prostitutes (if prohibited), breach of security,	Laws of friendly governments (esp. as defined by "Status of Forces Agreements")

TABLE 1. (cont.)

SYSTEMIC CONTEXT OF DEVIANCY	CRIMES AGAINST PROPERTY	CRIMES AGAINST PERSON	CRIMES AGAINST PERFORMANCE	SOURCE OF FORMAL SANCTIONS
system)				(also U.S. Military Law)
(Enemy civilian social system during combat or occupation)	Looting, plundering, and pillaging ("liberating")	Atrocities and massacres ("cleaning villages," "wasting," "pacification," "reprisals," "rooting out the infrastructure")	fraternization or unauthorized marriage (if prohibited), collusion with civilians to defraud U.S. Army ("tight with Herman")	Laws established by occupation authorities (also see U.S. Military Law)
Inter-occupational (Enemy military system)	Misappropriation or unauthorized destruction of captured enemy supplies and equipment. Illegally taking personal property of POW's. ("taking souvenirs")	Mistreatment, torture, or murder of POW's. ("military expediency") ("body count")	Aiding the enemy, subordinate compelling surrender, misconduct as prisoner, cowardice in the face of the enemy ("bugging out")	International treaties (Geneva Convention), Law of Land Warfare (FM-27-10), etc. (also U.S. Military Law)

Loci of Occurrence

(although the military itself might be the indirect victim in some instances). Furthermore, the civilian population might be of the same nationality as the military, the home population, as it were, or it might be the civilian population of a friendly allied nation, such as when vast American forces were stationed in Great Britain during World War II. Finally, in some instances the civilian population might be that of an enemy nation, such as was the case when German troops occupied parts of Russia or U.S. troops occupied parts of Germany during World War II.

The military, by virtue of its mission, may often be in contact with an enemy military, either in battle or in a less violent mode of interaction such as a siege situation or an instance of entrenchment on both sides of a line awaiting battle. In such settings, violations of norms concerning correct and appropriate behavior in regard to the enemy may occur. Here the perpetrator of the deviancy is a member of the military and the victim is usually a member of the enemy military, or the enemy military itself. In some instances, however, the deviant behavior of the offender may victimize his own parent military, but in these cases the vagrant pattern of behavior involves the enemy in a principal and significant fashion. The deviant mode always involves both militaries or members of both militaries. It can accordingly be labeled *inter-occupational military* crime.

Thus khaki-collar crime, in addition to the three-category typological division mentioned earlier, can also be further divided vertically into five loci of occurrence, dependent on the systemic context of its commission. As articulated, these are: (1) intraoccupational; (2) extraoccupational: a. American civilian, b. foreign friendly civilian, and c. enemy civilian; and (3) interoccupational. In way of illustration, the various categories of such crime will be discussed briefly within each of the different systemic contexts within which military deviancy occurs.

Intra-Occupational Military Crime

Much of the deviant behavior committed by members of the armed forces is internal to the U.S. military system itself. Such deviance is directed against the military and may involve theft or misuse of government property, interpersonal violence, and inappropriate military behavior.

CRIMES AGAINST PROPERTY

The protection of an appropriate allocation of supplies and equipment is especially important to the efficient implementation of the military mission. Servicemen, however, may seek to supply themselves or their units with government-issued property not normally authorized or available, as a means of enhancing their comfort and contributing to their survival. The result is widespread theft and misappropriation of government property, often involving elaborate illicit barter (Zurcher 1965)) and "scrounging" systems, or theft simply redefined as "moonlight requisitioning." Intraunit theft based on need and rivalry is an endemic practice.

In recent years a new variation of crime against military property has emerged—exploitation of the PX system. The military post exchange and commissary system is the third largest merchandising enterprise in the world and operates as a private business, and as such is not subject to normal military scrutiny and control. Recent congressional investigations into charges of graft in the system, especially in Vietnam, uncovered an incredible chronicle of "corruption, criminality, and moral compromise" (Rugaber 1971) involving kickback payoffs, black-market operations, and Swiss bank accounts, and implicating a number of general officers and the first soldier to hold the rank of sergeant major of the army.

The U.S. military, with its inordinate amount of relatively accessible goods and equipment plus additional opportunities for internal theft for those strategically located in the system, affords full scope for the commission of a variety of economic crimes.

CRIMES AGAINST PERSON

The social organization of the military rests on an elaborate set of formalized status relationships involving highly specific and circumspect subordinate-superordinate roles. Interaction between superordinate and subordinate should not involve physical coercion or violence. The imposition of authoritarian discipline can be onerous, however, and the behavior demanded may be distasteful or excessively dangerous. Subordinates, in their pique and frustration, may rebel and assault their superiors. In Vietnam, for example, it was reported that "fragging" (throwing a fragmentation grenade at disliked officers) was endemic in many units (Linden 1972).

Similarly, some officers may define physical abuse as necessary or desirable in their interaction with their subordinates. The military is equally specific in its proscriptions concerning the physical abuse and maltreatment of subordinates. Extremely serious sanctions may be invoked in the event of violations of these regulations. In spite of the existence of such regulations, there are evasions of the rules, particularly in basic training. In some instances, also frequently in training, there is a systematic attempt to approximate maltreatment with various types of intimidation and routines without actually exceeding the limits of the regulations. It is often assumed that such treatment facilitates the transformation from civilian to "warrior," and in a sense the intimidation is implemented as kinds of *rites de passage,* albeit against military regulations. Perhaps more flagrant examples of physical abuse or maltreatment of subordinate personnel may be encountered in regard to the inmates of military prisons and stockades, and individuals arrested by military law-enforcement personnel. Military custodial facilities have had a historical and well-deserved reputation for severity in treating inmates.

If power corrupts, then military power seems to have had a particularly corrupting influence on some individuals who occupy positions of authority, particularly if they come to define physical abuse as necessary or desirable for the accomplishment of their mission. By the same token, the exigencies of war and military life are such that they seem to promote in some subordinates the aggressive acting-out of their privations and frustrations.

CRIMES AGAINST PERFORMANCE

The effectiveness of the military in successfully discharging its mission of defending society from aggression from both outside and within may well lie with its ability to function in an orderly and concerted fashion, and thus also with the inherent functioning of its constituent parts down to the individual member. Discipline is clearly essential to the operation of the military, and the appropriate discharge of individual duties and responsibilites is therefore considered a mandatory requisite of overall success. It is therefore not surprising that the military places a high premium on appropriate performance and severely sanctions crimes against performance.

The specificity of expected military performance is such that a variety of deviations from the extensive statutory norms concerning the obligations and duties of the individual member constitute criminal offenses. These norms are frequently violated, even though violations often are punishable by prison sentences, fines, loss of rank, or dishonorable discharge. Military personnel on occasion desert, go AWOL, malinger, and incapacitate themselves with liquor or drugs. Other crimes against performance include misbehavior of a guard or sentinel, dereliction of duty, bringing discredit to the armed forces, conduct unbecoming an officer and a gentleman, insubordination, and—most serious of all—mutiny.

No military establishment is more effective in its mission than it is in the maintenance of discipline and obedience among its ranks. Great armies have floundered without it and small ones have been vanquished because of it. Any abridgment of the formalized "chain of command," any rejection of order or authority, any attempt to evade or to be derelict in one's military duty, any disorders or neglects to the prejudice of good order or discipline, or any conduct of such a nature to bring discredit upon the armed forces constitute crimes against performance.

The strains of military life and particularly combat duty are great. Many young men especially are often not equiped physically or temperamentally for these stresses. Some, in their anxiety and frustration, rebel, while others flee physically by deserting or going AWOL. Still others seek chemical release through alcohol and drugs, often incapacitating themselves for effective duty in the process. This latter type of release is historically and globally endemic to almost all military systems.

In the final analysis no intraoccupational deviancy is more critical than crimes against performance, and few violations are more severely sanctioned. Significant numbers of individuals in the armed services do violate the norms concerning performance and become, in effect, khaki-collar deviants.

Extra-Occupational Military Crime

Military personnel, while members of a separate social system, are also frequently involved with civilian society both here and abroad. In the course of their interaction with civilian society, American, allied, or enemy military personnel sometimes commit crimes involving abuse of civilians, whether their own, allied, or enemy, by directing acts of theft and violence against them. They may also behave, in a civilian setting, in such a way that their actions are prejudicial to the military, and thus directly or indirectly handicap the military in the discharge of its mission.

CRIMES AGAINST PROPERTY

In order to maintain proper toleration, respect, support, and cooperation from the U.S. civilian population as well as from foreign, friendly, and occupied enemy civilian populations, their property rights must be assidously observed and the occasional circumstances necessitating acquisition of their property must be rigidly defined and regulated in regard to due process and justification. Accordingly, it is perhaps not surprising that the legal constraints and regulations governing the relationship of military personnel to armed forces, civilian, and enemy property are elaborate, specific, and severely sanctioned. In spite of this, violations of formal property norms are frequent, flagrant, and often supported by the informal structure and subculture.

Where property crimes against American and friendly foreign civilians committed by servicemen occur, they are most likely to include damage to property as a residual effect of brawling or disorderly conduct. Soldiers or sailors may become involved in brawls or fights that damage bars or restaurants, or they may destroy property as part of a drunken shore leave "spree." Property crimes involving the violation of financial trust, such as defaulting on debts and cashing worthless or insufficient bank fund checks, are also not infrequent. When U.S. troops are stationed abroad they may also commit crimes against civilian property, such as vandalism and destruction of property as a residual product of altercations with foreign nationals. Such brawling may be precipitated by hostile rivalry, not infrequently involving disputes and jealousies concerning local females and American troops and their spending habits. American troops often violate currency and exchange laws of the country involved, inasmuch as this is one of the few economic crimes of which the commission is encouraged and facilitated by their occupational circumstances.

In wartime among foreign civilians, troops may commit crimes against property in the form of "looting." Today's wars are ostensibly political in motive, rather than economic, and the members of the armed forces involved are often well paid, especially the American military, thus booty and plunder take on more of a symbolic than real value. In actual practice, however, American servicemen may be among the worst offenders in the violation of military prohibitions against looting. With their cultural preoccupation with material goods, it is perhaps not surprising that our servicemen often were (and are) flagrant looters. McCallum (1946) reported that in World War II, 80 percent of the men in his company were looters. Regardless of the values held by the individual servicemen concerning theft prior to joining the military, the situation can be adequately redefined by both the informal peer group and at times by military authorities themselves so as to permit looting with little or no personal discomfort. American servicemen do not loot, they "liberate" or "appropriate" enemy civilian property that is "abandoned." When they do so, it is only because of "military expediency" as an aid to comfort and efficiency.

CRIMES AGAINST PERSON

Because the military constitutes a separate and "alien" social system, adversity, if not antagonism, is natural between servicemen and civilians, whether American, foreign friendly, or enemy, which sometimes results in altercations and violence. Servicemen may assault civilians in the course of fights and brawls in bars and taverns, as well as roll drunks and "queers" for "fun and profit." Sex crimes involving military personnel and civilians also occur with some frequency and create significant problems for military authorities. Young males cut off from traditional informal controls, bolstered by a masculine and aggressive military subculture, and faced with a situation of relative unavailability and inaccessibility of females, are prime candidates for sexual crimes. Members of the military may feel, or be instructed, that foreign enemy civilians and even foreign friendly civilians are "inferior" or "subhuman," and thus be more inclined to commit offenses then would otherwise be the case.

After hostilities the enemy civilian population, subject to occupational rule by the opposing military, may have to endure beatings, rapes, and murder at the hands of military personnel. The military normally undertakes to try and prevent or minimize military crimes committed against enemy civilians, and especially crimes against person. It does so in the belief that enemy territory will be easier to occupy and its population will be easier to control if they feel secure against harm from the invading army. Proscriptions against harming enemy civilians are sometimes laxly enforced by military commanders, and such norms are frequently and widely violated. In Vietnam, perhaps more than any of our wars in the past with the exception of the Indian campaigns, atrocities involving civilian victims, such as the so-called massacres at My Lai and Son My, were flagrantly committed. In the final analysis, it is often difficult for military commanders to restrain their troops from availing themselves of the aggressive privilege of the victors, and troublesome, if not impossible, to convert finely honed combat soldiers into nonaggressive occupation troops.

CRIMES AGAINST PERFORMANCE

In an effort to win public support and approval for the armed services, the military is particularly strict about public deportment of servicemen in this country and in allied countries where American servicemen are stationed. Military regulations dictate appropriate norms of dress, conduct, and transactions with civilians. Members of the armed forces do, however, create public disturbances and nuisances, or dress or comport themselves inappropriately, in violation of civilian law and/or military regulation. The military is perhaps even more distressed over its personnel becoming involved in public scandals that erodes the military image of integrity. It has recently become public knowledge that some U.S. astronauts have been involved in some unethical practices for profit, and have accordingly violated military regulations concerning appropriate conduct for officers. Perhaps far more prevalent than looting civilian property, black marketeering and currency manipulations in a foreign civilian setting constitute the largest incident of crime against performance. Members of the armed forces are also often prone to violate military regulations concerning fraternization and transactions with enemy civilians. Even marriage to a foreign enemy civilian without permission may be a violation of military conduct.

Inter-Occupational Military Crime

War is a venerable and (at least at one time) honorable social process. Like other kinds of large-scale social interaction, it has historically operated within a normative framework of sorts. As with most "sports," war has traditionally been waged according to various rules and "laws," which devote considerable attention to the conduct of armed forces vis-à-vis the opposing forces and the various contingencies attendant to combat and its aftermath. The exigencies of war and the predilection of individual members of the military, however, often engender deviant behavior directed against members of the enemy military system.

CRIMES AGAINST PROPERTY

The treatment of enemy military personnel and the disposition of their equipment is rigidly specified by U.S. military regulations and international treaties such as the articles of the Geneva and Hague conventions. Violations of these laws and regulations are severely sanctioned, and punishment may emanate from either U.S. military authorities or belligerent military authorities, if the offender is captured. Just as looting from a friendly or enemy civilian population is forbidden by military regulation, so, too, is the appropriation of enemy military property by the individual soldier. When enemy military personnel are captured, according to regulations, certain personal items, such as watches, medals, and keepsakes, may be retained by the POW's. In actual practice, American (and soldiers of other nations as well) servicemen have often been quick to dispossess the captured enemy troops of "souvenir" material. In some instances this has been confined to the retention of various personal items from individual POW's by U.S. servicemen. In other instances "souvenir" collecting has taken on the aspects of large-scale systematic plundering and theft of items of significant economic worth. American troops for a number of wars have had the reputation of being ingenious and pragmatic when it came to diverting captured enemy supplies and equipment to their own needs. In some instances enemy souvenirs have even been counterfeited and sold fraudulently to other servicemen as battle trophies. War may not be fun, but some servicemen attempt to make it more bearable—in terms of all the comfort and luxury that can be effected under the circumstances—if not profitable, with the enemy paying the bill.

CRIMES AGAINST PERSON

Combat between honorable men is subject to a variety of treaties, codes, and traditions. Various weapons have at one time or another been formally outlawed—"dum-dum" or expanding bullets, poison gas, and, since World War I, shotguns. The rule has been bent to some extent in both Korea and Vietnam, with the U.S. military employing tear gas and other nonlethal chemical agents. In both Korea and Vietnam some servicemen allegedly borrowed shotguns from MP units or Special Services stockrooms and utilized them in combat.

In the World War I era there was a residue of chivalrous *camaraderie* between aviators on both sides, but by World War II there were incidents of shooting fliers in their parachutes by both Axis and Allied pilots. In all of our recent wars, troops on both sides have fired on forbidden targets such as hospitals. Accepted military practice today calls for shooting paratroops before they touch ground, where possible.

Prisoners of war are theoretically entitled to humane and dignified treatment according to treaty. In the interest of "military expediency," the proprieties of regularized warfare cannot always be observed. Killing prisoners of war, because there is no practical means of transporting them to a rear area (as in the Malmédy massacre, for example), systematically mistreating or depriving them of the essentials of life, or torturing them to obtain intelligence information have sometimes been considered necessary and efficacious. (It was reported that in Vietnam occasionally a captured Vietcong prisoner would be dropped to his death from a helicopter in order to "loosen the tongues" of other prisoners who observed his treatment.) The mutilation and beating of Vietcong prisoners by American troops was reported to be common practice. The nature of the guerrilla-type fighting in Vietnam was such that combat servicemen were prone to violate regulations concerning captured enemy soldiers, in some instances with the tacit (or open) approval of their superiors. The fact of survival in a combat situation or the context of war is such that humane values apparently are often eroded in the face of the exigencies of combat necessity, and there is sometimes minimal reluctance to perpetrate crimes of violence against prisoners of war.

CRIMES AGAINST PERFORMANCE

A serviceman's overriding responsibility is to acquit himself honorably in his performance vis-à-vis the enemy and, in this regard, the military is quite specific in its prescriptions and proscriptions. He should obey orders and, if necessary, close with the enemy, killing or being killed in the process, if his orders so dictate.

To fail in the discharge of this responsibility, or to be guilty of cowardice, desertion, or dereliction of duty in a combat situation represent some of the most serious of all military crimes and call for the most severe sanctions, including imprisonment, dishonorable discharge, or even death. To surrender without good reason, to fail to comply with a combat order, or to "bug out" in the face of the enemy are all extremely serious offenses against military performance. In World War II, Pvt. Eddie D. Slovik deserted in the face of the enemy, was court-martialed, and subsequently "shot to death by musketry" at the hands of an American firing squad, finally being buried in an unmarked grave. In some armies such behavior may result in execution on the spot by the commanding officer or field police.[2]

Nor does the responsibility for obedience, loyalty, and bravery incumbent upon military personnel cease upon capture and imprisonment. In the U.S. Army, the POW servicemen are bound to obey the highest-ranking POW in their camp, to attempt to escape where possible, to avoid cooperating with the enemy beyond that required by treaty (such as necessary work details for camp maintenance), and to refrain from giving information to the enemy that would be helpful in pursuing the war. The Code of Conduct constrains American POW's from collaborating with the enemy, giving "confessions" of American war crimes, or acting to the detriment of other POW's. Breach of the Code would constitute a serious violation of military norm. Captured military personnel should not behave in such a way as to cause harm to their fellow POW's or refuse to render such aid as they can. The most severely sanctioned offenses committed while a POW are those involving crimes against fellow POW's (such as neglect, theft of food, or actual physical violence), or betraying the United States through collaboration with the enemy.

In Korea, POW escapes were nonexistent and attempts were rare. For almost the first time, U.S. POW's did not obey orders, stole from each other in some instances, killed each other, in many cases gave valuable information to the enemy, and collaborated to the extent of making peace statements and condemning the U.S. Several even elected not to accept repatriation. Some that were

---

[2] Russian officers in World War II not infrequently took such action where discipline was breaking down, and the German army in retreat before the Russians often hanged straggling deserters to "stiffen resistance" in their own troops.

returned were court-martialed and punished. In Vietnam, the long period of imprisonment and the conditions of privation may have motivated some violations of the Code and other military regulations as well.

Social Control in the Military

THE RULES OF WAR

The military, like all social systems, effects a variety of social control mechanisms to enforce and sanction its operant norms. These norms and the attendant sanctionative mechanisms operate at various levels of formality, specificity, and explicitness. Additionally, the military is also subject to normative systems and social controls that are external to its own structure, and that rely on other kinds of sanction for enforcement.

Military rules are perhaps as old as intergroup hostility. Tribal groups in the prehistoric era, in more recent historical times,[3] and even today have had elaborate sets of norms and rules covering war and conflict, and the appropriate role of the warrior. Violation of such rules may evoke serious sanctions. All of the ancient civilizations attempted to regulate warfare and combat and to control the behavior of the members of their military units. There were even norms and rules concerning the treatment of captured enemy warriors and enemy civilian populations. As early as 2000 B.C., the Egyptians and Sumerians waged war according to rules (Friedman

---

[3] One of the most vivid examples of tribal military discipline was the Prussian-like discipline of the Zulu regiments under Cetshwayo, Shaka, or other great chiefs, late in the nineteenth century. Discipline in the Zulu *impis* was absolute. Young warriors were forbidden to have sexual intercourse with any female until the King (Chief) awarded the "head-ring" for bravery in combat to them, at which point they could set up their own kraals and take wives. They trained, worked long hours, and perfected their military skill. In combat they were fearless. In a battle once an *impi* was in motion, in the charge, no warrior was permitted to hesitate, hold back, or even pause to throw a spear. On the other hand, no warrior was permitted to speed ahead of the *induna* (unit leader) in the charge. To do so was a terrible breach of discipline and would evoke the death penalty—death by having wooden pegs hammered up the nostrils into the brain. Zulu military discipline was harsh and death was the commonest of punishments. The death penalty was accomplished in a variety of ways, including being clubbed or speared, being thrown to the crocodiles, or being castrated, flayed, and buried in an anthill (see Clive 1973).

1972:3).[4] Later, among the Hittites and in ancient China, war and military operations were elaborately circumscribed by formalized rule, tradition, and chivalric custom. Friedman relates that Sun Tzu in his classic treatise, *The Art of War*, written in the fourth century B.C., spoke of the rules and norms of war. Similarly, the Hindu *Book of Manu* contained rules regulating land warfare. The Babylonians and the ancient Hebrews abided by a variety of rules and customs governing warfare. Over the years, the concept of regulated warfare and the rigidly circumscribed role of the soldier evolved and took on more specific form and thrust. The protocol of war became nearly as complex and convoluted as in modern times. There were armistices, safe-conduct passes, and cease-fires to bury the dead. From Friedman we learn that poisoned weapons were proscribed, as was the practice of poisoning the enemy's water supply. War required a formal declaration, there were prescriptions to conduct war with restraint, and prisoners were to be treated according to normative and humane custom, in order to permit their ransom or exchange. There were, of course, individual violations of all such norms.

After the Christian era, new ideological constraints on military behavior appeared. According to Friedman (1972:6):

> With the spread of Christianity, the laws of war took a new turn. The principles of pacifism and non-resistance which lay at the heart of Christianity, were balanced by the development of the just war doctrine—the need to spread and then protect the true faith against attack by outside enemies. Antimilitaristic precepts appeared in many of the early canons of the Church.

Thus the Christian soldier now assumed the need for compliance with the Christian philosophy, as well as the burden of penitence for some actions in war, in addition to the need for compliance with traditional military discipline. "From the sixth through the twelfth centuries, the canons dictated that soldiers do penance for any killing" (Friedman 1972:7). While the Church attempted to ameliorate the excessive violence and cruelty of war, the chivalric code governing the conduct of knights and noblemen also developed and added a new dimension to military social control. The chivalric "code called for single combat among nobles of

[4] Friedman is perhaps the definitive work on the history of the laws of war and, accordingly, we have drawn on his exposition to a considerable degree. The material here is largely a paraphrasing and condensation of part of his discussion.

a certain rank, specified conditions of ransom for captured officers, and defined the division of spoils after victory" (Friedman 1972:10). The code was indeed binding in time of "just war."

Nonetheless, there was widespread violation of all the formal, philosophical, and traditional norms of war. Friedman records that Joan of Arc indicated to the British that her troops would give no quarter. Many of the Balkan and middle-eastern wars of the tenth and eleventh centuries involved widespread slaughter and atrocities against military prisoners and civilians. The rules of war were often ignored, but there was a persistent thrust, particularly from the Christian Church, to humanize war. Slings and arrows, for example, were prohibited in Christian wars. Furthermore, "the heraldic courts also preserved the notion of an international law of war to which all soldiers were bound and which could be enforced by every Christian prince" (Friedman 1972:11). Friedman goes on to say that, by the fifteenth and sixteenth centuries the various bodies of military rule, law, custom, tradition, and philosophy were being compiled, analyzed, sythnesized, and articulated in formal treatises such as Francisco de Vitoria's *On the Indies and the Law of War*. Friedman also mentions that other such definitive treatments on the law of warfare also appeared over the years, such as *Three Books on the Law of War and on the Duties Connected with War* by Balthazar Ayala, who, in the sixteenth century, acted as judge advocate of the Spanish armies in the Netherlands. In the seventeenth century a Dutchman, Hugo Grotius, was to author perhaps the most monumental exposition to date on the law of war. Grotius' three-volume masterpiece, *On the Law of War and Peace*, was to provide the foundation for our modern-day international constraints on excessive military behavior in war. According to Friedman (1972:15), "many of his suggested restraints were later written into international law as part of the Hague and Geneva conventions."

In the late 1700s the newly independent United States entered into a series of treaties with the Netherlands, Prussia, and France, which contained provisions on war between the signers. Friedman notes that after the Crimean War, because of differing practices among nations in regard to the maritime law of capture, the leading maritime powers had a conference in Paris to establish the rule that henceforth neutral ships and goods would not be captured in time of war. The suffering and treatment of the sick and wounded during the Franco-Austrian War of 1859 prompted the convening of the Geneva Conference of 1864 to establish "protective principles for Red Cross personnel and others engaged in helping the wounded" (Friedman 1972:151). An international conference in St. Petersburg in 1868 addressed the problem of explosive bullets and resulted in a formal agreement to prohibit the use of such bullets. In 1899 the first Hague conference was called, at the suggestion of Nicholas II, to limit armaments and weapons. Friedman indicates that at the conference such issues as poisonous gas, "dum-dum" bullets, and the launching of bombs from balloons were addressed. Additional conferences were held in 1904, 1906, and 1907, resulting in more comprehensive rules on war and treatment of the wounded. After World War I, the Versailles Peace Conference called for war trials for the German leaders. The Hague Conference of 1922 and subsequent international agreements in the years following "regulated the use of submarines and banned the use of asphyxiating gases" (Friedman 1972:154). The Geneva conference at the end of the decade produced further proscriptions and prescriptions on the treatment of the sick and wounded and prisoners of war. The Kellogg-Briand Pact signed in Paris in 1928 outlawed war, and the 1930 Treaty of London put further restrictions on the conduct of submarine warfare. After World War II there was another Geneva conference in 1949 at which 110 nations of the world agreed on a set of comprehensive rules of war. Over a number of years the United Nations promulated many resolutions concerning respect for human rights in armed conflicts. In 1971, because of the experiences of the Vietnam War, another conference in Geneva was called to study the problem of noninternational armed conflicts.

The direct impact of Hugo Grotius's legal contribution to present-day military constaints on the behavior of individual soldiers in the U.S. military, as well as the integration of traditional philosophies of humane warfare into official military doctrine, can be largely attributed to the Lieber code (Taylor 1972:xv).[5] Francis Lieber, a German by birth, and a veteran of the Prussian Army in the Napoleonic wars, "studied philosophy, mathematics, and law at Halle, Berlin, and Jena, where he received a doctorate" (Taylor 1972:xv). Taylor relates that he emigrated to England and subsequently to America, settling in Boston, and

---

[5] Taylor contributed an extremely erudite forward to the Friedman treatise, and his discussion provides the main basis for our comments here on the Lieber code. My account here draws heavily on his material.

became a citizen in 1832. He developed an acquaintance with a number of famous and influential people such as Henry Wadsworth Longfellow. In 1835 he became a professor at South Carolina College in Columbia. After more than two decades there, he left and took a post as professor of History and Political Science at Columbia College. The new Law School was being organized at that time and Lieber was appointed to its first faculty.

According to Taylor, during the Civil War Lieber had occasion to go to Washington, as a representative of Columbia, to confer an honorary LL.D. upon President Lincoln. While there he became acquinted with Attorney-General Edward Bates. Later he went west and met General Henry W. Halleck, who at one point had practiced law and had authored an important treatise on the laws of war, *International Law, or Rules Regulating the Intercourse of States in Peace and War.* In time Halleck was called to Washington to serve as "General-in-Chief"—in effect, chief of staff to the president. Halleck had an abiding interest in clarifying the rules and laws of war and sought Lieber's advice about guerrilla warfare and the treatment of captured guerrilla troops. Lieber provided the requested advice and proposed to Halleck that "the President appoint a commission to prepare, a set of rules and definitions providing for the most urgent cases, occurring under the Law and usages of War, and on which our articles of war are silent." (Taylor 1972:xvi).

Taylor points out that Lieber moved ahead on his own and prepared and delivered a series of lectures at Columbia on the "Laws and Usages of War." Subsequently General Halleck did appoint a board under the presidency of General Ethan Allen Hitchcock, on which Lieber was appointed as the only civilian member. The board was "to propose . . . a code of regulations for the government of armies in the field as authorized by the laws and usages of War" (Taylor 1972:xvii). Lieber subimtted a draft of such a code; after some "emendations" by General Hitchcock, the Lieber code was adopted. It was issued as General Orders No. 100, *Instructions for the Government of Armies of the United States in the Field,* in May 1863, and for many years remained as the definitive rules for U.S. forces for the conduct of war. The agreements of the Hague conventions of 1899 and 1907 drew heavily on the Lieber code (Taylor 1972:xvii).

The Civil War produced the Lieber code, but as Taylor (1972: xviii) relates, it also saw another significant event in military justice:

The notion of command responsibility was plainly enunicated in General McClellan's order of 1861, to the Army of the Potomac, warning his officers that they would "be held responsible for punishing aggression by those under their command" and directing that military commissions be established to punish violations "of the established rules of warfare."

The defense of superior orders was subsequently used by members of the military to counter charges of war crime—usually without success. Captain Henry Wirz, the Confederate commandant of Andersonville prison during the Civil War, claimed he had only acted under orders, but was sentenced to be hanged in spite of this defense. In the war crime trials after World War II, the defense of superior orders—the so-called Nuremburg defense—also proved to be unsuccessful in most instances. In more recent years the My Lai incident and the subsequent court-martial of Lieutenant Calley saw Calley unsuccessfully use the defense that he was acting under orders. Calley, of course, ultimately served only a fraction of his sentence, and under the most minimal of restrictions. Many higher-ups in the military who shared some element of responsibility in the My Lai killings escaped punishment entirely. The American people were shocked and outranged by the event, suggesting a strong public belief in humane warfare and military discipline to this end. Almost 70 years earlier much the same thing had occurred in the Philippines when Brigadier General Jacob H. Smith and two other officers were court-martialed in circumstances similar to that of Calley, and with a similar outcome. Smith and others were found guilty but received the most minimal of punishments. Also as in the Calley case, there was great public shock and outrage. Public sentiment everywhere was beginning to mitigate for constraints and controls on military behavior in war, and increasingly the military of all nations became more sensitive and responsive to public and thus political pressure.

MILITARY JUSTICE

As mentioned earlier, all military entities have attempted to enforce discipline and compliance with orders with regulated sets of norms and a system of sanctionative military justice. The Greeks and Romans had detailed systems of military justice (Knudten

1970:472),[6] and the Romans even had the equivalent of modern-day military police, which they called camp police, to enforce order and military regulations (Robinson 1971:19). Errant Roman legionnaires might well be fined, subjected to extra duty, or even flogged for infractions of the rules or dereliction of duty. Later in the Middle Ages, the Crusaders apparently had a relatively formalized military code. Various European nations, over time, developed formal codes of military justice derived from the authority of the king as chief executive and commander-in-chief of the armed services.

On June 30, 1775, the U.S. Continental Congress adopted a set of Articles of War derived from several sources, including portions of the code of Gustavus Adolphus of 1621, the British military code, and the Massachusetts articles of war. This set of articles was the first national code of military justice. General Washington encountered little more than a "disorganized and undisciplined mob" when he assumed command of the Continental army on July 3, 1775. He subsequently moved to implement the new Articles of War and vigorously effected military justice (Maurer 1964). There were various revisions of the Articles of War in subsequent years. Many of the revisions had to do with the relative authority of the military commander, the Congress, and the president in regard to the power to convene courts-martial, and the process of appellate review. During the period of time when the army was known as the Legion of the United States, military justice was "harsh and severe" but it was also very uneven, arbitrary, and inconsistent (Knopf 1956). Severe punishment for violation of military regulation continued to be the prevalent posture of military justice during the War of 1812 (Hare 1940).

By the time of the Civil War, the new military situation necessitated additional revisions, and resulted in the Articles of War of 1874. A major change was the new provision that "the commander was empowered at time of war to execute certain death sentences upon confirmation of the department commander or the commanding general in the field" (Knudten 1970:473). The Articles of War underwent further extensive revision in 1916. The revisions primarily addressed judicial procedures and the authority

---

[6] This portion of our discussion draws heavily on the Knudten source, which is very comprehensive and extremely well documented. For a more detailed legalistic account of the development of military justice see Ujevich (1969).

of certain commanders to courts-martial. In 1920 the Articles of War were again revised. In this revision the major thrust was to dilute the commander's authority, in effect requiring him (Knudten 1970:474):

> to share his decision-making authority with noncommanders, to forward the file of an accused to the staff judge advocate prior to trial, and to consult with his staff judge advocate for an opinion concerning the legality of the proceedings before taking any posttrial action.

The commander was also further constrained in his judicial prerogatives in yet other ways.

After the end of World War II, in 1948, the U.S. Articles of War were again significantly revised. Among the changes with significant import were the creation of a separate Judge Advocate General's Corps that could "insure independent legal action and advice" (Knudten, 1970:47). For the first time, enlisted men were empowered to sit as members of a court-martial if requested by the accused. Perhaps most important, individuals who sit as members of a court-martial were enjoined to "use their independent judgment free of commander influence and without fear of censure in later court-martials."

In 1950 the extant system of military codes in this country was thoroughly overhauled and the new U.S. Uniform Code of Military Justice appeared. According to Knudten, this code incorporated elements of the earlier Army and Navy codes portion of the United States code. It articulated a wide range of military offenses encompassing our categories of crimes against property, crimes against person, and crimes against performance. It also specified the appropriate procedures for alleging military violations and the subsequent charges and specifications. It additionally restricted the type of sentence that could be given, but did not restrict the type of offense that could be tried. Knudten goes on to describe three classes of courts-martial that were provided:

1. The *summary court-martial*. This type of trial is conducted by a single officer and makes no provision for a defense counsel or prosecutor (in recent years counsel has been permitted). This court is intended for enlisted men and is not empowered to try officers. The punishments that may be levied are limited to one month's confinement, limited

reduction in grade, and forfeiture of two-thirds of a month's pay. Knudten (1970:475–76) has equated it to a civilian police court.

2. The *special court-martial*. This type of trial is convened for more serious offenses, but generally must be convened by a person with the authority to convene a general court-martial (there are exceptions to this rule). A special court-martial shall consist of any number of members not fewer than three, and a military judge who is not a member of the court (in special instances the court-martial could consist of a military judge alone). Such a trial also permits a trial counsel and a defense counsel (defense counsel must be a lawyer if trial counsel is a lawyer), plus appropriate assistants, as well as a court reporter. Special courts-martial may try persons subject to the code for any noncapital offense made punishable by the code (and again in some special circumstances may be referred to a special court-martial for trial). The special court-martial may prescribe or adjudge (Dept. of Army 1969:4–5):

> Any punishment not forbidden by the code except death, dishonorable discharge, dismissal, confinement for more than six months, hard labor without confinement for more than three months, forfeiture of pay exceeding two-thirds pay per month, or forfeiture of pay for more than six months.

A bad-conduct discharge may not be adjudged by a special court-martial except under certain circumstances.

3. The *general court-martial* is convened for the most serious offenses and is empowered to prescribe the most serious punishments. A general court-martial shall consist of any number of members not fewer than five and a military judge (in special instances a general court-martial shall consist of a military judge alone). Such a trial also permits a trial counsel and a defense counsel, both of whom must be lawyers, plus appropriate assistants, as well as a court reporter. General courts-martial may try persons subject to the code "for any offense made punishable by the code." They can also try persons for offenses and crimes against the law of war, and for crimes or offenses "against the law of the territory occupied as an incident of war or belligerency whenever the local civil authority is superseded in whole or

in part by the military authority of the occupying power."
The general court-martial can adjudge any punishment not
forbidden by the code (within certain limitations).

In the instances of minor offenses against the Code of Military
Justice, or other relatively inconsequential violations of military
rule or norm, the local commander (generally a company commander in the army or ship captain in the navy, for example) may,
at his or her prerogative, administer nonjudicial punishment instead or referring the offender to court-martial. Nonjudicial
punishments, which are imposed under Article 15 of the Uniform
Code of Military Justice, may assume one of the nine basic forms as
articulated by Knudten (1970:481) for trial.

1. admonition and reprimand
2. restriction
3. extra duties
4. reduction in rank
5. forfeiture of pay
6. arrest in quarters
7. correctional custody
8. confinement on bread and water or diminished rations
9. detention of pay

The offender does not normally have to accept punishment under
Article 15, but may instead request trial by court-martial.

In addition to nonjudicial punishment and the various levels of
court-martial, there are several levels of administrative review, including boards of review maintained by each military service,
which serve as an "intermediate appellate tribunal to review matters of fact and of law and to affirm only that part of the approved
sentence which seems appropriate" (Knudten 1970:482). Beyond
that, the U.S. armed services also have a supreme court of the
military in the form of the court of Military Appeals, which is composed entirely of civilian judges of whom "no more than two may
be of the same political party," and who "must be appointed from
the membership of the Bar of the federal court or the highest state
court."

After the experience of the Korean War, in which, as noted
earlier, some U.S. servicemen captured by the North Korean forces
and confined in POW camps provided "confessions" to their captors, collaborated with them, committed offenses against their

fellow POW's, and even refused to be repatriated, the armed forces were compelled to effect new norms proscribing this kind of behavior. On August 17, 1955, President Eisenhower issued Executive Order 10631, Code of Conduct for Members of the Armed Forces of the United States, which specifically forbade certain kinds of collaborative or inappropriate behavior while a prisoner of war (Knudten 1970:480).

All other nations have some form of military apparatus that attempts to enforce conformity to the various systems of military rules and norms and administer appropriate sanctions when indicated. Relatively speaking, forms of official mechanisms of military justice have changed little in centuries, and vary little from nation to nation. The militaries of some nations are, of course, more vigorous in the enforcement of military law and norm then others, and may have more severe punishments for offenders. Overall, however, military justice universally has had essentially the same characteristic parameters.

In the United States there has been, concomitant with the general trend of further democratization of society and an ongoing effort to effect greater social equality, and to render the individual civilian member of society less subject to governmental authority through the erection of additional constitutional protection and the development of more elaborate and insulative due processes, a similar trend to dilute the absolute authority of the military, to ameliorate the restrictive and punitive nature of military justice, and to afford the individual serviceman an enhanced opportunity to insulate himself against military sanctions through the further civilization of military due process. Toward this end, in recent years, U.S. military justice has had its share of critics and detractors, and numerous aspects of the contemporary system have been attacked. The traditional practice of punitive separation as punishment has been attacked as ineffective and inequitable (Bednar, 1962). Such discharges have always, however, served as serious sanctions for military offenders, as the same author points out in quoting an English writer of the seventeenth century who observed that "A soldier should fear only God and Dishonor." Other writers have faulted the administrative discharge for failing to guarantee "fundamental fairness [and] due process when subject to involuntary separation" (Lynch 1970:169), for the broad discretion often present in the administration of military justice (Everett 1972), and for lacking appropriate constitutional due process, especially in regard to the rules of evidence and the right of cross-examination, as well as effective appellate review procedures (Suskind 1965). There has also been the assertion that the administrative discharge has served as a means of "circumventing the requirements of the Uniform Code" (Dougherty and Lynch 1968:19). Some have addressed the constitutional equity of the summary court-martial (Grove 1977). Yet other critics of U.S. military justice have simply taken the posture that military justice and militarism stress "discipline" while law stresses "legality" and "justice," and thus "the existing Articles of War represent a confused and confusing attempt to reconcile those irreconcilable elements." (Morgan 1946:97).

The Vietnam War era probably saw more criticism of the extant system of military justice than any other time in history. Contemporary generations simply expected more personal freedom and prerogatives than military discipline could sustain, and many attacked the very concept of arbitrary discipline in the military, and the necessity for the loss of some liberties that military service entails. In this regard some writers have attacked our military justice system in general (see Bishop 1970). As one critic phrased it (Sherrill 1970:1):

> It is one of the ironies of patriotism that a man who is called to the military service of his country may anticipate not only the possibility of giving up his life but also the certainty of giving up his liberties.

No less a critic of contemporary military justice than Senator Sam Ervin, then chairman of the Senate's Constitutional Rights Subcommittee, occasioned to complain that (Sherrill 1970:68):

> The primary purpose of the administration of justice in the military services is to enforce discipline plus getting rid of people who think they are not capable of contributing to the defense of the country as they should.

The widespread resistance to the Vietnamese war, the very vocal critics of the military in general during this period, and the various trials of radicals, war resisters, and military personnel accused of crimes against Vietnamese civilians and enemy prisoners, all focused a critical scrutiny on the system of military justice in our country. It was not overlooked, for example, that there was a 94 percent conviction rate in the military as compared to only 81 percent in the federal courts for civilians (*Newsweek* 1970b:18). In recent years even some church groups have taken umbrage at what they perceived as the injustice of the military justice system (Times Wire Dispatches 1975). Without question, there have been considerable changes in the structure and process of U.S. military justice over the past half century, and especially in recent years. Many of the efforts at reform of the military justice system have aimed at the furtherance of the civilianization of military law.[7] An important decision in this connection was that rendered by the Supreme Court in the *O'Callahan* v. *Parker* case, "which ruled that—subject to some possible exceptions—even offenses committed by servicemen could not be tried by court-martial unless those offenses were service-connected" (Everett 1972:213; see also *Journal of Criminal Law, Criminology, and Police Science* 1970). Interestingly, some of the efforts at such reform have come from within the military. In World War I such a movement was led by General Samuel A. Ansell, the acting judge advocate general of the army. General Ansell seems to have been sincerely disaffected with military justice when he observed that "the existing system of Military Justice is un-American, having come to us by inheritance and rather witless adoption out of a system of government which we regard as fundamentally intolerable" (Sherman 1970:5). In spite of the efforts of General Ansell and other reformers, the process of civilianizing the U.S. system of military law has moved surprisingly slowly. As Sherman (1970:103) has characterized it, "the movement for civilianization of military law has achieved only limited success in the 50 years since General Ansell proposed an overhaul of the court-martial system." Nevertheless, there have been important alterations to the U.S. system of military justice that have tended to strengthen due process, provide for more effective appellate review, limit the arbitrary authority of commanders, and broaden court membership. Proper military order does not appear to have been significantly diluted or affected as a result of these alterations.

[7] It should be noted that as recently as World War I, military justice actually reached out and embraced U.S. civilians in some instances. During World War I a number of civilian individuals who were employed by the American Expeditionary Forces, hired by contractors doing work for the army in France, or working for the army in camps in the United States or ports of embarkation, were charged with violations of military law or regulation and tried by military court-martial. Appeals by these "camp followers" to civilian courts were turned down. It was only in decisions in 1957 and 1960 that the U.S. Supreme Court held that it was "unconstitutional to court-martial either civilian employees or dependents" (Maurer 1965:215).

It is true, however, that the individual in the military of this country (as in any other nation) is stripped of most civilian rights and freedoms and is subject to an extraordinary degree of discipline and restraint, reforms not withstanding. As Knudten (1970:487) has phrased it:

> The serviceman is not like his civilian peers. He is unable to quit his job and go home or to convince others to strike against working conditions. He does not enjoy the right to trial by jury or even the right to bail guaranteed under the Eighth Amendment, since he is continually under the control of his superiors. Because he lives publicly in a barracks with other men, the Fourth Amendment guarantee against unreasonable search and seizure offers only limited value. Practically, the serviceman exists within a welfare state committed to order and to discipline in order to accomplish a defense function. And yet, this state is the most undemocratic of all institutions.

Nevertheless, the mission of the military dictates a degree of unparalleled hardship, effort, and sacrifice from its members. Members of the military may experience starvation, searing heat, freezing temperatures, disease, accident, disfigurement, blindness, deafness, paralysis, or death as a result of combat, or even training for combat. They have to respond to orders when their own logic may tell them that the order is without logical basis, or that it will lead them into disaster. The work of the soldier is violent and not all have the proclivity or the stomach for mayhem and butchery. Clearly, rigid discipline is an essential component in assuring that all members of the military behave and respond in a predictable fashion and in a manner most efficient to the fulfillment of the military mission. In this sense, military law cannot readily parallel civilian law or tolerate civilian prerogatives and freedom. As Knudten (1970:479) phrases it:

> Civilian criminal justice and military justice serve different purposes. While the civilian criminal code seeks to prevent antisocial acts, the military code enforces the military demand that the soldier perform disagreeable and often dangerous responsibilities rarely asked of civilians.

Thus the military context must be a situational loci of excessive social control, rigid specificity of behavioral norms, and severe sanctionative mechanisms, in order to insure that members of the military do what they might not otherwise be inclined to do, and to cause the military social system to function with near machine-like predictibility, if not efficiency. This social control encompasses all of the various formalized laws, articles, rules, and regulations previously discussed, as well as the several institutionalized mechanisms for sanctioning violations of military discipline, such as nonjudicial punishment and the different levels of courts-martial.

Social control in the military does not only operate at the formal level, nor are all norms explicit and codified. Superiors may use extralegal sanctionative means on subordinates to enforce compliance with discipline. Subordinates, likewise, may employ informal if not extralegal devices to effect some control on the behavior of superiors and to moderate their excesses in the application of discipline. Inasmuch as the military is a work system and formal organization, like all other work systems and formal organizations, there is an elaborate informal social system integral to the formal structure. This informal structure possesses its own normative system and employs its own pressures, persuasions, and sanctions to insure peer compliance with the norms. There are even informal normative systems of expectations based on custom and tradition that simultaneously embrace members of opposing militaries. Finally, there are implicit codes of conduct embedded in cultural history, tradition, and ideology, which are components of basic socialization and military socialization in particular, and which, once inculcated, tend to dictate certain elements of military behavior, and result in significant erosion of self-image if violated. The member of the military endures rigidly contained and circumscribed behavioral alternatives, and is subject to an inordinate number of compliance pressures. In spite of the existence of this formidable system of social controls, members of the military continue regularly, routinely, and endemically to ignore, resist, evade, subvert, and violate military normative control, thereby becoming khaki-collar criminals as a result of their deviant behavior.

CHAPTER TWO

The Facilitation of Khaki-Collar Crime

To fight you must be brutal and ruthless and the spirit of ruthless brutality will enter into the very fibre of our national life, infecting Congress, the courts, the policeman on the beat, the man in the street.
Woodrow Wilson

Crime in the military has not been totally overlooked by behavioral scientists. Some researchers in Britain and the United States have examined the interface of military behavior and deviancy from a number of perspectives. Mannheim (1940:204–205) viewed war itself as a kind of crime, and asserted that there was "a strong affinity between the causes of war and those of crime." War and the attendant social conditions tended to increase the rate of crime and juvenile delinquency, although various crimes of violence sometimes decline in wartime inasmuch as war may be "a more impressive form of violence," and thus war may act as a substitute for crime.

Trenaman (1952) studied military offenses and the effectiveness of rehabilitation in the British army in World War II. He primarily addressed the etiology of "waywardness" in offenders and felt that there was little difference in the tendency to commit military or civilian crimes. The roots of military offenses like other kinds of delinquency lay within various sociopsychological and sociocultural background characteristics culminating in a kind of role inadequacy.

Gibbs (1957:255–256) studied delinquency in the British army and concluded, while military offenses arose from "a multiplicity of factors," that "any predisposition to military delinquency lies in the recruit's pre-service personality development, this being a product of biological and social influences." For Gibbs, military delinquency resulted from predisposition, and precipitating factors such as situational stress. In research conducted by Shainberg (1967: 243,253), fifteen hundred prisoners who passed through the Psychiatric Department of the Third Naval District Brig in Brooklyn were studied concerning their motivation for a variety of offenses, mostly unauthorized absences. His findings suggested that the majority of the men came from broken homes and had lived disrupted lives. Some 90 percent of the subjects had "severe difficulties with their fathers." The men had made poor adjustments to military service in general and the "impersonal military hierarchy" in particular. The military became, in effect, a "second failing father, and their resentment of all the past years was re-ignited." For Shainberg, military crime of this variety was essentially the result of psychological problems. Schneider and LaGrone (1945) studied five hundred soldiers whose military delinquency had resulted in their confinement in an army rehabilitation center. In analyzing various developmental and environmental group characteristics of these men, the researchers concluded that the majority of their army delinquents had been delinquent before entering the army. Military delinquency seemed to be simply a continuation of prior delinquent patterns. The majority of the delinquents they studied had stressful background characteristics such as having come from broken homes, and having had poor school adjustment and incompleted secondary education. Additionally, the majority were below average in intelligence, had never been married, exhibited personality disorders, had only limited job skills, and had experienced serious emotional disorders as a child or adolescent. Again, military crime is seen to be largely the result of a criminally predisposed category of persons.

Hakeem (1946) has explored the notion that military service and the attendant training and combat experience may be a contributing factor to criminality in some persons. It has been hypothesized that military training may make some persons more aggressive or cause them to develop a criminalistic orientation. On the basis of a study of a group of servicemen who had been admitted to a penitentiary and a control group who had no military ser-

vice, Hakeem concluded that there does not appear to be any support for assuming that military service is a contributing factor in
criminal activities.

Most of the literature in the area of military crime has,
however, focused almost exclusively on war atrocities as crime. In
his detailed analysis of military atrocities and the contributing factors, Karsten (1978) spoke to a number of elements including the
ethnocentricity and ideology (i.e. overly aggressiveness and ruthlessness) of the soldiers involved as well as their character and personality traits (sadism or excessive brutality). He also discussed external forces such as the combat environment which may place extraordinary stresses on the men involved in the fighting, as well as
weak or ineffective leadership and weaponry which tends to make
killing more impersonalized or depersonalized (i.e. saturation
bombing or air strikes).

Yet other authors addressing military atrocities as crimes have
talked of some similiar contributing factors and have also introduced others. One psychiatrist (Gault 1971:450), in discussing
military attrocities mentioned six principles contributing to
"slaughter." These included ". . . the universalization of the
enemy; the 'cartoonization' of the victim; the dilution of responsibility; the pressure to act; the natural dominance of the
psychopath; and the ready availability of firepower."

The limited literature on military crime has tended to be nar-
row in its focus on the offenses committed and has not addressed
the full range of behaviors deviant to military norm and regulation. Furthermore, this literature has tended to view such deviancy
more as an idiosyncratic pathology than the more endemic interpretive distortion and social role subversion, constituent to the
military context, that it represents. Khaki-collar crime should be
appropriately conceptualized as a universal mode of institutional
deviancy largely precipitated by structural considerations and contingencies.

Military criminals, like most other criminal offenders, are
made, not born. The genesis of deviant behavior in a military context must be traced to an unusual set of social circumstances and
exigent conditions characteristic of, and unique to, this particular
work system. The military traditionally recruits or impresses a
population of individuals who are especially prone to unconformity
(as opposed to nonconformity) if not antisocial behavior, although
they may well be prime candidates for intensive secondary military

socialization, which itself may indirectly, if not directly, contribute to deviant tendencies. In this regard, military socialization may be a major factor in inculcating deviant values and behaviors. The military possesses an inordinate opportunity structure for crime as well as a unique culture and milieu that is conducive to and facilitative of certain characteristic forms of illegal activity. The unusual routines, pressures, stresses, and problems endemic to military existence would appear to contribute to individual motivation for the violation of military norms, and to induce and encourage illicit behavior.

The Military Population

The military represents a large social entity of distinctive characteristics and unique circumstances. The military is normally made up of a population that is inherently more difficult on which to impose social control than is the general civilian population at large. From a demographic standpoint, the military is disproportionately made up of single males in their younger adult years.[1] Such individuals have just rejected, or are in the process of rejecting, parental control, and are substituting peer control. Although in time they are likely to submit more readily to other institutional control, these young men in their late teens and early 20s are in a particularly formative period in terms of their adult socialization.

At this juncture in their life, when they are between spheres of social control (family and work organization, for example), they are perhaps most prone to antisocial behavior, and particularly behavior hostile toward authority. In order to prevent these young people, with their frustrations experienced in the process of attaining meaningful adult statuses (i.e., occupational, conjugal), from becoming a disruptive element in society, they have in many societies been absorbed temporarily into tightly structured military

---

[1] While it is true that the U.S. military is still predominately male, the fact is that increasing numbers of females are entering all of the services, at both the officer and enlisted levels. Only time will tell whether they will tend to reflect the resistance to social control characteristic of young males in our society. A recent study of females in the military (see Schreiber and Woelfel 1977:18) suggests that females are discharging their military responsibilities satisfactorily and that ". . . the performance of U.S. Army Companies is independent of the proportion of women that they contain (up to 25 percent). . . ." Females may well accept military socialization more readily and more effectively than males.

or paramilitary organizations. (This is or was equally true of preliterate groups like the Masai and Zulu of Africa as of modern societies.) In this way they can be better controlled, monitored, and kept under surveillance during the period of their service. In this sense, the military constitutes a kind of custodial institution. Interestingly, in the presumably sham *Report from Iron Mountain on the Possibility and Desirability of Peace,* this latent function of the military is discussed in some detail (Lewin 1967:41–42). As the report of the "Special Study Group" put it:

> The most obvious of these functions is the time-honored use of military institutions to provide antisocial elements with an acceptable role in the social structure. The disintegrative, unstable social movements loosely described as "fascist" have traditionally taken root in societies that have lacked adequate military or paramilitary outlets to meet the needs of these elements. This function has been critical in periods of rapid change. The danger signals are easy to recognize, even though the stigmata bear different names at different times. The current euphemistic cliches— "juvenile delinquency" and "alienation"—have had their counterparts in every age. In earlier days these conditions were dealt with directly by the military without the complications of due process, usually through press gangs or outright enslavement. But it is not hard to visualize, for example, the degree of social disruption that might have taken place in the United States during the last two decades if the problem of the socially disaffected of the post-World War II period had not been foreseen and effectively met. The younger, and more dangerous, of these hostile social groupings have been kept under control by the Selective Service System.

The aggression of the youth can be channeled toward more socially acceptable behavior, such as the waging of war or the training for war. In addition, young men can more quickly and effectively be socialized as adults and their acceptance of adult roles and responsibilities can be facilitated. To some degree the military system itself represents a kind of rehearsal system for civilian status competition in terms of achievement and recognition. In this sense the military may be viewed as a mechanism of general social control aimed at a specific segment of the population.

It may also be argued that military service for the young is functional for society in that it keeps a sizable proportion of the population out of the labor force temporarily, thus contributing to a fuller employment rate. To some degree, the military also delays many men in marriage until a later age, affording a larger selection of potential spouses to the slightly older males who have previously served and facilitating the culturally desirable age gap between husbands and wives.[2]

In addition to a population of young, single, aggressive, and potentially antisocial males, the military is also made up in large measure of lower- and lower-middle-class individuals who were more likely to be drafted, lacking college deferments, or to elect enlistment as one of a limited number of occupational alternatives. The majority of the enlisted personnel in the United States Army (and in almost all other armies) tends to be minimally educated (frequently high school or less), and often of lower and lower-middle socioeconomic status. It is true that in periods of large-scale mobilization with a draft system, all walks of life may be represented in the enlisted ranks. The fact remains, however, that college graduates do not, as a general rule, if given their choice, elect to join the military at the enlisted level. Traditionally, the military has provided a vocational haven for those persons for whom many other occupational opportunities are closed, and for persons who may be viewed as more "expendable" than some others in the population.[3] It is interesting to note that as part of the military draft system, certain persons, such as those in "essential" work deemed critical to the war effort, are exempted or deferred from being drafted into military service. So, too, are young men enrolled in college often deferred, while young men who did not pursue a college education are not. This is not necessarily a modern condition of military demography. Again the *Report from Iron Mountain* cogently observed, "It must be noted also that the armed forces in every civilization have provided the principal state-supported haven for what we now call the unemployable" (Lewin 1967:43). The *Report* goes on to quote Fischer (1932:42–43), who asserted that the typical European standing army of 50 years ago

---

[2] In earlier periods it was customary for young Cossacks to serve in the military for up to 20 years before marrying. When they returned to their home village after discharge, they would receive a parcel of land and could appropriately marry. The 20-year age gap was considered appropriate and desirable. With the Masai of Kenya, the young men serve as Moran or bachelor warriors for several years before they are allowed to marry.

[3] This ideological view expressed by many, was very well articulated by Harris (1979:F–3) who opioned, "At first, it was hardly noticed. Those who died (in Vietnam) were regarded as unessential to the national defense in the eyes of the Selective Service System. They were uninfluential, disproportionately black and brown and it took a significant number of them dying to make political waves."

consisted of "troops unfit for employment in commerce, industry, or agriculture, led by officers unfit to practice any legitimate profession or to conduct a business enterprise."

Thus historically, as today, the ranks of the military have been filled largely with young men of lower and lower-middle income and socioeconomic level, frequently of below-average educational level, and often essentially unemployable or with minimal skills and capabilities appropriate to meaningful vocational employment. Such youths may be lacking in the emphasis on control and channelization more characteristic of the upper and upper-middle class, particularly in regard to aggressive behavior. These kinds of individual are prone to operate more on an emotional level than persons of more education. Being less articulate, they are more likely to resort to overt hostility or violence when frustrated. (A lower-class youth may be more likely than an upper-class youth to resort to violence in settling arguments, for example.) Such youths may be more disposed to immediate rather than deferred gratification and generally more disposed to peer influence in their deportment than are upper- and upper-middle-class youths, who may be more sophisticated and independent in their behavior. The general picture that emerges is a population of young men who, in terms of socioeconomic characteristics and sociocultural predisposition, may be prime candidates for subculturally determined deviant activity and, at the time, are equally favorable candidates for authoritarian discipline. They are less equipped for self-discipline, logical examination, or rational concerted action—in the absence of external control. It is for these reasons and others that military discipline is necessarily imposed. While it is not axiomatic, there does seem reason to believe that the less sophisticated are the troops in the military, the more stringent and authoritarian will be the system of military justice. Some of the Russian armies in World War II had recruits that only a short time earlier had been Mongolian tribesmen. Such illiterate masses required ironlike authoritarian discipline, and the European Russian officers provided it to the extent of sometimes shooting recalcitrant enlisted men. Many Asiatic armies, recognizing that their conscripts may not always be the most rational with which to deal, often delegate even to noncommissioned officers the prerogatives of using physical violence on the enlisted man. Military discipline is necessary because of the nature of the population being disciplined.

To compound the matter, the armed services are frequently used by judicial mechanisms as correctional "dumping grounds" for adjudicated delinquents and deviants, or for young men who may face trial. Judges, law-enforcement officers, and parole personnel frequently "encourage" or order young offenders to enlist in the military as an alternative to facing trial or serving a jail sentence.[4] It must be admitted, however, that programs such as the one in World War II that paroled large numbers of inmates from prison into the military tended to be relatively successful. In one such program in Illinois, "the violation rate for Army parolees was 5.2 percent compared with a violation rate of 22.6 percent for civil parolees" (Mattick 1954:49). This success was explained on the basis of several factors, including the army's tolerance of misconduct being "so apparent that a 'lenience factor' was demonstrated to be at work favoring the 'adjustment' rates computed for parolees as compared with similar rates computed for the controls" (Mattick 1954:51). The parolee also enjoyed a degree of anonymity in the army in regard to his past criminal record. Additionally, it was pointed out that "the Army, being an all-male culture, informally tolerates certain male behavioral excesses to a greater degree than mixed civilian society" (Mattick 1954:54).

The Stress of Military Existence

Individuals neither live nor work in a state of tranquility or equilibrium. Rather, they are subjected to a variety of disruptive

---

[4] A typical example of this practice was described in our local newspaper several years back. The paper reported that a local circuit court judge had two 18-year-old youths appear before him and plead guilty to felony charges. The judge offered the youths the "choice" of joining the army or being sentenced to prison for two years. The judge further stipulated that if the youths did not serve the full enlistment time, went absent without leave while in service, or were not honorably discharged, they would be returned to his court for formal sentencing (see *Bowling Green-Park City Daily News* 1970).

The U.S. military officially deplores such action. Army Regulation 601–201 specifically prohibits the enlistment of an individual as an alternative to further prosecution or a means of avoiding incarceration or other judicial punishment. Letting young persons accused of a crime avoid prosecution by joining the military is still a widespread practice in some courts, however. Some prosecuting attorneys say they have "such a request about once a month." Because of the new volunteer system, there may be some decline in this practice (see Coombs 1976). Pipelining civilian offenders into the military has not been without consequences. It has been reported (Johnson and Wilson, 1972:36), for example, that "part of the reason for rising crime in Germany, according to Army investigators, is the influx of gangsters coming into the Army—some of them sent there by judges as the alternative to going to jail."

stresses, conflicts, and disaffections. Particular kinds of occupational specialty and work systems may expose their member practitioners to characteristic configurations of such stresses and disruptions. The disequilibrium may be both chronic and unique to the particular work setting. The attempt on the part of the individual to evade, ameliorate, cope with, or compensate for these strains may take the form of pathological or deviant behavior, either antisocial or self-destructive. The hazards, dilemmas, and discomforts of a job are as much a part of the fabric of work as are the benefits, affections, and satisfactions that accompany the occupation. Military life possesses certain inherent stresses and dissaffections.

For many, military existence is oppressive in its authoritarian discipline and rigidity.[5] Individualism is suppressed, and individual freedoms and prerogatives are eroded. The requisite subordination to persons of higher rank and to military discipline in general is demeaning to some individuals who chafe under the constraints of the military role, and find the constituent system of repressive social control, and the attendant punishments, dissaffective and repugnant. U.S. culture emphasizes personal freedom and choice, as well as initiative , novelty, and individuality. All of these characteristics are essentially antithetical to the traditional military posture. Persons who do find the oppressive element of military life intolerable may react with a rejection of discipline and authority, such as insubordination, disrespect, or failure to carry out orders. They may also attempt to escape from what they perceive as an odious situation. The attempt to escape may assume an objective form such as going AWOL or desertion, or be more of a subjective effort such as overindulgence in alcohol or narcotics. There are even suicides in the military that can be traced to a reaction to an intolerable situation of discipline and authority. On the other hand, other members of the military may develop informal systems of behavior that effectively blunt, dilute, subvert, evade, or thwart the formal proscriptions and prescriptions, much in the fashion of the fictional characters of the television series "M*A*S*H." In all such instances the disaffected individuals, by virtue of their

---

[5] It has been traditionally believed that rigid discipline and harsh punishment prevent or at least minimize the violation of military norm. A very recent study (Hart 1978:1456), however, reveals that increasing punishment does not deter crime, rather "recipients often respond to this punishment with a feeling of injustice, which then incites them to break the law more frequently, resulting in more serious problems on a delayed basis."

unauthorized and proscribed behavior, violate formal norms and become military deviants.

Military discipline is necessary because of the nature of the military mission. Not every individual is sufficiently imbued with either the warrior spirit or the patriotic zeal to motivate him to risk death or terrible infirmity in battle or to kill and maim others. Military discipline removes from the individual the necessity of making a choice in the matter. If conscripted and ordered into combat, the individual has no recourse but to follow legitimate orders, even if they mean death. Failure to do so constitutes a violation of military regulation and is appropriately punished, in the previously discussed case of Pvt. Eddie Slovik. Many military authorities, including one of the legal officers who reviewed the court-martial record, contended that Slovik was shot "not as a punitive measure nor as retribution, but to maintain that discipline upon which alone an army can succeed against the enemy" (Huie 1954:10–11). Close-order drill is traditionally retained in military systems not so much for the purpose of preparing for orderly movement from place to place or for aesthetically satisfying parade-ground performance, but rather to instill in the troops a reflexive obedience to order that will carry over into combat, insuring an immediate and complete obedience to command regardless of the circumstances. The violence of combat and war has a severe traumatic impact on most individuals. In some instances exposure to the violence of battle not infrequently produces or precipitates psychosomatic illness or mental disorders. In World War I, servicemen who were mentally traumatized by violence were sometimes referred to as "shell-shocked," while in World War II the phrase "combat psychosis" was more frequently used. Even for those who do not succumb to psychological withdrawal, combat and violence cause stress to the point of dysfunction and pathology and, not infrequently, exhibition of escape behavior. According to Blake (1970:335):

> Specifically, this passage shock [confrontation with combat] will lead either to an inability to accept the experience of combat, or action-out-of-place. Examples of the former include various forms of flight behavior (panic, "bugging-out," etc.) as well as some form of what is commonly called shell-shock (cornering in a hole, "neurotic" behavior, etc.), i.e., inability to accept as meaningful the experience of the battlemoment [cf. Hemingway 1968:17: "Cowardice . . . is almost always simply a lack of ability to suspend the functioning of the imagination."].

The stresses of war and combat may linger with the individual long after the cessation of the violence itself. In this regard Kroll (1976:63) has commented:

> The prolonged indoctrination in basic training toward efficient killing sets the stage, but does not come close to preparing the young men for the full horrors of the combat experience, especially one in which the civilian population is so inextricably involved. More recently, studies have appeared documenting the difficulties the veterans have as a result of their Vietnam experiences (Borus 1973; Lifton 1973; Shaton 1973).

Kroll and other researchers have asserted that war and combat have a lasting traumatic impact on individuals. He contends that even if they survive the war physically they will "see and react to the world differently as a result of their wartime experiences," and thus be "victims of the war," as it were. The stress of battle affects individuals in unusual ways. In Vietnam some black servicemen apparently experienced considerable anxiety as a result of combat, and this anxiety sometimes manifested itself in inordinate hostility and aggression toward white soldiers. Kroll (1976:62) has observed that:

> From the black point of view, it was the white man who had placed them in such a vulnerable situation. Their resentment, both immediate and delayed, was toward the white man, and also toward themselves for agreeing to fight in a white man's war, and consequently exposing themselves to the feelings of fear and helplessness which arise in combat.

This combat stress experienced by blacks contributed to the fact that "twice as many black soldiers as white were incarcerated for refusal to go out to the field for combat." Similarly, "twice as many black soldiers as white soldiers were incarcerated for violent crimes against other U.S. soldiers." Thus the stress of combat triggers a variety of reactions, including aggressive behavior directed at persons other than the enemy. Other kinds of actions include being unable to stop killing (Marshall 1947:200) and excessive brutality toward enemy POW's, all of which could constitute military offenses in some instances.

In a study of 293 servicemen who had served in Vietnam, committed criminal offenses while there, and then been sentenced to the U.S. Disciplinary Barracks at Fort Leavenworth, Kansas, Kroll (1976:63) concluded that these servicemen "did not appear to be different from other soldiers in Vietnam." The only thing that distinguished them from other men that had served in Vietnam was that "these men put into action some of the fears, hostilities, and temptations that all men felt in Vietnam." In short, the stress of war in Vietnam had somehow manifested itself in the commission of military crime.

The rigidity of military discipline and the trauma of combat are not the only stresses attendant to military existence. As a large, impersonal, and rigid bureaucratic organization, there is a relative loss of identity and autonomy in the military and less opportunity for individualization and self-expression than in many other settings, with attendant dissaffection, stress, and erosion of self-image. This may precipitate antisocial or self-destructive behavior.

Noncombat military duty can also be stressful. The routine repetitiveness of training and drill, the monotony and drabness of garrison life or naval-base duty, with the attendant ennui and tedium of day-to-day military existence, may all drive the individual to seek respite in the form of drugs, alcohol, or flight, or in some instances to the extent of aggravating and encouraging the violation of military rules and norms.

Opportunity Structure

The inordinate number of norms and legal statutes in the military make it difficult to avoid their violation. Beyond the existence of such a morass of legal proscriptions and prescriptions is the further factor of opportunity based on the ubiquitous abundance of military equipment and supplies, the interactive frequency of subordinate and superior, and, in combat, the anomic isolation and insulation from mechanisms of social control.

Vast amounts of rations, supplies, and equipment must be appropriately allocated and used if the military mission is to be accomplished. The traditional verse about the battle's being lost for want of a horseshoe nail has considerable validity in military fact. The abundance of material in the military means that its control and maintenance of security is difficult to effect. For this reason, a significant proportion of military regulations concern themselves with offenses against government property, and in this regard military justice is often severe. To maintain proper equipment allocation, considerable effort is expended by military systems to insure appropriate equipment accountability in terms of both units and individuals. In spite of these elaborate configurations of supply controls and regulations in military systems, the fact remains that military existence is often one of deprivation. Military personnel not infrequently resort to misappropriation of government property for their personal or group use, with the intention of improving their comfort, effectiveness, and chance of survival. Where property and supplies are accessible and abundant (maintained in dumps and warehouses), even if not equitably distributed, there is a likelier chance of misappropriation.

In occupied countries with a flourishing black market and a desperate shortage of food and consumer goods, military supplies and equipment take on an inordinately high economic and social value to the indigenous populations. American GI's who initially occupied Germany in World War II discovered that a mere carton of cigarettes or case of C-ration might readily be traded for a variety of German family heirlooms, bring a handsome price in invasion marks, or support a fräulein for a month or so in relatively luxurious style. The temptation was too much for many American military servicemen, who undertook to acquire lucrative incomes from black-market activities and advantageous currency exchanges.

The rigidity of military authority also provides opportunities for violent crimes against persons. The opportunity to abuse subordinates, such as the young recruit in basic training, is present to a degree unparalleled in civilian life, and is often exacerbated by the pressures and stresses attendant to command and responsibility. Given the oppressive authoritarianism of the military structure, inappropriate responses or reactions from subordinates that violate rules or laws are not unexpected, but the military offers some unusual opportunities for extreme reaction to perceived grievances or dissaffection. The enlisted man who thinks his platoon leader to be a petty tyrant, for example, can easily avail himself of a grenade or claymore mine in a combat situation and deal with his oppressor through the simple expedient of "fragging." Similarly, an officer who wishes to deal with a recalcitrant private who constantly foments trouble can readily have the private serve as point man for the unit in a mined area, until the private has the misfortune to step on a mine. The extremely dangerous context in which the military often operates simply provides an opportunity structure for violence directed at peer, superior, or subordinate, and the violence can be easily disguised. Moreover, combat is a social situation separate and apart from normal existence. Conventional norms of behavior and civility are suspended, as it were, and the individual soldier finds himself in an ephemeral anomic situation. Even military social control is often absent or diluted to the point of nonexistence. The soldier could not loot if he were not in a combat or occupied area where there is little or no effective social control to prevent it. In a war situation, under the strain of physical and psychological trauma, the soldier may shoot prisoners or murder civilians as a necessary expedient for sheer survival. Atrocities are committed because they can be committed, often with no residual evidence. The military offers an opportunity structure for all manner of deviant acts, perhaps exceeding all other work systems in this regard. The occupational opportunity structure offers absorption or concealment of deviance, avoidance of stigma, or neutralization of guilt, as well as opportunity for the commission of the deviance itself.

Military Culture

To cope with their environment, provide for their needs and wants, and accomplish their social goals, work systems develop distinctive patterns of behavior and attendant material artifacts and accessories. As in the larger society, the totality of these behavioral and material configurations constitutes a culture for the work system. The military is no exception to this rule. Work culture represents an elaborate way of coping with the problems of work, including getting the job accomplished; making the process endurable, if not rewarding, for those involved; and developing a social justification and individual rationalization requisite to the continued existence of the work system. The culture of a work organization may, for example, define the appropriate routine and tempo of work for the workers. In time they will internalize these norms and values and thus be shaped by the culture of their work.

Work culture also defines social conformity and thus, to an extent, morality in that it provides reason and rationalization for certain kinds of job-related behavior, as well as clarifying, obscuring, or modifying the individual's perspective of social control and sanction. Work cultures provide elaborate myth systems that in turn may initiate, support, sustain, and perpetuate various kinds of deviant behavior attendant to the occupational efforts.

The work culture may, either formally or informally, define and prescribe effective appropriate buffering agents to ameliorate the stresses and strains of work. The harried businessman has relied on drinking to maintain the executive pace, and research indicates that the physician uses various kinds of drugs to endure the tempo of his work. Both semiformally and informally, the military traditionally has relied on alcohol for between-combat respites or to alleviate the monotony of garrison duty. But in recent years, especially in Vietnam, the informal culture has dictated marijuana as the preferred relaxant, although it is sternly forbidden by formal military regulation. In addition to being readily accessible in Vietnam, marijuana is in a sense a "protest" drug and symbolic of the counterculture.

Work culture may also define the appropriate image of, and value stance toward, customer or clientele. In the military the clientele may be the enemy military, or civilians, either U.S., foreign friendly, or enemy. Or work culture may define an appropriate means for workers to deal with the boredom of their work. The diversion may be as innocuous as simple games constructed out of variations in the work routine itself. It may take more reprehensible forms, such as frequent and intense amorous and sexual liaisons with employees of the opposite sex, and even involve atrocity behavior, where soldiers, in an attempt to alleviate the personal strain of war, may while away their spare hours sniping at isolated civilians or seeking to rape and plunder the indigenous population.

At a formal level work culture may identify an expected standard of work performance, but at an informal level it may articulate the means by which the members of the work system may appropriately and successfully evade or subvert the formal norms. Informal work culture may also impose an alternate set of work-level expectations and specify the sanctions for violators of the norm. Because work culture defines for the individual many of his perspectives of reality and thus shapes his existential experience, in effect it provides him with an awareness of opportunities for deviant behavior within his work and a motivation and justification or rationalization for engaging in such behavior.

Military culture is structured around the constituent characteristics of a "total institution." Goffman (1961:xiii). In paraphrasing these various characteristics, (Zurcher (1965:390) has written that in a total institution:

1. All aspects of life are conducted in the same place and under the same single authority.
2. Each phase of the member's daily activity is carried on in the immediate company of a large batch of others, all of whom are treated alike and required to do the same thing together.
3. All phases of the day's activities are tightly scheduled, with one activity leading at a prearranged time into the next, the whole sequence of activities being imposed from above by a system of explicit formal rulings and a body of officials.
4. The various enforced activities are brought together into a single rational plan purportedly designed to fulfill the official aim of the institution.
5. There is a sharp split between the supervisors and the members, with social mobility between the two groups being highly restricted.
6. Information concerning the fate of the member is often withheld from him.
7. The work structure in the total institution, geared as it is to a twenty-four-hour day, demands different motives for work than exist in society-at-large.
8. There are usually real or symbolic barriers indicating a break with the society "out there."

Members of the military are constrained to act in a concerted and uniform, collective fashion under bureaucratic authority, in the form of a series of commanders. All activities are carried out in a systematic, scheduled manner according to a set of formal rules, regulations, and norms. The organizational and status cleavage between the enlisted and officer's rank is sharp and decisive. Similarly, there is considerable separation and differentiation, both real and symbolic, between military and civilian society. The individual, especially at the lower ranks, is seldom privy to any significant information about "his fate." The military operates on a much different set of motives from those that exist in the larger society. In this connection, Zurcher (1965) has drawn a detailed analogy between the naval vessel and the concepts of the total institution. According to Zurcher (1965:391), "the ship *at sea* is a total institution." Military culture is very much an embellishment of the themes of the total institution.

The military is bureaucratic to a fault. There are pressures to operate with ultimate efficiency, but in actuality this is seldom the case. There is a heavy emphasis on responsibility and accountability. One result of this is the tedious reliance on paperwork as a means of formally assigning and identifying responsibility and accountability. Another counterproductive result is the development of elaborate systems and mechanisms, formal and informal, for evading or subverting responsibility and accountability. Military culture incorporates values that encourage "passing the buck." A company commander who may be derelict in obtaining some required supplies or equipment can shift the blame for his dereliction by formally requisitioning the supplies or equipment through official channels. The shortage can then be attributed to supply channels, and the commander is secure in the defense that the equipment is "on requisition." In effect, compliance with the bureaucratic mandate for absolute accountability is elaborately subverted through various subterfuges that are usually dysfunctional for the military mission, although successful for the individual.

The extreme emphasis on bureaucratic structure and procedures tends to produce a posture of rigidity and almost pathological concern with (although not necessarily adherence to) the rules.[6] "Doing things by the book," or as it is phrased in the U.S. Army, "doing things by the numbers" (for training purposes, even relatively simple activities are broken down into component acts and numbered sequentially so that the neophyte can more easily inculcate the procedure), often becomes a value of almost compulsive dimension. The emphasis on rigid adherence to procedures and rules, aside from often being inefficient and cumbersome, also sometimes evolves into a kind of dramaturgical chicanery. Things are done for appearance's sake, or to deceive a superior. A common phrase in this regard is "eyewash," meaning something that is for superficial deception or camouflage purposes only. Thus dramaturgical presentation, deception, and conceal-

---

[6] The story has been told that during the Japanese attack on Pearl Harbor on December 7, 1941, some U.S. soldiers at Schofield barracks grabbed their rifles and went outside, prepared to shoot at the low-flying Japanese planes that were strafing the base. Needing ammunition for their rifles, the soldiers asked the sergeant in charge of the ammunition storeroom to open the lock. He is said to have refused on the grounds that the rules flatly stated that in the absence of a directive from his superiors, he could not unlock the storeroom "except in an emergency."

ment are all informal cultural themes in the military and may, in some instances, contribute to deviant behavior.

The military, traditionally composed primarily of males and concerned with violent and aggressive behavior, has a strong value orientation of manliness (i.e., *macho, machismo*) and virility.[7] "Toughness" and aggressiveness are highly favored characteristics and are often equated with "leadership." Good soldiers must be stoic and, on occasion, brutal. Such an ideological posture tends to produce a degree of insensitivity, fatalistic determination, and daring, all of which may be the pregenitors of deviancy. In a related vein Berger (1946:86) has observed that:

> Simulated grimness and toughness are of a fiction soldiers accept, for these qualities are traditionally soldierly. The leader, too, is always constrained to show his leadership and he does this (except in combat) mainly by an assumed attitude of hardness and unconcern for regulations.

Berger (1946:85), in his commentary on law and custom in the army, has also pointed out that among other cultural themes are the need for complete uniformity and the presence of extreme and endemic rivalry. Rivalry is an abiding and carefully cultivated attitude in the military. It breeds agressiveness and initiative for battle, but it also opens the door for interunit, interservice, or even interpersonal hostility, violence, and theft, as well as precipitating other kinds of proscribed behavior.

Berger also has asserted that the emphasis on hierarchical rela-

---

[7] Early in World War II, the story was told that an officer was inspecting the footlockers of his men in a barracks when he came across a jar of deodorant in one soldier's footlocker. "What is this?" asked the officer. "Deodorant, sir, for my body odor." Deodorant was relatively new, not widely used, and used primarily by females. The officer is said to have replied, "Soldier, if you're going to stink, you're going to stink, but dammit, you're going to stink like a man! Get rid of that stuff."

A recent study of females in the military (see Schreiber and Woelfel, 1977:6) raises the question of whether or not the adjustment of females in the military will be handicapped by the all-men environment and the training emphasis on manhood and masculinity. In effect, will the strong masculine orientation be a hostile value system for women. As the researchers phrase it: "It might well be, then, that the psychological climate of the U.S. Army experience would prove to be uncongenial for woman soldiers and that this uncongeniality would negatively affect both their enthusiasm and their motivation for performing Army tasks."

On the other hand, it may well be that in time, the increasing number of females in the military may well effectively erode or dilute the masculine culture and a new uni-sex of uni-gender culture may become the prevailing value system in the military.

tionships has generated the attitude that in the army (and no doubt in the other armed services as well) it is considered "unmanly" to offer excuses. Berger says, "An attempt to excuse one's error is considered an attempt to avoid the consequences for having committed it." As he goes on to explain, "To excuse one's self or to explain an error is to criticize, in some degree, the superior for having pointed out the error." Perhaps related to this is the preoccupation with status differentiation so characteristic of the military everywhere. Even relatively minor differences in rank and status are often exaggerated, and the superior-subordinate relationship is stressed to a considerable degree. This overemphasis on differential statuses may contribute to feelings of frustration, deprivation, and hostility on the part of subordinates, and could be a factor in acts of aggression or violence directed at superiors. The most obvious such status cleavage is the officer/enlisted distinction. By way of illustration, one enlisted man in World War II was reported to have complained, "What's the matter with us enlisted men, are we dogs?" (Vidich and Stein 1960:495).

Berger (1946:84) has also asserted that "while theoretically not tolerant of errors in official duties, the Army is very tolerant of certain excesses generally believed to be owning to the weakness of the flesh." In this sense there is an ideology of toleration in the military based on the idea that "men will be men." Berger additionally speaks of the "cult of the rifle" as an old tradition. This concept might be broadened to encompass the "cult of the weapon," for the military revolves first and foremost around the weapon, be it rifle, cannon, fighter plane, or warship. The individual is, in effect, subordinated to the weapon. Perfection in use of the weapon is perhaps the highest value of military life, and individual proficiency with the weapon is one of the most desired personal goals. The purpose of the weapon is to destroy, by the rules of war if possible, but otherwise, in any way that is expedient. In Vietnam some soldiers kept in practice for combat by shooting at civilians.

Finally, attention must be directed toward the considerable distinction between soldier and civilian that is inculcated by the military. The work, mission, and motivation of the soldier contrast so sharply with those of the civilian that the civilian who enters the military must be totally transformed. He must literally acquire a new self-identity, a new ideological posture, and a much different set of perspectives. In order to accomplish this effectively, military culture emphasizes the distinction between soldier and civilian and even attempts to exacerbate the contrast. Members of the military are segregated from civilian life, and are involved in a social enterprise of different dimensions and tempo. The soldier, by design and training, comes to enjoy a different existential reality. Conceptualizing the world differently, the soldier can more readily do those things that are required of the soldier but that may be antithetical to his original cultural value stance. Once the new conceptual perspective is accomplished, however, the individual may be able to redefine any act from deviant and antisocial to expedient and normatively correct. If killing in war ceases to be murder, then stealing from the quartermaster dump can easily be rationalized on the basis of group imperatives.

Military Socialization

The mission of the military is of such a nature, and the role responsibilities of individual members so demanding, that the socialization process must be extraordinarily intense, totally comprehensive, and effectively convert the civilian into a noncivilian in terms of values, beliefs, and perspectives, as well as behavior. Civilian value systems and military value systems are often antiethical, and the average civilian may well be dissaffected to the point of immobility at the prospect of violence and mayhem, killing and/or being killed, and the necessity for blind obedience to orders from superiors. The civilian must be converted into that which he was not—a warrior with warlike proclivities. Zurcher (1967:85), in his study of navy boot training, has spoken of the neophyte coming to the navy with a "presenting culture, an elaborate set of values, beliefs, roles, norms, and expectations which lead him to behave in certain ways with regard to certain perceived social stimuli." It is this "presenting culture" that must be diluted and washed away. He must come to leave behind his "civilian frame of reference" and the "set of cultural values and expectancies that are not compatible" with the military's objective and organization, and be transformed and reoriented in his behavior "to the military standard" (Zurcher 1967:88). In this connection military training must be painful and traumatic. As Zurcher (1967:91) describes it: "Assault after assault is being made on the new recruit's 'presenting culture' self. It seems that many of his responses to situations which had served him well in civilian life are now inappropriate or ineffective."

Zurcher's review of the literature (1967:88) in this regard reveals that military training has been described as "shock treatment" (Stouffer 1949), a "crisis" (Janis 1945:159), and "personally degrading" (Brotz and Wilson 1946:372–74). Some individuals are not able to endure the change or to meet the required expectations. They may drop out of training and be discharged, rebel and be court-martialed or otherwise punished, develop schizophrenic or other mental health problems (Erikson and Marlowe 1959), or in some instances, even commit suicide. Military training requires major adjustments of all who do succeed (Weinberg 1945:272; Hollingshead 1946:440). The successfully socialized military neophyte has shifted roles, self-conceptions, value systems, and perspectives. Seeing the world from the new vantage point of military service, certain situations and behaviors are now redefined, and that which was viewed as deviant may now be viewed as merely expedient or consistent with military culture, custom, and expectation.

The major goal of military socialization is to remake the civilian into a killer, and one who follows orders in doing so. According to Vidich and Stein (1960:498):

> Since such ideological incentives as patriotism could not be counted upon, the training-period had to create incentives that would fit the established purposes of the military machine, particularly, acceptance by the recruit of the self-image of a combat soldier.

Military training may imbue the individual with mystical notions and exaggerated beliefs about his new self, and this may have implications for his new interpretations of morality and normative behavior, as well as for his relationship with other servicemen, civilians, and even the enemy. Weiss (1967:25), in his account of training in the army airborne forces, points out that "They [paratroopers] consider themselves superior to all other such groups—not only in their military virtues but in their vices as well. A paratrooper is supposed to be able to outdrink, outbrawl, and outwhore any other member of the armed forces." Military training, by intention, does often enable the individual to develop identification with, pride in, and loyalty to a particular service, branch, or unit, which in turn may permit him to rationalize personal offenses that he has endured. Lyon (1969:223) has observed that "In order to justify to himself the severe initiation of recruit training, the Marine recruit has to assign high value to the group joined (or devalue the harshness of training)." A high degree of identification with a unit usually encompasses a high degree of identification with the values and mission of the unit. Lyon (1972) tells the story of one of his new staff psychiatrists who masqueraded as a marine recruit in order to monitor the program. His DI (drill instructor) would not allow his platoon enough time to use the toilet facilities. In desperation, the doctor abandoned his masquerade in order to be able to use the toilet. Years later, the psychiatrist had forgotten the indignity and sadism of the DI in not giving recruits a chance to use the toilet, and instead was prone to speak of the "purifying" aspects of marine training. Physical and psychological brutality in military training, especially where there is an acceptance of it, tends to brutalize the individual being socialized.

Military socialization and existence tends also to inculcate a strong reliance on, and identification with, the informal group. Thus peer-group influence, good or bad, becomes an important factor in the behavior of members of the military. Shils and Janowitz (1948), in their study of social solidarity in the German Wehrmacht in World War II, have convincingly demonstrated that interpersonal relationships in small military units—the primary group—are significant influences on individual behavior. The primary group aids in survival and provides personal gratification. It also dictates norms and values, and provides the definition of the situation. In many instances the informal organization assumes primacy over the formal in influencing and ordering individual behavior, thus encouraging violation of the military norm. One writer (Anonymous 1945–46:365) has stated that:

> The informal social organization of the enlisted men actually controls many army activities theoretically governed by the formal army organization. . . .Customs which may contradict or reinforce formal army regulations are developed in the informal group to control many of the details of army life.

Official Toleration of Military Deviancy

As a means of effecting efficiency, some degree of norm violation is tolerated and even tacitly encouraged by the military, although it must never come to public attention. In a similar vein, considering the mission of the military and the tasks expected of its members, a major problem is maintaining morale, neutralizing frustration and anxiety among the troops, and motivating personnel to channel aggressive goals properly. To accomplish this also requires some relaxation of the strict and pervasive norms that govern military life. The troops may have to "let off steam" as a discipline safety valve, and to do so may mean letting them "beat hell out of some 'slopes.' " As Elkin (1946:409) noted of the servicemen of World War II:

> One aspect of this negativism, whose ill-effect on international relations will remain incalculable, is that our immediate allies became the primary scapegoat for the G.I.'s need for self-assertion. Just as the Germans, servile and compliant in their own life, came to feel strong and important by venting their pent-up aggression on "inferior" Jews, Poles, and Russians, so the G.I. "took it out" on "damned Limeys" and "dirty Frogs," but *not*, interestingly enough, on the Germans and southern Italians who directly gratified his self-esteem by behaving toward him as a conqueror. A correspondent from China recently wrote that G.I. drivers go out of their way to splash mud on Chinese trudging along the side of the road![8]

Crimes against property may be tolerated in the interest of efficiency, and crimes against person may be treated with leniency in the interest of morale and motivation. Crimes against performance, however, are usually viewed with more seriousness and punished with more severity, inasmuch as the commission is almost wholly antithetical to the military mission.

Subversion of Military Training

In addition to a unique demographic base that is prone to certain kinds of deviance and an informal subculture that tends to

---

[8] Attitudes of U.S. servicemen had changed little by the time of the Vietnam war. Members of the U.S. military in Vietnam tended to view ARVN soldiers as "faggots" and not infrequently would take out their frustrations with the war on some ARVN soldier (Levy 1971). Their attitude toward Vietnamese civilians was such that U.S. soldiers riding in a truck past civilians on bicycles would sometimes hold their rifles over the edge of the truck in an attempt to knock the hats off the civilians or the civilians off the bicycles (Kroll 1976:58).

promote it, the formal training strategy and specific objectives of the U.S. military may contain latent dysfunctional elements that tend to facilitate and encourage the violation of formal military regulations.

The military may often operate in a noncombative context and may also frequently undertake responsibilities of a peaceful nature, but basically it stands as a work system whose unique function is to implement political decisions by force of arms or threat of force of arms. Its mission, therefore, must include the development of an effective capability to wage war. This is accomplished through concerted training efforts. As the U.S. Army officially states its training mission (Dept. of the Army 1967):

> To attain and maintain the Army at a state of operational ef-
> fectiveness which will assure the capability of closing with and
> destruction of the enemy through prompt and sustained combat
> operations on land, along or jointly with the Navy, Air Force, or
> both, and to conduct effective counterinsurgency operations in-
> cluding the support of friendly or allied counterinsurgency opera-
> tions.

To effect this training mission and "its supporting tasks," the U.S. Army further articulates five basic objectives (Dept. of the Army 1967:3): military discipline, health, strength, and endurance, technical proficiency, teamwork, and tactical proficiency. These particular objectives, while patently functional to the attainment of the stated training mission and subsequently to military performance (especially combat performance), would also seem to be dysfunctional in the sense of contribution to the commission of khaki-collar crime. As indicated in Table 2, their contribution to khaki-collar crime may well grow out of a subverted

TABLE 2. Structural Subversion of Military Training

United States Army Basic Training Objectives	Residual Dysfunctional Training Elements Facilitative to Military Deviancy
Military discipline	Authoritarian indoctrination, reflexive discipline, and unhesitating obedience, while desirable for military purposes, may also lead to a dilution of personal responsibility and misinterpretation of goals.

TABLE 2. (cont.)

United States Army Basic Training Objectives	Residual Dysfunctional Training Elements Facilitative to Military Deviancy
Health, strength, and endurance	The attainment of fitness and confidence may result in "toughness." This may in turn breed insensitivity and brutality. Regard with health often leads to overconcern with comfort and luxury, even if illicitly obtained.
Technical proficiency	Overemphasis on mechanical expertise and efficiency, particularly with weaponry and in combat skills, leads to "overkill" and adroitness in the violation of regulations.
Teamwork	Overreliance on informal structure, for accomplishing formal expectations as well as for personal support, leads to excessive influence of informal groups in determining norms and effecting sanctions.
Tactical proficiency	The attainment of military goals and military activities in general is conceptualized as a "game." The violation of formal norms also becomes a "game."

interpretation and relevancy and the process of making the training objectives operational in an exigent nontraining situation.

MILITARY DISCIPLINE

Military indoctrination and socialization revolve around absolute discipline and mental and physical control of the individual. The extent of physical control is such that marine recruits, for example, are "not permitted a bowel movement for the first week of boot camp" (Levy 1971:18). The product of successful training will, according to military design, "recognize and respect authority and give unhesitating obedience to that authority." Such reflexive discipline tends to permit the individual to transfer to his superior the responsibility and, thus, the guilt for any action ordered, even if in violation of social, if not military, norm. A disciplined social system is essentially an unreasoning social system. Crimes such as theft of equipment from other units or even the murder of prisoners may be committed by an individual when ordered or even if he thinks such action is desired by his superior. Lt. Calley, for example, is alleged to have said to a subordinate, "You *know* [italics added] what I want you to do with them (My Lai civilians). . ." (Hersh 1970:65).

HEALTH, STRENGTH, AND ENDURANCE

Requisite to the obvious military need for boldness and endurance on the part of individual servicemen is fitness, strength, and confidence (including determination and aggressiveness), and to this end a significant proportion of military training is devoted to developing stamina and confidence. Many of the physical fitness "obstacle" courses are labeled "confidence" courses. The bayonet course, also called a "confidence" course, involves much yelling and grimacing, which is supposed to develop determination and aggressiveness.

Fitness and confidence, however, often militarily defined as "toughness," may breed insensitivity and antisocial aggressiveness. "Elite" combat troops, such as paratroops, rangers, and marines, famed for their "toughness," are also notorious for their fighting and brawling with civilians and other troops, both American and friendly foreign, as well as their savage combat ability. "Tough" units take what they want from civilians and other units, and frequently "do not take prisoners."

Ancillary to the emphasis on confidence and aggressiveness is the training concern with health, and thus collaterally with hygiene, food, shelter, medical treatment, and recreation. A significant proportion of training is devoted to these topics, thus underscoring the American preoccupation with creature comforts and physical condition. American troops are conditioned to anticipate a high level of logistical luxury. Unlike Oriental armies, which may fight poorly clothed and meagerly fed and with little else but a weapon, the American armed forces anticipate and demand being superbly equipped regardless of where they go or fight. When the formal bureaucratic channels will not provide the appropriate items of equipment and supplies for individual or unit comfort and survival, informal, clandestine, unauthorized, or illegal means of obtaining these materials will be employed, including elaborate systems of "scrounging" and barter and various means of theft, misappropriation, and black marketeering.

Similarly, American troops, in their preoccupation with material affluence, may also illegally confiscate, acquire, or misappropriate foreign friendly or enemy property, or captured enemy equipment.

TECHNICAL PROFICIENCY

The military man, no different from his civilian counterpart, derives intrinsic satisfaction and personal pride from expertise in his occupational skill. The bombardier may take justifiable pride in the accuracy of his bomb drop, and the quartermaster officer may derive occupational satisfaction from the knowledge that his equipment accounting records are above reproach. In the navy appropriate occupational skills may justify a rating. It is significant to note that the annual evaluation reports on U.S. Army officers are known as efficiency reports, and commendations of various kinds are frequently awarded for jobs performed well. Purely military skills are particularly emphasized and excellence in skill is recognized. The MOS (Military Occupational Specialty) is awarded after demonstration of proficiency in the given specialty. Proficiency in weaponry is recognized by awarding appropriate Marksman, Sharpshooter, or Expert badges after demonstration of a specific level of competence with particular firearms.

The ultimate aim of military skills, however, is effectiveness in combat, which implies destructiveness. Historically, the military man has taken pride in his destructive ability. John Hersey (1947:144), for example, in his novel *The War Lover*, has his protagonist, Buzz, the B-17 pilot in World War II, proudly proclaim: " 'I like to fly,' he said. 'I like the work we're doing. . . .' 'Listen,' he said, with flashing eyes, 'Bowman [his co-pilot] and I belong to the most destructive group of men in the history of the world. That's our work.' "

In his detailed analysis of violence as a military process, Blake (1970:338) has pointed out that military socialization involves equipping the soldier to be an efficient combat killer. As he put it:

> The opening phase of the socialization process begins shortly after recruitment and entails the attempted destruction of previously held roles and the preliminary fitting of the actor to the role of organizational killer. This latter entails two analytically distinct processes; first, instilling the military rationale into the actor and second, giving him the technical training required to make him a proficient killer.

Proficiency in destruction acquired in training is frequently reinforced in a combat situation. It was reported, for example, that in Vietnam "one brigade commander ran a contest to celebrate the unit's 10,000th enemy kill" (Hersh 1970:55). Such a practice was common in many units. With such competitive zeal, the troops were not always particular about identification of the enemy. In Vietnam there was a saying, "Anything that's dead and isn't white is a VC" (Hersh 1970:56). Technical proficiency, even in killing, apparently provides some measure of intrinsic satisfaction. Referring to the incident at My Lai, Hersh reports, "Some GIs were shouting and yelling during the massacre. Carter [a participant] recalled: 'The boys enjoyed it. When someone laughs and jokes about what they're doing they have to be enjoying it' " (Hersh 1970:55). He also relates the story of an American battalion commander who listed his "kills" of Vietnamese by stenciling rows of conical hats on the fuselage of his helicopter, which he named the "Gookmobile" (Hersh 1970:55).

Interestingly, as war has progressed technologically, the actual contact between fighting man and enemy has become more mechanical and depersonalized, and the enemy is essentially dehumanized. Blake points out that those troops who are most technologically removed from the enemy and who thus are more prone to think of the enemy in dehumanized terms are the ones who require the least socialization as killers (Blake 1970:339). The bombardier never sees his victims, and therefore he need not acquire the "killer" spirit to the same degree as, say, the marine who may have to meet the enemy bayonet to bayonet. Philip Slater speaks of "extermination at a distance" and comments, "Flying in a plane far above an impersonally defined target and pressing some buttons to turn fifty square miles into a sea of flame is less traumatic to the average middle-class American boy than inflicting a superficial bayonet wound on a single soldier" (Slater 1970:4).

In Vietnam members of the armed forces could sometimes see the enemy, but often only from the vantage point of a "Huey" gunship (a helicopter equipped with machine guns, rocket launchers, and sophisticated aiming devices) where people are reduced to ant proportions. The pilots who strafe enemy troops, and sometimes civilians believed to be guerrillas, speak of "rabbit shoots," "barbecuing" peasants, and "hosing" a suspect with machine gun fire until he "blows up like a toy balloon" (Slater 1970:38–39). Being a good shot in a "Huey" is perhaps not unlike being expert at skeet shooting. The line between effective combat proficiency and war atrocities is a thin one.

So, too, is the line between shrewd quartermaster administration and misappropriation of government equipment. Embezzlers in civilian life are frequently highly skilled accountants who become "overly proficient" at their trade. Their skill affords them an opportunity structure not often available to the less skilled, plus an attitude of impunity. Some confidence men are so good at their criminal specialty that they cannot resist the chance to con someone, even if only for a few dollars. The expert is tempted to exceed the limits imposed on him for the sake of personal perfection or continual demonstration of his expertise. The master craftsman, even a military craftsman, looks for new work worlds to conquer; he seeks to experiment even at the risk of violating the rules. Some of the most able surgeons in America, for example, have been accused of undertaking operations that had no hope of success simply because they were "challenging." They were, in effect, using patients unethically as surgical guinea pigs to demonstrate their technical expertise. The expert is often overzealous to a fault. He may violate the norms of propriety in his enthusiasm for efficiency. As Hersey reflected, "Genius in flying, as in the performance of music, lies not in precision, not in being exactly on pitch and in time, but rather in the ability to perform with absolute accuracy and then to *break the rules by inspiration for the sake of a higher perfection*" [italics added] (1947:55).

The individuals who are most adept at breaking the rules are the "old-timers" and the ones most steeped in military know-how. Familiarity with technical routine can breed boredom with, if not contempt for, the normative structure.

TEAMWORK

Warfare historically has been essentially a collective enterprise. Military activities, even at the most elementary level, involve concerted effort and coordinated behavior. From the Macedonian Phalanx to the "crew-served" weapons of recent wars to today's sophisticated electronic weapons systems, the military apparatus is a man and machine system. It is, therefore, not surprising that the military emphasizes teamwork in its training and operations.

The development of strong teamwork linkages in the formal

organization also tends to engender equally strong symbiotic relationships at an informal level. Reliance on the informal structure is intensified by the fact that the military, as a bureaucratic enterprise, is sometimes ponderous and rigid. Not infrequently, as Zurcher (1965) suggests, the informal organization employs "patterned evasions"—regularized ways of getting around the demands of the formal organization, usually with the result of accomplishing the formal expectations in a quicker and more efficient way. The formal organization tolerates and overlooks, if not accepts, these patterned evasions in the interest of efficiency and end results. Zurcher (1965:393) has pointed out, for example, that on board ship there are numerous informal behaviors or "secondary adjustments" employed by members of the crew to subvert the regulations and official procedures and obtain favored treatment or living conditions for themselves. Over time the illicit procedures employed at an informal level become ritualized as part of the informal culture. Dornbusch, for instance, has pointed out that in the U.S. Coast Guard Academy, a first classman might dispatch a "swab" on an illicit errand. If caught, the swab would receive demerits. The first classman, to compensate the swab, would informally tell his classmate to withhold the same number of demerits from the swab for other offenses (1955:317). The informal culture of the military becomes in many instances a deviant culture with an elaborate value system that defines ways of violating formal military and civilian norms, as well as providing the rationalization and support for such violations.

The informal structure serves as a particularly potent reference group for another reason. Initial training in the military attempts and often succeeds in separating the neophyte from his former identity and ties. Military discipline is demanding and often oppressive, and military life not infrequently stressful. Enduring and coping with military discipline and life is made easier by the presence of a strong supportive informal structure.

TACTICAL PROFICIENCY

War, unlike most other forms of human hostile behavior, and certainly unlike other varieties of work (if war is, in fact, work), has been most often analogously compared to a game. As late as the Crimean War (and to a limited extent during the American Civil

War), some civilians went to witness specific battles, and even carried picnic lunches and refreshments. War was a sort of spectator sport. Military maneuvers are often referred to as war games, and practically all armies periodically have their senior-level officers engage in map exercises or map games. Much formal military training is structured in a game format; similarly, informal training often takes on the characteristics of a game. Not infrequently, some of this informal training actually involves the violation of various military regulations. Thus, "moonlight requisitioning" may be used as a means of instilling aggressiveness and resourcefulness in recruits. Initiative, resourcefulness, aggressiveness, and decisiveness—all characteristics developed by stealing equipment from other units—are also traits that contribute to tactical proficiency, and thus the effective soldier. Coincidentally, these characteristics appear to make for an equally effective criminal. A thief stealing an automobile may employ tactics similar to an infantryman on combat patrol. Einstadter (1969:77), in his study of armed robbery, concluded, "Military experience of a certain variety, for example, lends itself readily to robbery."

Armed with the game orientation acquired from the emphasis on tactical proficiency in military training, some individuals make a game of many of their military activities, including looting enemy property, wheeling and dealing on the black market, escaping from the military police after a raid on a brothel, outwitting a superior officer, or skillfully misappropriating military property for personal use. In all instances it is essentially a game where the object is to violate the rules and not get caught. It is interesting that this has been a recurring theme on several popular television shows, such as "McHale's Navy" and the "Sergeant Bilko" show. In such programs the sly servicemen constantly outmaneuver their superiors in a game of wits. For many individuals, military life itself becomes a game one plays, using various kinds and degrees of subterfuge. The good tactician can maneuver just as well in breaking the rules as in combat.

Summary

The military has a special problem of social control. It has a population difficult to control, but a primary mission that requires highly specific normative behavior. It also has a number of secondary aims and goals that call for a considerable degree of conformity on the part of its members to its own norms as well as norms imposed by a variety of other social systems. The opportunity structure of the military, however, is such that norm deviation is facilitated, and the informal subculture tends to promote this. Although, in theory, the military seeks to enforce its formal norms rigidly with severe sanctions, in actual practice it often finds it expedient to ignore or tolerate some degree of deviancy, especially where such behavior involves crimes against property or persons. Furthermore, the informal structure of the military is sufficiently effective to harbor and insulate the offender from both detection and sanction.

In the final analysis, certain kinds of deviant behavior on the part of military personnel, and conditions and circumstances that foster deviancy, actually are latently functional to the mission of the military and, as such, are tacitly if not actively endured and even promoted.

PART TWO

Intra-Occupational Crime

The importance of law as one of the forces in the maintenance of discipline in the Services needs no emphasis. "A member of the Fighting Forces undertakes additional liabilities—the deprivation of a considerable part of his personal liberty, the obligation of obedience to lawful commands and the whole catalog of duties summarized in the word 'discipline.' Without discipline the Fighting Services would perish."
Quoted in John C. Spencer, *Crime and the Services*

CHAPTER
THREE

Crimes Against Property

*An interesting phenomenon is the widespread
"appropriating" of various types of Navy property, and
making it one's personal possession. The sailor does not
consider such things as smuggling off the ship parts or
tools for his car or hobbies to be stealing.*
Louis A. Zurcher, Jr.

The question of property has always been of vital concern to the
armed forces. The protection and appropriate allocation of its own
supplies and equipment are especially important to the efficient
implementation of the military mission and attainment of its
goals. Modern warfare has taken on a technological complexity
that mandates elaborate and predictable, thus carefully regulated,
logistical support for military activities. The enormity of the
modern armed forces enterprise has necessitated "the unification of
all power of command by the government and the resulting
monopoly of property in arms and military equipment by the
State" (Heberle 1936:3).

Monopolistic ownership of military equipment by the government has not always been the case. Until relatively recent times,
individual soldiers generally furnished their own individual arms
and equipment, although various intermediate commanders may
have been responsible for unit equipment paid for with personal
funds. Heberle (1936:4), for example, has pointed out that" in the
Middle Ages each knight had to supply his own armour, and com-

manders of larger units of mercenary troops had to secure the
means of equipment and supplies themselves. . . ." Various tribal,
and especially nomadic, peoples, such as some of those of the
Asiatic Steppes and in feudal Ethiopia, rallied to their chieftains
and tribal leaders, usually furnishing their own horse and necessary
weapons. In our own country, it would appear that the Second
Amendment to the Constitution and its phraseology concerning
"well-regulated militia units" was to make legal provision for an
armed citizenry in case of military emergency. Indeed, in some colonies such as Massachusetts every man between the ages of 16 and
60 was required by law to possess a gun and its proper complement
of ammunition and accessories, and to be enrolled in the company
of his own township. He was supposed to turn out at certain inter-
vals, perhaps four times a year, with the rest of his company for
training; hence the common appellation, "trainbands" (Ward
1952:29).

In general, the militiaman of Revolutionary times supplied his
own rifle, power horn, bullet pouch, bullet mold, and perhaps
some shot, powder, and flints. He frequently also supplied his
"uniform," which might be little more than normal civilian
clothes, often homespun, as well as blanket and haversack. He
might in turn be issued food, additional powder, flints, and lead
(Ward 1952:78–85). The custom of each soldier supplying his own
weapon continued to some degree until the time of the Civil War.
Various volunteer groups who fought in the War of 1812 and the
Mexican War brought their personal weapons with them. In the
Civil War, the Confederates, being generally less well supplied,
fought with their personal weapons in some instances. The standard issue weapon in both the Confederate and Union armies was
the single-shot, muzzle-loading musket, but there were far more effective firearms available at the time, including Henry and Spencer
lever-action repeaters, and even the Sharps breech-loading single-
shot rifles. A number of units on both sides did purchase repeating
rifles commercially, by individual subscription. Sometimes there
was a unanimous purchase by all men in the units, while in some
instances a few individual soldiers bought the weapons.[1] Some

[1] Sidearms were more traditionally personally owned weapons, and this practice
was not unknown even in World War II. Colonial officers owned their own
swords and pistols, as did officers in various of our wars after the Revolution. In
the Civil War this fact was taken for granted to the extent that Grant, in his letter
stating terms of surrender to Lee at Appomattox, specified that the requirement
to have Confederate arms and equipment turned over to Union authorities "will
not embrace the sidearms of the officers." After the Civil War, sidearms increas-

units so equipped achieved a degree of fame and glory, e.g., Col. John T. Wilder's Confederate cavalry unit, which became known as "The Lightning Bridge" (Wiltsey 1961).

The Revolutionary soldier, in general, provided his own horse—bought or borrowed. Personal ownership of weapons and equipment, including horses, apparently tended to make the individual soldier more concerned with the care and protection of his own equipment. Ward (1952:87–88) provides an illustration of this solicitousness when he relates an incident that occurred just prior to the Battle of Bunker Hill:

> The other newcomer was General Seth Pomeroy—old Seth Pomeroy, carrying his nearly seventy years as lightly as he bore the musket which he himself had made and carried at the siege of Louisburg thirty years before. He had ridden to the Neck on a borrowed horse. As it was not his own, he would not submit it to the raking fire there, but dismounted, crossed on foot, and trudged all the way to the rail fence, where he took his place with the others amid an enthusiastic welcome.

The private ownership of horses by the individual soldier has continued up until modern times. In the American Civil War, the men of the Confederate army often supplied their own mounts. As the practice has been described (*American Heritage* 1960:357–58):

> Quite literally, the Confederate trooper rode to the wars on his own charger, cavalry horses not being government issue with the Richmond administration. In the beginning this was an advantage, for many Confederate squadrons were mounted on blooded stock that could run rings around the nags which sharp-

---

ingly became an item of standard issue to officers, and since World War I, all except senior officers tended to rely on the issue Colt .45 automatic. Higher-ranking American officers were issued various kinds of smaller-sized pistols, but some, such as Gen. George C. Patton, preferred to carry their own personal weapons. For a detailed exposition on Patton's sidearms, see Collins (1971:30–34, 80–81).

During World Wars I and II (and between the wars), in foreign armies, there was a stronger tradition for officers, especially field grade or higher, to purchase and own their own sidearms. Many German officers, for example, during both world wars were prone to carry privately owned pistols. Another case in point is Japan, where all Japanese officers had to provide their own sidearms. Some individuals purchased foreign weapons, but many bought theirs from the Japanese military. The so-called "Baby" 7 mm Nambu, designed as a scaled-down Model 14 Nambu and produced at the Koishigawa plant of the Tokyo artillery arsenal from 1902 to 1921, was intended solely as a suitable pistol for purchase by officers. For an authoritative account of this pistol and its function, see Strengholt (1962:158–60).

shooting traders were selling to the Yankee government. In the
long run, though, the system was most harmful. A trooper who
lost his horse had to provide another one all by himself, and he
usually could get a furlough so that he might go home and obtain
one. Toward the end of the war replacements were hard to come
by.

This was not the case in the Union army. When negotiating with
Grant at Appomatox, Lee had to call to his attention the fact that
cavalrymen and artillerymen in the southern forces owned their
horses and would need them for spring plowing when they returned home. Grant accordingly specified, in his letter to Lee lay-
ing out the terms of surrender, that "private horses or bugguge
[*sic*]" could be retained by the owners, as could the sidearms of the
officers.[2] In the British Indian Army, for many years, the *silladar*
system prevailed in the cavalry regiments (Glover 1973:8). Under
this system the recruits had to provide their own mounts. Feed for
the horse was supplied through regular issue, and if the horse was
killed in action, the soldier was compensated by military
authorities. If, however, the horse died or became unfit for duty
because of neglect or age, the cavalrymen was required to replace
the animal. The *silladar* system persisted until World War I. It was
superseded by another arrangement under which the recruit was
issued a horse by the army, but had to pay a deposit on it, which
was refunded only when he took his pension.

Although historically it was the personal equipment such as
firearms, horse, and uniform that the individual soldier owned, in
some instances larger pieces of equipment, including artillery or
even warships, have been privately owned. During the American
Revolution, some privately owned ships manned by an employed
crew were authorized as warships by the Revolutionary government, and fought as naval vessels under the American flag; hence
the name "privateers."

War, like work, however, was subject to the impact of
technological change. With the passage of time the tools of war
became increasingly more complex and expensive. As with the
worker who could no longer afford to own and maintain the tools
of his trade after the Industrial Revolution, the soldier lost the
economic ability to own and maintain the tools of war. Where at
one time the cost of a horse and a gun might be less than $100, by

---

[2] From Grant's original letter of Terms of Surrender as reproduced and distributed
  by the United States Parks Service.

the time of the Vietnam conflict a weapon might cost hundreds, if not thousands of dollars; a tank might represent a value of hundreds of thousands of dollars; and an airplane might cost millions. Modern warfare and the requirements attendant to the massive bureaucratic operations of the contemporary military enterprise have rendered inappropriate, and in large measure unworkable, the practice of private ownership of weapons and equipment by members of the armed services. Any bureaucratic apparatus as vast as that of the military is necessarily based on nearly complete predictability and maximum efficiency of all constituent parts. Predictability coupled with efficiency can afford effectiveness, but predictability is based on uniformity, and efficiency is built on utility. Heberle (1936:4), in commenting on the need for military uniformity, has observed that:

> The complete uniformity of clothing and arms is the symbol of the modern type of military. There is no other way to secure a continuous supply of modern technical arms. Arms and other technical equipment have to be produced by mass production in huge quantities of equal and thus interchangeable parts. This, however, is only possible through centralization and uniformity of requirements.

No military commander could rightfully assign a mission to a subordinate unit, with any assurance of their success, without having a verified knowledge of the unit's arms and equipment capabilities, as well as military skills. For this reason, every particular type of military unit has a generally precise makeup in terms of numbers of individuals of various ranks and categories of military specialty skills, as well as arms and equipment. In the army this is known as the TO&E, or Table of Organization and Equipment—a master pattern for the formation and equipping of every specific unit. Not only is size, composition, and equipment of every variety of military organization known, and thus its capability, but also the uniform design and quality of each type of military arms and equipment. Thus the commander at each level can make tactical decisions based on a rational assessment of the capability of the troops under his command. Again, as Heberle (1936:4) has observed: "In the modern military equipment and supplies are taken care of by Central Ordnance and Quartermaster Units, and these units watch with extreme vigilance over every button, just as they control the consumption of paper in the administrative offices."

The effective control and stewardship of military equipment not only requires an elaborate system of bureaucratic monitoring and accountability. It also requires an equally elaborate set of institutionalized norms prescribing and proscribing the specific and appropriate allocation and use of any and all equipment and supplies utilized or expended by members of the armed services. Such norms are generally enforced by rigid, often severe, sanctions. In the American military, a significant number of the Articles of War address themselves to the question of inappropriate use of military property, and a substantial proportion of judicial and nonjudicial punishment activities in the military, including the various levels of courts-marital, are concerned with sanctioning military property offenders. Crimes against property are particularly endemic to the military in spite of vigorous efforts by military authorities to prevent and expose such offenses. Although all such property offenses are theoretically subject to statutory sanction, some configurations of crimes against property are dealt with severely when they occur, while other varieties of property misuse or misallocation are tolerated or at least endured, if not tacitly encouraged, because of their organizationally functional nature. Tolerated crimes against property have become integrated into the culture and tradition of the U.S. military. However, the offenders in such instances, if "officially" caught, may still be subject to formal sanction.

The Dispossession of Military Property

This type of property offense results in the loss, unserviceability, or deterioration of government property, and is therefore viewed both formally and informally as dysfunctional to the military mission. It is seen as a particularly serious violation of military norm and regulation and is generally dealt with in a vigorous and severe fashion.

DELIBERATE DAMAGE TO MILITARY PROPERTY

From time to time individuals who are not in sympathy politically with the current military mission may undertake to sabotage or destroy government equipment. Such persons may occasionally be in the employ of enemy nations, but more frequently they may merely be individuals who are disgruntled with military life (perhaps they were drafted against their wishes) and are simply striking back at what they perceive as an oppressive organization. This type of motivation is vividly illustrated by Hodges's account of "dud behavior" in the army (Hodges 1974:27–43). He tells of the escapades of a group of army draftee malcontents who expend considerable time and energy in attempting to sabotage the military in various ways, including damaging, destroying, and/or losing government property, but who manage to avoid punishment by appearing to be inept. Some of their nefarious schemes included: dropping and breaking $150 tank batteries; attempting to tear up $85,000 motors out of armored howitzers; and dropping live artillery shells on an iron floor as a means of getting out of the job of howitzer loader. Dud behavior may be viewed as an adaptive mechanism in that "it may serve as a device for attacking discomforting institutional control over the occupational members" (Bryant 1974:19). It may also be functional to the morale of some personnel while dysfunctional to the organization. (Dud behavior will be discussed in more detail in Chapter 5). Sabotage to military property may, in some instances, involve enormous economic costs. Several years ago, for example, an apprentice seaman on board the navy aircraft carrier Forrestal started a fire that subsequently caused more than $7 million in damages. Some acts of sabotage may result from incapacitation because of alcohol or drugs rather than from personal or political disgruntlement.

Sabotage to military property, whether because of political persuasion or personal disgruntlement, is perhaps more characteristic of unpopular wars and/or a period of conscription where considerable public opposition to the military mission exists. In a peacetime situation, members of the military are generally volunteers and thus could hardly be said to be involved against their desire or conviction. During a popularly supported war, sabotage of property becomes a violation of patriotic norms as well as military regulation. In addition, damage to property may even jeopardize one's own chances of survival in combat. In the Vietnamese conflict, the conditions were at their most favorable for intraorganizational sabotage. The war was unpopular, politically and because of a generally antiwar and antimilitary mood prevalent among much of the population. More important, the draft, extremely dissaffective to many young men, in conjunction with the conflicting political values involved, prompted many to take out their frustration on government property. During World

War II the German army conscripted many individuals from captured or occupied countries to work in factories, in labor battalions, and even in military units. The problem of damage and sabotage, especially in the building of fortifications along the Atlantic Wall by disgruntled persons impressed into service, was enormous.[3]

MISUSE OR LOSS OF MILITARY PROPERTY

As a result of the specific and binding system of accountability in the military, even the accidental or unavoidable loss or damage of government property may lead to the application of sanctions, especially if culpability, dereliction, or negligence can be demonstrated. Armed services personnel may be liable for the financial costs of any equipment or supplies lost or damaged, and criminal sanctions may be involved where dereliction is present.

The military attempts to assign accountability for enormously expensive equipment, such as aircraft or ships, at all times; usually the accountability rests with the pilot or with the captain. A captain may, on occasion, relinquish operational control of his ship temporarily to an OD (Officer of the Deck), who becomes, as Duty Officer, the acting captain of the ship. Should a naval ship have a mishap or accident causing the loss of or damage to the ship, such as running aground, colliding with another ship, or sinking, both the ship's captain and the OD may well have to undergo a Board of Inquiry. If negligence is demonstrated, they may both be court-martialed. One such case occurred when a freak wave 80 to 100 feet high struck the U.S. naval battle cruiser *Memphis* while it was anchored in approximately 50 feet of water in Santa Domingo Harbor in August 1916. Before it could get up enough steam to maneuver, the ship was smashed and sunk, leaving 200 injured and 43 dead. There were several inquiries, including a Board of Inquest, and two Courts of Inquiry. As is traditional, the captain, Edward L. Beach, Sr., stood court-martial (for a more detailed account of this disaster see Beach 1966). As the chronicler of this disaster has observed (Beach 1966:279):

> Tradition, in the Navy, is important and tradition dictated
> that except under the most unusual circumstances he, the cap-

---

[3] A favorite trick among disgruntled members of impressed labor battalions was to put sugar into the cement being used to make fortifications. The sugar caused the concrete to carbonize and become brittle and fragile. The first artillery hit might well destroy a bunker completely.

tain, must stand trial and, unless his every action and every preparation were adjudicated perfect, must suffer some punishment.

Although the other officers of the Memphis managed to avoid court-martial through the captain's absolving them of all blame, he was tried and found guilty of one of the counts—not having enough steam available to get under way on short notice. The sentence was relatively light, but it still meant the effective end of a 32-year naval career.

A similar case more recently involved the U.S. naval cruiser *Belknap*. While on maneuvers in November 1975, the *Belknap* collided with the U.S. aircraft carrier *John F. Kennedy* off Sicily. The fiery collision killed eight men and injured 48. Damages were in excess of $100 million. Lt. (j.g.) Kenneth M. Knull, who had been OD when the collision occurred, was tried by court-martial, as was the ship's captain, Walter R. Shafer.[4] The captain was tried for dereliction of duty resulting in the hazarding and loss of a navy vessel, and was subsequently cleared of all charges. Knull was tried on several charges and found guilty of two—negligence that led to the collision and disobeying orders—but, because of his previous exemplary service record, was sentenced to no punishment. His naval career, of course, ended.

Although the charges in such cases are usually couched in terms of dereliction or inadequacy of performance, these offenses must be viewed as crimes against property, inasmuch as the question of appropriate behavior is really incidental to the larger question of the destruction of government property. The enormity of the cost involved simply dictates that the blame be laid somewhere. Even where an accused officer is cleared officially, the loss of property remains, and this stigma generally serves as a deterrent to further career mobility, if not worse.

The impairment of government property is always a crime against property, regardless of the degree of negligence involved. In general, concern with attaching blame for impairment of larger and more expensive items of equipment appears to be more prevalent in peacetime. During war, military property, by virtue of its abundance and its potential expendability, becomes devalued, and its protection is less critical. Then, too, every loss of

[4] The *Belknap* collision and trial was well documented by wire-service accounts in numerous newspapers and periodicals around the country. For some such accounts, see Associated Press (1976a; 1976e; 1976f).

property can usually be legitimated as related to the war mission and destruction of the enemy. Thus a ship sunk in combat is simply expended in the manner for which it was intended. As one naval officer has phrased it (Beach 1966:275):

> A captain who loses his ship during war as the result of enemy action need only fear that somehow his handling of her in combat might be open to criticism; but a captain whose ship is lost or damaged from any other cause, or from any cause whatever in time of peace, must expect that he will at the very least suffer a most searching Court of Inquiry, as the legally constituted investigating body is called, in which his every move and order will be inspected for its complete and perfect adequacy, his every action under the stress of emergency inquired into at leisure and at length, the full benefit of hindsight brought to bear upon it. . . .

Crimes against property involving misuse or negligence do not necessarily have to involve million-dollar ships. The actual cost of the property lost or damaged is of secondary concern to the mere fact of military property being lost or damaged, and thus losing its utility in accomplishing the military mission. Even an item worth only a few dollars may be viewed as a critical piece of equipment and its deterioration or loss may well constitute a serious breech of military regulation. The fictional account of Capt. Queeg's indefatigable search for the missing strawberries is far from ludicrous, and contains considerable validity as a reflection of reality in the military, especially preoccupation with the security and care of property, and the appropriate expenditure of supplies (Wouk 1951).

While the loss or damage of any military equipment is always a serious matter, the loss or damage of a personal weapon is considered to be an unusually serious offense, with severe consequences. The weapon becomes more than mere equipment, and loss of or damage to a weapon becomes more than simply economic. The individual weapon (presumably a rifle in most cases) is the serviceman's principle survival tool, and the seminal instrument in the waging of war, especially in the United States military.[5] To lose a weapon or to have its effectiveness impaired is to demonstrate one's ineptness as a soldier, and to dilute the military capability of the unit to accomplish its mission. Berger has

---

[5] In some foreign armies, such as the German army, the tactical emphasis has traditionally been on the crew-served weapon, such as the machine gun or mortar. In the American army, tactical emphasis on the individual riflemen remains.

labeled this preoccupation with the individual weapon and the attendant symbolizations as "the cult of the rifle" (Berger 1946:86–87). Even the most minute damage to a rifle represents a normative offense at both the formal and informal level. Berger (1946:86) relates that:

> Similarly it is an unpardonable sin, one that brings on endless ridicule, if a soldier should ever drop his rifle. Besides enduring the shame, the soldier who drops his rifle is likely to get a weekend restriction as well for his clumsiness.

To leave a weapon unattended and thus vulnerable to theft, or to allow it to rust or otherwise suffer from neglect, may precipitate company punishment,[6] and the loss of a weapon through negligence may result in a court-martial. Not only does the loss of a weapon often mean punishment for the individual serviceman, but various of his superiors may also be sanctioned for not exercising appropriate monitoring and control procedures.[7]

The loss or misuse of equipment other than weapons is frequently viewed by the military as more than simply an economic loss. It may be interpreted as dereliction of duty, incompetence, or even cowardliness in combat. The loss of equipment within this interpretive context may elicit severe sanctions. Guy Sajer's account of his service with the German army on the Russian front during World War II provides a vivid illustration of such an instance. Sajer (1972) relates that when the German army was in full retreat

---

[6] Punishment in the U.S. Army may be administered at the judicial level through the mechanisms of various types of court-martial. It may also be administered at the nonjudicial level in an arbitrary fashion by the unit commander, as provided for under the Fifteenth Article of War. In the army, this is generally accomplished at the company level by the company commander, and is accordingly known as company punishment. The equivalent nonjudicial punishment device in the U.S. Navy is known as captain's mast.

[7] During my service with the Military Police several decades ago, I encountered a unit whose company commander, a lieutenant, apparently was very much disliked by members of his company, particularly the noncommissioned officers. Suddenly, weapons began to disappear—several a week—in such a fashion that blame or negligence could not be attached to any particular person. Rifles, for example, simply turned up missing after they had been placed in locked stacks in the company armory room. An appropriate investigation was made by an army CID team, but no clues to the missing weapons were found. Subsequently, the company commander was relieved of his command and transferred. In the absence of some specific accountable person to whom fault could be attached, the company commander was implicitly accountable and thus took the blame, as it were. As soon as the disliked officer had left, all of the missing firearms mysteriously returned to their locked stacks.

before the Russian onslaught and many units were destroyed, fractured, or dispersed, some members simply wandered about in an
aimless fashion, seeking their units. As was the custom, German
Field Military Police personnel observed and monitored the stream
of retreating soldiers, searching for deserters and stragglers. When
they encountered such soldiers who could not satisfactorily explain
their presence and justify their retreat, they might summarily mete
out military justice. Deserters, when they could be identified, were
usually shot or hanged by the side of the road as an example to the
retreating units. Similarly, persons who had stolen food or supplies
from army supply sources were also executed. Stragglers, if they
were far away from their units or could not account for being
separated from them, were generally sentenced to penal battalions
that had the most dangerous duty, such as forward positions or
mine clearing. Sajer (1972:333) tells of a German lieutenant who
was apprehended by the Military Police as a straggler. He explained to his interrogators that his entire unit had been wiped out.
Not satisfied, the MP continued to seek fault with the straggler
lieutenant:

> Further, it appeared that the lieutenant was missing a great
> many things. This fact obsessed his interrogator. It didn't matter
> that the man in front of him was effecting a miracle simply by
> staying on his feet, and had lost at least thirty pounds since enter-
> ing the army. The M.P. only noted that the Zeiss fieldglasses,
> which are part of an officer's equipment, were missing. Also miss-
> ing were a map case, and the section telephone, for which the
> lieutenant was responsible. In fact, the lieutenant, who had
> managed to save only his life, was missing far too many things.
> The army did not distribute its papers and equipment only to
> have them scattered and lost. A German soldier is expected to die
> rather than indulge in carelessness with army property.
>
> The careless lieutenant was assigned to a penal battalion, and
> three grades were stripped from his rank. At that, he could think
> himself lucky.

Sajer (1972:472–474) also recounts how he and some men from his
unit, all starving, stumbled across a wrecked German supply truck
full of food, wine, and cigarettes. They plundered the truck, each
taking a sack of supplies. Unfortunately, two of the group were
shortly thereafter apprehended by Military Police with bottles of
wine under their arms. The following day Sajer and the members
of his unit came across their two luckless comrades hanged from a

tree limb. One had a sign tied to his broken neck that read, " I am a thief and a traitor to my country."

Crimes against property involving the misuse or loss of supplies or equipment appear to be more common during wartime. In peacetime, equipment and supplies are usually in short supply and extremely careful stewardship is exercised in regard to these resources. Very tight security procedures are usually enforced with strict and vigorous supervision over the distribution and use of equipment and supplies, thus diminishing the opportunity for loss or misuse of property. In wartime, especially in the American military, equipment and supplies are usually in much greater abundance, and control of such property is often lax, with less severe sanctions applied for the misuse or loss of property. The exception to this situation is those occasions when an army is under siege or otherwise beleaguered, or when it is in retreat, such as the German army on the Eastern Front during World War II. Then, of course, equipment and supplies are in short supply and the loss or misuse of property becomes a significant and serious offense.

THEFT OF MILITARY PROPERTY FOR PROFIT

While the armed forces of all nations have no doubt had individuals in their ranks who undertook to steal military property and sell it for profit, this type of crime is seemingly relatively infrequent. Certainly in the history of the U.S. military until recent years it has tended to be uncommon. Nonetheless, there have been some bizzare exceptions. During World War II, one of the chaplains of the First Special Service Force was discovered selling communion wine to the men on the way to Kiska, and was quickly transferred out of the unit (Adleman and Walton 1966:112). In World War II, there were also some instances of gangs of U.S. deserters stealing vast amounts of military supplies and selling them on the black market (see Chapter 10, note 5). In general, military property was in little demand outside the military and thus had little economic value. Sometimes military equipment, such as firearms, was even inferior to similar equipment available through civilian channels. The close scrutiny and control exercised by military authority also reduced opportunity for theft, making it a difficult crime to commit, but easy to detect. Military thieves of conventional bent have traditionally been relatively easy to apprehend.

The situation has changed, however, in recent years. Beginning in World War II, and continuing on through the Korean War, more individuals in the military found it easier to steal government property and convert it to profit, usually on the black market of occupied countries. With the Vietnamese conflict, theft for profit became a major pattern of property crime in the military; graft and corruption became relatively common. This showed up particularly as a new variation of crime against military property—exploitation of the PX system.[8] The military post exchange and commissary system, with its hundreds of retail outlets, represents the third largest merchandizing enterprise in the world. Inasmuch as military retailers operate as private entrepreneurs rather than with congressionally appropriated funds, such stores are not subject to normal military scrutiny and control. As official government operations, the PX's have a variety of price advantages, including tax exemptions. This, plus the remoteness of some military base locations, affords them a "captive" group of customers. Congressional investigations into charges of graft in the system, especially in Vietnam, uncovered an incredible chronicle of "corruption, criminality, and moral compromise," involving kickback payoffs, black-market operations, and Swiss bank accounts, and implicating a number of general officers (United States Senate Committee on Government Operations 1971).

Along with PX corruption, there have been a number of other incidents in recent years involving crimes against property, where the motive and circumstances clearly indicated theft for profit. One such case involved former Brig. Gen. Earl F. Cole, who was convicted in 1973 of defrauding the military while he was head of the army's personnel administration in Vietnam (Washington *Star-News*, 1973). Among other particulars, he was charged with helping his secretary collect overtime and take unauthorized business trips from Saigon to the United States. He was subsequently sentenced to three years in prison. Another case uncovered three years later was an army meat fraud scheme of substantial proportions (Associated Press 1976c). Two meat-packing firms were substituting beef knuckle cut to look like sirloin on an army meat

[8] The military PX scandal received considerable publicity when it broke. For one detailed newspaper account, see Rugaber (1971). News of the scandal also prompted the writing of a novel, with considerable basis in fact, that deals with corruption in the PX system during the Vietnamese conflict (Moore and Collins 1971); a later novel also included many valid details of military corruption in Vietnam (Blankenship 1974).

contract. Inasmuch as the army was paying approximately $2.40 per pound more for sirloin than knuckle, each day up to $192,000 in illegal profits were accruing to the meat packers. Several military meat inspectors were bribed with gifts, favors, and even the free services of prostitutes, for "refraining from nit-picking and not creating disputes," and, of course, for not exposing the fraudulent scheme.

In 1972 it was reported nationally that army investigators had uncovered what they considered evidence of "possible criminal misconduct by senior Pentagon officials in the awarding of a $40 million advertising contract (Associated Press 1974b,1974c). Rather than turn the case over to the Department of Justice, the army chose to refer the matter to its own inspector general, with the goal of "improving management controls," and closed the criminal aspect of the investigation when the commander of the Army Criminal Investigation Division, "in consultation with military lawyers," found "no evidence of criminality."

In another example, in 1969 the United States Senate Permanent Subcommittee on Investigations, in the course of its PX inquiries, and specifically because of their interest in the efforts of then retired Maj. Gen. Carl C. Turner's efforts to prevent the CID from investigating the activities of certain senior NCO's who were alleged to be involved in irregularities in open mess systems, discovered that he had obtained a number of confiscated weapons under questionable circumstances (United States Senate Committee on Government Operations 1971:59–67). The subcommittee subsequently discovered that General Turner, while occupying the position of Provost Marshal of the United States Army, had taken possession of 493 firkearms confiscated by various civilian police departments. General Turner had solicited the guns from various police departments "obstensibly to turn them over to the U.S. Army for training purposes or to use them as displays from his gun collection in lectures he gave to civic groups on gun safety." Turner had turned over only 56 to the army, had sold 23 to a gunshop in North Carolina, and could not account for the remaining 414. It also appeared that 195 firearms confiscated by the U.S. Customs Bureau at El Paso, Texas, were acquired by the Provost Marshal of Fort Bliss, Texas, and shipped to General Turner's home in Springfield, Virginia, in December 1967. Some 59 of these weapons were turned over to the army, but the remaining 136 were unaccounted for. A number of questions were raised by the subcommittee concerning the propriety of the transfers themselves, the conversion of the firearms into personal profit, and the implications of General Turner's firearms transactions for his federal income tax returns.

Even the traditional, albeit illicit, practice of military units exchanging equipment and supplies has, in some instances, involved a motivation for personal profit. In 1973 in Oklahoma, for example, two army reserve officers, who were also full-time reserve employees, were tried in federal court on charges of conspiring to steal approximately $100,000 in government property (*Daily Oklahoman* 1973:16). Testimony in the case suggested that "excess" equipment in the army reserve units involved was "traded" with other units, and that some such equipment was converted to personal use.

The plethora of military property crimes for profit in recent years, especially during and after the Vietnam conflict, would seem to result from the military's increasingly taking on the characteristics of a commercial or industrial enterprise and conducting much of its business in a commercial fashion, thereby affording a much enhanced opportunity structure for theft and corruption. The conduct of the Vietnamese conflict and the unusual relationship between our military and that of South Vietnam permitted kickbacks and graft that had not always been possible in earlier wars.[9] Then, too, the military population during the 1960s and 1970s has probably not represented the dedicated career commitment of earlier eras. As opportunity for military property crime for profit has increased, the potential illicit profit has also soared. The less committed personnel, perhaps more sensitive in recent years to unfavorable economic comparisons with civilian careers and life styles, and often politically disenchanted with the contemporary military mission, appear to have been lured more easily into criminal intent, and then facilitated in perpetrating crime, by the opportunities available.

THEFT OF PROPERTY FROM OTHER SERVICEMEN

Although seldom involving significant economic value, the theft of property from a fellow member of the military is often

---

[9] During World War II, in the China-Burma campaign there was reported to be widespread corruption and theft in the Chinese Nationalist Army. American aid was furnishing most of the weapons, equipment, and even payroll money for the Nationalist forces. It was alleged that some Chinese commanders sold equipment and supplies on the black market, sold weapons to the Chinese Communist forces, and sometimes pocketed the payroll funds intended for their men.

viewed as a particularly serious offense, informally as well as formally. Its perceived seriousness is based more on the principle of betrayed trust than on economic loss. Inasmuch as members of the military seldom have in their possession much in the way of economic value, there is usually little to steal. An individual might conceivably steal a modest amount of money, personal effects such as a watch, or perhaps some military items or supplies issued to a fellow soldier. Aside from the paucity of things to steal, there is a modicum of opportunity to steal what is available. Members of the military live in close proximity, with almost constant mutual observation by each other and ongoing monitoring of activities and behavior by superiors. There is also only negligible means of hiding what is stolen. Nevertheless, theft of property from fellow military members has been a continual occurrence, although not with nearly the same frequency as theft of government property.

Theft of fellow servicemen's property tends to occur where there is a minimum of group cohesion, often in units staffed with transient troops, such as holding companies or replacement companies. It is also more prone to occur where the victims are more vulnerable, such as when they are sick or wounded and may be in a strange unit such as a hospital.[10] Theft from fellow servicemen in the same unit is relatively rare where there are permanent personnel and thus the likelihood of strong unit cohesion and affective interpersonal relationships. When individuals are caught stealing from another serviceman, the sanctions are likely to be severe. In the Civil War, for example, a soldier that stole from a fellow soldier might have his head shaved and be drummed out of camp by a squad carrying reversed arms. The offender would also have a sign tied around his neck proclaiming his crime. His reception outside of camp would undoubtedly be less than hospitable. In time of military crisis, such as a siege or a retreat, the theft of food from a fellow soldier, or even the hoarding of food, may be provocation enough to cause an individual to be killed by members of his unit. Sajer (1972:468) describes the starving condition of the German troops, and recalls that some men "were beaten to death because they were suspected of hiding food." He tells of one soldier who had his head kicked in, and was found to have "a few handfuls of crumbled vitamin biscuit" in the bottom of his pack. To steal or

[10] At the Battle of Waterloo, British regimental bandsmen served as stretcher-bearers taking the wounded to the rear. It has been reported that they were "notorious as plunderers" (Keegan 1976:198). They presumeably stole from their own wounded colleagues as well as from the enemy wounded and dead.

hoard is to violate the sacred trust of military camaraderie, and invites the retribution of one's comrades, as well as the formal sanction of military authorities.

The Subversion of Military Property

All crimes against military property are sanctioned, but some are sanctioned more often and more severely than others. Unlike property crimes involving malice, individual ineptness, or personal profit, those that appear to involve simply an innovative or expeditious reallocation of equipment or supplies may be viewed as residually functional to the military mission, and thus are often informally countenanced to a degree.

MISAPPROPRIATION OF MILITARY PROPERTY

Although specifically proscribed, and officially sanctioned if observed, the unauthorized distribution and reallocation of equipment and supplies is an abiding characteristic of military social organization everywhere, and perhaps especially the American military. Misappropriation of property represents a response of the informal structure to organizational disequilibrium and in some contexts is functional to both individuals and constituent units, as well as the larger military mission. It is because of this that there is a considerable degree of tacit toleration of such deviant patterns of property involvement.

The U.S. military, by virtue of America's industrial productivity, is perhaps the best supplied (in terms of quantity) armed force in the world. There are virtually mountains of supplies and acres of equipment at every military base or installation. A bureaucracy as large as the U.S. military, with its myriad tasks and consequent material requirements, is obligated to be exact and theoretically judicious in the allocation, distribution, and accountability of those supplies and equipment. Cohen (1966:79), for example has stated that:

> An elaborate system of War Department directives, memoranda, and tables of organization and equipment (T/O and E) specified in great detail what each type of unit was entitled to in the way of supplies and equipment, and in what quantities and at what intervals, and prescribed elaborate clerical and book-

keeping procedures for ordering, issuing, and keeping track of supplies. It goes without saying that things cannot be otherwise, when everything is in short supply and some method must be found for allocating scarce goods among a multitude of would-be users.

The military mission of individual units, however, may produce an immediate need for certain types and quantities of supplies that may not be formally authorized or available through regular channels, and the success or failure of the mission may hinge on the ability to secure these supplies. Inasmuch as comfort and/or survival belongs to the "fittest," individuals or units often resort to informal, clandestine, and unauthorized or illegal means of obtaining that which they want or need. Leckie (1957:129–30), for example, relates the occasion when he was in the marines in the South Pacific campaign during World War II, and robbed the PX. A portable tent PX was set up in the jungle for a new marine unit that had just arrived. Leckie and a friend managed to slip past the guards and steal a copious supply of cookies and cigars, which they selfishly refused to share with others who wanted some. These means by which government property is misappropriated may include widespread barter and begging systems defined in the military as "scrounging." In some instances the scrounging is represented by a more permanent and structured network. Such a barter system on board a navy ship is described by Zurcher (1965:399), who related:

> We were assigned to a shipboard shop which was fully equipped with electronic testing equipment and components. As such, we became the radio, T.V., and electrical appliance center for those members of the crew we considered to be our friends. In return for parts for and services to the personal property of the crew members who came to us, we were rendered what goods and services they could supply. One of the cooks gave us fresh ground coffee for the perculator and hot plate one of the electrician's mates had given us. A yeoman saw to it that our personnel requests were always processed rapidly. One of the storekeepers made certain that our spare parts bin was always full, and not only with components called for in our formal inventory. The medical department, ordered to give us a certain amount of alcohol per month for the cleaning of antennas, had a chief who was the "buddy" of the chief of our shop and who would never ask questions when we returned for a refill before the end of the month. We, in turn, would treat two of our boatswain mate

friends to a little something extra in their coffee, and they, reciprocating, would have their work details take extra care with the maintenance of our work spaces. If an officer whose T.V. we had repaired was the inspecting officer for the week, we could expect an "excellent" inspection rating.

In other instances, the scrounging is more of an emphemeral or erratic practice, although it may constitute substantial transactions. Cohen, for example, mentions the problems of trying to obtain supplies to establish a battalion school for civilian skills in a chemical mortar unit in the Philippines after the Japanese surrendered. Cohen (1966:79) reminisces that:

> Practically none of the equipment needed for this hastily improvised school was authorized by any regulations.
>
> However, the school quickly materialized, and so did the necessary equipment. I spent one day a week traveling about the island of Luzon, "requisitioning" equipment. ("Requisitioning," as practiced in the armed services, can mean (1) properly requesting, (2) confiscating, or (3) just plain stealing—sometimes referred to as "liberating.") This day was dedicated to the violation of regulations not only by me but by scores of supply sergeants and officers in dozens of Army, Navy, and Air Force installations. Requests were not granted perfunctorily: I had to explain my bizarre requests for cameras and other photographic equipment; for books, automobile engines, stationery, and so on. But when I did this, I met with understanding and cooperation. Of course this procurement activity was largely furtive, involving a great deal of illegal falsification of records, and it was not without some risk to those involved. But the school was successful. (Some months later the War Department caught up with events and issued regulations authorizing the issuance of supplies that I had only been able to obtain illegally.)

In many cases scrounging is clearly beneficial or functionally efficient to the military mission. In other instances it becomes equally dysfunctional by informally diverting supplies and equipment from the formally intended recipient unit. It also creates hidden shortages and deficiencies, as well as defective material (where parts have been pirated), which may be detrimental to the military mission.[11]

[11] It is an almost endemic condition in the military that, from time to time, many units are chronically "short" certain equipment that they have bartered off or expended and for which they have not received a replacement issue. To cover such temporary shortages some units borrow from other units, and display the bor-

Military scrounging, as a criminal collusion system, presumes some expertise with military organization but, more important, presumes a contact network.[12] Thus the more experienced noncommissioned officer may be more adept at this than the neophyte serviceman. Lacking the necessary contact network, the serviceman or unit may have to resort to more open theft to obtain the desired property. Military subculture redefines the situation, however, and relabels the activities so that theft or misappropriation of government property do not constitute stealing as such but are rather thought of as "moonlight requisitioning." The new recruit is informally indoctrinated with this new definition of the situation in the course of his military socialization and thus can easily avoid or dilute any residual feelings of guilt or anxiety associated with stealing. Moonlight requisitioning may be used as a means of instilling

---

rowed items or supplies to whoever may be inspecting the unit. The inspecting officer is satisfied, the borrowed equipment is returned, and the deficiency is perpetuated. Such a shortage may be critical in an emergency, such as lacking fire extinguishers if a fire breaks out, or not having cold-weather gear if the temperature drops suddenly. Furthermore, the process of trying to cover up shortages by chicanery is often deleterious to the equipment or supplies as well as being dysfunctional to the larger organization and mission. Some years ago in the army it was customary to have all of the blankets in units laundered periodically by turning in dirty blankets and being issued clean blankets simultaneously. Inasmuch as the blankets were turned in at the military laundry in truckload lots, usually wadded up and counted rapidly in front of the laundry personnel, many supply sergeants used the expedient of tearing some blankets in half to get a double count. The laundry, on the other hand, was equally notorious for issuing half-sized clean blankets for full count. Over a period of time some of the blankets were reduced to the size of dog blankets.

[12] Truly effective scrounging often relies heavily on a more or less permanent contact network and attendant trading relationships. As a company commander in the old "brown shoe army" in the early 1950s, I was faced with the problem of obtaining for my Military Police unit extra amounts of olive drab paint, which was only obtainable in limited supplies through regular channels but was needed to keep our equipment looking pristine for inspection purposes. My supply sergeant and I uncovered a defect in the quartermaster regulations that let us retain the winter overcoats of men being discharged in the summer months without reporting these to the battalion G-4 (supply office) or showing them on our inventory. Armed with an oveage of overcoats, we traded them to neighboring infantry units who had a shortage of overcoats for their excess soap, which we in turn traded to the mess sergeant in a nearby service unit for coffee. Coffee was an excellent barter item, so we traded coffee to the post engineer units for olive drab paint, of which they had a surfeit. The trading arrangement persevered over time, and our interunit relationships were enhanced because of our mutual collaboration and collusion in the scheme. Thus we had, in effect, established a "khaki kula ring." This refers to Malinowski's classic account of the "kula" or trading system of a group of South Sea Island people (1961).

aggressiveness and resourcefulness in recruits. In basic training, for example, the various training companies are in fierce competition for performance and appearance recognition.[13] Brooms, mops, garbage cans, and lawn and office furniture are usually in short supply. Cadre noncoms may "commission" some of the recruits to "find" some extra garbage cans. Of course, the recruits can only accomplish this by stealing the cans from neighbor units. These expeditions simulate combat patrols to a degree and are often tacitly approved by the company officers. The company noncoms (and officers) look favorably on the recruits who are successful in such theft. The neophyte soon learns that he will gain recognition, support, and often material reward (such as passes or other privileges) for playing his new military role, including the larceny component, in the appropriate prescribed informal as well as formal manner. Although much moonlight requisitioning is an individual or collective endeavor in behalf of a unit or buddies, it also occurs for personal use. Zurcher (1965:399) comments on this:

> An interesting phenomenon is the widespread "appropriating" of various types of Navy property, and making it one's personal possession. The sailor does not consider such things as smuggling off the ship parts or tools for his car or hobbies to be stealing. In fact, the informal organization has a legitimized euphemism for this acquisition—"to cumshaw" (a Chinese word, meaning a gratuity or tip; a phrase of thanks used by a beggar). This connotes a "by gosh I deserve it, because I have certainly done enough for them" attitude. It is understood that one does not turn in his shipmate to the authorities for such conduct.

Unauthorized misappropriation of military property, although superficially resembling the theft of military property for profit, is not the same, and a distinction should be made between them. The individual who commits theft of military property for profit generally has criminal intent and willfully undertakes to defraud the military for personal economic gain. Scrounging or moonlighting requisitioning for one's personal use is more an instance of

---

[13] Competition is a dominant theme in military culture, and in this instance encourages and facilitates military property theft. Berger has observed that "Rivalry between units, from the largest to the smallest, is the keynote of the army." He also has commented (1946:85) that "In cooperative group life the group loyalties are strong. The army does not have to instill the competitive spirit into soldiers; they have it in large measure the day they put on the uniform, and the army uses this spirit extensively in the training of individuals and units."

redefined situation. Much as factory workers sometimes redefine certain raw material in the factory as "scrap" in order to appropriate it for their own use, the individual in the military simply views the equipment that he misappropriates as surplus or something that would not be needed or missed, that he is putting to more productive use—his![14] In attempting to convert government property to their own productive, but not necessarily profitable, use, military personnel have misappropriated practically every conceivable type and variety of equipment and supplies.[15] In World War II, in the European Theater, members of the First Special Service Brigade on several occasions stole ambulances from other U.S. units, and at least on one occasion stole a major general's private jeep. An inventory of the force revealed that it

[14] For a detailed account of blue-collar theft through the redefining of desired raw material as "scrap" see Horning (1970). Sometimes the distinction between "scrap" and that which is good leads to some interesting variations of misappropriation of governmental property. Once, some years ago in the military, I saw an instance of redefining government property as "scrap" and then redefining it as useful in a clandestine fashion. At that time the army operated on a master food menu. Shrimp was on the schedule for a particular day and was delivered to the various units on the post where I was stationed. It was customary for the post veterinarian to inspect seafood for freshness. He was away on a trip and his assistant, a young inexperienced lieutenant, came around to inspect the shrimp. The shrimp had a particular "fishy" odor and the lieutenant jumped to the wrong conclusion and decided that they were spoiled. He ordered all the shrimp to be thrown away and authorized the issuance of new rations of another kind. My own mess sergeant—a man wise in years and experience—did not follow orders and dispose of the shrimp. Instead he cleverly hid them in the meat freezer. When the post veterinarian returned to camp, he examined a specimen of the shrimp that had been saved for him and declared that there was nothing whatsoever wrong with the shrimp. The army had lost $50,000 in shrimp that were thrown away. The lieutenant assistant post veterinarian was in hot water. Most of the units on post never got to eat the shrimp, but the men in my unit, thanks to the crafty old mess sergeant accomplished to have shrimp cocktails with their meals for quite some time.

[15] The Military Police sometimes conduct "shakedown" searches at the gates of military posts when servicemen who live off post leave to go home. I, as an MP officer, often saw whole piles of materials confiscated in such searches, including furniture, food, and weapons, and know of one instance where a serviceman was trying to leave the post with an "army" pig stolen from the camp stockade farm. A classic case was one the author studied in Military Police Officers School concerning a sailor who stole a U.S. government tractor in Japan and managed to get it back to his farm in Kansas. On a bet, he had simply walked past a guard at an equipment depot, driven the tractor out the gate down to the waterfront, and bribed a petty officer on board his ship, a carrier, to have the tractor hoisted aboard and hidden on the hangar deck. He did the same when the ship came back and had the tractor shipped home by rail. It took the CID considerable time to track it down.

had almost twice as many jeeps as were authorized (Adleman and Walton 1966:169, 220, 238).

INAPPROPRIATE USE OF MILITARY PROPERTY

In addition to being misused, damaged, stolen, or redistributed in an illicit fashion, military property can also be used in an inappropriate fashion—either productive or deleterious. The main element of such property crimes is that the equipment is used in a way that is not helpful to the military mission, or supplies are expended in a wasteful manner. Deleterious misuse of military property might include such practices as joy riding in military vehicles, putting a "hair" trigger on weapons, or making unauthorized use of supplies or equipment, such as "jury-rigs."[16]

It goes without saying that there is a strong disposition to ritualism and routine in the military, perhaps growing out of the very complex nature of military organization and procedure. Routinization and ritualism become, in effect, coping techniques for bureaucratic survival. It is doubtful, given this complexity, that the military mission could be accomplished if all rules and regulations were complied with to the letter. As Berger (1946:83) pointed out:

> It is tacitly agreed by everyone that the Army's requirements are extremely difficult, if not impossible to satisfy. If an officer were to make all the checks and inspections as thoroughly as prescribed, he would have little time left for his principal duty and for himself. The Army's top directors apparently recognize these facts; a complete and intensive check is rarely made upon all the work of officers in the field.

Because of the difficulty of complete and sincere compliance, the appearance of compliance becomes an important coping mechanism. In this regard, military ritualism often becomes a kind of superficial exercise aimed at the maintenance of *appearance*. Appearance becomes a seminal military preoccupation, and existential reality often comes to revolve around this veneer of compliance.

A military organization not infrequently operates more on the basis of the appearance of efficiency than on that of real efficiency. Administrative monitoring, particularly from the higher levels of

[16] Zurcher (1965:394) defines "jury-rigs" as "using unofficial, pirated, or homemade parts to maintain machinery in full operation."

supervision, is often perfunctory, and as a result, the actual conditions or situation extant are sometimes camouflaged—i.e., disguised or misrepresented—through the use of dramaturgical props, contrived performances, or deceptive accounts or reports known as "eyewash." In this connection there is considerable logistical misappropriation and inappropriate use of equipment and supplies toward the end of dramaturgical efficiency. To effect such deception not only involves the use and/or misuse of government property and supplies, but also expends the time and effort of military personnel in a wasteful, nonproductive manner. Such practices that misuse or waste property and effort are clearly forbidden, but the desire to appear efficient and avoid criticism and reprimand from superiors may well outweigh the proscription against misappropriation. A vivid fictional account of such practices (but clearly a valid reflection of reality) is provided in Robert Lowry's novel about World War II, *Casualty*. Lowry describes the machinations of an American Air Force photo reconnaissance unit stationed in Italy during the closing days of the war. The personnel of the unit were subject to minimal supervision from "upstairs," and as a result were normally left to their own devices and their own rate of work. When the situation demanded, however, they could mobilize their resources and provide a creditable dramaturgical appearance of work and efficiency. As Lowry (1971:60–61) depicts it:

> At nine o'clock Captain Blake came into the drying room excitedly and announced that "there was going to be an inspection at any moment by a general from MAFF." He conferred with Master Sergeant Anderson, a red-headed serious boy of twenty-three who'd been a garage mechanic in Denver before joining the army and learning photography, and then dashed out. Within half an hour prints began to come through for the dryer, and when at eleven o'clock the General finally arrived, with Colonel Polaski looking very official right beside him, the drying room was a busy place, turning out fourteen-inch aerial photographs at mass production. The prints as Johnny Conkle and Master Sergeant Anderson and Captain Blake and Colonel Polaski knew, were phonies—made from old rolls that had already been used. They were a waste of print paper and of seventy men's time. But the General didn't know and the effect was all that was ever demanded in the army before superiors. The dryers looked busy, and the General would undoubtedly think the Wing was a very good outfit indeed.

Lowry (1971:69–70) has the ruse succeed, as it no doubt would in real military life:

> "Well, PRO is in the clear," Pinkerton said. Joe felt it wasn't a personal remark but directed to the room in general. "I just talked to Major Barnes—he told me the General thought this office one of the liveliest-looking he'd visited. Seemed very pleased. That's what a few photographs on the wall will do."

Sometimes the efforts to create a desired appearance or "front" may require more energy and supplies than the genuine activity and, in this sense, be dysfunctional to the military mission. Occasionally such practices may even be deleterious to equipment or create a hazardous condition.[17]

Property is so critical to the unit mission, rivalry so keen, and conceptualization of property so proprietary that some unit commanders have gone to the extent of hoarding badly needed supplies and equipment even if it meant hiding them from other units and from higher command. There are also instances of unit commanders actually dismantling equipment as a means of keeping it from being transferred out of their control. Such practices are, of course, serious infractions of military regulations, and if discovered would be viewed as a serious property offense as well as antithetical to the attainment of the larger military objective.

In World War II, for example, after the allied forces had landed in Normandy and were pushing up through Belgium and Holland, Gen. Wilheim Bittrich, commanding the II SS Panzer Corps, was ordered to have one of his divisions entrain and return to Germany, where it would be refitted and brought up to strength. The Ninth Hohenstaufen Division was named as the division to be moved. General Bittrich told SS Obersturmbannführer (Lieutenant Colonel) Walter Harzer, who was the division commander, "to transfer as much of his transportation and equipment as he could" to the other division that would remain. Bittrich's reasoning was that any shortage of equipment in the Ninth Division would be replaced in the refitting progress. It was, as he saw it, more expeditious to cannabalize Harzer's division before it left than to wait for normal supply channels to provide what was

---

[17] As a example, during my army experiences I knew a company commander who "acquired" bolts of target cloth and "panneled" over the roof studs in the company supply room, and then sprayed the tightly stretched cloth with airplane dope. The effect was aesthetically not unpleasing, but in view of the fire hazard, was clearly in violation of post fire regulations.

needed in the division that was to remain. It is doubtful that such logic would have been appreciated or honored by the German High Command in Berlin, had they been privy to this information in its entirety. Lieutenant Colonel Harzer, however, felt that if he did give up any of his tanks or armored vehicles, even to help the remaining division, which was desperately short of armor, he was not likely to have it all replaced because of shortages of material even in Germany itself. According to historian Cornelius Ryan, Harzer did not protest the order but rather undertook to use subterfuge to protect the proprietary interest of his division. As Ryan (1974:150) describes his actions:

> Harzer had long ago learned to husband his division's resources. He had more vehicles than even Bittrich realized—including American jeeps he had captured during the long retreat from France. He decided to ignore the order by "some paper maneuvering." By removing caterpillar tracks, wheels or guns from his vehicles, he could make them temporarily unserviceable until he reached Germany. In the meantime they would be listed on his armored strength returns as disabled.

Summary

The military, with its inordinate amount of relatively accessible goods and equipment, plus ample additional opportunities for internal theft, misuse, and misappropriation of property for those strategically located in the system, affords full scope for the commission of a variety of criminal offenses.

Crimes against military property assume a number of configurations, are motivated by a range of intents and considerations, involve a variety of individuals and offices, are tolerated by the formal structure to varying degrees depending on the residual expediency and function of the activities, and are subject to widely differing kinds of sanctions at both the formal and informal level.

Historically, the value system of the individual soldier and the larger military entity in regard to property have been in conflict. When private ownership of the tools of war gave way to corporate ownership, much of the personal motivation for maintaining equipment and weapons was diluted. The military places a high priority on the proper maintenance and care of its corporate property. If property is to be effective and reliable it must be in good operating condition. A battle may hinge on the serviceability of certain equipment or weapons. Much of this corporate military property must be entrusted to the stewardship and care of the individual soldier, and proper maintenance of the equipment is prescribed by military regulation and custom. Individual soldiers, however, do not always hold the same proprietary attitudes toward the equipment with which they are entrusted. They may view the maintenance of equipment not their own as an onerous chore. They may be derelict, negligent, or lackadaisical in protecting and maintaining the equipment and weapons they have been issued, with the result that the military property becomes lost, damaged, inoperative, or deteriorated. As a result of such dereliction or negligence, or even ineptness, carelessness, or unpropitious or unfortunate circumstances, individuals in the military may be held responsible for damage or loss of military equipment or supplies, and sanctioned accordingly. In such an instance the individual becomes a military offender for his crimes of omission.

Members of the military may on occasion, because of political persuasion, or disgruntlement with or hostility to the military, undertake to damage, destroy, or otherwise sabotage property or equipment. A disaffected soldier may externalize his pique and hostility by purposely damaging or destroying equipment or weapons.

On the other hand, members of the military sometimes become overly proprietary about the corporate property they are using and undertake to keep it on a permanent basis. Many a GI in recent wars was successful in retaining some of his personal gear or even weapons when he was separated from the service. It may be that the materialistic bent of our society has tended to make members of the U.S. military a bit more larcenous in this regard than persons in other armies.

A major variety of property offense is the dispossession of military property. Increasingly in recent years, and especially during and since the Vietnamese conflict, some members of the military have, with criminal intent, stolen or otherwise converted military property and supplies into personal economic profit. In some instances actual theft has been involved, while in other instances more indirect means have been employed, including graft, kickback payments, and bribes. Graft and corruption have always been constituent to some militaries, but in recent years, and especially in the Vietnamese war, there was almost an endemic problem of theft and embezzlement from the PX system, a widespread pattern of kickbacks and payoffs from military contractors, extensive activity involving currency manipulation, and, perhaps most frequent of all military property crimes, the conversion and misappropriation of government property for profit on the black market. The U.S. military has increasingly conducted its affairs in a commercial fashion, which has enhanced the opportunity structure for corruption and theft.

Although relatively infrequent, theft of property from a member of the military by another member of the military does occur on occasion, more often in units of transient troops than in the more permanent and socially solidified units. Crimes involving the dispossession of military property are generally more dysfunctional to the military mission than are other types of property crime, and are accordingly severely sanctioned if discovered.

Another major category of crime against property concerns those involving the subversion of military property. Most militaries in recent times, and especially the U.S. military, have been extremely well supplied, at least on a collective level. The distribution and allocation of equipment and supplies, however, is often inefficient, inequitable, and niggardly, if not illogical.[18] Individual servicemen and even small units may be sufficiently dissatisfied with the distribution arrangement that they undertake to improve on it through clandestine and unauthorized activities involving misappropriation of government property. In effect, property may be reallocated or distributed in an illicit fashion. This illicit redistribution of military property often assumes highly routinized and institutionalized configurations of various forms of bartering, or "scrounging," as such practices are known. The misappropriated military property may sometimes be simply stolen, but the theft is redefined and made less serious by conceptualizing it in a more innocuous and innovative fashion as "moonlight requisitioning" or some similar euphemism. Military property may also be used in an inappropriate fashion and thus misused, damaged, or

[18] During the Russian siege of Stalingrad in World War II, Von Paulus's belieguered Sixth German Army was starving for lack of food, freezing for lack of warm clothing, suffering for lack of medical supplies, and possessed of only the most meager supply of ammunition. This is to say that at the level of the individual soldier, there was a great shortage of supplies and equipment. At the collective level, however, the quartermaster units of the Sixth German Army were burning and destroying enormous stores of food, clothing, equipment, and ammunition, in order that it not be captured by the Russians when they broke through and overran the city.

wasted in an unproductive manner. Such inappropriate employment of military property might be for personal use, or more likely
for the preferred use of some unit or organization. Sometimes
misappropriation of military property is a survival mechanism, but
more often it is simply a device for insuring a greater degree of
creature comfort and convenience, a striving for luxury in an
otherwise spartan and deprived existence. On occasion, misappropriated military property is something of a status symbol.

Whether purely for personal use or for unit use, the misappropriation of property may have both function and dysfunction
for the military mission. Sometimes supplies or equipment crucial
to the success of a military action can be obtained only through illicit channels. However, in addition to being a violation of military
law and regulation, misappropriation of military property is also
an offense against one's fellow serviceman, inasmuch as other individuals and other units may be deprived when someone misappropriates property in order to oversupply himself or his unit. In
any event, such forbidden activity, while perhaps functional on an
informal level, is clearly dysfunctional to the formal military mission in that it creates hidden and thus unpredictable shortages,
which are dangerous. In general, subversion of military property is
more tolerated by military authorities than is dispossession of property, and even tacitly encouraged in some circumstances.

The allocation, storage, maintenance, and employment of
equipment and supplies are extremely critical processes in the
military and vital to the military objective and purposes. Any activities that prevent, interfere with, or otherwise disrupt or subvert
those processes represent crime against property of serious import
and sanctionative consequences.

CHAPTER
FOUR

Crimes Against
Person

*Class hostility of enlisted men versus commissioned
officers is exacerbated by the continual allocation of
privileges and scarce resources to the officers. The
theory is that the separation enhances discipline and the
class hostility will be displaced onto the enemy. Soldiers,
according to this view, fight because they hate, not
because they love (other soldiers).*
Lawrence B. Radine

The social organization of the military rests on an elaborate set of
formalized status relationships involving highly specific subordinate and appropriate superordinate roles. By necessity, the interaction of military personnel, particularly between individuals of
lower and higher rank, must be circumspect, formalized, and
based on legitimately assigned authority relationships. Under no
circumstances should interaction between superordinate and
subordinate involve physical coercion or violence, either on the
part of subordinate in response to an onerous order or command,
or on the part of superordinate in an attempt to reinforce or insure
the carrying out of his command. The issuance of orders and their
subsequent implementation must be in accordance with military
protocol and based on disciplined obedience. Where tribal military
groups, or armies in an earlier era, may have tended to rely on immediate physical coercion, the modern military organization of
most countries relies on a bureaucratic structure where authority is
constituent to the status system, and violence is unnecessary.[1]
Clearly, there are exceptions to this rule. Some foreign armies, in

[1] There is something of a parallel between early industry and the military of a
former time in this regard. In the nineteenth century and during the first few

relatively recent times, have tacitly permitted some use of physical
force or violence on the part of superiors when dealing with subordinates.

An interesting and insightful account of physical coercion is
contained in an autobiographical account of service in the Spanish
Foreign Legion in Africa, prior to World War II. Arturo Barea
(1972:304) describes the commanding officer addressing a unit of
new recruits to the Spanish Foreign Legion. The lieutenant colonel stops in front of a newly recruited private—a mulatto—and
asks "Where do you come from, my lad?" The surly private replies,
"What the devil's that to you?" According to Barea, the officer
replies:

> You think you're brave, don't you? Listen here, I am the
> Chief. If anyone like you speaks to me he stands to attention and
> says: at your orders, sir. I don't want to say where I come from:
> and that's as it should be. You've perfect right not to name your
> country, but you have no right to speak to me as if I were the likes
> of you.

The private, still defiant, retorts, "and in what are you more than I
am?" The officer answers, "I——?" he goes on, "I am more than
you, more of a man than you!" He then seizes the private by the
shirt collar, pulls him out of ranks, and strikes him in the face with
both hands. The mulatto fights back, but the lieutenant colonel
beats him viciously and leaves him lying on the ground, battered
and bleeding. He calls the private to attention, claps him on the
back, and tells him, "I need brave men at my side tomorrow. I suppose I'll see you near me." Barea describes the response: " 'At your
orders, sir.' Those eyes [those of the mulatto], more bloodshot than
ever, more yellow with jaundice, held a fanatical flame." Failure
to submit to military authority, and violations of regulatory proscription and prescription, may elicit punitive action, but response
to military order is reinforced by legitimated norm and regulated
sanction, usually involving the withdrawing or withholding of
privilege, or a punishment of inconvenient or extra duty, rather
than physical violence.

---

decades of the twentieth century it was customary, in some industries, for lower-
level supervisors to reinforce and legitimate their authority with "ax-handle
foremanship." The foreman or supervisor literally used his fists or a club to keep
recalcitrant or obstreperous workers in line. In more recent times, of course,
bureaucratic devices employing more symbolic sanctions are used to insure appropriate work behavior and role compliance.

To allow an enlisted man to do physical violence to a superior, for example, would clearly impair the enlisted man's future responses to orders and directions, and possibly infect other enlisted men with a seditious attitude or a propensity to violent response in the face of lawful orders. Additionally, officers are key personnel in the military bureaucratic structure because of skill and training, and, as such, are sufficiently valuable to the military mission that violence against their person by subordinates cannot be tolerated. Accordingly, the military severely sanctions any assaults or other use of violence or attempts at violence on a superior officer, or warrant, noncommissioned, or petty officers. The Ninetieth and Ninety-First Punitive Articles of War are most emphatic about this (U.S. Government 1969:169b-170d). Violation of these articles would likely justify a general court-martial. If convicted, the accused could well be sentenced to a term in a military prison, plus other possible punishments, such as fines and/or dishonorable discharge.

Violence and Aggressive Behavior Against Superiors

In spite of the severity attendant to physical attack of a superior, violations do occur. Military life, and especially combat, may be stressful and unpleasant, and officers and noncommissioned personnel may be unpopular. Many servicemen, in a fit of pique or frustration, often while intoxicated, have struck or struck at a disliked officer or sergeant. In a few isolated instances, crimes of violence against superiors have been essentially symbolic and motivated more by humor than hate. A few years ago, for example, a U.S. Navy Seebee, Leon L. Louie, was court-martialed for assault on a noncommissioned officer, charged with throwing a pie in the face of a chief warrant officer at morning mast at Port Hueneme, California (*New York Times* 1974). The enlisted men in his unit thought that the pie throwing might serve as a humorous morale-booster and "nominated" this individual to perform it. After a hearing, the charge was dismissed on a technicality, but the military prosecutor indicated that he might have the charge refiled.

Violence or aggressive behavior toward a superior officer or noncommissioned officer, however, is seldom a matter of humor. More frequently there are violent outbursts involving physically or

verbally assaulting the superior, which may well occur spontaneously in a situation of frustration, stress, and/or confrontation.
Actually, the Punitive Articles of War include the "raising in a
threatening manner" or lifting up of a firearm or club, or
"anything by which a serious blow could be given" as being within
the description of assault (U.S. Government 1969:169b). The
Punitive Articles also proscribe the use of "contemptuous words"
against public officials such as the president, vice president,
secretary of defense, a governor, or a group such as the legislature
of any state (U.S. Government 1969:167–68). Similarly, "disrespect
by words," "opprobrious epithets, or other contemptuous or
denunciatory language," or "disrespect by acts" against officers is
prohibited, as is similar behavior directed toward warrant officers,
noncommissioned officers, or petty officers (U.S. Government
1969:168–171b).[2]

Violence or aggression directed toward superiors has often attended insubordination. This was particularly true in instances of
mutinies and revolts, both on land and at sea.[3] In his psycho-
historical analysis of shipboard existence during the eighteenth and
nineteenth centuries, McKee (1978:293) provides an account of the
mutiny on board a British warship on September 21 and 22, 1797:

> The crew of the British frigate *Hermione*, goaded to the
> breaking point by the sadism of their captain, mutinied. With
> cutlasses and tomahawks they brutally hacked to death and/or
> threw overboard to drown, the captain, three lieutenants, the
> lieutenant of marines, a midshipman, the purser, the surgeon, the
> boatswain, and the captain's clerk. In all, ten officers died in this
> bloody orgy of revenge for injustices past.

There had been other, earlier mutinies, of course, including the
now famous mutiny on HMS *Bounty* in 1789 (for a detailed exposition on the events of this mutiny, see Hough 1973). Some of the
earlier mutinies, like that on the *Bounty*, had not entailed the same
overt violence toward the ship's officers and crew loyal to the captain. In the *Bounty* mutiny, Fletcher Christian and his mutineers

[2] Recently, however, a military court dismissed a charge against a sailor for using
profane and abusive language against a base policeman. The military judge ruled
that the charge against the sailor was "in conflict with speech protected by the
First Amendment of the Constitution" (Associated Press 1974a).

[3] Riots, mutinies, insubordination, and other forms of disorders and behaviors prejudicial to authority and discipline will be examined in detail in Chapter 5. We
mention them here because of the violence directed toward superiors by mutineers that often attend such disorders.

put Captain Bligh and 18 of his loyal officers and crew in the *Bounty's* 23-foot long launch (which had a normal capacity of 15) with some belongings and food and water for no more than a week, and set them afloat. In many ways it was a sentence of death, for Bligh and his men could easily have drowned, starved, or been killed by hostile natives on some of the islands in that part of the ocean. They were not physically harmed by the mutineers, however, as were the unfortunate ship's officers on the *Hermione*. The *Bounty's* mutiny had been precipitated by a number of factors, including short rations, oppressive living and working conditions aboard ship, and Captain Bligh's general treatment of his crew. As was the custom in the British Royal Navy at the time, Bligh had ordered various of his men flogged for infractions of naval rules, including desertion. On one occasion of desertion, he ordered 12 lashes for one man and 24 for two others. Ten days later he had the punishment repeated (Hough 1973:125). By the standards of the day this was not excessive punishment.

After the bloody events of the *Hermione* mutiny, the threshhold of paranoia for ship captains in many navies dropped significantly. McKee (1978) has argued that the *Hermione* mutiny was the basis for preoccupation with "mutiny and murder" among seamen in the U.S. Navy.[4] McKee (1978:294) relates that on May 10, 1800, on board the U.S. frigate *Essex*, one "William Ash, forecastle man, harangued the crew of the ship and urged them to fall on the officers and serve them 'as we did on board the *Hermione* and serve them right.' " The captain of the Essex put Ash in irons and 110 days later Ash, still in irons, was writing the captain, claiming he had been intoxicated when he made his inflammatory remarks, and insisting that his words were only the talk of a drunk rather than a would-be mutineer. McKee (1978:294) also tells of a Seaman Quinn on the U.S. frigate *President*, who in 1804 wrote a "pseudonymous" letter to the ship's captain, berating him for his treatment of the crew and complaining about the working conditions on board. He ended his letter with the thinly disguised threat, "The *President* is arrived to such a pitch as to exceed the *Hermione*. . . . [signed] Unhappy Slaves."

----

[4] According to McKee (1978), the horror of the *Hermione* mutiny was presumably on the minds of ship's officers as well as a fantasy preoccupation of seamen. It was this knowledge of mutinous retribution by the ship's crew that prompted ship captains and officers to employ such harsh and oppressive discipline as a means of forestalling any mutiny attempt.

Seaman Quinn's identity was discovered, and such was the concern with possible munity that he was subsequently sentenced to have his eyebrows and head shaved, and his forehead branded with the word "Mutinus." He was also "to receive 320 lashes with the cat-o-nine-tails, and then to be drummed on shore in a boat with a gallows erected in it." McKee relates the comment of an officer who observed the punishment and said, "I have no idea that he [can] survive the whole of it, but must die under the operation. It is, to be sure, most cruel punishment, *but the very existence of the Navy require[s] it*" [italics added].

There have been large-scale, land-based mutinies that involved violence to superiors. Perhaps the most infamous of these was the sepoy mutiny in British India, which began in 1857. (For a definitive account of this mutiny and the subsequent military campaign see Edwards 1973). For a variety of complicated reasons there was disquietude and resentment among some segments of the British Indian Army. On May 10, 1857, at the military base at Meerut, the unrest and complaints of the native sepoys (soldiers) broke into open rebellion. Some native troops murdered their officers and departed for Delhi. On May 30, 1857, sepoys of the Seventy-First Native Infantry mutinied, murdered their officers, and set fire to their huts and bungalows. Within a few weeks the uprising had spread widely. Across the province of Oudh, other similar occurrences were taking place. In some instances the wives and children of British officers were attacked and murdered as well as the men. The subsequent siege at Lucknow took the lives of numerous other British and other European men, women, and children. The original mutineers at Meerut had killed a number of women and children and thus set a precedent of brutality on both sides. In speaking of this brutality one authority (Glover 1973) has related:

> The massacre at Cawnpore served to heighten the horror. The troops who recaptured the place were not to know that the mutinous sepoys had refused to carry out the mass killing of women and children and that butchers had had to be hired to do the execution. The British, and the loyal Indians, uncertain of themselves and horrified that their former comrades could behave in such a way, overreacted and few captured mutineers escaped with their lives.

Some captured mutineers were court-martialed and hanged, and others were summarily shot. According to Glover (1973:19), "it was the custom to execute mutineers by blowing them from the muzzle of a cannon." Some of the sepoy offenders undoubtedly met their fate in this fashion.[5]

Other than the group mutinies and uprisings where officers or other persons of superior rank have been abused, assaulted, or killed, there have been some instances in our armed forces and others, in various wars and in the peaceful interims, of individual servicemen attacking or murdering a disliked or distrusted superior. As Linden (1972:12) has commented:

> In World War I, World War II, and Korea, the typical fragging took place in the field and for the most part during skirmishes and firefights. An inexperienced or overly zealous lieutenant would be shot by his own men while the platoon or squad was preoccupied with the enemy. The victim would be listed as killed in action. The killing generally followed a cold reckoning by the men in the unit that the lieutenant was a danger to them. Albeit ruthless, this type of murder at least can be understood as the result of a life or death assessment.

Such an incident was apparently never a frequent occurrence in the U.S. military before Vietnam. In World War I, for example, even though there were more than 4 million Americans in the military, there were fewer than 370 cases of violence directed at superiors that resulted in court-martial (Linden 1972:11). In Vietnam, however, violence directed at superiors was reported to be widely prevalent among our troops. Furthermore, the assaults against officers were often precipitated by irrational reasoning or relatively minor incidents, sometimes involving nothing more than an officer's reprimanding an enlisted man. These attacks also often occurred in rear-echelon areas, not just in combat situations. The practice of killing or wounding an unpopular or overly strict officer often took the form of "fragging" (so-called from the practice of throwing a fragmentation hand grenade at the disliked officer). Some accounts suggest that if the practice itself was not endemic to American troops fighting in Vietnam, it was *believed* to be by many servicemen (*Newsweek* 1971). In any event, during 1970 and 1971 there were upwards of 500 cases of alleged assaults with explosive devices, and it was estimated that "only about 10 percent of fraggings end up in court" (Linden 1972:2).

[5] Such a punishment may have been "more humane than the slow hanging then practiced"(Glover 1973:19).

Fragging apparently results from several different kinds of stress and hostility. Sometimes an individual might undertake to murder an officer for ostensible reasons of personal revenge or animosity, but in such instances the officer victim might only be a symbol of a larger hated entity. Moscos (1973:11), in describing such individuals, has observed that they

> have developed a diffused resentment against the whole military system rather than toward a specific person—though a particular noncom or officer might come to represent symbolically the system. These are cases in which the perpetrator is likely to be personally unbalanced or psychologically disturbed at the time he resorts to violence.

A number of such cases were brought to trial with such an explanation offered by the defense. One such instance was the court-martial of Pvt. Billy D. Smith, who was accused of murdering two officers in Bien Hoa, Vietnam (Associated Press 1972e). Smith, a 24-year-old black from the Watts area of Los Angeles, allegedly pushed a fragmentation grenade into the quarters of the officers. The defense attorney accused the prosecution of "tragic tunnel vision" in the fragging case, and went on to say that "the prosecution has proved only a motive for wanting to get out of the Army and not a motive for murder." The defense attorney went on to imply that Smith was "*discontented with his soldier's life* [italics added]." Moscos (1973:11) has estimated that fragging of this motivational variety probably accounts for less than 20 percent of all incidents. According to Moscos:

> In this type of fragging no collusion with others is involved, little if any warning is given, the lethal instrument is usually one's personal weapon, happenstance often determines the ultimate victim, and the culprit makes little effort to hide his identity.

In some instances, an individual soldier might simply have overreacted to an aggressive officer or noncom who reprimanded him, or interfered with some proscribed behavior in which the soldier was involved. Such a case was described in a *Newsweek* (1971:34) account of the Vietnam War. In this news story, a captain in the First Air Calvary Division made a night inspection tour of his unit's perimeter and found all of the men asleep in five bunkers in a row. His patience exhausted, the captain began waking up the men and taking names. As he was walking away, one of the men yelled, "I'm gonna kill you, you motherf——." The captain heard the angry soldier pull the pin from a grenade and, in his words:

> I went down fast into a ditch. The frag sailed right past me and went off a few feet away. As soon as the dust cleared, I was right back on top of that bunker, and I really whaled on that guy. I think I would have killed him, but people pulled me off. The other men testified against the guy, and he's in the stockade now. I hope he stays there.

As Moscos (1973:11) points out, there is another mode of fragging that is more common than that involving an individual culprit. This variety of fragging, he asserts, "systematically involves small group processes." He goes on to specify that "these fraggings occur in response to soldiers' groups believing their integrity has been violated in some way." Group-motivated fraggings, he suggests, may be articulated into three subvarieties: (1) racially inspired fraggings; (2) "dope hassle" fraggings that involve reprisals against officers who vigorously enforce antidrug regulations; and (3) fraggings against an officer or noncom who is considered to be too "gung ho" and thus is endangering the lives of his men.

In some instances it has been alleged that pooled money has been put up as "bounty" on some unpopular or "hard-line" officers and NCO's, with the result that bounty-hunting has become something of a group sport in the unit involved. Linden (1972:13), for example, tells of a second lieutenant who refused to obey an order to storm a hill. A sergeant told him later that his men had placed a $350 bounty on his head thinking he was "hard-line," but removed it when they heard him refuse the order. There have been a few cases of out-and-out group combat assaults by disgruntled enlisted men on officers' quarters or clubs. Linden (1972:13) recounts the incident of an officers' club in the 2/11 artillery area at Camp Eagle, north of Hue, being attacked by "between twenty and thirty enlisted men." The men used a well-organized assault technique when they attacked the building. They first stoned the building, and then attacked the officers with gas and smoke grenades when they came out to see what the disturbance was. The enlisted men had planned to use M-79 grenade launchers at this point, but, fortunately for the officers, this part of the plan was abandoned. It may be that, similar to the way stealing ceases to be theft when it is redefined as "scrounging" or "moonlight requisitioning," and the killing of the enemy becomes "wasting Charlie" or "neutralizing," the act of murdering a superior somehow loses its enormity when it is redefined as simply "fragging." Many of the men caught for fragging have not been able to think of themselves as criminals and have vehemently resented being so labeled at their court-martial. As Linden (1972:15) phrases it:

> The basic question remains: Why murder? The answer is that for many fraggers, the act is not murder and the victim is not human. Private First Class Walt Ross (again, a pseudonym) tried to murder his commanding officer because the PFC was "irritated."

Linden goes on to describe the soldier's attitude after his court-martial:

> Ross was asked during his post-trial interview whether there was anything in his trial that he thought was unfair. There was one thing that irked him, Ross admitted, and that was that the prosecutor when summing up for sentencing had made him "sound like a criminal." Ross still could not believe that he had committed a crime.

Linden argues that in Vietnam there were no convincing arguments for killing people (the enemy or civilians), and thus officers could also be killed without convincing arguments. To the combat-stressed soldier, the "gung-ho, nit-picking officer is as inhuman and remote as the gook." An account in *Newsweek* (1971:30) told of a unit in Vietnam where the men cheered enthusiastically when they heard that two of their own officers had been killed in a Vietcong ambush.

THE GENESIS OF VIOLENCE

There appear to be similar themes or strands underlying violence directed at officers or superiors, regardless of the historical period or the specific military context. The most prominent theme or factor contributing to such violence would seem to be the basic antagonism attendant to class differentiation and conflict. The distinction between enlisted and officer ranks has historically paralleled social-class differences. There has been a persistent pattern of privilege and deference attendant to officer rank, and an equally persistent pattern of subordination, harsh discipline, and deprivation bearing on the enlisted ranks. In most foreign armies, especially prior to the twentieth century, and particularly the

British and European military, caste distinction between officer and enlisted ranks was explicit and pronounced. It was perhaps less extreme and more implicit in the American military than in the European military during the same period, but the caste system did exist and was rigidly undergirded with iron discipline and ruthless punishment. As McKee (1978) pointed out, there was a rigid social caste system vis-à-vis officer and enlisted sailor in the U.S. Navy of the eighteenth and nineteenth centuries, and discipline was maintained with "systematic, brutal, physical punishment" that included frequent floggings and having men branded, chained, and confined to the brig for long periods.

Treatment in the navies of other countries was no different, and discipline was maintained in the U.S. Army in much the same way. Flogging with a wire rope—sometimes 100 lashes or more—was a "standard sentence" in the late 1700s (Knopf 1956:232–38). In addition to the formal punishments, such as the British naval practice of "flogging around the fleet"—having the offender tied in a boat and rowed from ship to ship to be lashed by the boatswain's mate of each vessel—it was also the custom of the time to permit petty officers to "start" the men on their tasks with a knotted rope end (Ellacott 1970:41). Conditions for the enlisted personnel both on board ship and in army units was harsh and spartan, especially in contrast to the privileged lot of officers. Class distinction went beyond mere differences in accommodations and standards of discipline. There was a pronounced attitude on the part of officers toward the social inferiority of enlisted personnel. As McKee (1978:301) describes it:

> But violence alone could not have done the job. Another element maintaining order, discipline, and subordination was old ethos of deference; that is, the philosophy or world-view so common in the eighteenth century that most men were no more conscious of it than of the air they breathed: namely, that God (or Nature) had ordained a social and economic hierarchy in which some men were placed high and others low; that those who were placed higher had a right and a duty to command and to lead; that it was the duty of those placed in subordinate stations to obey these social leaders and to be content with their lowly station in life; and finally, that the good of the whole social order depended on respecting this hierarchical social structure, for without that ordered ranking anarchy, destruction, and other unnamable evils would appear.

He illustrates this attitude by recounting an incident on board a U.S. naval vessel in the early 1800s when a sailor tried to address the captain of the ship. The captain angrily responded, "Begone—I don't allow a sailor to speak to me *at all!*" McKee (1978:299) also tells of a sailor who made a pension application to Congress as a result of having been "kicked in the genitals by a boatswain or boatswain's mate and knocked down the ladder to a lower deck in the process."

Over time, the differential in privilege between officer and enlisted ranks was significantly reduced. The American Civil War, for example, saw officers on both sides from a wide range of social strata. In contemporary times, in the American military, the officer/enlisted bifurcation has much less often reflected social-class origin, but the caste distinction in terms of privilege and prerogatives, which include higher pay, better living conditions, greater freedom of individual expression, and stronger legal rights, tended to persist, especially into World War II. In this regard, Stanton (1973:474) has observed:

> In World War II much of the hostility that is today directed toward the "lifer" was then aimed at commissioned officers, and NCO's were united with lower-ranking enlisted men in harboring this resentment. This animus revolved around the "caste" system and the differential treatment of officers and enlisted men in which officers were considerably the more privileged of the two.

Class differential and subsequent antagonism had not completely disappeared. During some periods of World War II, for example, even some junior officers had enlisted orderlies. Moskos (1973:3) has pointed out that Stouffer's *The American Soldier* studies during World War II revealed "widespread discontent among enlisted men." Moskos cogently observed:

> While it would take us far afield to give a summary of the findings of *The American Soldier*, it is sufficient to note that there was little acceptance of the military system on the part of enlisted men. Indeed, it appears that resentment toward the "caste" system of the army and the differential treatment of officers and enlisted men generated the strongest feelings about army life. The tenor of the gripes. . .was succinctly typified by one of the interviewees: "What's the matter with us enlisted men, are we dogs?"

Nor did social-class consciousness and subsequent antagonism abate after World War II. In Vietnam the hostility between officer and enlisted ranks may have reached its zenith. In this regard, Linden (1972:13) has observed:

> Thus, in the rear, the enlisted men become acutely aware of the authoritarianism of the system and the privileges and luxuries enjoyed by officers; yet, they see little immediate justification for the discrepancies in status because both officers and enlisted men are doing essentially nothing. This resentment sometimes erupts into skirmishes that resemble class war.

Racial tension has also been a major basis of interrank hostility and violence. Until the middle of the Korean War, the U.S. military was, by and large, racially segregated, but most black units were commanded by white officers, and the frictions between enlisted ranks and officers, intensified by racial antagonisms, did sometime result in attacks on officers. According to Laffin (1973:165):

> Young Negroes who believed that by putting on a uniform they could buy more respect were sadly disappointed; even colored officers found no change in white attitude. White officers were constantly complaining about Negro servicemen, from General Mark Clark, who called the 92nd Negro Division "the worst division I had" to the young lieutenant who daily ran the risk of being shot by his own men, "those God-damned trigger-happy children."

Although the U.S. military was racially integrated during the Korean conflict, and the number of black officers and noncommissioned officers subsequently increased substantially, the relative proportion of black to white remained small into the Vietnam War. By the time of Vietnam, only a relatively insignificant percentage of the officer corps was black. As of about 1970, there were 971,872 enlisted men in the army, of whom 138,693, or 14.3 percent, were black. At the same time there were 130,261 officers in the army, of whom only 4,661, or 3.6 percent were black (Johnson and Wilson 1972:91). The emergent interest of black servicemen in black pride and power in the 1960s has tended to intensify the racial hostility that has become especially characteristic of the U.S. military in recent years. The white officer, in effect, became symbolic of the racial status differentiation of the military, and the frustrated black soldier often directed at the white officer his hostility and aggression toward the military and the social system in general. Such racial hostility has not always been historically one-sided.

Since the American Civil War, and even before, the U.S. military has displayed a traditional theme of hostility toward black and enlisted personnel. White officers and noncommissioned officers historically have tended to question or underrate the military ability, especially in combat, of black troops. With a few notable exceptions, black troops have frequently been used as stevedores, truck drivers, in construction battalions, and as service workers, rather than in line units. Thus black enlisted men have been put into the position of providing a self-fulfilling prophecy. During World War II, both British and French recruited blacks for the military from their colonies. With the English particularly there was great concern about the fact that their African troops would be "in a position to meet vast numbers of ordinary Englishmen, and not just those thoroughly versed in colonial etiquette" (Headrick 1978:511), and thus there was fear about the loss of "the prestige of the white race." The contact that black soldiers might have with white prostitutes was also a concern. The black colonial troops, on the other hand, were disturbed by the disparities in pay, work conditions, food, housing, and recreational opportunities, as well as racial discrimination in general. Morale of the black troops deteriorated and there were frequent breaches of discipline, which subsequently resulted in a revival of flogging in the British army (Headrick 1978:510).

Such a military racial posture, and resultant racism among white officers, was hardly new to the British army. Edwards (1973:217), in his detailed account, tells of an incident during the sepoy mutiny involving a captured native soldier and a British soldier:

> One captured sepoy, who got down on his knees and begged for his life, was told by a man of the 78th: "You black rascal, do you think we are going to carry your ugly face all over the face of the blessed earth?" The soldier then drove his bayonet through the man's heart.

Prior to the mutiny, the sepoys had been loyal members of the British military, and had presumably been worthy of respect. However, the attitude of the British soldier was no doubt reflective of his officers' attitudes.

Racism conflict, social class, and caste have historically been major factors in officer/enlisted hostility, but there have been other equally divisive kinds of differentiation tendency inherent in the social structure of the military. By the time of Vietnam, for example, there were yet other cleavages that exacerbated the hostility between officer and enlisted men. As Stanton pointed out, the Vietnam draftees often developed more animosity toward individuals who were military careerists and thus presumably derived benefit, if not satisfaction, from the war. As he described this cleavage (1973:474):

> Today a greater proportion of the vocalized objection comes from college-educated enlisted men who resent being ordered around by people they consider their intellectual inferiors; indeed many of them appear to be disgruntled because they do not themselves enjoy a commission. This, then, is less an objection to the military caste system on intrinsic grounds as much as it is an egalitarian struggle combined with a schism between career and noncareer soldiers.

Interestingly, Moscos (1973) has asserted that in the Vietnam War, where there was a significant percentage of college-educated draftees, such individuals often had less identity with their lower-class enlisted peers than with college-educated officers.

In Vietnam, the draftees felt that the "lifers" were enjoying the war, which they themselves felt was unjustified and immoral, as well as a personal imposition. As Linden (1972:16) put it:

> The hardnosed officer and career NCO believe in discipline, often enjoy combat if only as a game, drink beer and whiskey, and distrust the alienated and unmotivated crop of draftees that are sent over to Vietnam to fight. Conversely, the grunts and rear-echelon draftees often feel that they are helpless, that they have no avenue of redress of grievances, that the structure of the Army is stacked against them, and that they were railroaded into Vietnam at a time when we have admitted it is a horrible mistake and are pulling out.

The enlisted men often felt that their situation, and the arbitrary discipline of the military that they experienced, were part of a conspiracy perpetrated by "lifers." In this regard violence directed at superiors meant getting even with the career conspirators.

Thus it would appear that, overall, violence against superiors arises from a number of factors, including the frustrations attributable to incipient (or overt) racism, the bifurcation of values separating the draftee and military careerist, and the pronounced differential in deference, privilege, and reward constituting the class or caste separation of officer and enlisted ranks. These frustrations are often exacerbated by cruel or oppressive treatment or conditions imposed or implemented by superiors or the military establishment, and also by a military situation that fails to provide men with a will to fight, hope for survival, or a sense of unity and purpose. Violence against superiors is often simply a means of venting frustrations. As one writer (Linden 1972:55) has so aptly phrased it, "*First* the soldier takes out his frustrations on the enemy, then his superiors, then anyone."

VIOLENCE AND AGGRESSIVE BEHAVIOR AGAINST PEERS

The dissafections of military existence, whether the monotony of garrison life or the anxiety and fear of combat, often create inordinate stress for individuals in the armed services. As pointed out earlier, this stress may precipitate aggressive behavior or physical attack against officers or superiors. In other instances, however, stress may lead to violence between military peers. No military organization can operate with any degree of effectiveness that does not maintain internal discipline to the extent that all members act in harmonious concert to effect the mission. Any disruption to the teamwork capability and internal discipline is usually severely sanctioned. Fights and assaults between peers, as well as altercations between subordinates and superiors, represent such disruptions. Such violence has historically not been confined exclusively to enlisted ranks, but has also, on occasion, included officers. Officers might lose control of their composure and fight with a brother officer, but in an earlier era disputes were probably settled in a more formalistic fashion, through duels. Although duels may have represented a codified, and thus more "civilized," means of fighting, they, too, like common brawling and fisticuffs, were disruptive to discipline, good order, and unit equilibrium, and were accordingly banned by the U.S. military and practically all other militaries.

If duels or fights between fellow officers tended to be infrequent, fighting and brawling in the enlisted ranks of the U.S. military and other armed forces have been more common in all of our wars. Frequently such fighting and brawling was part of a larger pattern of drunkenness and unruliness growing out of the frustration of garrison duty. During the Civil War, in the Union army, offenders had their wrists tied about their heads to tree limbs and a bayonet tied in their mouths to serve as a gag (see Ketchum 1960:II, 381). In more recent years such offenders are more likely to be punished under Article 15, or given stockade sentences.

Some violence directed toward peers is spontaneous and related to drunkenness or irritation. In other instances, the violence, even murder, may grow out of some long-standing grudge or dispute.[6] In garrison situations, where wives and families are present, assaults and murders of fellow soldiers may grow out of jealousies and sexual affairs.[7] Not infrequently the sexual jealousies and violence may erupt over the favors of a prostitute, as well as the fidelity of a spouse. An instance in point is the case of Sp4c Leroy McDowell of the U.S. Ninth Infantry Division during the Vietnamese conflict, which received national publicity (*Newsweek* 1970a:21). McDowell persuaded a fellow soldier to take guard duty for him, so that he could smuggle a native girl onto his fire base. Later that night another soldier became involved in a quarrel with McDowell over the girl, and subsequently McDowell shot and killed the other soldier. He was court-martialed and found guilty of voluntary manslaughter. Sexual rivalries involving military personnel of different races is particularly prone to precipitate interpersonal tension, if not violence. In this regard Moscos (1970:123) has observed that "the most overt source of racial unrest in the military community centers in dancing situations." White soldiers frequently take offense at black soldiers dancing with white girls and altercations sometimes subsequently occur. Moscos goes on to assert that "in many noncommissioned officer (NCO) clubs, the likelihood of interracial dancing partners is a constant producer of tension."

[6] In Rudyard Kipling's (1940:395–96) "Danny Deever," Deever the soldier is hanged for shooting a sleeping comrade, but the poem never relates the details of motivation for the killing.

[7] Military garrison life is an encapsulated social existence, and military personnel and their families are, accordingly, more cut off from the outside than is the case with nonmilitary people. Flirtations, romances, and sexual liaisons may sometimes be precipitated as a result of this social segregation and the "togetherness" it fosters. Infidelity and violence directed at the lover would seem to be a familiar theme in military existence. Rudyard Kipling (1940:415) makes reference to such an eventuality in the British army. In his poem, "The young British Soldier," one stanza advises:

If the wife should go wrong with a comrade, be loth
To shoot when you catch 'em—you'll swing on my oath!—
Make 'im take 'er and keep 'er: that's Hell for them both,
An' you're shut o' the curse of a soldier.
Curse, curse, curse of a soldier . . .

Sometimes violence and the killing of a fellow serviceman may result from horseplay, or accident, or from some insignificant personal transgression. In 1977 a U.S. Marine guard was court-martialed and sentenced to 30 years confinement at hard labor and a dishonorable discharge for having shot a fellow marine guard. The victim was apparently sitting on the offender's bunker and the guilty marine shot him five times (Associated Press 1977b).

Perhaps the most frequent mode of military peer violence grows out of interunit or interservice rivalry. Military training and culture tend to inculcate unit and service branch ethnocentrism, and a competitive spirit. Historically and globally there has been a tradition of fighting and brawling between personnel of different armed services, different branches of the armed services, and different units within a service; in some instances officers have been involved. Braham (1961), for example, related the drinking and brawling patterns of off-duty fighter pilots in England during World War II. Enlisted men have more characteristically been involved in such brawling, however. In World War I the American doughboys would fight and brawl with each other as well as with British and French troops. During World War II our GI's not infrequently became involved in bar fights and altercations with members of other services and units, as well as with civilians and personnel from all of the other Allied militaries. This pattern did not change in the Korean or Vietnamese conflict. The incidence of interservice and interunit fighting and brawling has been endemic to our military (and those of other countries) since its creation.[8]

Certain types of military unit would appear to have more of a propensity for fighting and brawling. There is a strong stereotypical image of naval personnel as being inclined to become involved in bar fights and altercations. If this is so, and it is difficult to document such a stereotype, it may well be because sailors are often confined to relatively cramped quarters, and have to endure monotonous living routines on board ship while on sea duty.

---

[8] Again turning to Kipling for documentation of behavior in the Victorian era British army, his poem "Belts" is most insightful (Kipling 1940:412). The poem relates an account of a brawl between members of an Irish regiment and an English Cavalry unit. There was a history of brawling between members of these units, which normally involved fighting with their belts. On one occasion, however, tempers got out of hand, and one man "drew his side-arm" and "Hogan took the point an' dropped." The soldier, Hogan, died and a number of the men involved in the brawl were punished.

Alcoholic beverages are not even permitted on U.S. naval vessels. Thus the sailor has little opportunity for a respite from his duty. He cannot easily "blow off steam," or enjoy "a change of pace." The soldier in garrison duty can usually go to the PX or service club for beer at night, and he can get frequent weekend passes. The sailor, on the other hand, may only escape his shipboard routine every few months, if that. When he does obtain liberty (shore leave), he is likely to be in a mood that might incline him to become involved in fights simply for the excitement involved, not to mention the fact that he may be less emotionally disposed to self-control than might normally be the case. The sailor experiences a special situation of ethnocentrism. His social entity is the ship, and the ship and its crew experience considerable social as well as physical distance from other military units. The ship, perhaps more than any other type of military setting, represents a total institution with its constituent characteristics (see Goffman 1961). The "fleet" is a relatively diffuse social entity for identification. Accordingly, the sailor has a strong sense of in-group identification with a relatively small social group, and tends also to have a strong sense of out-group competition or conflict. Zurcher (1965), in his analysis of shipboard behavior in the U.S. Navy, has stressed the identification of the crew with the ship and the strong sense of involvement with the informal organization. On shore leave they may scatter widely, singly or in small groups, becoming an even smaller social entity in a potentially hostile port. In-group cohesion and identification become even stronger. Encounters with members of other armed forces or other service branches may then result in disputes over territoriality (perhaps in bars), females, or assertions of relative superiority of unit, service, or country.

Other categories of military personnel that appear to have a propensity for fighting and brawling might include various kinds of elite or "crack" troops such as U.S. Marines, army paratroopers, and army rangers or Special Forces personnel. As with sailors, there is a strong sense of identification with unit that promotes ingroup cohesion, and often out-group conflict. In the case of such elite troops, however, a major factor in their involvement in interunit or interservice fighting and brawling is their training and the resultant self-image it inculcates. Training for combat and war necessarily involves a socialization into violence (for a detailed analysis of this process see Blake 1970:331–50). Infantry, and especially "shock troop" infantry such as rangers, marines, paratroops, and commandos, have to be trained to sustain and accomplish more violence than do most other military personnel. Elite troops must acquire a greater sense of aggressiveness or "fighting spirit," as well as a greater sense of esprit de corps. To accomplish this, recruits for such elite units must develop a self-image as superior to other kinds of military personnel, and as more competent in the skills of violence. Their training is often more strenuous and the discipline more harsh in order to effect this self-image. Thus paratroopers and marines, for example, come to see themselves as "tougher" and "better" (and "worse," too) than troops in regular military units. According to Weiss (1967:25), "[Paratroopers] consider themselves superior to all other such groups" in military virtues as well as vices. A similar ideological posture exists in the U.S. Marine Corps. Stack (1975) obtained a number of responses from a questionnaire administered to a set of marine recruits at the end of their training periods that revealed the same kind of sense of superiority in violence. When asked who and what are the marines, some of the recruits answered: "The most efficient killing organization in the world—efficiency meaning killing more than you have [had] killed." "It's just people like you or me who've been made experts in aggressive assault" And, perhaps more succinctly: "Nasty dudes that nobody fucks with."

With such an attitude, members of elite military units are often, in effect, "spoiling for a fight," and not infrequently become involved in altercations as a means of asserting their superiority in violence and legitimating their claim to, and fame for, "toughness." If necessary, they will provoke the fight, if they cannot induce someone else to start it.[9] Fighting and brawling become

[9] Several decades back, while I was serving as the commanding officer of a post Military Police detachment on an army base, we had occasion to have an airborne regiment pass through our base and bivouac there for the night. Although the paratroopers were encamped some distance from the barracks area of the base, some paratroopers undertook to sneak up to the barracks area and silently attempt to assault armed sentries and steal their weapons. Apparently it was something of a game to the paratroops and a test of their combat skills. Since they could easily have been shot and killed, it was also something of a hazardous undertaking. A number of paratroopers must have been involved inasmuch as a number of assaults and attempted assaults were reported. Several of the sentries were injured and some fired shots at their would-be assailants. We were never able to determine if any of the paratroopers were actually hit by the gunfire. Only after doubling the guard, arming them with shotguns, and appealing directly to the commander of the airborne unit did the attacks cease.

symbolic forms of combat and represent a means of maintaining a high degree of aggressiveness. In this regard, commanders of units of airborne infantry, commandos, marines, and so on, may well tolerate, if not tacitly encourage, fighting and brawling on the part of their men as a functional mechanism to enhance in-group cohesion and promote combat readiness. It does not appear that most foreign armies have the same toleration for interunit fighting and brawling. Discipline appears to be a more important consideration than aggressiveness. It should be recalled, however, that in many foreign armies, such as the German army, the emphasis has traditionally been on the crew-served weapon rather than the individual rifleman, as in the U.S. military. Thus, there would logically be more concern with discipline and precision teamwork than with individual initiative and aggressiveness.

In recent years in the U.S. military, racial conflict and hostility have precipitated a significant amount of peer-directed violence. As discussed earlier, there has been a long history of racism and racial discrimination in the U.S. military and in various of the European armed forces, such as the British and French military. Far from being merely an informal prejudice, racial discrimination was institutionalized and rationalized by an official ideology of racial superiority. In World War II, for example, a British publication called *Service Overseas* gave the following advice to the newcomer Englishman in colonial service and interacting with "native" troops or citizenry (Headrick 1978:511):

> In all contact with the natives, let your first thought be the preservation of your own dignity. The natives are accustomed to dealing with very few white people and those they meet hold positions of authority. The British are looked up to, put on a very high level. Don't bring that level down by undue familiarity. . . . To do so does not increase your standing, it does not elevate them. All it does is to make them perplexed, and lower your prestige along with that of the Empire.

The employment of large numbers of African troops in the British and French armies during World War II was not without incident. There was widespread discontent among some of the African troops because of discrimination, and differential privileges and treatment. Headrick (1978:512) has reported that in 1943, in the Middle East, a company of East African troops sent a petition to their commanding officer requesting an improvement in wages and an end to the color bar. There were also some incidents of racial clash between units of different racial makeup, and between individual servicemen.

Similarly, in the U.S. military there were occasional black and white racial clashes involving both units and individuals. These were sporadic until the Vietnam era, when racial violence in the military became endemic.

Contrary to popular belief, fraggings were not only directed at disliked officers, but frequently involved black and white enlisted men. Racial hostility would often erupt into open conflict and assaults, even to the extent of ambush shootings and fraggings. Sometimes these incidents would involve only two soldiers of different race, and in other instances large numbers of military personnel would be involved. *Newsweek* (1971:37) reported a racial flare-up at Chu Lai, headquarters of the Americal division. In this incident, a shooting spree broke out at an enlisted men's club, involving some 400 black and white soldiers. One white GI was killed and several whites were charged with conspiring to kill blacks. The McDowell case mentioned earlier involved a black soldier and a white soldier. Linden (1972:14) told of visiting Vietnam in 1971, when two race riots erupted in the Danang area alone. When the MP's came to quell one of the riots, they discovered that both whites and blacks had hidden caches of M-60 machine guns, fragmentation grenades, and ammunition around the base. A short time later the act of a white replacement who unwittingly sat down at a table that black soldiers traditionally reserved for themselves precipitated two days and nights of racial fighting in which five men were injured. Both whites and blacks have been the perpetrators of fraggings. After the racial clash at Chu Lai, a black private, G.D. McLemore, heard a white voice outside his "hootch" (barracks) say, "The nigger lives here, let's get him," and then he heard the pin being pulled from a grenade (Johnson and Wilson 1972:91–93). At this point McLemore grabbed his M-16 rifle, went outside, and killed the man bending over his window, holding a grenade. The grenade went off, proving to be only a red smoke-signal grenade. McLemore was subsequently court-martialed, convicted of voluntary manslaughter, and sentenced to 18 months imprisonment at Fort Leavenworth, Kansas. These authors reported that racial assaults have caused many units, even in the field, to take grenades away from everyone, and to issue firearms only to those on patrol or guard.

Racial hostility in the U.S. military generated new forms of informal segregation. Blacks would eat at one mess table, whites at another. In Vietnam there were often black bunkers and white bunkers, even in combat units. Off duty, there were white bars and clubs, and black areas like "Soul Alley" in the Saigon slums, where whites were not supposed to enter the bars and brothels unless they wanted to invite a racial attack (*Newsweek* 1971:36–37). The black troops often wore special amulets in the form of a clenched black fist, and had a ritualized handshaking custom known as the "dap" or the "liberation handshake."

Racial clashes and violence against peers in recent years have not been confined to combat situations. There have been a number of racial clashes and fights in military garrisons in the United States and abroad. Some Marine Corps training bases were the site of a particularly endemic pattern of racial conflict. Gangs of blacks or whites would go through barracks systematically attacking men of the opposite race. In some instances it became necessary to post guards in the barracks, and have the men move about in groups to forestall attacks. In 1972 the U.S. aircraft carrier *Constellation* had to interrupt maneuvers at sea to put 237 crewmen (all but only a few black) ashore. The men had staged a protest on the ship "to complain about what they called 'calculated racism' on the part of the ship's officers in administering discipline and work assignments" (*Roanoke Times*, 1972). After the men were put ashore, the captain subsequently ordered them back aboard, and 130 of the sailors refused the order.

The same year a bloody riot between white and black sailors took place aboard the carrier *Kitty Hawk* and lasted more than five hours; 46 crewmen were injured, and 21 black sailors were arrested and held for court-martial or disciplinary action. Like many altercations, this one had been preceded by a long-standing problem of strained race relations and racial hostility on board the *Kitty Hawk*. There had apparently been concern on the part of the ship's command about the tendency of the black crewmen to congregate during off-duty hours to talk and "pass the dap" or "pass the power." There was a controversy concerning whether or not the captain ordered the shipboard marines to disperse groups of blacks larger than three. When the marines did attempt to disperse the blacks, fights broke out. Subsequently it was claimed that groups of blacks roved about the ship attacking white crewmen. Ultimately the marines did contain the disturbance and a number of black offenders were confined (for a detailed documentary program of the *Kitty Hawk* incident consult Pacifica Tape Library 1973).

Racial tensions among U.S. troops stationed in Germany have also been disruptive, and peer racial violence has been common. There continue to be numerous incidents of attacks and muggings by both blacks and whites inflicted on soldiers of the opposite race. As in the Marine Corps training bases in this country, sometimes gangs of soldiers move through the barracks assulting men of the other race. At an even more serious and sinister level, there have also been reports (Johnson and Wilson 1972:31–51) of small gangs of black soldiers going into barracks and robbing soldiers at knife point, and mugging and robbing soldiers on the street. In some instances the robberies resulted from the failure of the victim to pay extortion money for a protection racket.

The racial violence in the U.S. military in recent years perhaps arises from a number of sources. The civil-rights movement of the 1960s made minority-group members more aware of and defensive about discrimination. It also produced a kind of backlash from some whites who felt that blacks and other minorities were getting too many concessions at their expense. The subsequent black-power movement facilitated and encouraged a strong social cohesion among blacks. In addition, the subsequent ritualized behavior attendant to the movement, such as the clenched fist and the "dap," tended to promote a degree of hostility and aggressiveness toward nonblacks, and elicited a hostile response from some whites, especially the "rednecks," as the blacks termed them. Thus the black servicemen, with their increased racial consciousness, have become more critical of the authoritarian command structure of the military and what they perceive as various kinds of "insidious forms of institutional racism in the military." White servicemen (especially lower-ranking enlisted men), on the other hand, have come to develop "a real fear of black hooliganism" (Moscos 1973:19). Thus peer violence will probably continue and possibly even increase in incidence in the future, the military's efforts to ameliorate racial tension, promote racial equality, and eliminate racial discrimination and prejudice notwithstanding. Such disturbances are costly and deleterious to the prompt and efficient discharge of its mission, however, and the military will probably employ its most severe sanctions to minimize or eliminate such disruptive breakdowns of discipline, and the erosion of military cohesion and morale.

Violence and Aggressive Behavior Against Subordinates

Some individuals may come to define physical abuse and violence as necessary or desirable in their interaction with their subordinates. In some foreign armies even today, officers and even noncommissioned officers may be authorized to slap, strike, beat, or even kill an enlisted men. If not authorized, such behavior may be tacitly tolerated. In times past, violence directed at subordinates as a means of reinforcing discipline and insuring obedience was widespread. Some European military establishments, as well as the U.S. military, however, have tended to discourage the use of physical coercion of subordinates and to rely more on the bureaucratized authority of superior status to obtain compliance with orders. The U.S. military is quite specific in its proscriptions concerning the physical abuse and maltreatment of subordinates. Article 93 (U.S. Government 1969) "provides for the punishment of any person subject to the code who is guilty of cruelty toward, or oppression or maltreatment of, any person subject to his orders." The assumptions underlying such proscriptions are that mistreatment of subordinates would erode or destroy discipline and obedience rather than enhance them, and that such mistreatment is antithetical to the democratic principles of our society, of which the military is but an instrument. Extremely serious sanctions may be invoked in the event of violations of these regulations. A famous case in point is the World War II incident of Gen. George Patton slapping the soldier in the field hospital because he believed the man was malingering. Patton was ordered by General Eisenhower to apologize publicly to his troops, which he did. He also did not receive a command for which he was in line. Only his high rank, his former military accomplishments, and his popularity with the public prevented far more serious sanctions being applied. In spite of the existence of such regulations, there continue to be widespread violations and evasions of the rules in the U.S. military. One of the most frequent contexts for violence against subordinates is that of basic training.

TRAINING AS CONTEXT FOR VIOLENCE AGAINST
SUBORDINATES

The object of military training is to prepare men for combat,
and to render them capable of accomplishing the military mission.
Blake (1970:335–37) addresses the process of socializing the soldier
into violence, and speaks of the trauma or "passage shock" that the
military individual experiences as he moves from one reality (the
world of noncombat) to another, that of combat and the "battle
moment." Thus to equip individuals for the "passage shock" of battle and violence, training must be made realistic, and the rigors of
the experience must be strenuous. The training of elite or "shock"
troops (e.g., paratroops, U.S. Marines, Waffen SS in Germany in
World War II) must be made even more grueling and
physiologically and psychologically demanding than most, inasmuch as it is these units that will often bear the major brunt of
combat and will experience the greatest degree of battle violence.
In general, however, all recruits receiving infantry training must
become inured to violence if they are to become effective combat
troops. Blake (1970:340) points out that there are several ways of
exposing the recruit to the results of violence. Troops from these
elite units frequently are exposed to such violence during their
training. In Neumann's account of service in the Waffen SS
(1958:65), he points out that training included field maneuvers
with live ammunition fired overhead, and on at least one occasion,
two recruits were killed. He also relates (1958:71–72) having to dig
a foxhole within 20 minutes and then having a line of armored cars
drive over the recruits lying in the holes. Such an exercise was not
without injury. As he phrased it: "Of course, some of our chaps are
killed. But none are cowards. Thus do we learn courage—at the
risk of our lives."

It is not unusual to have accidents, and even fatalities, in
military training. In order to make the training as grueling as possible, some training instructors become too enthusiastic or too brutal
in their efforts. Basic training in the military is often extremely
demanding by design. Hours are long, the physical routine is ex-
hausting and painful, and the psychological pressures are severe.
Typical requirements include long forced marches, seemingly
unending exercise, and physically punishing activities. Neumann
(1958:64), for example, tells of the Waffen SS recruits being
ordered not to use the washrooms, but instead to run a mile-and-a-

half and wash in an icy stream. The recruits also had to go out in the snow in the middle of the night and do physical jerks (a form of strenuous exercise). Because of some breach of discipline, half of the recruits' meals were eliminated throughout an entire month. Discipline, by design, is ironclad during training, and training personnel are often harsh and oppressive in dealing with trainees. In this regard, Levy (1971:18) relates that "[the Marine] drill instructors achieved on a psychological level the same control that they had on a physical level when, for example, the men were not permitted a bowel movement for the first week of boot camp."

In actuality, most armed services, and certainly our own, attempt to specify, define, and regulate the processes and conditions of military training so as to insure that acceptable limits of harshness and physical demands are not exceeded and the basic rights of recruits are not abridged. In spite of the existence of such regulations, there are evasions of the rules and regulations pertaining to training and the treatment of recruits.

There is often a great deal of competitive rivalry between and among training units, and the officers and cadre personnel may push the recruits beyond acceptable limits as a means of achieving superior performance ratings. In effect, the status of "winning" becomes more important than the goal of training the men correctly. Some training personnel develop a real sense of hostility toward their charges. The recruits are outsiders, and as newcomers they are military neophytes. They are accordingly often viewed with disdain by the experienced noncommissioned officers. This disdain may initially be feigned or superficially contrived as a training ploy, but over time some noncommissioned officers sincerely come to hold such a hostile attitude. By labeling Marine Corps recruits, for example, as "maggots" or "faggots" or other derogatory names, the metamorphosis from civilian to warrior may be facilitated, but the labelers may come to think of those being labeled in a pejorative sense. The *Marine Notebook* (quoted in Stack 1975) states that "Profanity, swearing, and verbal filth is discouraged. A person who must resort to profanity demonstrates his inability to verbally express himself in a socially acceptable fashion." Such verbal abuse is, however, quite common in training units of the U.S. Marines, Army, and, perhaps to a lesser degree, Navy. The drill instructors may admit such verbal abuse but often rationalize it as simply a dramaturgical aspect of training. As one marine drill instructor put it (Stack 1975):

You know something, I think I could get out of the Marine Corps and become an actor.

Yes I think I could become a good actor. Because that's all we're doing down here, we're playacting 'cause we tell these privates we hate them, we call them all kinds of names, but we don't really mean it. We don't mean that they are the worst things that walk the face of the earth. We call them these names because if they should ever become prisoners of war, somebody is going to call them worse names than we call them. So if they can't take it here, they won't be able to take it over there. This brings out self-discipline.

Nevertheless, the acting sometimes takes on the property of stark reality. The recruit who cannot tolerate the abuse may be the first to experience the transition from dramaturgical labeling to real hostility. If the recruit returns the verbal abuse or strikes at the NCO, or even reacts in a hostile fashion, he may experience the wrath of the drill instructor and his colleagues, even to the extent of physical assault. If the recruit displays weakness or ineptitude, he becomes the prime candidate for more verbal abuse or physical punishment. The weak recruit invariably takes the brunt of the hostility and punishment from his superiors. Tauber (1971:31–33) relates his experiences during basic combat training in the U.S. army, and tells of a fellow recruit who fell into such a mold. This soldier was "short, fat and sweaty, dark and ugly." He was also a Brooklyn Jew and clumsy. He tripped, he fell, he fell asleep in classes, his belt came loose, and he broke his glasses the first day in camp and had to wear prescription sunglasses instead. He had a bed that would not stay straight, boots that wouldn't stay shined, a fly that wouldn't close, was always out of step, and was grossly overweight and immature. The army drill sergeants called him "Piggy," "Porky," and "Bitch". One drill sergeant in particular seemed to have it in for this individual and had him spend each evening in the low-crawl pit on an obstacle course that called for a 40-yard crawl to be made in 30 seconds through a sand trough on one's belly. According to Tauber, the unfortunate soldier collapsed, crying, the second night in the pit.

Some noncommissioned officers engage in particularly abusive or even brutal treatment of recruits, to the point of sadism. Barnes (1971:63–64) reports an instance of a college-educated Jewish recruit in boot camp at Parris Island who was labeled as a Jew by his drill instructor and called "Jewboy" and "bagel." Subsequently the DI painted a Star of David on the recruit's forehead. Another DI, of German extraction, told the recruit, "You know what we Germans think of you Jews." Under such a regimen of abuse, the recruit began to have delusions that he was in a concentration camp, and after seven and a half weeks he cracked up and had to be given a psychiatric discharge. Other instances of abuse that Barnes mentions include making recruits do exercise inside wall lockers, ordering recruits in a "Dempsey Dumpster" garbage container and pounding on it with baseball bats, or making a recruit who was caught smoking eat cigarette butts or drink water from canteens in which ashes have been dumped. "Thumping" or striking a recruit as punishment has not been an uncommon practice in all of our armed services, but is particularly prevalent in the Marine Corps, although regulations clearly prohibit such abusive behavior. Marine Corps regulations explicitly proscribe "maltreatment, oppression or cruelty towards recruits."

In some instances, noncommissioned officers may endanger the lives of their subordinates, or negligently contribute to their injury or death, by underestimating the hazards of a situation, or being insentive to the physical limits of a given recruit. One widely reported case was that of Pvt. Lynn McClure, a 110-pound marine recruit who died as a result of injuries sustained in a pugil stick contest during training. The padded pugil sticks are used as rifles in simulated bayonet practice. According to the Associated Press report (1976b), he suffered "massive skull and brain damage" after being battered by "pugil sticks." His marine drill instructor, S. Sgt. Harold Bronson, was subsequently tried by court-martial on charges of disobeying orders, dereliction of duty, involuntary manslaughter, and assault. The general court-martial trial board found him innocent of all charges. The chief prosecutor, Maj. John Fretwell, said of S. Sgt. Bronson, "In an effort to make a marine out of this man, he ran roughshod over the regulations" (Associated Press 1976i). It was alledged that McClure was mentally handicapped—that in fact, in civilian life he had "lost a job as a shoeshine boy because he could not remember how to make change for a dollar" (McGrory 1976).

The death of recruit McClure was not the first instance of death resulting from brutality and mistreatment in basic training. A few years ago, one recruit died of "routine stress" after being run to the point of exhaustion (McGrory 1976). The DI involved in that case was given a $100 fine and transferred to another post. The marine training program, perhaps more so than that of any of the other armed services, has been criticized and attacked for its excesses, abuses, and brutality, all expressly against military regulation. Specific charges have included instances of recruits being slapped, handcuffed hand and foot to drain pipes, kicked, shoved, slugged, made to swallow canteens full of water and then beaten, and whipped (Jeffers and Levitan 1971). Seventeen marine recruits died between January 1968 and September 1969 alone. The reasons for death included suicide, drownings, kidney failure, cardiac arrest, pneumonia, heart failure, brain abscess, and pulmonary embolism. Given the strenuousness of the training, death by natural causes might well stem from abuses of one kind or another. Between 1964 and 1966, 120 DI's were relieved of duty at Parris Island, of which 73 were specifically because of recruit abuse or maltreatment (Jeffers and Levitan 1971:11).

Perhaps the most widely publicized incident of recruit abuse in the Marine Corps was the McKeon case. One night in April 1956, S. Sgt. Matthew McKeon, a drill instructor at Parris Island, marched his 75-recruit platoon into Ribbon Creek, a marshy tidal area. Six of the trainees drowned, and McKeon was subsequently court-martialed for "oppression of his men and negligence leading to their death," and for "possession and consumption of alcohol in marine barracks" (*Life* 1956:29; see also *Time* 1956:12–14; Jeffers and Levitan 1971:14). Perhaps the definitive exposition on the McKeon incident is McKean (1958). McKeon was ultimately found guilty of negligent homicide and drinking in recruit barracks. The court sentenced him to a bad-conduct discharge, nine months at hard labor, reduced him to a private, and levied a $270 fine. Higher authorities late reduced the penalties, and three years later McKeon was discharged for medical reasons (Jeffers and Levitan 1971:9). McKeon became something of a folk hero to marines who felt that he had simply been trying to instill discipline in the recruits. At about this same time there was another incident relating to the mistreatment of army recruits that attracted a lot of publicity. This case involved an army company commander and some of his sergeants who struck recruits, made them climb rough-barked trees while naked, and subjected them to a variety of physical abuses.[10] The abuse of recruits appears to be endemic to some degree in all of our armed services.

Perhaps more flagrant examples of physical abuse or maltreatment of subordinate personnel may be encountered in regard to the inmates of military prisons and stockades, and individuals arrested by military law-enforcement personnel. Military custodial facilities have a traditional and well-deserved reputation for severity in treating inmates. Some years ago, there was a practice of selecting the largest and most aggressive prisoner (as well as most tractable) and making him an "upside-down sergeant." His task was to intimidate and brutalize the other prisoners as a means of maintaining order and discipline. The "sweat box" was also a common military penal device of the times. James Jones, in his novel about pre-World War II life in the "pineapple army," *From Here to Eternity* (1951), provided an unsavory picture of army prisons and the mistreatment of inmates. A decade after the Korean conflict, some theatergoers were electrified at the events portrayed in a play called *The Brig* (Brown 1964) which purported to depict life in a marine prison. An equally sordid picture of prisoner maltreatment in a naval and marine brig emerged from Jere Peacock's novel of the Korean War, *Valhalla* (1962). In this fictional but presumably representational account, prisoners are denied water to the point of dehydration, and systematically beaten at "parties" conducted by the brig personnel. During the Korean campaign the so-called "Big-8" stockade in Japan developed a particularly infamous reputation. The "Big-8" was known for its rigid discipline, and its military guards were reputed to be especially severe in their treatment of prisoners.[11] As with basic training, however, the Marine Corps has the reputation of exceeding the other armed services in the abuse of prisoners in confinement facilities. At the marine brig in Camp Pendleton in California, there have been reports of inmates being exercised to the limit of their endurance and then beaten, handcuffed to a chain-link ceiling and left hanging for hours, and confined to a cagelike building that became unbearably

---

[10] When I was in the army at about this same time, I knew of a sergeant in my training battalion who often made recruits eat lighted cigarettes and occasionally had them buried up their necks in the woods and left them overnight. In the true Mertonian sense, such individuals become pathological in their ritualism and often turn their own frustrations against recalcitrant or inept recruits.

[11] The stateside Military Police detachment that I commanded in the early 1950s had several men who had served as guards at the "Big-8." When these men were guarding prisoners in our stockade, it was necessary constantly to admonish them against abusing the inmates, since they viewed such behavior as normative. I also observed that if we arrested servicemen from units that had recently returned from the Far East, an officer from the unit not infrequently came to the station house to stay with the arrested soldier for fear my MP's might physically assault him.

hot during the day and very cold at night. There have been other incidents reported in which prisoners had their mouths taped shut in a way that made it difficult for them to breathe, and in which guards bound prisoners' heads like mummies to keep them quiet (Jeffers and Levitan 1971:135, 139). The problem of maintaining the level of discipline believed necessary to the successful execution of the military mission has always skirted the edge of abuse and maltreatment.

If power corrupts, then military power seems to have a particularly corrupting influence on some individuals who occupy positions of authority, particularly if they come to define physical abuse as necessary or desirable for accomplishment of their mission. By the same token, the exigencies of war and military life are such that they seem to promote the aggressive acting-out of the privations and frustrations of some subordinates. In the final analysis, as General Chapman, then Marine Corps commandant, observed, "when discipline breaks down, brutalization sets in" (Jeffers and Levitan 1971:189).

Summary

The social organization of the modern military is hierarchical and bureaucratic, with rigidly structured subordinate-superordinate relationships and attendant roles. Rank and command prerogatives are based on legitimately assigned authority. Discipline is maintained by socialized obedience and an elaborate system of formalized and codified sanctions, rather than by violence and phsyical coercion. In order to insure proper military order and discipline, violence, force, and belligerence against other members of the military are proscribed by law and regulation, and violations of norms are severely sanctioned.

The stresses of military existence and the general circumstances and conditions of the military context often precipitate violations of the regulations proscribing violence or physical force against superiors, peers, or subordinates.

Perhaps the most serious of such offenses are those directed at superiors. Throughout history, and in all militaries, there have been instances of individuals who could not control their frustrations and hostility toward some disliked officer or noncommissioned officer, or have found the exigent discipline oppressive to the point of intolerance, and have directed violence and force at their superiors. Sometimes such violence has taken the form of coordinated mutinies and insurrections in which whole categories of superiors have been harmed, but in other cases it has been more of a spontaneous emotional outburst directed at a single superior. Sanctions invoked for attacks on a superior have historically been extremely severe, in the belief that only the harshest punishment would serve to deter such offenses. In Vietnam, a new pattern of furtive and clandestine violence was directed at some officers and noncoms. In those instances the disgruntled individual would secretly try to kill or injure a disliked officer with a grenade or bomb. This practice, called "fragging," was reported to be extremely widespread throughout the war. There were also some instances of small groups of enlisted men attacking officers in well-organized assaults on officers' quarters or clubs. This type of violence in Vietnam seemed to be symptomatic of the general malaise that infected the whole military system during that period, and included racial conflict, officer-enlisted caste hostility, a general breakdown in discipline, and a dissaffection with the war and the attendant political motives.

The inherent competitiveness and rivalry constituent to the military combined with the stresses of military life, have sometimes produced acts of violence directed at peers. Brawling and fighting are disruptive to discipline and good order and dysfunctional to the military mission, and have accordingly been prohibited along with other forms of violence toward peers. Violence sometimes grows out of a long-standing dispute or conflict or may simply erupt out of the boredom and monotony of military existence, perhaps exacerbated by alcohol or drugs. In recent years, racial hostility has been a major factor in precipitating interpersonal violence in the military.

Although equally proscribed along with violence toward superiors, violence and abuse directed at subordinates is not infrequent in the military, especially in the training phase of military life. Individuals of all rank, even up to general, have sometimes been guilty of abusing subordinates, and have been sanctioned accordingly. In the training process, however, there is often an overzealousness to produce men who are inured to the dangers, hardships, and deprivation of war, and some members of the military may come to abuse and brutalize the trainees. Having such complete power over individuals when they are so vulnerable perhaps brings out an element of sadism in some persons in positions of authority. The pressure to produce "hardened" and effective "warriors" not infrequently drives some noncoms and officers to violate regulations and mistreat and endanger the trainees in their charge. Similarly, inmates of military correctional facilities are quite vulnerable and, as offenders, are viewed in a most negative fashion by their keepers, who may vent all of their hostilities on the inmates. Again, having such authority over the inmates, and enjoying insulation from outside influence, military correctional guards sometimes systematically abuse and brutalize the inmates.

In spite of all regulations, proscriptions, and sanctions to the contrary, the military context contains such an opportunity structure for violence toward other members, as well as stresses and anxieties that precipitate it and an informal value system that countenances it, that crimes against persons are essentially endemic to the military.

CHAPTER FIVE

Crimes Against Performance

*While I certainly would not say that every instance of
AWOL or disrespect to an officer is an act of political
dissent, some of this sort of activity can be considered
primitive or prepolitical forms of rebellion.*
Lawrence B. Radine

The mission of the military may be critical to the continued well-being and the very survival of a society. The effort of the military
in discharging its mission successfully may well lie with its ability
to function in an orderly and concerted fashion, and thus also with
the inherent functioning of its constituent parts down to the individual member. Discipline is clearly essential to the operation of
the military, and the appropriate discharge of individual duties
and responsibilities is, therefore, considered a requisite of overall
success. It matters not what the cost is to the individual member in
discharging his responsibilities; the performance itself is the major
concern. Armed forces, almost universally, have traditionally
prided themselves on the "crack" discipline and dependability of
certain of their units. Such units could be counted on to hold positions, take ground, or attack units superior in size and firepower.

Because of its concern with discipline and predictability, the
military places an extremely high value on rigid role playing and
scripted behavior and, to effect such behavior, has developed an
elaborate system of normative proscriptions and prescriptions that

135

narrowly constrains the range of behavioral prerogatives. The specificity of expected military performance is such that a variety of deviations from the extensive statutory norms concerning the obligations and duties of the individual member constitute criminal offenses. These norms are frequently violated, however, even though violations often are punishable by prison sentences, fines, loss of rank, or dishonorable discharge. The range of activities that may constitute crimes against performance is formidable and the attendant sanctions are severe.

Inappropriate Appearance and Nonuniformity

The overriding and abiding characteristic of the military as a large, formal, social organization is uniformity. Like most formal organizations, it operates on the basic principle of interchangeability of parts, particularly at the lower ranks. One soldier is essentially like another soldier. Soldiers are not so much individuals as "warm bodies," thus the oft-used phrase in the military, "I need three warm bodies for a ditch-digging detail," or "Get five warm bodies for a patrol." The assumption is that any soldiers can do the job equally well, and that there is a complete interchangeability of men for any job. Nonetheless, even at the lowest rank there have always been specialists. In the past there were dragoons, hussars, lancers, sappers, pioneers, grenadiers, and so on. Today, even in the infantry, the individual soldier possesses what is known as an MOS (military occupational specialty). A soldier might be trained in the use of the machine gun, flame-thrower, or some other crew-served weapon, but basically he is trained as a combat infantryman and light weapons specialist. Within the generic rubric, all infantrymen in the army are essentially as alike as peas in a pod. When there are casualties, men can be shifted from unit to unit and position to position as needed, with complete flexibility. Thus the essential need of the military, in order to maintain the necessary flexibility and capability of interchangeability of parts, is uniformity in its members in terms of training, capabilities, equipment, and appearance.

A major mechanism for insuring uniformity in some areas is the uniform. Everyone must have the same clothing and equipment to insure the uniformity of the individual soldier. The military uniform, of course, plays a number of other equally significant functions for the organization. Wood (1966:139) points out that the use of a uniform in a formal organization "aids in the administration of a large body of persons," and the wearing of distinctive but similar dress "emphasizes the solidarity of the group and maintains morale." The uniform, in effect, serves as a kind of symbolic control. Control over the clothing worn by members of the organization represents control over their behavior. The uniform relates one member of the organization to the other members, and also insures social distance from outsiders. It defines appropriate ways of behaving by establishing a role. Additionally, the uniform projects a suitable image of the organization. In essence, the uniform facilitates formal social relationships and thus enhances efficiency. As Wood (1966:141) phrases it:

> The importance in certain situations of physical signs which defy error is exemplified by the army, which must remain organized even in the confusion of battle. Persons must be instantly recognizable so that orders may be given and carried out speedily and effectively.

Wood (1966:143) also points out that the uniform prevents "the individual from projecting many of his personal characteristics." Individuality is the antithesis of conformity, and conformity is essential to the predictible behavior necessary for the efficient operation of the military. According to Joseph and Alex (1972:723), "the uniform suppresses individual idiosyncrasies in behavior and appearance." Thus the uniform serves as a kind of "quality and quantity" assurance in the sense of identical components.

In another regard, the uniform specifies and guarantees the authority of a status. If a person dressed as an officer gives an order to an enlisted man, the enlisted man can move immediately to implement the order, secure in the knowledge that the person was, in fact, an officer and accordingly empowered to give orders. In the confusion of battle, everyone must be sure of the cast of characters and who has each appropriate part. The uniform, as Joseph and Alex (1972:725) put it, "validates the claim." It is for this reason that a most serious crime against performance is to wear a uniform or badge of rank of a person of higher status. Impersonating an officer or noncommissioned officer is falsifying a status and is therefore subject to severe sanction. If allowed to persist, the credibility of the entire authority system would be undermined. In addition to misrepresenting one's authority, it is also a serious crime against performance to wear any unauthorized badge of status.[1]

Uniform violations may well be the most numerous form of crime against performance. In various of our wars, members of the United States military have sometimes been charged with wearing no uniform, having buttons not fastened, not wearing a coat, or wearing a coat as the case may be, not wearing a tie, having a dirty uniform, or wearing a uniform not appropriate to the time and circumstances (i.e., wearing field fatigue uniform to a place where a class-A dress uniform is appropriate). In recent years, however, there have been numerous incidents of members of the military violating appreareance norms by growing beards, or letting their hair grow longer than regulation requires. One such case was that of First Lieutenant Matthew R. Carroll, who in 1974 grew his hair long after the fashion of General Custer (Whitney 1974; Swift 1975). Carroll refused to cut his hair on constitutional grounds, and the army court-martialed him.

Some members of the military sought to subvert the regulations on hair length by growing their hair long and tucking it under a wig with short hair. This way they could conform to the civilian fashion of long hair when off duty, and the military standard of short hair when on duty. The military banned wigs, however. Several naval reservists challenged the constitionality of the navy's ban on wigs in federal court after receiving "unsatisfactory reports at drills for wearing wigs rather then having their hair cut" (Associated Press 1973b:3; see also Associated Press 1975b). Military regulations require that reservists complete 90 percent of their 48 annual drills with a satisfactory report. Failure to do so would subject them to involuntary recall to active duty.

---

[1] Some years ago when I was in military service, I had occasion to see an unusual instance of such an offense. There was a captain who commanded a Leadership Company in my regiment. He was a very impressive individual who wore the patch of Merrill's Marauder's in which he had allegedly served in World War II. He also wore a number of decorations for gallantry, both American and foreign. He had the legend and reputation of being a war hero and tried to live up to his image as a dashing hero. A visiting general met him and noticing his decorations decided to have him assigned to him as an aide. In checking on the Captain's record, however, he discovered that the Captain had fradulently altered his record to indicate various awards for bravery in combat. He was not entitled to any of the decorations or patches. He was, in effect, impersonating a hero. The army viewed his actions as a serious crime against performance. He was subsequently court-martialed, and sentenced to a dishonorable discharge, loss of rank, forfeiture of all pay and allowances, and two years at hard labor in a disciplinary barracks. Whether any part of the punishment was ever rescinded or reduced on review, I am not sure.

A few years ago, Adm. Elmo R. Zumwalt, Jr., became chief of naval operations for the U.S. Navy and undertook to liberalize naval regulations concerning dress, hair length, beards, and so on. His actions were not enthusiastically supported by many high-level naval officers. In 1976 the navy moved to return to a more traditional standard of hair length and style (Associated Press 1976g:2). In this instance, the newer post-Zumwalt regulation prescribed hair no longer than "four inches in length and two inches in bulk," which is defined as "the distance that the mass of hair protrudes from the scalp." Although the U.S. Navy did change its regulations to permit beards under some circumstances (such as while at sea), the U.S. Army did not. Since the Vietnam period, when beards have been popular, a number of military servicemen have tried to grow them and were usually sanctioned as a result. In 1974 a navy airman technician in California was court-martialed, his rank reduced to airman recruit, and given an honorable discharge for refusing to remove his beard, and also his turban (Blau 1974). He had been converted to the Sikh religion, which requires that the faithful leave their hair unshorn and wear a turban. Several other servicemen were in the same circumstances, including two army privates who converted while on duty in Germany, and who were subsequently court-martialed, sentenced to three months of hard labor at Fort Riley, Kansas, and given general discharges. Attorneys for the American Civil Liberties Union took their cases, and federal court appeals were planned on the basis that the army regulations violated the First Amendment on religious freedom. Interestingly, in another case the same year, another Sikh convert, this time a Sikh minister, was given special permission by the army to wear his turban and beard after he became a soldier (Associated Press 1974d).

At a time when the American army has been trying to maintain relatively traditional standards of dress, appearance, and demeanor, the military services of some other nations have moved in the opposite direction. The most signal example is that of the Dutch army. For a number of years there has been a Union of Dutch Conscripts in the army there, and the union has been responsible for abolishing the military regulations requiring shining of shoes, saluting of officers except on formal occasions, shaving of beards, and trimming of hair (*Newsweek* 1974:45; *Parade* 1973). Members of the Dutch army frequently have beards and long hair hanging to their shoulders. They may, on occasion, wear dirty leggins or rumpled uniforms while in an honor guard. They even won the right to stage political meetings and discuss their grievances. A planned military parade honoring Holland's Queen Juliana's twenty-fifth anniversary was canceled because it "would not fit the mentality of our people," according to a government spokesman. Holland's "hippie army," as it has been called, could hardly be expected to have a different attitude when Defense Minister Henk Vredeling has said (Swift 1975): "My whole life I have been against discipline. . . . I do not have a feeling of solidarity with respect to military people. I am in fact absolutely allergic to uniforms." The Dutch army has become so unmilitary that when President Leopold Senghor of Sengal visited in 1974, there was an honor guard for him. The honor guard was from a crack unit of the Dutch army—the Guards Brigade of the Limburg Hunters—but the appearance of the soldiers was such that President Senghor turned to Queen Juliana and whispered, "Your Majesty, is this really the Dutch army?" (*Newsweek* 1974:45).

It is doubtful that any other military in the world would tolerate such an unmilitary appearance of its soldiers. The uniform is symbolic of the organization and should ideally inspire confidence and respect on the part of the public. The uniform also is perceived as a kind of indicator of attitudinal posture and behavioral utility to the organization. As Wood (1966:142) phrases it:

> Those who are slovenly in dress are presumed to be undisciplined in their actions; thus they cannot be relied upon as intrinsic parts of an interdependent network organized around formal rules. In that this concept is believed to be in the minds of the public also, the administrators feel that individuals whose uniform is not maintained in good condition will damage the image of the institution.

The military role is a complete role demanding the full attention of the individual. The uniform aids in imposing the complete identity on the occupant of the military status and, in effect, insulates him from external influences that might dilute the military identity and erode the individual's ability to perform the role appropriately. In this connection, according to Joseph and Alex (1972:722):

> The explicitness of the uniform as a status indicator depends upon its monopolization. While he is in uniform, indicators of all other statuses of a citizen are suppressed. An as extreme example,

Army regulations discourage officers in uniform from carrying packages—the ultimate indication of domesticity.[2]

The uniform, then, is an important dramaturgical component in the military context. Uniform and appearance rules and regulations are seen as being equally important.[3] Violation of such norms is a crime against performance, and the military exerts considerable effort to insure that such deviancy is minimized.

Deliberate Ineffective Behavior

The individual in the military is part of a man-machine system in which everyone is expected to behave and perform in the most capable, efficient, and effective manner. Lack of efficiency and effectiveness in the military, in some instances, is formally sanctioned. Some individuals fail in their performance becuase of personal ineptness, or role inadequacy, where they are not sufficiently prepared to conform to the work role expectations. Other persons may fail in their performance or underperform because of unfavorable circumstances, inappropriate facilities or equipment, or insufficient resources. Still others are not able to achieve an effective level of efficiency and effectiveness because of negligence on their part. An individual who, through some personal and obvious negligence, allowed himself to become incapacitated and thus unable to discharge his responsibilities appropriately would be guilty of a crime against performance. For example, an individual

[2] Although officers in uniform are theoretically discouraged from carrying packages, many of them do. Some years back when I was in the service I had a field first sergeant of genuine sadistic bent toward officers. A principal source of recreation and amusement for him was to go down to the post PX and wait outside the front door hidden by some shrubbery. He would wait until he saw an officer come out of the PX with his arms full of packages. Then he would step out from behind the shrubs and throw the officer an inspired and precise salute (the sergeant possessed considerable military bearing, and he also had long arms; his salutes, which were glorious to behold, seemed to start at ground level). The officer, startled by the sudden appearance of the sergeant and awed by the precision and correctness of his salute, invariably would fumble the packages, often dropping them, in his awkward and hasty attempt to return the salute.

[3] The question of tatoos has also entered into the appearance code of the U.S. military in some instances. Traditionally, candidates for Annapolis were not admitted if they had tatoos. Until quite recently, the Marine Corps did not allow female marines to have tatoos. They recently discovered, however, that they had five female marines with tatoos, offered waivers, and undertook to revise their policy to apply equally to men and women (New York *Times*, 1979:E9).

who stayed out on the beach sunbathing too long and let himself become so severely sunburned that he was unable to wear a pack and go on a training exercise the next day might be formally punished for negligence. A stockade guard who took some medicine that made him drowsy, thereby permitting a prisoner to escape, might also be guilty of negligence. Some individuals in the military, however, deliberately attempt to perform in an inadequate, inappropriate, or ineffective manner.

The classic military example of deliberate ineffective performance is malingering, or pretending to be sick or injured. In the military, the "sick" role must be verified by a person competent to make such an interpretation before it can be legitimated (Little 1956). Usually this determination is made by the medical officer, or in some instances by a corpsman or a pharmacist's mate in the navy. The military, accordingly, has an elaborate set of rules and procedures that govern the shift from "duty soldier" to "sick soldier." There are various screening devices, such as the morning sick call, when individuals can present themselves as ill and undergo an initial examination. Subsequent examinations and screening mechanisms might be involved before the individual would be conceptualized as "completely sick," and admitted to a hospital. A "sick" soldier is a soldier not available for the military mission, and is thus a liability. For this reason, the sick role is usually viewed as deviant. The military medical officer is, in effect, socialized to inculcate the "negative definition of the sick soldier as a deviant social role" (Little 1956:24).

The time and circumstances may dictate the resistance to certifying the soldier for a sick role. During or just before a battle, every soldier is needed, and there is a tendency for some individuals to avoid the battle by reporting as sick. The medical officer may therefore be less inclined to accept the claim of sickness at such a time. Medical officers may be under pressure from peers and superiors to limit or minimize the number of persons who are "sick," and so may simply refuse to certify an ailing soldier as actually ill. Even with a genuine illness, the sick soldier is always a deviant to some degree. In some instances, the medical officer who was too lax and lenient in certifying soldiers as sick might himself be considered a deviant, expecially by the commanding officer of the parent unit, who might need every available man for combat. The medical officer operates to monitor the process of changing roles and represents the social control to minimize the process. At times it may be necessary for the military to reject practically all claims to sickness. When General Patton slapped the shell-shocked soldier in World War II, he was simply refusing to accept the soldier's claim of psychological infirmity, and physically sanctioned the individual for being a medical deviant, The character "Clinger" on the TV series "M*A*S*H" is constantly claiming all kinds of ailments, in addition to the more obvious ostensible pathology of affecting transvestitism. No one believes him, his pathologies are ignored, and he cannot successfully convert his role to that of "sick soldier." When a person deliberately feigns illness or infirmity, he is guilty of malingering, and has committed a serious crime against performance. Similarly, if an individual intentionally inflicts self-injury to avoid work or hazardous service, he is also guilty of malingering. A favorite act is to shoot oneself in the foot or leg. The injury may also be inflicted by nonviolent means, such as voluntary starvation.[4] In any such event, offenders are usually tried under the 115th Article of War.

Although it may have always been component to the military context, recent years have seen the emergence of a modal pattern of ineffective behavior in the U.S. military, in which the individual deliberately misplays or sabotages his correct military role. Role sabotage is not unknown in contexts other than the military. The young person who does not wish to attend college, but begrudgingly goes because of parental pressure, may seek to solve the dilemma by sabotaging the role via poor academic performance, and subsequently flunking out. Some years ago, a researcher documented the existence of role-sabotage behavior among delinquent children in a treatment camp (Crain 1964). Some of the children were "forever playing, ignoring staff demands, or screaming with real and put-on pain," and they "all played and clowned, [and] did foolish spur-of-the-moment things." Such children were labeled as "chronic mess-ups" or "dings." Presumably such "fool" behavior was an adaptive mechanism.

In some situations, "fool" behavior or role sabotage may be representative of an adaptive pattern, as a means of maintaining morale and mental equilibrium. Daniels and Daniels (1964) relate

---

[4] Self-inflicted injuries are not uncommon in some other contexts, especially in other total institutions such as prisons. Some of the prisons in the southern states of the United States have historically consisted of prison farms, with relatively rigorous work for the inmates. Some inmates have attempted to evade work by disabling themselves in such ways as chopping off their toes or cutting the tendon in their ankle.

the account of a group of recruits in air force basic training during World War II and their experiences with one member of their flight who, because of his "fool" role performance, frequently kept the other members of the unit in difficulties with their superiors. This individual's role sabotage, however, was also functional to the men in the flight, in that the "fool" often acted as a buffer between them and the depredations of their superiors. His behavior demonstrated the vulnerability of the military system, and thus he stood for the men as a symbol of individualism, albeit irrational individualism, in the face of regimentation. This "fool's" behavior also represented a form of boundary maintenance and helped spell out the limits of tolerated deviancy for the others. The "fool" also was continually breaking military rules and was guilty of crimes against performance. For an elaborate discussion of "fool" behavior, see Klapp (1962).

Deliberately ineffective or "fool" behavior may not always be functional to the group or to the organization, and it may not always be based on personal awkwardness. It may serve as a device for attacking discomforting institutional control over the occupational members. In an essay published a few years ago, Hodges (1974) relates a pattern of deliberate ineffective behavior on the part of some U.S. servicemen who were drafted into the military and were very dissaffected by their circumstances. He examines a variety of role sabotage in which the violation of role requirements represents a deviant form of adaptive mechanism for coping with unwelcome and uncomfortable regimentation and restrictions on individualism. The unhappy draftees view the army as a repressive total institution, and some of them become the kind of rebel who sabotages his work role by emulating the inept. Such behavior is labeled "dud" behavior (after the artillery shell that does not go off). Nonconformity to army norms concerning workrole behavior is severely sanctioned if identified and defined as deliberate, and dud behavior is really a premeditated and serious crime against performance.

Dud behavior violates the role norms, but in such a manner as to evade the sanctions for deviance. The "offender" manages to escape the consequences of his crimes through an elaborate and contrived set of dramaturgical machinations. The dud soldier ordered to perform some onerous task like loading heavy (and expensive) tank batteries would drop one and break it and pretend to be clumsy and inept. The NCO in charge of the detail would then be likely to take the dud off of the work detail lest he drop another tank battery (Hodges 1974:35–36). The disguise of ineptness provides a high degree of immunity from the formal processes of social control. It may be a means of striking back at a work system for the enforced occupancy of a work status, and may also constitute an effective vehicle for evasion of the norms pertaining to work performance. In this regard the dud or "goldbrick" may not only use his deliberate ineffective behavior as a device to externalize his hostility and resentment toward the military or his situation; goldbrick behavior sometimes operates as a kind of symbolic role model for the collective disaffected of the larger group. Vidich and Stein (1960:499–500) have reported that:

> The role of goldbrick or Schweikism in general, which usually took the form of devoting excessive time to assigned tasks and other minor forms of "sabotage" against efficient operations, was a permitted form of resentment response. In fact, the goldbrick who did not make more work for others was held in high esteem, particularly by other enlisted men, and exceptional talents along these lines usually brought considerable prestige from all but overzealous officers. Such forms of sublimated resentment, given content in assigned tasks from instituted authority, served to define the psychological profile of those who elected the goldbrick style of personality.

As a de facto violation of military work norms, and a demonstration of patent ineffectiveness, such deviancy represents inappropriate occupational behavior, and consequently crime against performance. Similar kinds of ineffective behavior but perhaps of a less serious intent or consequence are practices such as goldbricking or "goofing" on the job.

Conduct Unbecoming and Inappropriate Behavior

The militaries of all nations have historically insisted on circumspect and proprietous behavior on the part of all of their members, but especially officers. Officers (and to a lesser degree enlisted men) were expected to be exemplary models of honesty, integrity, and correct social behavior. "Conduct unbecoming" an officer and a gentleman was not countenanced, and sanction was often swift and severe. Over the years various kinds of behavior have been prohibited, such as dueling, public drunkenness, openly notorious, lewd, licentious, or wanton behavior, not paying bills or gambling debts, and dishonesty or unethical behavior of any kind.

Perhaps one of the most incongruous examples of the violations of the norms of circumspect behavior involving a military officer (although serving in a civilian organization at the time) was the space program scandal of a few years ago. The astronauts in the program had a public image of having the very highest moral and ethical standards, in addition to being outstanding examples of young American armed services officers.[5] They were seen as being brave, intelligent, able, dedicated, and motivated by unimpeachable altruistic, scientific, and patriotic reasons. The American public was understandably disappointed to discover that their idols and heroes had feet of clay, and the military was understandably outraged.

In one instance, three astronauts, Alfred M. Worden, David R. Scott, and James B. Irwin, shipped to a German stamp dealer 100 of the 400 postal covers they had carried to the moon (*Los Angeles Times* 1972:1). (It is interesting to note that authorization to carry 232 souvenir postal covers to the moon had been given by Donald K. Slayton, chief of Astronaut Activities. The smuggled 400 were in addition to those.) Although it was already too late, the astronauts apparently had second thoughts about the transaction and had a friend call the German stamp dealer and try to stop the sale of the covers. However, the dealer had already sold 99 of the covers for a total of $150,000, keeping one for himself. The postal covers were said to be a "philatelic dream." They all carried the autographs of the astronauts (two of whom had autographed them on the moon), they displayed the Apollo 15 emblem, and had been canceled twice, once at Cape Kennedy upon launch, and again on the recovery ship, USS *Okinawa*, upon splashdown. One of the explanations was that a trust fund for the children of the astronauts was to have been set up with the astronaut's share of the profits. All three astronauts were reprimanded by NASA. The air force had

---

[5] In the case of the space program, military officers from various armed services were assigned to NASA. Although NASA is technically a civilian organization, I am using it as the context of some behavior which violates military norms. NASA has its own norms, of course, but the officer astronauts serving in NASA were not freed from their responsibility to adhere to military proscriptions and prescriptions concerning circumspect behavior and normative military comportment. The officer astronauts were still members of the military obligated to conform to military rules, and were theoretically subject to military sanctions if they were deviant or derelict in discharging their duties and responsibilities.

nominated the three to receive the General Thomas D. White U.S. Air Force Space Trophy, but subsequently withdrew the nomination (Associated Press 1972b). Later one of the astronauts, Alfred M. Worden, was transferred out of the astronaut office to another space agency center as a research engineer and test pilot (Associated Press 1972c).

Other improprieties were to emerge. It appeared that 15 astronauts had been selling autographs at $5 per signature (Associated Press 1972d). Each astronaut received $2,500 for the autographs from the same individual who had arranged the sale of the postal covers. This individual was a former Cape Kennedy, Florida, contractor employee. Five of the astronauts were reported as having donated their receipts from the autographs to charity, while the other ten retained the money. The signatures were on stamps, postcards, and other philatelic material, and NASA indicated that the signatures might be "commercialized at some future time." Since no misuse of government property or personnel was involved, and inasmuch as it is questionable as to whether the government has the right to question the disposition that the astronauts make of their own signatures, no formal punitive action against the astronauts was taken. NASA did subsequently tighten the provisions of its regulations concerning the personal and souvenir material that could be carried on the space flights.

On top of all other disclosures of improprietous commercialization of the space program, yet another questionable incident was revealed (Associated Press 1972a:4). A Belgian artist, Paul Van Hoeydonck, had created a tiny piece of sculpture, resembling a stylized astronaut, which he offered to provide to the crew of the Apollo 15 to be left on the moon as a memorial to astronauts and cosmonauts who have died in space projects. It was accepted with the understanding that the action was not to be commercialized. Furthermore, NASA did not want the sculptor publicly identified for a year. Subsequently, however, the Belgian sculpture produced 950 copies of the statue, which were offered for sale as representative of the "first art on the moon." The name of the artist also leaked out prematurely. NASA was understandably irked but it was impossible to stop the sales of the duplicate statues.

Sometimes the individuals involved in the unauthorized activities to commercialize the space program for personal profit were in direct violation of various NASA regulations, but in other instances their behavior was more a violation of the spirit rather than the letter of the law. Because of this and the enormous publicity involved, NASA and the air force chose to invoke only mild sanctions. Without question, however, these activities did erode public confidence in the integrity of the individuals involved, and no doubt caused the loss of some public support for the program. Inasmuch as such behavior reflected badly on the air force (and the other services from which the astronauts had come), and, in effect, brought discredit to the various armed services, it was "conduct unbecoming" and a crime against performance, even if relatively minor.

Historically, officers in some armies have been severely sanctioned for seemingly minor indiscretions that were officially viewed as conduct unbecoming an officer and a gentleman. One such instance in Britain during the reign of Queen Victoria was the case of Colonel Baker of the 10th Hussars, who was accused of kissing a young lady on a train. This act, although relatively innocuous by today's standards, was seen as very serious then. The colonel was cashiered from the military, tried, and imprisoned. The trial judge described the colonel's behavior as "a gross outrage," and a member of Parliament called it, "one of the most scandalous and atrocious crimes ever committed." Edward VII, then Prince of Wales, helped the colonel obtain a senior post in the Turkish army after his release from prison (Johnson 1979:34).

Perhaps one of the most bizarre instances of alleged deliberate conduct unbecoming an officer and gentleman in the U.S. military is the case of Cadet John Whittaker. In 1881, Whittaker was a cadet at West Point, at that time the only black cadet in the corps. Racial prejudice was rampant then, and Whittaker had been effectively ostracized by his fellow cadets. One morning Whittaker was discovered tied hand and foot to his bed, cut and bleeding and unconscious. Whittaker claimed that he was the victim of three masked assailants. The superintendent of West Point ordered a court of inquiry to investigate the case. The court of inquiry ultimately concluded that Whittaker had faked the crime to obtain sympathy from the professors at West Point and from the general public, and that he was the sole perpetrator. Subsequently, Whittaker was tried by court-martial and ultimately found guilty of both conduct unbecoming an officer and a gentleman, and of a second charge, conduct prejudicial to good order and discipline. He was sentenced to be dishonorably discharged from West Point, fined $100, and sentenced to serve one year in confinement at hard labor. The latter two penalties were remitted. President Arthur eventually voided the remainder of the sentence, but Whittaker was discharged from the academy because of deficiency in the examination that had been given before the court-martial (see Marszalek 1972).

Sexual Misconduct

The military as a social organization has a special set of problems in regard to sexual behavior. On the one hand, the military is composed of a vast aggregation of adult males in their most sexually active years, who are largely cut off from the normal and usual heterosexual outlets. Furthermore, the general cultural ethos of the military is aggressive masculinity, which in turn tends to promote or encourage sexual activity. The question of sexual offenses against the civilian population will be treated in chapter 7. Similarly, the problem of fraternization with females, especially prostitutes, in an occupied country, in direct violation of nonfraternization regulations, also will be taken up later in chapter 7. From the standpoint of the intra-occupational perspective, the military is concerned about promiscuity and venereal disease. Promiscuity is seen as dysfunctional for three reasons. First, promiscuity, particularly if it involves the spouses of other military personnel, may be disruptive to the social equilibrium of the post or community and divisive to the solidarity and cohesion of the military unit. Sexual rivalries are not conducive to organizational harmony and teamwork, especially in combat. For this reason, the military attempts to minimize adulterous liaisons with the spouses of others. [6]

[6] While I was a young officer in the military 20 years ago, I heard an old colonel relate an interesting story in this regard. When he himself was a young officer in the army before World War II, he was stationed in the Canal Zone as part of the "banana army." Duty was relatively light and there was a good bit of time for recreational activities, such as horseback riding. Inasmuch as the officers themselves had staggered duty hours, they might find themselves able to ride at a time when their spouses were doing something else. In effect, a captain might be free to ride in the afternoon, but his wife might have a bridge club engagement in the afternoons and be free to ride only in the mornings. A lieutenant might only be able to ride in the mornings, but his wife's schedule might only permit her to ride in the afternoons. Thus the captain might go riding with the lieutenant's wife in the afternoon, and the lieutenant in turn might go riding at the same time as the captain's wife, in the morning. The bridal paths were long and meandered through the jungle, and riders tended to ride in pairs. Thus the opportunity for flirtations, romances, and even sexual affairs was available and even flagrant.

Second, promiscuity may be viewed publicly in an unfavorable light, and there is concern that it brings discredit upon the armed services and is ungentlemanly and, therefore, unlike an officer. Promiscuity must be conducted in an extremely discreet fashion if it is to be tolerated. In 1966 Capt. Archie C. Kuntze, U.S. Navy, who for a time has been chief of Headquarters Support Activity in Saigon—in effect the "American Mayor of Saigon"—was court-martialed for various financial irregularities, and for certain inappropriate commercial activities (DiMona 1972:188–221). This individual, at the time estranged from his wife in the states, had a "lovely Chinese girl" who had spent most of her time in his villa, serving as his "hostess" and presiding at dinner parties and official functions. As a result, Captain Kuntze was also charged with "wrongfully and dishonorably permitting Jannie Suen, an unmarried Chinese National female, about twenty-six years of age . . . to reside openly and notoriously in his official quarters." This was, in fact, one of the charges of which he was convicted.

Male members of the military are not the only ones to be sanctioned for promiscuity. In 1975 a female marine, 2d Lt. Mary C. Niflis, was to be court-martialed for "allegedly having sexual relations with six enlisted men" (Associated Press 1975c:12). She was charged with "conduct unbecoming an officer and a gentlewoman" as a result of the alleged intercourse. She was also charged with sodomy and "fraternization with enlisted personnel on terms of military equality." The lieutenant resigned from the service, thus canceling the court-martial she was to have faced.

Finally, the military in this country and elsewhere takes an official posture against promiscuity because of the hazard of venereal disease and the fact that such disease can be extremely handicapping and debilitating to its mission. Some years ago, one social scientist underscored the military's concern with venereal disease (Berger 1946:84) and observed that:

> This is best seen in the Army's campaign against venereal disease. Soldiers are educated against promiscuity. Houses of prostitution

---

Concern about their spouses caused a morale problem with the officers. The commanding general, in his wisdom, solved the problem deftly and diplomatically by the simple expedient of requiring appropriate riding habit, including jodhpur breeches and high riding boots, for both officers and spouses. The riding breeches and boots were hard to get on and even harder to get off, thus serving as chastity belts while the riders were on the bridal paths. Decorum, sexual propriety, and social equilibrium were thus presevered.

are closed, and gathering places for loose women are placed "out of bounds" to soldiers. It is pointed out to soldiers that fornication is evil and dangerous. The soldier is told that the only sure way to avoid venereal disease is to avoid sexual contact with any woman but his wife.

For a considerable time, it was a punishable offense for a member of the military to contract venereal disease. The individual simply did not have the right to incapacitate himself through sexual negligence. After May 17, 1926, military regulations provided for disciplinary measures and loss of pay to be imposed as penalties on persons in the military who contracted venereal disease (Winick and Kinsie 1971:225). The result was that many individuals in the military did not report their infections and instead sought private treatment. On September 27, 1944, Congress eliminated the military penalties for contracting venereal disease.

The American military has often taken an ambivalent approach to prostitution. It has been recognized that sexual outlets must exist for the troops. If the civilian population is not to take the full brunt of the sexual drive of the members of the military and morale is to be maintained, prostitution must be tolerated. In some instances the military has actually encouraged prostitution, facilitating it or at least providing medical monitoring in the vicinity of military installations. During World War II, in North Africa, the military placed some brothels off limits, but provided free access to others that could be medically supervised (Winick and Kinsie 1971:226). There was even one, "The Sphinx," reserved for Allied officers in the evening. A brothel for Fifth Army troops was maintained by the military in Naples. Similarly, in Cherbourg, brothels were run for American troops. In all of the theaters of war in War World II, brothels were at least tolerated some of the time, if in fact they were not maintained by the military, and the prophylactic station was a ubiquitous military establishment. The U.S. military usually attempted to maintain a system of segregated brothels—one for officers, one for white enlisted men, and a third for enlisted black men. Many foreign militaries, including the German and Japanese in World War II, have had field brothels constituent to some of their units.

If the U.S. military has tended to be tolerant of prostitution in some instances, it has also at times been vigorous in proscribing it and sanctioning violators. During World War I, pressure from Congress and the military succeeded in closing the red light

districts in New Orleans, San Francisco, and New York (Winick
and Kinsie 1971:219). When American troops first went to Europe,
General Pershing encouraged unit commanders to grant leaves and
furloughs to Paris. When venereal disease began to be a problem,
however, General Pershing, on December 18, 1917, issued his
General Order #77 placing houses of prostitution off limits to
troops (Winick and Kinsie 1971:220). Later the British did the
same. In World War II Roosevelt signed the May Act, which prohibited "prostitution within such reasonable distance of military
and/or naval establishments . . . needful to the efficiency, health,
and welfare of the army or navy." The act was invoked on several
occasions in the United States (Winick and Kinsie 1971:224). In all
theaters of World War II, the military would tolerate prostitution
at one time, as noted, then change its posture and put them off
limits, arresting any GI who was caught in one.[7] By the time of
Vietnam, General Ky had established an American brothel section
at An Khe, and prostitution was encouraged at rest and recupera-
tion centers such as Taipei on Taiwan. In general, the U.S.
military has historically recognized the functionality of prostitution, and often tolerated if not tacitly encouraged it at an informal
level. At an official level, however, prostitution has usually been
condemned and forbidden, and military personnel who have fre-
quented brothels have sometimes been sanctioned for their crimes
against performance, especially if their sexual peccadillos resulted
in venereal disease.

The military has traditionally proscribed other sexually related
behavior. Historically, for example, West Point or Annapolis
cadets could not marry while they were cadets; marriage itself was
grounds for dismissal. Over the years various cadets have married
and tried to keep it secret. Cadet Donald M. Boyd almost made it
to graduation but an anonymous letter advised the commandant at
West Point that Boyd had been secretly married the year before
and that he had an 11-month-old daughter (Andelman 1974). Boyd
was denied permission to receive his diploma and his commission as
a second lieutenant. Technically the sanctions were for lying about
his marital status, not for violating the rule against marriage. Both
are, however, crimes against performance. Boyd filed suit in U.S.
District Court charging that the West Point ban against marriage

---

[7] During the Korean War, combat boots with zippers down the side were known as
"short-time" boots because they could be worn to a brothel and taken off easily,
but could be put back on in a hurry in the event of a raid by Military Police.

was an unreasonable infringement on his constitutional rights. At the Air Force Academy, female cadets, like their male counterparts, cannot marry. Until recently they could not be pregnant either. The rule has now been changed and an unmarried pregnant cadet who does not resign must take an extended leave after her baby is born.

Sometimes the sexual folkways and mores of the military take on an amusing dimension (except, of course, to the sanctioned offender). In 1975 a U.S. nuclear sub, the USS *Finback*, was about to put out to sea on an extended voyage. As a reward to the crew, the skipper, Comdr. Connelly D. Stevenson, had given approval for a local topless go-go dancer, 23-year-old Cat Futch, to do her act on the deck of the submarine. The sub subsequently went out to sea, but when navy brass heard about the performance, they signaled it to return home to port. There Commander Stevenson was promptly relieved of his command, reprimanded, and grounded at a desk in Norfolk, Virginia. He appealed on the grounds that the Navy "overreacted" (*Newsweek* 1975:33).

Of all forms of sexual behavior, the military seems to have been more concerned with preventing and sanctioning homosexuality than any other form of sexual persuasion. This rigorous attempt to proscribe homosexual activity apparently grows out of several factors. The first is that the military of most countries tend to have a highly conservative and moralistic outlook. The moralistic posture is certainly consistent with discipline, tradition, loyalty to authority, and an ethnocentric view of the status quo, philosophically or otherwise. Homosexuality simply appears more unnatural and therefore less moral than other modes of sexual expression. Second, homosexuality definitely erodes the atmosphere and image of masculinity component to the military. Homosexuality is, from the military standpoint, antithetical to assertiveness, leadership, toughness, and virility, all qualities deemed desirable if not essential to the military role.

Finally, it would appear that some settings may also contribute to, or facilitate, homosexuality. The military, particularly the navy, may well be such a setting, at least in times past. If homosexuality is apt to be prevalent in such settings, extra diligence and efforts may be necessary to prevent or at least minimize its existence. The military, then, abhorring homosexuality, strives mightily to combat it.

Winston Churchill, just before World War I, had occasion to

comment that the traditions of the Royal Navy were, "rum, sodomy, and the lash." The isolation of military personnel, especially those on naval ships, often tended to cut them off from normal heterosexual encounters, causing some to seek homosexual outlets. Some arrangements, such as the "cabin boys" on many ships, were institutionalized. Legend has it that men who were isolated on ships and bounced by the waves were sexually aroused. Accordingly, it has been long-standing naval custom never to assign men to work alone in pairs where it could be avoided (Trip 1975:222–23).

Interestingly, it has often been within the military or naval context that the most severe sanctions for homosexual acts have been administered. In the British Royal Navy, for example, prior to 1861, sodomy was punishable by death. In fact, on February 1, 1816, on the orders of Edward Rodney, captain of HMS *Africaine*, four members of the ship's crew were hanged for buggery (Gilbert 1974:111). The same day, two other crewmen were punished for "uncleanliness," a euphemistic term for all sexually deviant behavior. One of the men received 200 lashes while the other received only 170 out of the 300 lashes to which he was sentenced, because the ship's surgeon warned that his life would be endangered if he received all 300. In more recent times, in the British navy and our own military, the punishment is not so severe, although homosexuality is still a court-martial offense, and the U.S. military particularly is unusually vigorous in attempting to identify homosexual offenders and invoke statutory sanctions. Williams and Weinberg, who have made a detailed study of homosexuality in the U.S. military, have spoken of "the zealousness with which the military seeks out and prosecutes homosexuals" (Williams and Weinberg 1971:203). This is done, they say, "based upon the magnitude of their perceived threat to good order." They relate the army's position (quoted in Williams and Weinberg 1971:203):

> The army considers homosexuals to be unfit for military service because their presence impairs the morale and discipline of the army and that homosexuality is a manifestation of a severe personality defect which appreciably limits the ability of such individuals to function in society.

Furthermore, the military usually makes no distinction between a confirmed homosexual and an individual who commits a single homosexual act. Even persons who have "strong tendencies toward homosexuality," which may even mean persons who associate with homosexuals, may be liable for discharge. When a serviceman is suspected of homosexuality or caught in the act, according to Williams and Weinberg, he is "processed to confess and thus avoid a hearing" (Williams and Weinberg 1971:216). This causes minimal problems for the organization. The serviceman charged with homosexuality may be incarcerated in jail or in the hospital, and may be segregated from other inmates. In the army, if he is to receive an undesirable discharge, the individual will be reduced to the lowest rank. Those convicted usually lose accumulated leave pay and veterans' benefits, and are told that they can expect "to encounter substantial prejudice" after discharge. Such treatment is facilitated by the fact that the serviceman is usually encouraged to incriminate himself, and thus actually participates in his own discharge process.

In contemporary times, homosexuality in the military is apparently not just a problem for the U.S. armed forces. Recently it was reported that a homosexual vice scandal was discovered in the Queen's Household Cavalry, an elite English military unit. As many as 100 soldiers were said to be involved in homosexual activities. Some of the soldiers were apparently earning extra money as male prostitutes and for posing in "suggestive fashions" for different "gay" magazines (*Roanoke Times* 1976).

In recent years, some homosexual servicemen (and women) have resisted punishment or separation after discovery, and some have even deliberately revealed their sexual persuasion and invited confrontation. Many of these cases have attracted national news coverage. A recent incident involved air force T. Sgt. Leonard P. Matlovich, who became something of a *cause célèbre* when he announced his homosexuality in a letter to his base commander (Duberman 1975:16–17, 58–71; Mathews 1975). Other recent homosexual service people who have fought to stay in the service include WAC Pfc. Barbara Randolph and her lover, Pvt. Debbie Watson, as well as air force S. Sgt. Rudolf S. (Skip) Keith, Jr. (see *The Advocate* 1975).

Another case of military homosexuality receiving widespread notoriety was that of Ensign Vernon Berg III, a graduate of the U.S. Naval Academy, who was the first navy officer to admit his homosexuality publicly (Associated Press 1976d, 1976h). Ensign Berg was subsequently dismissed from the navy with an "other than honorable discharge." At his hearing by a discharge board, Berg estimated that over 200,000 homosexual men and women are in the military. Berg's father, a career navy chaplain, testified "that he had known of officers up to the rank of rear admiral who are secretly homosexual."

There have been other instances of sanctions taken against homosexuals. In 1975 a naval reserve commander in southern California was recommended for discharge, although an honorable one, by a three-man navy fitness panel because of homosexuality (Associated Press 1975a). The individual claimed that he was bisexual and filed a suit in federal court to stay in the naval reserve. He also asked damages, and that the Navy's regulation barring homosexuals from service be struck down. In another case, a female Sp. 4c., Marie Sode, was to be discharged (again honorably) from the army because of "homosexual tendencies" (Associated Press 1977a). Specialist Sode was apparently "married to a former WAC who claimed to be a transsexual male." Specialist Sode also went to federal court to try to block her discharge. The attorney for the army said that the case was "truly unusual" and might result in a servicewide policy on transsexuality, even though none now exists.

The military has historically viewed homosexual behavior as a serious crime against performance in that it violated the idealized role conception and expectations of the soldier. In many instances the offender was punished severely. In recent years the trend has been to separate the individual quickly from the service, even with an honorable discharge if necessary, but seldom to go beyond that in way of sanction. As one army psychiatrist (Druss 1967) explained the rationale:

> It is felt that the needs of the individual and of command are consistent as the dilemma is more apparent than real. The repetitive element in homosexual behavior and the temptations of military life combined with the possibility of serious punishment lead to the belief that it is for the individual's good that prompt separation be recommended. Separation is usually effected quickly and with no harm to the individual's future. With military customs and regulations as they are, prompt separation is protective of the individual.

Criticism of Authority

A military organization must operate on the basis of predictability of performance and loyalty of all of its members. It must function in a concerted fasion, with all components contributing according to their mission, and all members behaving as expected. Internal frictions are dysfunctional, and overt or covert conflict with subordinates cannot be tolerated. The military must always present a unified front to the public (and to its enemies). Therefore, internal dissension and/or criticism of superiors or the service itself is a crime against performance and is punishable accordingly.

The Vietnam War had been extremely unpopular, with only modest public support. It also had its detractors within the military. One such instance was that of Lt. Henry H. Howe, Jr., who in 1965 marched in a protest parade in El Paso, Texas (DiMona 1972:223). He carried a sign that read on one side, "End Johnson's Fascist Aggression in Vietnam," and on the other, "Let's Have More Than a Choice Between Petty Ignorant Fascists in 1968." This demonstration, along with others around the country, precipitated a response of outrage on the part of the military. Lieutenant Howe was subsequently tried under Article 88 of the Code of Military Justice, found guilty, and sentenced to two years at hard labor (later reduced to one year) and a dishonorable discharge from the army.

A signal example of sanctions imposed against a member of the military for criticism of authority is the now famous case of Gen. William "Billy" Mitchell. According to DiMona (1972:93), this "was the first major 'freedom of dissent' case in American military jurisprudence."[8] General Mitchell, offspring of a famous and influential family, had been an air ace and hero in World War I. Mitchell had been a leading exponent of the airplane as an offensive weapon, not just as an observation platform, and he had proved it in the battle of Saint-Mihiel, where he sent waves of aircraft (totaling 1,500) into battle, strafing and bombing the enemy troops. After the war he continued his fight for air power, against the generals and admirals who lacked sufficient vision to see and appreciate its military utility. He annoyed some high-ranking admirals by claiming that airplanes could sink a battleship. He arranged a test, however, and proved his point by having his airplanes sink several German ships, including the battleship *Ostfriesland*, captured in World War I.

Mitchell, to the consternation of his superiors, carried his fight for increased air power to the press and to Congress. The War

---

[8] My discussion in this section draws heavily on the DiMona source.

Department had enough problems obtaining funds for ground forces and the navy without going out on a limb for what seemed like a preposterous idea. To handicap Mitchell's press campaign, the secretary of war transferred him from Washington to San Antonio, Texas. Everyone thought he had been exiled to obscurity. A short time later, however, the navy dirigible *Shenandoah* crashed in a storm, and General Mitchell called a press conference. Military authorities had been saying that the crash of the *Shenandoah*, and the previous crash of three other unsuitable craft on a flight from Los Angeles to Hawaii, had proved that air power was ineffective and essentially worthless as a military weapon. Mitchell countered these assertions by issuing the following press release (DiMona 1972:96): "My opinion is as follows: These accidents are the direct result of the incompetency, criminal negligence, and almost treasonable administration of our national defense by the Navy and War Departments."

Mitchell had gone too far and had violated the expectations incumbent on a senior officer. A court-martial was ordered. He was to be tried for violation of the then-96th Article of War, which contained the "catch-all provision." This article provided that "Though not mentioned in these articles, all disorders and neglects to the prejudice of good order and military discipline, all conduct of a nature to bring discredit upon the military service. . . (DiMona 1972:99)—in other words, any act bringing "discredit" to the military service—would be subject to court-martial. According to DiMona, "Mitchell once said, an officer could be tried for tickling a horse" under this provision. Mitchell used his court-martial as a platform to expose his views of the role of air power in future wars. He and his defense attorney set out to prove that his comments about the military were true. Unfortunately, he was too much of a visionary for his time, and his opponents in the trial had the advantage of pragmatic rationalization. One of the prosecuting attorneys labeled Mitchell as a "loose-talking imaginative megalomaniac cheered by the adulation of his juniors who see promotion under his banner . . . and intoxicated by the ephemeral applause of the people whose fancy he has for the moment caught" (DiMona, 1972:113).

The court-martial, however, dealt in facts, not fancy, and found General Mitchell guilty of all charges and specifications. For his criticism of authority, and thus disloyalty to the service, he was sentenced to be "suspended from rank, command, and duty with forfeiture of all pay and allowances for five years." Mitchell had lost the fight and had been punished for his crimes against performance. He subsequently resigned from the army and retired to Virginia. Time and history vindicated Mitchell and his prognostications on air power, but the fact of his military crime remains.

In recent years one of the most publicized cases of a member of the military's being sanctioned for criticism of authority was that of Maj. Gen. John K. Singlaub of the U.S. Army (Weinraub 1977:1). In 1977 General Singlaub was chief of staff of American forces in South Korea. In that year President Carter announced his plan to withdraw United States troops from South Korea over a period of time. In response to the president's announcement, Singlaub commented in a newspaper interview in Seoul, "If we withdraw our ground troops on the schedule suggested, it will lead to war." The White House termed General Singlaub's comments "clearly inflammatory." The general was summoned to Washington, where he met with President Carter and Defense Secretary Brown. He was subsequently "ordered to report to the Chief of Staff of the Army for consideration for another assignment." Presumably this action signaled a stern reprimand for the general. Secretary of Defense Brown then issued an announcement that read: "Public statements by General Singlaub inconsistent with announced national security policy have made it very difficult for him to carry out the duties of his present assignment in Korea."

A year later, in 1978, President Carter announced that he would, at least temporarily, delay production of neutron weapons. Such weapons were designed to use radiation, rather than blast effect, in combat. Shortly thereafter, Major General Singlaub delivered a speech to Reserve Officer Training Corps cadets at the Georgia Institute of Technology in Atlanta, in which he labeled President Carter's decision to delay production of the neutron bomb "ridiculous" and militarily unsound (Associated Press 1978). In his speech, Singlaub also publicly disagreed with the Panama Canal treaties, saying that they were unnecessary. Within 24 hours the general was summoned to the Pentagon, met with Army Secretary Clifford Alexander and Army Chief of Staff General Bernard Rogers, and his retirement from the army was announced. As Singlaub phrased the action, "two strikes and you're out." In this instance, premature retirement was the sanction for criticism of authority, his crime against performance.

Disrespect and Failure to Obey Orders

Whatever else a military may be, it is an authoritarian organization. Orders are to be obeyed, and commands are absolute. Traditionally, the index of the well-disciplined military was the swiftness and exactitude with which orders were carried out. In this regard, the Prussian soldier was probably the epitome of iron discipline.[9] The real winner for absolute obedience, however, would probably have to be the army of Henri Christophe, the self-appointed King of Haiti in the nineteenth century (Pirtle 1974). King Christophe built a fortress inland in the mountains of Haiti, and 20,000 men died of exhaustion building it and the torturous, twisted road leading to it (it required 11 years and 200,000 men to do the job). King Christophe's approach to discipline and motivation was simple. If any of his men faltered, he had them shot: "That encouraged the others to do better." From the top of his fortress, the Citadelle, there is a sheer, 1,000-foot dropoff down the side of the castle. When a visiting foreign dignitary was visiting him, King Christophe is said to have marched a band of his troops off the side of the castle to their death in order to impress the dignitary with his army's discipline. Presumably, the punishment for disobedience was more fearsome than death.

Failure to comply with regulations and orders may take the form of relatively nonserious offenses, such as failing to salute an officer.[10] Other examples might be insubordination or refusal to obey an order. A relatively recent well-publicized example of

---

[9] The stereotypical image of the turn-of-the-century Prussian soldier was such that when movie producer Howard Hughes made a film about German dirigibles and the dirigibles needed to lose ballast in order to gain altitude, Hughes had the commander of the dirigibles order some of the crew to jump out—without parachutes.

[10] Early in World War II, a story relevant to this offense was widely publicized. It was related that a black officer passed a white enlisted man who failed to salute. The black officer stopped the enlisted man and rebuked him for not saluting. The white soldier explained that he was from the South, was not accustomed to paying deference to blacks, and could not bring himself to salute a black. Not wishing to escalate the confrontation, the black officer then proposed to remove his hat and hold it at arm's length for the white soldier to salute. Inasmuch as the salute is to uniform and insignia of rank and not the the individual personally, the soldier should have no reservation about that arrangement. The black officer held his hat at arm's length, the white enlisted man did, in fact, salute the hat, and the tradition and decorum of military discipline was preserved.

refusal to obey an order was the Levy case of the mid-1960s (DiMona 1972:223–24).

Captain Levy, who had been inducted into the military involuntarily in 1966, had been assigned to provide some basic training in dermatology to Special Forces aidemen at Fort Jackson. His superior discovered that Captain Levy was not providing the training and gave him a direct order to do so. Levy continued his refusal to give the training, since he felt that to do so would violate his principles and ethics. Captain Levy had also been an outspoken critic of the Vietnam War and had made many disparaging remarks about it to various persons with whom he worked. Levy was subsequently court-martialed on several charges, including refusing to train Green Beret medics, and having uttered or written statements "to promote disloyalty and disaffection" among the troops, which were "intended to impair loyalty, morale, and discipline," and were "to the prejudice of good order and discipline in the armed forces" (DiMona 1972:224). He was also charged with "conduct unbecoming to an officer." After a long, controversial trial in which many influential witnesses testified, Levy was found guilty of all five charges, although the court lightened two of them. He was sentenced to three years (the maximum penalty could have been eleven years) and dismissed from the service (DiMona 1972:243). Levy did go to prison, and subsequently another officer also refused to train airmen bound for Vietnam and was also court-martialed and sent to prison. Although massive protests and opposition around the country to the Vietnamese war, and disclosures of such events as the Green Beret murder of a Vietnamese national and the My Lai incident, may have tended to vindicate Captain Levy somewhat in the eyes of the public, the fact remains that he violated military norms and was punished for his crimes against performance.

Unauthorized Absence

All work systems depend on having their labor force available when they are needed. For the military, this need is essential. The military has to know where all of its members are at any given time. Inasmuch as war and battle do not run on a set schedule, the military may have to assemble its members within a very short time frame. For this reason, the movements of members of the military are carefully circumscribed, regulated, and monitored. To be absent on an unauthorized basis is a crime against performance that could result in severe sanction. The proscriptions and prescriptions bearing on absence and presence are perhaps among the most fundamental of all military norms, and among those that are most rigorously enforced.

The military everywhere, however, recognizes shadings and nuances of unauthorized absences. An endemic offense in the military is the pattern of temporary absence known as AWOL (absence without leave). The offender might simply have become drunk while on weekend pass, and not returned to the base. Sometimes soldiers have personal or family problems that motivate them to go "over the fence" or "over the hill," even though it may be anticipated that the individual intends to return within a reasonable length of time. Going AWOL in wartime or in combat is obviously a more serious offense than the same absence in peacetime or outside of a combat situation. Basically, then, AWOL is a situation in which any member of the armed forces is not at the place where he is required to be at a prescribed time, through his own fault. AWOL, not infrequently, is a function of unit morale, quality of leadership, and quality of life in the unit. The AWOL rate is often used as an index of unit condition and level of disaffection.

A more serious mode of unauthorized absence is missing a movement. The individual, by neglect or design, misses the movement of a ship, aircraft, or unit with which he is required to travel in the course of duty. Here there is a presumption of intent not to go with the unit and perhaps to avoid whatever duty lays ahead. A person on leave who intentionally failed to join his unit on a troopship about to embark for a combat theater would be committing such an offense. Also more serious than AWOL is attempting to desert. The mere fact of being absent on an unauthorized basis does not constitute desertion or even an attempt to desert. Attempting to desert involves not only the intent to be absent permanently, but also an overt effort to implement the intent. Even if the person subsequently desists voluntarily in his effort to leave permanently, the act of attempting to desert is complete.

The most serious of all unauthorized absence offenses is, of course, desertion. Desertion involves unauthorized absence of a member of the military with the intent to remain away from the organization or unit permanently, or to remain away with the intention of avoiding hazardous duty or important service. The deserter, in effect, wishes nothing more to do with the military. Desertion is a very serious offense and, even where it occurs outside of a combat situation, may result in severe punishment, perhaps including a dishonorable discharge and a long sentence in prison. Desertion is generally viewed as a serious crime against performance.

Insurrection and Mutiny

Insubordination, sedition, and failure to obey orders all stand as heinous crimes against performance, inasmuch as they tend to undermine the authority structure of the military and to erode its effectiveness. These offenses, however, pale almost to insignificance in comparison with insurrection and mutiny. Insubordination, sedition, and failure to obey orders are efforts to subvert or evade discipline and the authority structure. Insurrection and mutiny represent efforts to destroy the authority structure and to displace the extant system of discipline. In effect, insurrection and mutiny constitute counterattacks against authority and command. From this perspective, it is little wonder that insurrection and mutiny have been viewed historically as the epitome of military deviancy, and addressed in the most ruthless fashion. In some respects, insurrection and mutiny often constitute all three varieties of military crime. Inasmuch as military property may be stolen, destroyed, or misappropriated (such as the king's ship being taken by the mutineers in the *Bounty* mutiny), such offenses may be treated as crimes against property. They may also stand as crimes against person, since officers or loyal troops may be killed or injured in the process (such as in the slaughter that attended the sepoy mutiny). In the final analysis, however, insurrection and mutiny are crimes against performance because they violate the total set of behavioral expectations constituent to the military context. They represent a complete vagrancy from the traditional role of the soldier.

Insurrections and mutinies occur in a wide range of sizes, severity, and intentions. In some instances only one or a handful of individuals are involved. From time to time single individuals have been tried and severely punished for attempting or inciting mutiny. As mentioned in an earlier chapter, in 1804 an American seaman on the U.S. frigate *President* wrote an anonymous letter to the captain and implied a threat of mutiny (McKee 1978:294), for which he received harsh punishment.

Perhaps one of the oddest instances of mutiny in the U.S. military was the case of the "mutiny" aboard the brig *Somers* in 1842 (for a detailed account see DiMona 1972:43–71).[11] The *Somers*, under the command of Capt. Alexander Slidell Mackenzie, was a training ship, and sailed from the country on a training cruise in October 1842. On board was Midshipman Philip Spencer, who also happened to be the son of the secretary of war. Spencer was a high-spirited, mischievous, and imaginative young man. Apparently out of boredom, he spoke jokingly with members of the crew about mutiny, proposing that he, along with those who would join him, should kill the officers, seize the ship, and turn to piracy. Some of the crew believed him and evidently agreed to go along with his plan. Spencer, carrying his fantasy plot to extremes, actually kept a list of crew members that indicated the likelihood of each joining the conspiracy. One of the crew who agreed to help Spencer went to the captain and revealed the plan to him. Captain Alexander ordered Midshipman Spencer and two of the crew believed to be accomplices put in irons. The captain feared that a full-scale mutiny was at hand, and that somehow Spencer would manage to mastermind it. He consulted the ship's officers, who, no doubt under some pressure from the captain, advised that the would-be mutineers be immediately hanged—a suggestion that Captain MacKenzie followed. When the ship returned to port in New York, there was naturally a public furor about the incident. A naval Court of Inquiry cleared Captain Mackenzie, but because Secretary of War Spencer was pressuring for a civil trial in which the captain would be tried for first-degree murder, Mackenzie himself requested and received a court-martial. After a heated trial, the court acquited Captain Mackenzie of all charges and specifications preferred by the secretary of war against him. Mackenzie's sanctioning of Spencer's mischievous crimes against performance was supported by the military.

Some mutinies are really more a type of protest than an actual attempt to overthrow the traditional authority structure.[12] They

[11] Herman Melville, who was related to one of the ship's officers on the *Somers*, followed the trial closely. It was to provide the basis for his classic novel *Billy Budd* (1962).

[12] For a detailed analysis of the comparisons and contrasts between mutinies and some other types of protest and conflict, see Lammers (1969).

are often treated as mutinies, however, and sanctioned accordingly. The so-called Presidio "mutiny," in which a number of GI inmates of an army stockade in San Francisco staged a protest and created a disturbance, was such an instance (Sherrill 1970:4–61; Gardner 1970). The men "broke formation at the work lineup on the morning of October 14, 1968, sang songs and demanded to see the press, to see lawyers and to have an audience with the stockade commandant." (Sherrill 1970:4). Of the 27 men involved in the incident, "twenty-two were convicted of mutiny and two of disobeying an order, the other three having escaped prison and fled to Canada before their court-martial could be held." (Sherrill 1970:4–5). At the trial one of the Army prosecutors argued that it did not matter that the protest was peaceful, or that the men had grievances; the behavior of the men constituted an "attack on the system." During the Vietnam period there were numerous instances of protests, demonstrations, disturbances, and refusals to obey orders by members of the U.S. military, some of which were labeled as mutinies, with subsequent attempts to sanction them as such.[13]

Some mutinies have been incredibly bloody, such as the nineteenth-century sepoy mutiny described earlier, while others have been relatively free of violence. Immediately after the end of World War II, 7.6 million men of the U.S. armed services were left overseas, and were anxious to be returned home (Lee 1966: 555–71). Bringing the GI's home was a major undertaking, however, and could not be accomplished as quickly as had been hoped. An elaborate "point" system was devised that was to establish priorities for the men to return. There was great public demand in this country to bring the servicemen home quickly, and

---

A particularly interesting instance of a protest-type mutiny was the Invergordon mutiny in the British Navy in 1931. This mutiny was unique because it was spontaneous, without violence, and involved almost an entire fleet. On Friday 11, September 1931 the British Atlantic Fleet was assembled at Invergordon in Scotland. On Sunday 13th, the Admiralty in a Fleet Order announced that pay was to be cut by 25 percent. This cut would have also embraced the pensions of the men. The men of the fleet were outraged. They organized themselves and simply went on strike and did no work. The Admiralty was forced to give in and review the proposed cuts. A number of general reforms beneficial to the enlisted men of the Navy ultimately resulted and the only revenge for this breach of discipline that the Admiralty could ever effect was to have some of the ringleaders of the mutiny discharged (see Wincott 1974).

[13] For a lengthy discussion of protest in the U.S. military during the Vietnamese era, see Blake (1973).

some of the servicemen overseas began to demonstrate and protest in their impatience. "In Manila on Christmas Day in 1945, . . . 4000 men marched on the 21st Replacement Depot headquarters to protest against the cancellation of the sailing of a troopship" (Lee 1966:562). The personnel involved received only a mild reprimand from their commander. On January 6, 1946, in Manila, approximately 20,000 soldiers marched on command headquarters in the city hall to complain. There were mass letters and telegrams of protest all over the world, from India to France. Very few men were actually arrested or punished. So bad was the situation that "Senator Edwin C. Johnson wrote to his colleague Elbert D. Thomas, Chairman of the military affairs committee, declaring that Congress should take steps to prevent the army from degenerating 'into a mob' " (Lee 1966:567). In Hawaii, Lt. Gen. Roy S. Geiger, Pacific Fleet Marine Force Commander, ordered that the navy mutiny orders be read to marines stationed there. "He then forbade them to participate in any demonstrations" (Lee 1966:566). Subsequently 150 marines signed a protest petition and sent it to President Truman. Of the men who signed it, "six of the ring-leaders were broken to privates, and three of them were 'brigged' " (Lee 1966:566).

Some mutinies have historically been justified, after a fashion. The so-called Fort Jackson mutiny during the Civil War was certainly provoked if not justified, at least from the standpoint of the troops (for a detailed account see Harrington 1942:420–31). At that time, the Fourth Regiment Corps d'Afrique, a black unit, was stationed at Fort Jackson, a garrison south of New Orleans. Many of the white officers in black units were not of the first quality in terms of ability, motivation, and leadership. The white commanding officer of the Fourth Regiment was Lt. Col. Augustus C. Benedict, who has been described as "unstable, brutal, tactless." He used "foul language" and inflicted "inhuman punishments" on his black troops (Harrington 1942:421). He would strike them and kick them for such minor infringements as not having polished their brasses bright enough to suit him. He also had men whipped or tied by the thumbs and hung up with their toes just barely touching the ground. On December 9, 1863, Lieutenant Colonel Benedict had two men of the regimental band horsewhipped, with the troop assembled to watch the punishment. When they were dismissed, a "quarter to a half of the regiment" mutinied. They fired into the air, shouted and cursed, and demanded to be given

Benedict. Subsequently they released the guardhouse prisoners. They milled around in disorder, and in one instance a private lunged at an officer with his bayonet. Finally the white officers managed to get the troops under control, and Benedict escaped to his quarters. After this incident the conduct of the black troops was described as "unexceptionable" (Harrington 1942:423).

Although no real damage had been done, the demonstration was a "challenge to authority," and thus a crime against performance. The military moved to effect appropriate sanctions. Ultimately four of thirteen men tried were acquitted. Seven men received prison sentences ranging from one month to 20 years. Two of the men were sentenced to be shot, but the sentence was later suspended. Because Benedict's abusive treatment of his troops had been seen as a precipitating factor in the "mutiny," he was court-martialed for "conduct unbecoming an officer and gentleman," and for "inflicting cruel and unusual punishment to the prejudice of good order and military discipline" Harrington 1942:424–25). He was found guilty and cashiered from the army.

Although one of the best-known naval mutinies is fictional—the mutiny aboard the *Caine* as described by Herman Wouk (1951) in his novel, *The Caine Mutiny,*—there is a real-life counterpart. On March 31, 1966, Lt. Comdr. Marcus Aurelius Arnheiter was relieved from his command of the *Vance*, a destroyer escort relay on assignment off the Vietnamese coast, for "certain irregular practices" (Sheehan 1971:10). Like Wouk's protagonist Captain Queeg, Arnheiter was described as eccentric, tyrannical, and paranoid. According to one book-length account of his behavior and of the entire affair (Sheehan 1971:frontispiece):

> He purchased a speedboat with the crew's recreational funds, installed a machine gun, painted the bow with shark's teeth and sent it out to draw Viet Cong fire. He filed false position reports, wrote fictional press releases, enforced discipline with a martinet's fetish for shined belt buckles, made his officers recommend him for a Silver Star—and then contested his dismissal countercharging that he was the victim of an ingenious mutiny.

Arnheiter's behavior was irritating and dissaffective to his officers and crew to the point of intolerance and even illness (some were developing ulcers and other nervous disorders). Finally some of them complained to higher authority, and the navy realized the true state of affairs aboard the *Vance* and moved to relieve Arnheiter. Arnheiter in turn charged that he had been the victim of a conspiracy. An investigation was initiated and, after voluminous sworn testimony, the navy accepted the findings as evidence that Arnheiter had "destroyed the morale of the crew" and had also "exercised bad judgment and lack of integrity in so many important matters" (Sheehan 1971:10). The navy would not again give him command of a ship. His career was damaged beyond repair and he retired in 1971. In this instance his inappropriate behavior had triggered other inappropriate behavior from his men and almost precipitated a genuine mutiny. He was at fault, however, and was effectively punished for his crime against performance.

Fights between white and black groups, and to the prejudice of good order, are occurring with increasing frequency. Recently two major U.S. aircraft carriers have experienced disturbances allegedly stemming from racial discrimination (New York *Times*, 1972; Baldwin, 1974). The incident on the U.S.S. *Constellation* constituted a near mutiny, but the disturbance on the U.S.S. *Kitty Hawk* was a violent altercation that required the shipboard marine guards seven and one-half hours to quell. Large numbers of personnel were injured, some quite seriously.

Summary

The outcome of the war or armed conflicts may well hinge on the reliability of discipline in military units. It is therefore not surprising that all military organizations place a high premium on appropriate performance and severely sanction crimes against performance.

Personnel in the military are not supposed to misappropriate or misuse government property, or engage in physical violence or abuse against each other, subordinates, or superordinates; violations of these norms represent crimes against performance. The specificity of military performance is such, however, that a variety of deviations from the extensive statutory norms concerning the obligations and duties of the individual member constitute criminal offenses and are punishable in many instances by prison sentences, fines, loss of rank, and dishonorable discharge.

Basically, the individual serviceman is expected to be present, both physically and mentally, and to avoid rendering himself incapable of performing his duties either intentionally or through culpable negligence. The presence of the individual is rigidly regulated, as are the circumstances permitting or accompanying his absence. Missing a movement, absences without leave, or desertion (implying an intention to be absent permanently) constitute extremely serious although relatively common violations of the regulations concerning performance. Where one's presence is so critical, even the misappropriation of one's physical being becomes a violation of regulations. Where military personnel feign illness, disablement, or derangement, or intentionally inflict self-injury, they are guilty of malingering, a court-martial offense. Malingering, in effect, is misappropriation of one's performance utility. Even being sick may bring the individual into conflict with the military system, in that the "sick soldier" role may be defined as deviant behavior. In a similar fashion, incapacitating oneself with either liquor or drugs violates the punitive article prohibiting drunkenness on duty.

Even more specific than the regular role requirements of the serviceman is the prescribed behavior for sentinels, guards, or lookouts. These positions, although temporary, call for extraordinary alertness and vigilance. Failure to meet these obligations might theoretically endanger the ship or base, permit a prisoner to escape, or allow the enemy to attack unnoticed. Accordingly, the "misbehavior" of a guard, including being drunk, sleeping on duty, or in any way deviating from his "general orders" or special orders, makes the offender subject to extremely severe punishments. Any abridgment of the formalized "chain of command," any rejection of order or authority, any attempt to evade or be derelict in one's military duty, constitute crimes against performance. These are also codified under the punitive articles and range from the use of "contemptuous words" against military and public officials, through various degrees of disrespect and insubordination, to mutiny and sedition. Officers are especially admonished to be circumspect and honorable in their behavior; if found deviant, they may be tried for "conduct unbecoming an officer and a gentleman." In the event that the offensive behavior of any member of the armed services, officer or enlisted, is not specifically covered by any other of the punitive articles, the deviant offender may be tried by court-martial under the 134th Article of War for "disorders or neglects to the prejudice of good order and discipline," or "conduct of such a nature to bring discredit upon the armed forces." Homosexual behavior may lead to "less than honorable discharge."

No military establishment is more effective in its mission than it is in the effectation and maintenance of discipline and obedience among its ranks. Great armies have floundered without it and small ones have been vanquished because of it. In the final analysis no intra-occupational deviancy is more critical than crimes against performance, and no violations are more severely sanctioned.

In spite of the severe sanctions often applied for offenses against performance, such violations do occur, and with significant frequency. "Goldbricking" and malingering are endemic to certain types of military unit. The individual who has learned the "tricks of the trade" is often able to evade or minimize his work responsibilities. Insubordination and refusal to carry out orders have become increasingly prevalent in recent years. Black servicemen in particular have rebelled against orders and military customs, especially if they felt that racial discrimination was promoted by their superior officers.

The strains of military life and combat duty are great. Many young men are often not equipped physically or temperamentally for these stresses. Some rebel in their anxiety and frustration and strike back. In 1972 a seaman was accused of setting a fire on board the carrier *Forestal* that caused more than $7 million in damages. Others flee physically by deserting or going AWOL. Still others seek chemical release through alcohol and drugs, often incapacitating themselves for effective duty in the process. This particular type of release is historically and globally endemic to almost all military systems. As Bryant (1974) has pointed out, alcohol and drugs are often inextricably bound up in military custom and existence. Some, however, seek the ultimate release of death through suicide. It has been reported, for example, that there are an average of four suicide attempts per week at Fort Dix, New Jersey, a major training base, and nine actual suicides there during 1968 (Barnes 1972:105).

Considering the opportunity structure, the authoritarian interpersonal relationship structure of the military, which is largely alien to our American culture and civilian social system, and given the stresses and distresses of the military, it is not surprising that significant numbers of individuals in the armed services violate the norms concerning performance and become, in effect, khaki-collar deviants in their intra-occupational system.

CHAPTER
SIX

Crimes Against Performance: Alcohol and Narcotic Addiction

*The farther north you go in Vietnam, the more drugs
there are. Some of the forward fire bases are among the
worst. The men are using m_____uana, heroin, and
sometimes opium. In my unit, some of the medics were
on heroin, using needles from our own stores. You could
see the punctures right up and down their arms.*
First Sgt. Ernest R. Davis in *Newsweek*

The normative military structure mandates circumspect attention
to the nuances of prescribed and proscribed behavior. Voluntary
and purposive violation of the norms of performance are viewed in
a most serious light and are subject to severe sanction. Where an individual in the military voluntarily incapacitates himself through
the misuse of alcohol or narcotics, he is also guilty of a crime
against performance, even though he is involuntarily unable to
discharge his responsibilities. Alcohol and drugs are often inex-
tricably bound up in military custom and existence, and military
authorities have traditionally encouraged and facilitated some
degree of alcohol use, and, in some isolated instances, even the use
of narcotics. The military seeks only to insure that its members
have appropriate coping mechanisms for the stresses and disaffec-

An earlier version of this chapter was published as "Olive-Drab Drunks and GI
Junkies: Alcohol and Narcotic Addiction in the U.S. Military," in Clifton D.
Bryant, ed., *Deviant Behavior: Occupational and Organizational Bases* (Chicago:
Rand McNally College Publishing Company, 1974), pp. 129–45.

tions of military life and war. The military cannot afford the ineffectiveness of a soldier whose chemical respite deprives him of the will and capability to fight or respond to orders. Incapacitation, therefore, is a sanctioned state, and those members of the military who effect such a condition are, in effect, military criminals.

Alcohol and the Military

Military men drink. They drink off duty and sometimes on duty. They drink often and in quantity and, not infrequently, to intoxication. Alcohol figures prominently in military subculture in our society and in others, now as well as historically. As Vath (1965:1) has put it: "Military customs and tradition make up a large part of military life. Heavy drinking is one such custom." In a similar vein, West and Swegan (1956:1004), in commenting on the role of alcohol in military culture, have observed:

> In the old days it was traditional for the military man to be a hard-drinking fellow. The lore of the military service is filled with stories about alcohol, its consumption in large quantities, its procurement and concealment, and the various adventures associated therewith. The role of alcoholic beverages in military society was generally accepted and many aspects of social status were influenced by the use of alcohol.

Many nations have felt that alcohol was a desirable and necessary item of subsistence and morale, and have provided for a daily "ration" of some form of alcohol. The British navy, for example, traditionally issued a daily rum ration to its sailors. Some insight into the drinking patterns of the Royal Navy and Army can be derived from contemporary studies of delirium tremens in those services during the nineteenth century (Marjot 1977). It appears that mortality from delirium tremens averaged about 10 percent in the British army and 5 percent in the British navy. Of course, factors other than alcohol may have contributed to the mortality rate.

Similarly, the U.S. Navy at one time issued alcohol daily to each seaman in the form of "one gill of grog." A particularly vivid account of the practice of issuing alcohol rations on a man-of-war in the mid-nineteenth century is provided by Herman Melville (1966:56–57):

> In the American Navy the law allows one gill of spirits per day to every seaman. In two portions, it is served out just previous to

breakfast and dinner. At the roll of the drum, the sailors assemble around a large tub, or cask, filled with the liquid; and, as their names are called off by a midshipman, they step up and regale themselves from a little tin measure called a "tot." No high-liver helping himself to Tokay off a well-polished sideboard smacks his lips with more mighty satisfaction than the sailor does over his tot. To many of them, indeed, the thought of their daily tot forms a perpetual perspective of ravishing landscapes, indefinitely receding in the distance. It is their greatest "prospect in life." Take away their grog and life possesses no further charms for them.

The alcohol ration was of such significance to the sailor that its curtailment could be used as a punishment for violation of naval rules. As Melville (1966:144–145) comments further:

> It is one of the most common punishments for very trivial offenses in the Navy, to "stop" a seaman's grog for a day or a week. And as most seamen so cling to their grog, the loss of it is generally deemed by them as a very serious penalty. You will sometimes hear them say, "I would rather have my wind stopped than my grog!"

Today it is against Navy regulations to drink or possess alcoholic beverages aboard ship.[1] Drinking, then, in theory, occurs only on shore leave or liberty. For the armed services of some other countries, however, alcohol continues to be regular issue on and off duty.[2] Even where alcohol is not a normal issue, it is still distributed to the individual. Though no alcohol is normally served aboard ship, the flight surgeon on a carrier might routinely "prescribe" one or two shot-sized bottles (such as served on airlines) of medicinal brandy or whiskey to pilots after they return from a

---

[1] This rule is widely violated, especially by officers. The executive officer aboard the *Pueblo* related that the cooks on board the ship "on [Captain] Bucher's orders, were using wine and bourbon in the preparation of some of our meals." He also reported that he had been assigned "to triple the ship's alcohol allowance, on Bucher's instruction." Additionally, he told of the Thanksgiving mincemeat pies being spiked with brandy [again on Bucher's orders] (Murphy 1970:72–73).

[2] Wine is served with meals to some elements of the French army, particularly the French Foreign Legion. Wine concentrates were airdropped to beleagured French troops during the siege of Dien Bien Phu so that the Legionnaires might continue to enjoy their *vin ordinaire* with their daily meals. Schnapps was also parachuted to the German Sixth Army surrounded at Stalingrad during World War II. Curiously, the Russian navy permits its officers to drink in moderation on shore and even to drink white wine with meals while serving with the Black Sea fleet. However, it absolutely forbids Soviet sailors to drink at all, at sea or on shore (*Time* 1968:27). The U.S. armed services, while not providing a formalized

hazardous mission. After a particularly rough attack by the First Special Service Force during the Italian campaign in World War II, the commanding officer, Col. Robert T. Frederick, requisitioned and received "15 cases of Bourbon for medicinal purposes" from Fifth Army quartermaster (Adleman and Walton 1966:141).

Usually alcohol is readily available to military personnel. If they are stationed overseas, there are normally copious supplies of indigenous beverages at close hand.[3] Military posts in the United States sell alcoholic beverages by the drink or by the bottle at reduced prices because of tax reductions (this is an especially handy practice in "dry" areas). Drinks are dispensed in service, NCO, and officers' clubs. Prices are always reasonable, but frequent "happy hours" or "nickel beer hours" further reduce the cost to military personnel. In combat situations the military makes every effort to keep the troops supplied with their alcohol "rations." Even where cut off from normal alcohol channels, American military personnel have proved to be unusually resourceful at manufacturing their own with stills or, more frequently, concocting drinks from medical alcohol or "torpedo juice."[4] With alcohol readily available and reasonably priced, and with the social traditions of alcohol

---

alcohol ration, do attempt to provide a periodic informal ration in combat situations in the form of beer for the enlisted men and "Class VI" supplies for the officers. (In addition to the regulation five classes of supplies, officers' whiskey is designated informally as Class VI.) Even informally, issuing alcohol to U.S. troops has often been controversial. During the Korean War, for example, beer "rations" were often flown into front-line units. The WCTU objected violently to this, however, because it was "corrupting the morals of our boys."

[3] The Arab countries where alcoholic beverages are forbidden by Islamic law present something of a problem for both military and diplomatic personnel. With typical American ingenuity, however, the problem was solved in one major Middle Eastern country where a still was imported and set up in the American embassy. The marine guard detachment had the responsibility of running it, and the product was used for embassy social affairs and to supply diplomatic personnel and military officers attached to the embassy.

[4] One historically venerable form of alcoholic beverage concocted by ingenious U.S. soldiers was "spruce beer." In the absence of malt and hops, thirsty colonial troops in the Revoluntionary War made a beer-like brew from the fresh green tips of spruce boughs. It had something of a turpentine taste but it is said that one became inured to that in time. Spruce beer was also not without residual medicinal benefit. It was an antiscorbutic and was thus healthful because it was helpful in preventing scurvy. It was utilitarian in other ways also, in that it was said to be good for cleaning hats. During the Civil War, the Confederates made a beverage of which they were said to be fond. It was called "Pine Tops," and made from fresh young pine boughs. It was, of course, simply a variation of the old spruce beer (Beveridge, 1968:5, 19–20).

consumption, it is perhaps not surprising that military personnel drink, and often heavily.

Where alcohol is not available for regular issue or purchase through military channels or from civilian sources, individuals in the military may simply undertake to steal it. Adleman and Walton (1966:115) tell of one incident when the First Special Service Force was traveling by train through North Africa and pulled into a way station, where they found another train loaded with huge wine casks. They promptly stabbed the casks with knives and bayonets or shot out the plugs, drinking the wine by the helmetful as it spurted out. This same unit was prone to raid German-held wine cellars and operations posts during the Italian campaign, helping themselves to wine, cognac, and various foodstuffs (Adleman and Walton 1966:174–77, 215). These men were not even averse to stealing the alcohol from their own side. In one incident, a patrol from the force infiltrated the headquarters of Maj. Gen. Lucian K. Truscott. The general's headquarters, it seemed, was next to a captured wine cellar. They disarmed the general's sentries and made off with as many casks of wine as they could carry (Adleman and Walton 1966:195).

The use of alcohol apparently has several important functions that help account for its use (or misuse) by military personnel, and the sanctioning of its use under certain circumstances by military authorities.

ALCOHOL AND BOREDOM

Military garrison duty is monotonous, often uncomfortable, sometimes unpleasant, and frequently lonely. With nothing to do, nowhere to go, and often nobody (relatively speaking) with whom to do it, drinking becomes an institutionalized way of spending one's free time. "Fun" may have to be vicarious, and conviviality may have to be contrived. Alcohol facilitates these processes. From the standpoint of the authorities, alcohol serves to help solve the problem of morale and boredom and helps prevent the buildup of potentially disruptive frustrations.[5]

[5] Kipling, (1956:420) immortalized the soldier's preoccupation with alcohol while on garrison duty in the lines from his poem "Gunga Din":
>You may talk o' gin and beer
>When you're quartered safe out 'ere,
>An' you're sent to penny-fights an' Aldershot it;

ALCOHOL AND SEX

The large number of young single males concentrated in the typical military garrison makes it virtually a demographic impossibility for most of them to meet or date young single females—or any females, for that matter. Although many armies attempt to provide prostitutes (some even have prostitute units attached to military units), promote or encourage contiguous prostitution, or at least tacitly tolerate prostitution, this never provides an adequate range of sexual outlets for the troops. Alcohol serves the function of relieving the tension of or blunting sexual drives, acting as a kind of sexual anesthetic. It may be a substitute for sex, or at least make prostituted sex more acceptable. Alcohol functions to maintain morale from the standpoint of the individual and as a control device from the standpoint of the authorities.

ALCOHOL AND THE TENSIONS AND ANXIETIES OF COMBAT

The horrors of combat are frightening and traumatic to many military men, and difficult to live with both in terms of the personal dangers and the distasteful tasks of having to kill and maim, both before and after the fact of battle. Alcohol may prepare the soldier for the rigors of combat and let him deal with the unpleasant memories it leaves.[6] Alcohol serves to help those in the military prepare themselves for battle. Keegan (1976:326) suggests:

> Yet the prospect of battle, excepting perhaps the first battle of a war or a green unit's first blooding, seems always to alarm men's anxieties, however young and vigorous they be, rather than excite their anticipation. Hence the drinking which seems an inseparable part both of preparation for battle and of combat itself. Alcohol, as we know, depresses the self-protective reflexes, and so induces the appearance of courage.[7]

[6] This fact was alluded to by John Dryden (1969:484) in his classic poem "Alexander's Feast":

> Bacchus' blessings are a treasure;
> Drinking is the soldier's pleasure,
>   Rich the treasure,
>   Sweet the pleasure,
> Sweet is pleasure after pain.

[7] The term "Dutch courage," for example, came from the practice of issuing gin to Dutch mercenaries before battle to give them the necessary "bravery." Vath (1965:1) refers to some military physicians' encouraging the use of alcohol as a means of relieving the tensions and anxieties of combat.

Keegan (1976:181) has reported that drinking was a widespread activity at the Battle of Waterloo, and likely a significant factor in motivating the men to fight. In speaking of the factors that "sustained the ordinary soldier's steadfastness," he relates:

> Drink may certainly have been one of them. Tiredness, I have suggested, helped to inure the soldier to fear, and much of the army was tired. But many of the soldiers had drunk spirits before the battle, and continued to drink while it was in progress. Shaw, the slashing Lifeguardsman, was, in the opinion of Sergeant Morris who watched him guzzling gin at about noon, drunk and running amok when he was cut down by the French cuirassiers; Morris himself took three canteens, full of gin "for the wounded," but shared some of it with a friend; Sergeant Lawrence's officer in the 40th Regiment, kept running to him during the battle for a swig at his spirits flask; and Dallas, the Commissary of the Third Division, hailed by his general with the demand, "My brave fellows are famished for thirst and support, where are the spirits you promised to send them?," managed to get a cart forward and rolled a barrel into the middle of a square, where it was broached, and the contents distributed, during the closing stages of the battle itself.
>
> Almost every regimental memoir refers to drink being distributed. . . .

At the Battle of Agincourt, alcohol was also a factor that "sustained men in combat." Keegan (1976:113) points out that:

> Of the general factors, drink is the most obvious to mention. The English, who were on short rations, presumably had less to drink than the French, but there was drinking in the ranks on both sides during the period of waiting and it is quite probable that many soldiers in both armies went into the melee less than sober, if not indeed fighting drunk.

In the Battle of the Somme in World War I, some of the British units in the attack received a "strong tot of rum—Navy rum, and extremely alcoholic," just before leaving the trenches (Keegan 1976:241). Some men in the Eleventh Suffolks received the "teetotalers' share" as well as their own and allegedly drank themselves insensible. In the Sherwood Forester Brigade the leading wave, "through some error," also drank the rum intended for the second wave. Inasmuch as many men do not eat before a battle because of the possibility of being wounded in the stomach, the two rations of rum on an empty stomach caused some men in the first wave to be drunk.

ALCOHOL AND MILITARY CULTURE

Alcohol also occupies a significant ceremonial niche in military culture. Many official military social functions may involve both alcohol and mandatory or pressurized attendance. Examples might be receptions, unit cocktail parties, formal messes, banquets, and various military *rites de passage* such as promotions, retirements, or "prop blasts."[8]

ALCOHOL AND THE MASCULINE MYSTIQUE

The military role is a masculine role. In many cultures drinking may be a component of the male role. A "real" man can "hold his liquor." As Elkin (1946:410) points out: "Drinking in the Army, as in civilian life, was a symbol of virility and facilitated the forgetting of the self and the release of impulses of self-assertion and aggression."

Thus the ability to drink large amounts of alcohol is something of a masculine test and in some ways a test of suitability for the demanding masculine military role. One of the respondents studied by Janowitz (1960), for example, included alcoholic capacity as a requirement for success as a military officer. He states, "A man should be able to tell a good story but should not be a notorious braggart; a man should be able to *drink a lot*, but should not be an alcoholic. . . ."[9]

An interesting account of the masculine military drinking mystique is found in a popular novel about the Korean War. Here some marines are discussing Marine Corps heroes, and their stories concerning the famous Lew Diamond (a real-life Marine hero) are described as follows (Peacock 1962:51):

> Lew Diamond, in the Marine Corps, was a venerated legend;
> more so than Blackjack Pershing of the Army or two-time Medal

[8] "Prop blasts" are initiation ceremonies that celebrate the acquisition of jump "wings" after airborne school. For a full description see Weiss (1967). In effect, such military social events as mentioned above are also masculine *rites of intensification* and the constituent use of alcohol is one of the social mechanisms by which the masculine role performance can be legitimized.

[9] This is cited by Vath (1965:2). Vath also points out that the image of the soldier portrayed in many novels about the military, such as Michener's *Tales of the South Pacific* and James Jones's *From Here to Eternity*, is that of the hard-drinking soldier (1965:2).

of Honor winner in the corps, Dan Daly, who wound up as a guard in a bank. Lew Diamond, the Marine who was two thousand years old, a powerfully built man with a gray goatee and moustache who lived on slop-chute beer and never drank without his dog Piss Pot Pete right beside him every night of every year, both of them so drunk they had to be carried back to the barracks when the slop-chute closed.

Drinking and drunkenness were very much a constituent of Army life in the Indian wars of the American West. Ware (1960:23–24), for example, mentions that he returned to his army post after a hunting trip and discovered that his men had gotten some whiskey from a passing train, and that the whole camp was drunk. The commanding officer had to tie his men to wagon wheels to keep them from becoming violent. In order to get the soldiers to do extra hard work, such as building log buildings and forts, they were given a gill of whiskey in the morning and one in the afternoon as an inducement (Ware 1960:92–93). The soldiers of that era were hardworking and hard-fighting and therefore tended to be hard-drinking. Knowing the propensity of the men to get drunk at the first possible occasion, the officers often went to great lengths to keep them away from whiskey, but the soldiers apparently found a supply anyway, as Ware (1960:135–36) relates:

> I determined to set out a row of trees, principally box-elders, around the parade-ground, and I took Murphy [one of his soldiers who frequently got drunk and boisterous] out of the guard-house, gave him a spade, and detailed a corporal to keep him going. I got a corporal that did not believe in political democracy, and he kept Murphy digging day after day in good shape. But in spite of everything we could do, although Murphy was taken back to the guard-house, and was carefully watched, and kept digging day after day, he kept half drunk all of the time. How that man managed to get whiskey was one of the greatest of puzzles. It seemed that he could absorb it from the air, or suck it up from the sandy and arid plain.

EFFECTS OF ALCOHOL

Although the heavy use of alcoholic beverages is sanctioned by military tradition and subculture and tacitly approved by military authorities, excessive use of alcohol is officially discouraged, as Vath (1965:2) describes it:

Although military tradition favors heavy drinking, the official military policy is one of strong punitive action for drunkenness and alcoholism, especially when these conditions interfere with duty. This is made necessary by the seriousness of the military mission where drunken errors and impaired judgement cannot be tolerated. Compared with civilian law, military regulations prescribe harsh penalties for such behavior as being drunk on duty, being drunk and disorderly, and driving under the influence of alcohol. At times even moderate drinking is prohibited by regulation. SAC forbids drinking by aircrew members 48 hours prior to and during their being on alert. Navy ships are officially dry, and drinking on duty is a serious offense in all branches of the military.

This disruption that alcohol contributes to good order, discipline, and performance is most important to the military. Alcohol abuse contributes to insubordination or disrespect for supervisors or the service, and may impede or prevent the discharge of appropriate military role responsibilities. The fact that the military operates in a much more socially and politically sensitive milieu today than in the past, combined with the technological exigencies of the Cold War, render alcohol abuse particularly threatening to today's military mission. As West and Swegan (1956:1004) put it:

> The nature of the present peacetime military establishment requires a high level of alertness and a greater degree of individual responsibility than ever before. The irresponsibility that often comes with chronic alcoholism cannot be tolerated in an effective modern military organization. Thus punitive regulations have been evolved which place chronic alcoholism on a par with criminality and sexual perversion, subjecting the alcoholic to discharge without honor as unfit.

In addition to excessive alcoholic consumption constituting a violation of military regulations, heavy drinking patterns are often dysfunctional in other ways. While alcohol is supposed to relieve boredom and keep the men "occupied," it frequently promotes aggressive acts by removing inhibitions, and is thus often a factor in fights and brawls as well as in the commission of various crimes against persons and property, including rapes and assaults, exhibitionism, thefts, and vandalism.[10]

---

[10] While acting as Military Police duty officer in the army some years ago, I had occasion to investigate or process a wide variety of offenses. In the majority of

Military patterns of heavy drinking may also lead to actual alcoholism. Although studies are inconclusive, the patterns of heavy drinking that are part of the culture of military life may be a contributory factor to alcoholism in a man after he leaves the military, if not while he is still a member.[11] According to Vath, because alcoholism is a slowly progressive disease that may not reach the acute stage until late middle age, many potential alcoholics may have simply retired from military life before the onset of the disabling stage. Since the military exerts considerable control over the behavior of its members, the alcoholic can be "controlled" to a degree while the individual is still in service. In addition, the structure of the military is such that alcoholic patterns can be concealed better than in other work settings. The military can, in effect, "carry" or shelter the alcoholic as long as he is in service.[12] In any event, Vath (1965:21) did find that military veterans have a higher rate of alcoholism than nonveterans, on the basis of "their appearance in alcoholism treatment programs in greater numbers than expected from their distribution in the general population." Other researchers have also suggested that military drinking may lead ultimately to alcoholism.[13]

Narcotics and the Military

As with alcohol, there is a long historical association between narcotics and the military establishment. From ancient times until the present, military men, especially those engaged in actual fighting, have turned to chemical substances to prepare them mentally for the rigors of battle and to sustain them in the monotony of

---

cases, the apprehended individuals were drunk or had been drinking heavily when they committed the offense. Many used the excuse that because of their drunken condition, they had more or less lost control of themselves. For studies of the relationship of drinking to offenses of military personnel, see Cornsweet and Locke (1949); Blackman (1947).

[11] For a detailed study on this relationship, see Vath (1965).

[12] An excellent example was the "19-year" private in the recent movie *The Sergeant*, starring Rod Steiger. In the movie this character was an alcoholic "career" private with 19 years of service. His alcoholism had been covered up for years by his peers and superiors in order that he might be able to retire after 20 years and have a small income on which to live.

[13] Although the literature on military alcoholism is too extensive to list, see, for example, Wallinga (1956).

garrison duty. In previous wars, however, narcotics usage by military personnel did not pose a significant problem in terms of extent, although the number of veterans who were addicted was relatively high. The Vietnam War has produced a military drug problem of significant proportions. Some observers (Geller and Boas 1969:148) have reported that as many as three-fourths of the GIs there smoked marijuana, and even some official reports have indicated that 35 percent of the troops used marijuana.[14] A staggering number of military personnel in Vietnam were also apparently "hooked" on, or were at least heavy users, of hard drugs such as heroin. The problem is not confined to Vietnam. In this country there is evidence of a considerable drug problem on our military bases. One army authority (Lengel 1971:9) at Fort Bragg estimated that 50 to 70 percent of the men at the base "use marijuana and about 800 to 1,000 are strung out on heroin and amphetamines."

The military has traditionally been able to tolerate heavy alcohol use by its personnel. Alcohol consumption and the subsequent behavior of the drinker could be "controlled" to a degree, in the sense of setting firm limits. Furthermore, the recovery from inebriation is relatively rapid. Drug abuse and its subsequent behavior are much more difficult to "control." It is almost impossible to set and enforce limits in terms of narcotic behavior. The recovery from a narcotic state may be slow and, for the regular user, there may be no recovery. The military's prime concern is lowered efficiency or the inability to perform adequately or to discharge military responsibilities satisfactorily. From the army's standpoint, for example, the use of marijuana is incapacitating in terms of military duties. As viewed by the army (quoted in Cromley, 1971a):

> As a precautionary measure it is recommended that in general for administrative purposes persons may be considered voluntarily incapacitated for duty up to 12 to 36 hours after the use of marijuana, unless otherwise determined by medical or other appropriate authorities that a different time frame should be used in a particular case.

---

[14] Some authorities take issue with the assertions concerning both the extent and seriousness of the drug problem in Vietnam. Szasz (1972:4, 6), for example, suggests that military addicts are being used as "scapegoats," that the figures on heroin use among troops are being purposefully inflated in a kind of "pharmacological Gulf of Tonkin" manner, and that addicts may be able to function appropriately in many instances. For a fuller discussion of his view, see Szasz.

Several years ago in Vietnam, the then army provost marshal expressed his anxieties about GI marijuana smoking. "His biggest concern, though, was his conviction that the brain soaked in pot fumes would be dulled and unable to function in battle" (Geller and Boas 1969:148).

If the ultimate mission of the military, particularly the infantry, is to close with and destroy the enemy, anything that might hinder attainment of this goal or erode the efficiency with which it is accomplished represents a form of deviance highly dysfunctional to the military system. However, the military is largely, if indirectly, responsible for the drug abuse in terms of several factors that encourage, precipitate, or facilitate drug abuse among its personnel and are structured into the military system.

NARCOTICS IN MEDICAL TREATMENT

Because of the prevalence of wounds, injuries, and diseases encountered among military personnel, narcotics in various forms play a significant role in the attendant medical treatment. Narcotics are involved throughout the resultant treatment to a much greater degree than in civilian life. During World War II, infantrymen in combat situations often carried morphine syringes in their first aid kits. In Vietnam the drug problem was such that morphine was not generally issued to the individual soldier.

The principal medical strategy of the military is to "maintain" the wounded until they can be transported to a hospital facility with total medical resources. Narcotics will in all likelihood be administered to a wounded man for the pain, since there may be a delay in reaching a medical facility. Although the military does maintain relatively complete hospitals only a short distance from the combat area, such as Mobile Army Surgical Hospitals as well as hospital ships, the function of such facilities is to treat wounds of medium seriousness and perform preliminary surgical treatment on the wounded. Every attempt is made to transport the wounded serviceman to more sophisticated hospitals in the United States or in friendly countries. An elaborate system of transportation for the wounded has been developed by the military, including helicopter and transport planes and hospital trains. Lengthy narcotic sedation is often necessary during transport of the wounded man and while he awaits intensive treatment. The nature of combat wounds, with the attendant physical trauma and the often extensive surgical treatment, is such that the individual may require narcotics for a considerable time period. Although every attempt is made to prevent the possibility of addiction, some wounded servicemen do develop a dependence on narcotics that they continue during extended convalescence or after discharge, or reestablish at some later date. After our earlier wars, when medical authorities were less sophisticated about narcotic addiction, the problem was apparently quite severe. In the period after the Civil War and up to the time of World War I and even later, the so-called "soldier's disease" referred to narcotic addiction among veterans. In recent years with the Vietnam returnees, the military hospitals themselves have often become centers of drug traffic. As columnist Jack Anderson (1970) has described the situation:

> Venerable Walter Reed Army Hospital where Douglas Mac-Arthur and Dwight Eisenhower spent their final days has become a haven for narcotics users with patients briskly peddling a dizzying variety of drugs to fellow soldiers.
> Along the secluded walks of the famed rose garden, on the broad lawns and inside the buildings themselves, the bustling trade goes on even as a hospital spokesman denies vigorously that a drug problem exists.
> A reporter for this column, Sharon Basco, made two visits to the hospital in the nation's capital and learned from patients themselves that heroin, marijuana, LSD, mescaline, "speed," and demerol are all available for a price.

From the standpoint of the pusher, the military and veterans hospitals make ideal locations for their commerce because they have available a "captive" group of consumers with a high concentration of addicts or users, or at least individuals who may be familiar with marijuana and other narcotics as well as their effects.

THE PROPINQUITY OF NARCOTICS

The individual in the military finds narcotics more accessible than does his counterpart in civilian life. Fort (1966:77) comments, "Some of them [addicts] had had opportunities to steal morphine while in service; a favorite method was to steal the morphine syrettes contained in parachute first aid kits."

The sheer enormity of military medical supplies, and the problem of distribution, make it difficult to impose controls as rigid as those usually encountered in civilian life. Accordingly, an addict can more easily maintain a supply of hard drugs through illegal channels, and the marijuana user can more easily obtain hard drugs for initial experimentation. Other drugs such as "speed" (amphetamines) can often be obtained from army medical channels in the line of duty "if the soldier says that he needs to stay awake or requires extra energy for a tough mission" (Geller and Boas 1969:151–52).

Much military activity occurs in foreign countries. In such areas there may be more of a cultural tradition of using various kinds of narcotics, and they may be relatively available in the indigenous open market or from the often sizable addicted local population. As Fort (1966:77) observed, "A few of them [addicts] had become addicted while in service, sometimes through association with foreign addicts (for instance, in Japan)."

Some narcotics such as marijuana are relatively common in various tropical parts of the world, and may be used by significant numbers of the indigenous population. In some instances, historically, marijuana smoking may have been a cultural pattern into which American servicemen were socialized while stationed there. Such was apparently the case in the days of the "banana army." As Geller and Boas (1969:146) describe it:

> Back in 1925 the young American soldiers protecting the Panama Canal Zone were not much different from those scattered throughout the world today. It was a known fact that the men stationed in the Canal Zone had been smoking marijuana for some time, having picked up the habit from the local Panamanians. The military was aware of the practice, but they regarded it as a harmless diversion. However, the late twenties saw the emergence of the "marijuana menace" scare and, accordingly, pressure was placed upon the military to examine the drug's use in Panama.

Furthermore, marijuana may simply grow wild in quantity and be readily available "for the picking" in some areas of the world. Consider the experience of some of the first contingents of occupation troops in Japan after World War II. Bowers (1970:7) reports:

> The 11th Airborne Division was handed Yokohama until a few rapes and robberies and a couple of murders outside the New Grand Hotel (MacArthur's first temporary headquarters) caused

another "point of occupation" to be opened, Sendai in the out-of-the-way north. There, some of the wiser paratroopers immediately spotted acres of wild marijuana, and the first year of the occupation also saw the first big dope bust.

In the Vietnamese conflict, many of the American GI's had a history of marijuana use, and in some cases, harder drugs. Their continued use of marijuana and other drugs was much facilitated by the ready availibility of such formerly illegal substances.

The situation in Vietnam was particularly serious in this regard. Southeastern Asia has traditionally been a center for the raising of opium and marijuana as well as drug production and distribution. There is also a long history of drug use among some of the indigenous peoples there. Oriental organized crime found a lucrative market in the American servicemen stationed there. As one columnist (Cromley: 1971b) reported:

> So far as can be gathered, the principal bankrollers—the men who furnish the funds and rake in the bulk of the profits after agents, officials, transporters, and sellers are paid off—are an interconnected group of Chinese financiers in Hong Kong, Singapore, and Macao.
>
> These men are international, with business associates in Thailand, Laos, Malaysia, South Vietnam, Burma, and Communist China. In the main, however, the top men are themselves believed to be neither communist nor noncommunist.

This columnist also reported that an estimated 1,000 tons of opium a year moves out of Thailand, with most coming into South Vietnam. Furthermore, some of the highest quality marijuana—"Cambodian Red"—is grown in Vietnam near the Cambodian border and is available to the GIs from street vendors for a nominal price (Geller and Boas 1969:149–50). With marijuana and other narcotics freely available at low prices, a traditional background of narcotic usage in the region, a strong subcultural norm of marijuana smoking among the troops, and relatively lax enforcement of the regulations against drug use on the part of both South Vietnamese authorities and U.S. military authorities, it is perhaps not surprising that between 35 and 75 percent of our troops in Vietnam (depending on whose estimate) smoked marijuana, and a significant percentage were hooked on hard drugs.[15]

---

[15] Geller and Boas (1969:151) point out that: "Most MPs are taught to smell and otherwise establish the presence of marijuana. But since many of them turn on themselves, they tend to be casual about finding pot smokers except in cases

The incidence of drug use among the military in Vietnam was somewhat higher than in the age-eligible civilian population. According to Segal (1977:74), "this was due in part to overselection for military service of people who had used drugs in high school, and who continued their use in the Army." The Vietnam War simply brought about the lowering of standards for persons coming into the military, with the result that a larger percentage of persons who had been in trouble with legal or school authorities, or who had other characteristics associated with drug use, were inducted into the armed services. Segal also suggests, however, that the higher incidence of drug use in the military was the result of "drug use initiation with the military, as well as a carry-over of civilian patterns." He felt that "there is in all likelihood an additional effect due to being in the Army, driven both by drug availability and by peer pressure to use drugs."

NARCOTICS AND MILITARY STRESS AND DEMANDS

The military role is a difficult and demanding one. It is physically arduous and often mentally stressful and frustrating. It involves danger, fear, and depersonalization, and sometimes dehumanization. The individual may be subjected to regimentation, humiliation, loneliness, privation, and pain. Obviously some are not cut out to be soldier (or sailor). Others may be able to play the role successfully only with effort and difficulty. Few relish it. Marijuana and other narcotics, like alcohol, may serve as mechanisms to moderate the discomforts and stresses of the role. A marijuana user interviewed in World War II, for example, put it succinctly when he stated, "I ain't no soldier, and I ain't going to be one. When I want what I want, I got to have it. If I can't get any more reefers, I'm going A.W.O.L. again" (Marcovitz and Myers 1944:389). The army physician who interviewed this addict and others concluded that (Marcovitz and Myers 1944:389):

---

where the violation is glaringly obvious." They also speak of "the link between the Vietnamese police and the pushers." A young captain of the artillery, recently returned from Vietnam, told us in an interview that he had confiscated a large quantity of marijuana from some GIs and attempted to turn them and the marijuana in at a Military Police station. The MP's refused to accpt the soldiers, claiming there was no case against them, but offered to "keep" the marijuana. The captain refused.

The adjustment to military life was invariably very poor. In some cases this was due to a failure of adequate performance because of personal and character maladjustment. For example, many could not stand being reprimanded. Some could not endure being around other persons and liked to be off by themselves. Without his drug one claimed that he could not remember what he was supposed to do. Complaints of headaches and nervousness and inability to concentrate were exceedingly common and led to frequent visits to sick call and to the hospital. In fact, these symptoms were present in varying degrees in every addict whose case was studied in this series. In addition to inadequate performance there was difficulty in military adjustment expressed in the problem of discipline, especially as related to going A.W.O.L. and antisocial behavior toward fellow soldiers or superiors.

If the regimentation, routine, and social demands of the military role in peacetime or on garrison duty create adjustment and performance difficulties, the combat element of the military role in wartime poses special strains. Combat may involve suspense, intense fear, discomfort, or pain and personal revulsion beyond the limits tolerable to many persons. The soldier, of course, has no legal alternatives, and alcohol or drugs provide the only means by which he may moderate the stresses of combat and fulfill his military obligations. Alcohol may be unavailable or inconvenient to maintain in a combat situation. Marijuana, however, is light, convenient, and readily accessible to the troops. As a result, it is the preferred "escape" device. As Geller and Boas (1969:152) put it, "Marijuana found on dead and wounded GIs supplies ample evidence that smoking takes place under combat conditions." They also point out (1969:148) that:

> Newsmen, interviewing GIs after the story broke, found that many a pointman or rifleman on patrol in enemy territory turns on not because he's looking for a different kind of kick, but simply to overcome a basic human and particularly martial emotion: fear. The boredom of war coupled with fighting an elusive enemy make the conflict in Vietnam one where the guard at the gate, the sentinel at the barbed-wire perimeter, and the radio operator monitoring suspicious sounds play key roles in the conduct of the war. Lighting up a joint doesn't make time go faster but it does make a task of drudgery easier to bear, according to many GIs.

Like alcohol, various kinds of narcotics have long been used as a mechanism for coping with the stresses and dissaffections of combat. Keegan (1976:326), for example, informs us that:

Other drugs reproduce this effect, notably marijuana; the American army's widespread addiction to it in Vietnam, deeply troubling though it was to the conscience of the nation, may therefore be seen if not as a natural, certainly as a time-honored response to the uncertainties with which battle racks the soldiers. The choice of that particular army, moreover, had local precedents: the pirates of the South China Sea traditionally dosed themselves with marijuana before attacking European ships.

That any army today could train its men to feel comfortable in a combat situation is doubtful. While many tolerate it, for many others the only means of endurance is some form of chemical device for altering subjective reality.

MILITARY SOLUTIONS

In previous times the military more often overlooked occasional marijuana smoking as a trivial disciplinary problem or, when confronted with regular marijuana smoking or narcotic usage, viewed the practice as detrimental to the adequate performance of assigned military tasks and duties. Accordingly, such individuals were singled out for discharge under Section VIII of U.S. Army Regulations 615–368, which provides for release from active duty because of "ineptness or undesirable habits or traits of character," or courts-martial for breaches of discipline (Marcovitz and Myers 1944). Such disposition of the addict, however, serves only to hide the problem or transfer it to other responsibilities. It assuredly did not resolve it. As Marcovitz and Myers (1944:390) have commented:

> However, in our experience at least, most marijuana addicts avoid a general court-martial. At most, their breaches of discipline have led to special courts-martial, with sentences ranging up to six months in the guardhouse. The ones we have seen have never been led one step on the road to rehabilitation by such a procedure. On their release they immediately resume their use of marijuana and continue to be medical and disciplinary problems.
>
> Because they actually interfere with the efficiency of the Army and their potentialities for usefulness are slight, separation from the service under the provisions of Section VIII, AR 614–360 [later superseded by AR 615–368] eventually becomes necessary. However, it must be admitted that this merely released the addict to civilian life, where he continues to have his somatic and per-

sonality difficulties, with their expression in antisocial or criminal behavior, and he tends to foster the use of marijuana by others.

More recently, the military has drastically altered its views on the problem and now considers the use of marijuana and other narcotics as essentially a medical problem calling for treatment and rehabilitation. On this subject Cromley (1971a) has observed:

> The military services by now have perhaps more experience on a large scale with men affected by drug abuse—including marijuana—than any other institution in this country. . . .
>
> Whatever the regulations and whatever is said in policy statements, months of interviews convince that it is now U.S. Army policy at the highest levels to regard the use of marijuana (and other drugs) as a medical rather than as a legal problem.
>
> In Vietnam, Europe and the United States, American GIs physically or emotionally "hooked" on drugs are being encouraged to report themselves in for treatment with no penalty.

Unfortunately, the military's attempts at treatment and rehabilitation have been somewhat less than successful. Even where the addicts have been induced to undergo treatment under a "no bust" amnesty policy, the men have often been uncooperative, violated military discipline, continued their drug usage, and even engaged in a variety of other criminal activities. The following account illustrates this situation at one naval drug rehabilitation center (Holles 1971):

> Many of the patients—among them are enlisted men who became addicted to heroin while in Vietnam—have refused to accept authority and discipline or to cooperate with psychologists and therapists seeking to inquire into the root causes of their addiction.
>
> Some have flaunted their special amnesty status before other Miramar [the name of the center] enlisted men who are subject to more rigid discipline. This has led to what a spokesman called "confrontations" and what other sources described as near riots on several occasions. . . .
>
> As many as 20 of the center's 220 patients have been absent without leave at one time. Three were missing one day last week and another was in jail on suspicion of robbing a San Diego bank. Disciplinary action currently is being considered against 18 or 20 others suspected of smuggling drugs onto the base. . . .
>
> An increase in barracks thefts and shoplifting at the Miramar Navy exchange has been attributed, at least in part, to the drug trafficking.

Many servicemen addicts, especially blacks, remain suspicious of the amnesty program. Many of these men find that they can carry out their work even under the influence of drugs and without detection by authorities. In this sense the addicts are not taking advantage of the military's new enlightened attitudes toward drug use.

As one battalion executive officer in Vietnam articulated it (Emerson 1971:2):

> "You talk about the Army's amnesty program—that's three days maybe, what the hell," he added. "But they [GI drug takers] don't trust the Green Machine—they're afraid if they turn themselves in they'll be documented by the Veterans Administration, or maybe exposed by the Army."

Furthermore, while at one time the military made an effort to discharge its addicts, and even though rehabilitative treatment is now available, many individuals in the service are using their addiction as a means of obtaining a discharge. A recent newspaper account, for example (*New York Times*, 1971:35) states:

> American seamen appear now to be pleading drug usage rather than homosexuality as a quick way out of the service, Navy officials say.
>
> A statistical study of administrative discharges shows that while in 1964 the Navy released 1,586 men for homosexuality, compared with 42 for drug use, last year it discharged 5,672 drug users and 479 homosexuals.

Even in those instances where military personnel are confined as a result of disciplinary action, the authorities have been somewhat less than successful in cutting off their supply of drugs, as one account demonstrates (Geller and Boas 1969:148–49):

> One of the biggest scandals to emerge out of the Army's marijuana investigations was the discovery that the same GIs confined for pot offenses to the Long Binh stockade, twenty-five miles north of Saigon, were blissfully whiling away their sentences with a supply of grass. How the contraband substance entered the stockade gates is a matter of conjecture. Despite a massive ring of security, an inordinate amount of military goods still manages to get stolen and the Viet Cong learn of classified secrets. Pot, like water, finds its level even in tightly guarded premises. Undoubtedly, it was smuggled in, either through Vietnamese civilians employed in the camp or by way of the guards.

Although the military authorities have not enjoyed any great degree of success in their recent treatment and rehabilitation attempts, they have exhibited an enlightened attitude toward the problem. In the face of the fact that the use of marijuana and other narcotics by military personnel, with the attendant illicit traffic in drugs, often generates a significant crime problem in terms of thefts and antisocial actions, not to mention a morale and discipline problem, the military can ill afford not to continue exerting every effort. Most important, narcotic usage adversely affects the performance of troops, and the lowered efficiency, particularly in a combat situation, can hardly be tolerated without affecting the outcome of the conflict. Hence the military may be expected to turn even greater efforts and devote more resources toward finding a solution to the problem.

PART THREE

Extra-Occupational Crime

The citizen or native of a hostile country is thus an enemy, as one of the constituents of the hostile state or nation, and as such is subjected to the hardships of the war.
  Francis Lieber

CHAPTER SEVEN

Crimes Against Civilians

We was on a search and destroy mission; we was to completely overrun the village, leave nothing walking, crawling, or growing. We was to kill all the livestock. We was to leave no living thing when we left.

Charles West, a squad leader in the third platoon of the U.S. military force at My Lai

Military personnel, while members of a separate social system, are also frequently involved with civilian society both in their own country and abroad. In the course of their interaction with civilian society, military personnel sometimes commit crimes involving abuse of the civilians, whether their own, allied, or enemy, by directing acts of theft and violence against them. They may also behave in such a way in a civilian setting that their actions are prejudicial to the military and thus directly or indirectly handicap the military in the discharge of its mission. As a result, they may be guilty of crimes against performance involving inappropriate interaction with civilians.

United States Civilian Social System

The presence of a military installation usually means a large concentration of military personnel, often predominantly young, frequently single, relatively underpaid, and overly aggressive.

195

Contiguous civilian communities, while pleased to have the "payroll" that the military population represents, are frequently apprehensive if not outright hostile to the troops stationed there.[1] Much of this concern grows out of their fear of possible criminal behavior committed by the military population, who are not directly subject to the local mechanisms of social control, both formal and informal. It has been the traditional practice of military authorities to exercise especially stringent control over their personnel in regard to their relationships and activities with the local civilian population, so as to minimize possible crimes against civilians and their property. Toward this end, military personnel are often residentially segregated or restricted in their ability to live freely among the local population. Married officers and noncommissioned officers may, for example, have quarters available at low rent within the base limits. Married enlisted and noncommissioned personnel may live off base in civilian housing only with special permission. Unmarried enlisted and noncommissioned individuals may live off base only under unusual circumstances. For single persons living in barracks and other on-post housing there have traditionally been bed-checks and restrictions on being away from quarters after certain times at night. Through a system of passes and leaves, military personnel have been severely restricted and closely regulated in their travels off post and into the civilian communities. In many instances, military, shore, or air police still perform "town patrol" to assure the proper comportment of military personnel, and to make arrests if necessary.

Whether such control and monitoring of servicemen and their behavior in regard to their interaction with civilian society is necessary (or desirable) is debatable. Historically in the U.S. military (and presumably in the militaries of other societies) there has been a relatively low percentage of crimes of a civil nature as compared with crimes of a military nature (Gale 1970). Gale (1970:3), in his study of crime in the U.S. military, bifurcated crime into civil offenses such as "homicide, larceny, assault, sodomy, drug and mail offenses; acts prohibited in both military and civil life," and military offenses such as "acts [of] desertion, neglect of duty, insubordination."[2] Examining the number and

---

[1] A year or so before the start of World War II, *Life* magazine ran a photograph of a sign on the door of a drugstore in a small town near an army post. The sign read, "No Dogs or Soldiers Allowed."

[2] This study is not without defect in terms of relevance for our discussion. The author does not indicate whether the civil-type offenses are actually committed

percent of convictions at various levels of courts-martial for both types of offense over a number of decades, he concluded that, ·although there has consistently been a much higher proportion of military-type offenses than civil-type offenses, there has also been a trend toward the civilization of crime in the military.

In the pre–World War I period, for example, civil-type offenses constituted less than 10 percent of the convictions in general courts-martial in the marines, less than 17 percent in the army, and only 6.1 percent in the navy. By the late 1960s the percentage of general court-martial convictions for civil-type offenses had risen to 42 percent in the marines and 43.9 percent in the navy (there were no figures for the army in this study). Other figures given in the study supported such a trend.[3] The author attempts to account for the trend toward civilization of offenses in the military as a result of changes in the organizational structure and composition of the military labor force, leading to a more "civilianized" military establishment. There has been, for example, a declining ratio of combat and combat-related troops to support and technical troops. Interestingly, the author (Gale :2) points out that "at any given time, however, the more combat-prepared services are less likely to have offenses directed against its organization than the more civilian services." This appears to be the result of the "greater discipline and/or effective socialization in the more total of the military branches." Despite this trend toward civil-type crime, offenses against U.S. civilians committed by members of the military have not been nearly as much of a problem as have other types of offenses.

---

against civilians or simply other members of the military. Similarly, it is not known whether the offenses were committed in this country or abroad. Nevertheless, it would seem possible to infer that a substantial proportion of such offenses had been directed at civilians and, given the dates of some of the figures (i.e., peacetime), it would probably be safe to assume that most of the offenses occurred in this country. All in all, we think the study does support our point that offenses committed against U.S. civilians by servicemen have been relatively minor phenomena.

[3] The author draws his primary data from several sources including annual reports of the office of the judge advocate general of the Army and Navy, direct correspondence with the Navy and Marine Corps, and a Department of the Air Force report on court-martial activities. He did not fully account for the fact that certain army data for more recent years was not included in his table other than to comment, "given the gaps in time and service data." Some of the other figures in the article were derived from secondary data in various other previously published sources (Crowder 1919–1920; Chappell 1945; Boshes and Hermann 1947; MacCormick 1946; and U.S. Department of the Army 1952).

In any event, the military usually attempts to assume jurisdiction over the serviceman who commits a civilian crime, rather than allow the civilian authorities to hold sway and provide the unfavorable publicity of a civilian trial. The soldier or sailor who commits a civilian offense may stand subject to both civilian or military sanctions for the violation of civilian laws. The double sanctions along with the close observation and control by military authorities over their personnel have undoubtedly been factors in minimizing the incidence of crimes against U.S. civilian property or persons.

CRIMES AGAINST PROPERTY

In order to maintain the proper toleration, respect, support, and cooperation from the U.S. civilian population (as well as foreign, friendly, and occupied enemy civilian populations), their property rights must be assiduously observed and the occasional circumstances necessitating the acquisition of their property must be rigidly defined and regulated in regard to due process and justification.

Accordingly, it is perhaps not surprising that the legal constraints and regulations governing the relationship of military personnel to armed forces, civilian, and enemy property are elaborate, specific, and severely sanctioned. In spite of this, violations of formal property norms are frequent, flagrant, and often supported by the informal structure and subculture.

The property of military personnel, like their behavior, is closely observed and regulated. For example, lockers and trunks of enlisted men are inspected periodically. In the face of this control and restriction, it is perhaps more difficult for a military individual to commit certain types of crime against civilian property because of the lack of opportunity structure. The military person frequently does not have the time or freedom to commit theft, would not have physical or social access to a setting suitable for theft, would have limited placed for hiding stolen property, would not have the contact networks for disposing of stolen items, and would have only limited chances to use stolen property. Because of his relative isolation from civilian life, the military person cannot develop the same knowledge of theft situations or the same facilitative skills as can his civilian counterpart. Furthermore, there is reason to believe that the motivation to commit theft to obtain various civilian property may simply be diminished. As McCallum (1946:479) suggests:

> When a man enters to army, he no longer competes for the goods of the society, since his economic status is assured by the army. The struggle to get things and the social recognition they involve come to an abrupt end. One cannot overemphasize the psychological effect of this change from a situation in which a person is constantly striving to improve his social position in reference to those about him to one in which his position is predetermined.

Overall, it would seem that, as far as the U.S. civilian population is concerned, extra-occupational crimes against property are a minimal problem as compared with other kinds of khaki-collar crime. At least, this was apparently the case in relatively recent times.[4] Presumably, in addition to situational factors, the efforts of the military itself were relatively effective in minimizing the commission of civilian criminal offenses (especially property crimes) by military personnel. This may, however, have also been a function of the type of individual in the military in the past as compared with the present. Whatever the reason, the military may well see crimes against civilians' property attain a more significant frequency in the future.

On the other hand, military persons may be likely to be involved in the damage or destruction of civilian property or the violation of financial trust. Soldiers or sailors may become involved in brawls or fights that damage bars or restaurants, or they may destroy property as part of a drunken shore leave spree. They may on occasion default on debts[5] or cash worthless checks. Defaulting on debts or cashing worthless checks are crimes against property

---

[4] In my two years of service with the Military Police in the early 1950s, I never had occasion to observe more than one or two instances of a soldier committing theft of civilian property. Other kinds of crime, such as an assault against civilians or drunk and disorderly conduct, were somewhat more frequent. Data available to me at the time suggested that my experience was not unique and that the incidence of civilian property crime committed by military personnel was indeed generally low.

[5] The military takes a dim view of its personnel defaulting or being delinquent on their debts, feeling that such economic deviancy serves to "bring discredit upon the armed forces." Accordingly, pressure may be applied to induce the serviceman to honor his debts. Many merchants realizing this often permit a serviceman to become indebted to them beyond his ability to repay, and then try to use the military as a collection agency.

because of the economic loss to the victim, as well as crimes against performance in terms of the discredit they may being on the armed services (this will be discussed in more detail later in the chapter). The serviceman, having had practically all of his affairs managed for him by the military establishment, is often a poor manager of his financial resources and dealings, in addition to being relatively low paid. Economic problems sometimes resulting in excessive and unpaid debts, bad checks, and poor credit management have long been endemic to the enlisted ranks.

CRIMES AGAINST PERSON

In view of the makeup of the military population and in the face of the military mission, the armed services must effect a rigid system of social control over its members and their behavior. This is especially necessary in regard to deviant acts, particularly crimes against person committed against U.S. and foreign friendly civilian populations, if popular support and community approval for the military is to be maintained. If a serviceman commits an offense against civilian law, the military leaves no stone unturned in trying to obtain jurisdiction over the offender. The motivation is twofold. First, the military wishes to maintain its authoritarian presence, and allowing the civilian authorities to assume jurisdiction over a serviceman would erode that authority and violate boundary maintenance. The military attempts to preserve the image of a system beyond the influence and control of a civilian society. (This farce is, of course, incongruous in a democratic nation. The military must rely on artful manipulation of the civilian society, but at the same time it likes to preserve the myth of military power.) Second, by moving quickly to sanction servicemen who violate civilian norms, the military can avoid the angry wrath of civilian society and hope that it can maintain public support.

When I was in the military, many of the men in my company patronized a particular laundry near the post. The owner of the laundry would loan the men money in the last week or two before payday and then charge them exorbitant interest (as high as 25 percent for two weeks). To disguise his loan-sharking activities, he would make them sign credit slips for laundry as if they owed a laundry bill. When they could not repay the loans on time, he would come to me and insist that I threaten them with court-martial for not paying their lawful debts. Only when I threatened to have the post commanding general declare his laundry off limits to servicemen did he finally desist in his economic exploitation of my men.

Given the large concentration of unattached males in military installations in the proximity of civilian populations, some subcultural cleavage and attendant antagonism is perhaps inevitable. Fights and brawls in bars and taverns between military personnel and civilians are not infrequent (not to mention altercations between servicemen of different branches of the armed forces). The racial factor in some areas has no doubt been a contributing factor, as has been the equally inevitable competition for the pool of available females.

Servicemen have been known (as have other groups of young unattached males) to become predators, and to go out on expeditions seeking drunks and "queers" to roll for "fun and profit." Perhaps an anticipated problem area is sexual aggression toward females. If, as some researchers have pointed out (Kirkpatrick and Kanin 1957), there is a significant amount of male sex aggression on college campuses, there is reason to believe that similar behavior occurs with even more frequency among unattached military men. Such behavior ranges from simple offensive behavior in public in attempting to "pick up broads," through physical assaults and attempted rapes, to actual rapes and mayhem or sex-related murder.[6] Young males cut off from traditional informal controls, bolstered by a masculine and aggressive military subculture, and faced with a situation of relative unavailability and inaccessibility of females are prime candidates for sexual crimes against person.[7] Even prostitutes do not fill the void or evade being victimized, inasmuch as servicemen may on occasion refuse to pay and assault the girl if she protests.

CRIMES AGAINST PERFORMANCE

As the old saying goes, an army does "travel on its stomach." It exists, however, primarily on its image. This image may include its

[6] As a Military Police duty officer, some of the most frequent complaints with which I had to deal involved sexual offenses committed by servicemen against civilian females. Typical incidents that I recall include soldiers exposing their genitals to carhops in drive-in restaurants, molesting women in bars, and throwing a girl who "wouldn't put out" from a speeding automobile.

[7] Rape and other sexual offenses committed by military personnel against U.S. civilians have been a historical problem. It is recorded in George Washington's papers, for example, that on July 22, 1780, Thomas Brown of the Seventh Pennsylvania Regiment was sentenced to death for rape (Brownmiller 1975:31). It was apparently his second conviction for rape.

combat aggressiveness, morale, resourcefulness, loyalty, or rigid discipline. Discipline and loyalty, if not the other attributes, are often best exemplified, and best tested, by the circumspect behavior with which military personnel comport themselves in civilian settings. Accordingly, most military systems undertake to prescribe appropriate behavior in such settings, and violations of the formal expectations constitute crimes against performance.

In an effort to win public support and approval for the armed services, the military is particularly strict about public deportment of servicemen in this country (and in allied countries where American servicemen are stationed). Military regulations dictate appropriate norms of dress, conduct, and transactions with civilians. Military personnel are constrained to wear the appropriate uniform for particular occasions, to insure that the uniform is clean, well fitted, and worn correctly (no buttons unfastened, and so on), and to strive always for an image of decorum and military bearing. Fighting or brawling in public, drunkenness, vehicular violations, or any type of disorder or conduct that would bring discredit to the armed forces are sanctioned. Military personnel may, on occasion, need to let loose or let off steam, and soldiers on pass or sailors on liberty have a reputation for getting involved in disturbances and disorder. In spite of this propensity (or because of it), there are formal proscriptions that severely sanction such behavior.[8]

As mentioned earlier in the discussion, defaulting on debts or issuing worthless checks are considered by the military to be crimes against performance as well as crimes against property. Such behavior, it is felt, creates a bad image of the individual and thus the military. Offenses of this kind erode public confidence and trust in the military, and accordingly bring discredit to the services. Even a spouse or offspring engaging in such behavior may cause the husband in the military to be sanctioned.[9]

[8] Even though military regulations clearly prohibit public drunkenness and brawling, there have been instances where commanders might tacitly encourage a modest degree of brawling as a means of instilling aggressiveness and unit pride, as noted earlier.

[9] I know of one instance where the mother of the young wife of an army officer of my acquaintance gave her a monthly gift of a few dollars to help the young couple financially. On the first of each month, the mother would deposit the money in the wife's hometown bank account. In anticipation of this, and secure in the knowledge that an out-of-town check requires several days to clear, the wife was in the habit of writing checks against her hometown account several days before the first, even if there was no money in the account at the time. By the time the

In a similar connection, the military also becomes distressed over its personnel becoming involved in public scandals that erode the military image of integrity. The astronauts and their various clandestine profit-making activities were an example of such a scandal.

The military also discourages the involvement of military personnel with civilians of unsavory character, such as gamblers and prostitutes or women with a public reputation or loose morals. Accordingly, involvement in activities such as gambling or frequenting places where there is a likelihood of encountering unsavory individuals is also discouraged or prohibited. Such places may be placed off limits as being unsuitable for servicemen. Going to an off limits area or establishment is itself a sanctionable offense. Thus the military seeks to keep its personnel from being "tainted" by association and thereby cause the image and reputation of the military to be publicly sullied.

Foreign Friendly Civilian System

The presence of American troops in foreign friendly countries often generates the same welcome economic input and creates the same apprehensive concerns as their presence in this country. The military is usually equally anxious to maintain good relations with allies and avoid international incidents. Accordingly, observation and control of personnel by military authorities is often as pronounced, if not more so, as in this country. Being an alien, and a military alien at that, places the individual in a decidedly disadvantageous position in terms of the opportunity to commit crimes against property, such as theft or fraud, and, to a slightly lesser degree, crimes against person, inasmuch as the serviceman is more

---

check got to her hometown bank, her mother had deposited the money. On one occasion, however, she wrote such an out-of-town check in a store several days before the end of the month and asked the clerk if she could postdate the check to the first of the month. The clerk refused and the wife went ahead and wrote the check with that day's date. The clerk became suspicious and called the wife's hometown bank, which reported that her balance was insufficient to cover the check as of that day. The store viewed the incident as an attempt to pass an insufficient funds check, and notified the army post where the wife's husband was stationed. The husband was subsequently called before his commanding officer and given a verbal reprimand because of his wife's crime against performance.

conspicuous, is observed more closely, and has less opportunity for interaction with civilians. In spite of a diminished opportunity structure, crime committed by servicemen while stationed in other countries seems to have been on the rise in recent years. In 1970, for example, all crime in the United States climbed 10 percent over 1969, but during the same period crime among American GI's stationed in Europe went up 24 percent (*Newsweek* 1971:13). An allied army stationed in a foreign friendly country is, in effect, a guest in that land and can readily wear out its welcome, as it were. It is accordingly incumbent on the military to control the behavior of its personnel vis-à-vis the civilian population so as to minimize frictions and antagonisms. The problem of a military stationed or operating in a foreign friendly country is not unlike the problem of a guerrilla army needing to maintain tolerant, if not supportive, attitudes on the part of the civilian population. In this regard, the Chinese guerrilla general, Chu Tek, admonished in 1928 (quoted in Brownmiller 1975:91):

> Take not even a needle or thread from the people . . . return all straw on which you sleep before leaving a house; speak courteously to the people and help them whenever possible; return all borrowed articles; pay for everything damaged; be honest in all business transactions; be sanitary—dig latrines a safe distance from homes and fill them up with earth before leaving; never molest women; do not mistreat prisoners.

Members of the military are seldom so circumspect and diplomatic in their behavior toward friendly civilian populations. Crimes and offenses against friendly civilians are not infrequent.

CRIMES AGAINST PROPERTY

It is true that the opportunity structure for members of the military in a foreign friendly country to commit elaborate economic offenses such as embezzlement and grand theft is greatly diminished, but there are specific opportunities for minor crimes against property. Sometimes such offenses take the form of sport or "fun." When the U.S./Canadian First Special Service Force traveled by train across part of French North Africa during World War II, for example, they would cheat the local Arabs at every stop. As the train halted at various stations along the route, a number of men in the unit would sell their boots to Arabs who wanted to bargain. After they had sold their boots and were about to leave, the unit's MP's would retrieve the boots from the Arabs and return them to the sellers (Adleman and Walton 1966:114). Another trick used by members of this unit to swindle local Arabs was to offer to sell mattress covers (which could easily be made into clothing) to Arabs running alongside the train. When the train slowed to a crawl the men would hand the mattress covers out the windows to the Arabs and take their money. The men had heavy strings tied to the mattress covers and, after the sale, would simply yank the covers away and "reel them back in," reselling them at various stops further along the route (Adleman and Walton 1966:115).

Later in the war, the men of this same unit were still up to their old tricks of cheating the friendly civilian population. At one point, some of the men occupied a civilian villa in France. The men hired a local French electrician to repair the wiring in the villa, but when the civilian electrician submitted his bill they simply signed it and told him to send it to MacKenzie King (the prime minister of Canada). The Frenchman never got paid (Adleman and Walton 1966:236). In another incident, men of this unit were traveling by train in Europe and were cold. When the train stopped temporarily at a station, the men contrived to steal a hot wood stove from the trainmaster's shack and install it on their train. How they accomplished this feat is still a matter of conjecture. About this same time they also stole a bus to transport them in their advance through France (Adleman and Walton 1966:236).

When this same unit was in Italy they had occasion to bivouac close to the pope's summer residence near Albano.[10] Some of the men helped themselves to the contents of the papal residence, and soon the pope's furniture and statuary added a decorative touch to their bivouac area. Many of the men lined their sleeping bags with sheets "adorned by a papal crest." It required a general shakedown to recover the stolen items and return them to Vatican authorities (Adleman and Walton 1966:220).

Although many of the exploits of the First Special Service Force have the ring of mischievous college pranks, they were simply

[10] It is technically true that Italy was an enemy during World War II, but after the surrender of Italy, the civilian population was treated as a friendly civilian population more than as an occupied enemy civilian population, so this incident is included in this section rather than the next. In any event, the Vatican and all of its external territories were always a friendly, albeit neutral, nation.

looters on many occasions, even to the extent of looting from allied civilians. In one instance, in the campaign in southern France, a local French physician was treating some wounded members of the force while a platoon of the force holed up around the doctor's house. While the doctor and his wife were giving wine and brandy to some of the men, others were looting the house. When the platoon leader heard about the theft, he assembled his platoon, told them what had happened, and suggested that if the stolen goods were returned, no charges would be filed. The stolen goods turned up, the doctor and his wife were pleased, but the platoon leader mused that he hoped "that it wasn't restolen" as they left (Adleman and Walton 1966:234).

The First Special Service Force may have been a livelier unit than some, but certainly it was no significant exception. Members of the military in all wars (and in peacetime) and of all countries, not just the United States, have committed property crimes against friendly civilian populations, even if the theft was only that of a chicken or some foodstuffs. Although normally "foraging" or seeking supplies and foodstuffs is directed at an enemy civilian population and land, it sometimes encompasses stealing or extorting from a friendly civilian population. During the Civil War, for example, troops from both the Union and the Confederacy were sometimes motivated to steal foodstuffs from the local friendly civilians. The governor of North Carolina, Zebulon Vance, once wrote to the Confederate secretary of war and complained (*American Heritage* 1960:373): "If God Almighty had yet in store another plague worse than all the others, I am sure it must have been a regiment or so of half-armed half-disciplined confederate cavalry."

In Vietnam, U.S. troops on patrols and especially on "search and destroy" missions would go through peasant villages and routinely shoot livestock, destroy gardens and banana trees, burn down hootches and buildings, and even urinate on the sliced vegetables the peasants placed in front of their huts to dry (Vietnamese Veterans Against the War 1972:27).[11] The ARVN troops passing through peasant villages would not infrequently help themselves to a chicken (Schell 1967:65).

[11] There are probably no absolute exceptions to this generalization, but in some instances the friendly civilian population was so wretchedly poor that there was little for members of the military to steal. Such was apparently the case in Vietnam. As Brownmiller (1975:98) observed, "Raping and looting go hand in hand in warfare but there was little to loot in the villages of South Vietnam."

As even Victoria's soldiers knew, however, there may be more to loot than

Vandalism and destruction of property as a residual product of altercations with foreign nationals are usually increased because of hostile rivalry, not infrequently involving disputes and jealousies concerning local females and American troops and their spending habits. American troops often violate currency and exchange laws of the country involved, inasmuch as this is one of the few economic crimes of which the commission is encouraged and facilitated by their occupational circumstances. In some instances, American troops abroad may be subject only to the laws and regulations of the U.S. military, but more frequently today troops stationed in most friendly nations are subject to a "status of forces" agreement, and therefore subject to foreign civilian laws as well as U.S. military law.

CRIMES AGAINST PERSON

The problem of physical violence committed by servicemen against foreign friendly civilian populations is similar to that of violent crime against U.S. civilians. However, the strain of being in alien surroundings, especially in a combat or near-combat area, tends to compound the situation. The mechanisms of both formal and informal control may be weakened and the cultural division may tend to heighten antagonism. The stresses and dissaffections of foreign garrison duty or erratic combat involvement may prove frustrating beyond the tolerance level and result in physical violence directed toward members of the indigenous population.

The military system is large, rigid, and ponderous. As a means of effecting efficiency, some degree of norm violation is occasionally tolerated and even tacitly encouraged, although it must never come to public attention. In a similar vein, considering the mission of the military and the tasks expected of its members, a major problem is maintaining morale, neutralizing frustration and anxiety among the troops, and motivating personnel to channel aggressive goals. Accomplishment of this also requires some relaxation of the

---

first meets the eye, especially if one is persistent and persuasive in dealing with the natives. As Kipling immortalized it (1940:407–409):
"Now remember when you're 'acking round a gilded Burma god
  That 'is eyes is very often precious stones;
An' if you treat a nigger to a dose o'cleaning-rod
  'E's like to show you everything 'e owns."

strict and pervasive norms that govern military life. The troops may have to "let off steam" as a discipline safety value and to do so may mean letting them "beat hell out of some 'slopes.' " As Elkin (1946:409) described the servicemen of World War II:

> One aspect of this negativism, whose ill-effect on international relations will remain incalculable, is that our immediate allies became the primary scapegoat for the G.I.'s need for self-assertion. Just as the Germans, servile and compliant in their own life, came to feel strong and important by venting their pent-up aggression on "inferior" Jews, Poles, and Russians, so the G.I. "took it out" on "damned Limeys" and "dirty frogs," but *not*, interestingly, on the Germans and southern Italians who directly gratified his self-esteem by behaving toward him as a conqueror. A correspondent from China recently wrote that G.I. drivers go out of their way to splash mud on Chinese trudging along the side of the road!

Presumably, in earlier wars, members of our military would engage in some aggressive and competitive brawling and scrapping with allied troops, and no doubt with some of the allied civilians, perhaps in arguments about women or of some ethnocentric persuasion. Members of the military of other nations also undoubtedly became involved in altercations with their allied troops and civilians. In World War II the Germans took a jaundiced view of most of their allies, including the Romanians, the Hungarians, and especially the Italians, and there were incidents of German troops becoming embroiled in fights with and assaults on their own allied troops and civilians. Nothing, however, quite equaled the viciousness and endemic nature of the crimes against persons of the U.S. servicemen and their acts of violence and brutality directed at South Vietnamese civilians, even those not suspected of being Vietcong sympathizers or spies.

The range of violent offenses and depth of brutality directed toward South Vietnamese civilians is too detailed and convoluted to discuss comprehensively, but some selected illustrations may suffice to make the point. One white American soldier in Vietnam, for example, was riding in the back of a truck traveling between two bases when the truck passed some Vietnamese civilians on bicycles. The soldier wanted a Vietnamese hat to send home as a souvenir, so he extended his rifle from the truck to try to knock one off the head of a bicycler. Instead he fractured the skull of the rider. In this instance he was court-martialed, convicted of aggravated assault, and subsequently sentenced to a dishonorable discharge (suspended) and five years in prison (reduced to 11 months by the reviewing commanding general) (Kroll 1976:58). In some cases American servicemen would simply use Vietnamese peasant civilians for target practice as they moved through the countryside or through villages searching for the Vietcong (Vietnam Veterans Against the War 1972:43). The U.S. soldiers would sometimes shoot at civilian children who approached a military bivouac in order to beg C-rations or to scavenge (Vietnamese Veterans Against the War 1972:83). Sometimes they would throw phosphorus grenades into civilian bunkers (Vietnam Veterans Against the War 1972:84). One U.S. Marine reported that when he and some other men would haul their company's garbage to the dump, a number of Vietnamese civilians would jump on the truck and try to scavenge through the garbage. The Americans would beat them with their rifle butts and "just kick their ass all the way across the garbage dump." The same marine told of American troops taking a stock of canned foods with them as they rode in the back of a truck and, as children walking or riding bicycles alongside begged for food, throwing the heavy cans of food at the children and trying to hit their heads or knock them off their bicycles. Sometimes they would light heat tabs and drop them into the children's out-stretched hands (Vietnam Veterans Against the War 1972:91–92). When civilians suspected of being Vietcong or spies were inter-rogated, they were routinely tortured. One sergeant reported that one suspect was "held down under an APC [armored personnel carrier] and he was run over twice—the first time didn't kill him" (Vietnam Veterans Against the War 1972:43).

In another instance, a civilian suspect was staked out on the ground, cut open, and part of his insides pulled out in an effort to make him talk (Vietnam Veterans Against the War 1972:13). One soldier told of a civilian prisoner being interrogated by being tied up and hung from a tree. A string was tied around his testicles and when he did not give a suitable answer the interrogator would yank on the string, causing excruciating pain to the prisoner. He also mentioned having seen civilian prisoners with their ears sliced through with a knife, wounds carved on their bodies, and their penises burned with cigarettes (Vietnam Veterans Against the War 1972:11).

A soldier from the 101st Airborne Division reported that men of his unit had wounded and killed some women and children when they were going through a village. The next day, while the villagers were trying to conduct a burial ceremony, the soldiers on a nearby hill fired on them, killing still another person. The villagers simply rolled him in the hole with the other dead bodies and covered him up. The same day some of the U.S. troops came across two little boys playing on a dike and shot and killed both of them (Vietnam Veterans Against the War 1972:9). Sometimes U.S. troops would find a civilian in the woods and, to amuse themselves, fire close to him, forcing him to run back and forth dodging bullets. When they became bored of the game, they would kill him (Vietnam Veterans Against the War 1972:99).

U.S. troops apparently brutalized, wounded, or killed South Vietnamese civilians with great frequency and with no provocation. Some soldiers might shoot a civilian, man, woman, or child, with the casualness with which they might step on an insect. Helicopter gunships might routinely fire at any person seen moving on the ground. As mentioned earlier, some U.S. helicopter pilots who described their strafing of civilians suspected of being "guerrillas" spoke of "rabbit shoots," "barbecuing" peasants, and "hosing" a suspect with machine gun fire until he "blows up like a toy balloon" (Slater 1970:38–39). One officer told about a man and a woman who were machine-gunned from a helicopter while they were *having a picnic* (Schell 1967:60). Brutality visited on the civilian population seemed to become a matter of indifference.

As brutal as the treatment of supposedly allied or friendly civilians was in Vietnam, few acts of war directed toward an allied civilian population exceed the Ardeatine massacre in inhuman and criminal enormity (see Katz 1973). During World War II, a column of 156 SS police was attacked in German-occupied Rome by a band of sixteen Italian partisans. Some 33 of the Germans were killed and others were wounded. When Hitler heard about the attack, he ordered that Italian hostages be taken and executed on a ten to one basis. Hundreds of Italian civilians were rounded up, transported to the tunnels of the ancient Christian catacombs on Via Ardeatina. There 335 were summarily executed and the entrances to the caves were blown up and sealed. Ultimately, the Allies occupied Rome and the mass grave was found. Some of the perpetrators were subsequently tried and punished as war criminals.

As common among U.S. troops in Vietnam as the torturing, wounding, and killing of civilians was the raping of civilian females. In sweeps through villages U.S. troops would sometimes reach out and rip some or all of the clothes off a female, just for a laugh. Sometimes an individual or even a whole squad might seize a villager and rape her, perhaps even in front of her family. Often rape was rationalized by labeling the female as a "Vietcong whore." One GI informant told of an incident in which a Vietnamese female caught in a sweep of a hamlet was raped by an entire platoon. The whole platoon "caught her ass," as the soldier put it; "They all raped her . . . tore her up" (quoted in Brownmiller 1975:105). The woman later managed to escape and the rumor circulated that she was a North Vietnamese army nurse. The troops often had interesting ways of rationalizing and reconceptualizing rape. As one GI described it (Vietnam Veterans Against the War, 1972:12):

> When we went through the villages and searched people the women would have all their clothes taken off and the men would use their penises to probe them to make sure they didn't have anything hidden anywhere. And this was raping but it was done as searching.

It is difficult to accurately assess with any accuracy the true numerical incidence of rape in the Vietnamese war. According to Brownmiller (1975:98–101), the U.S. army reports a total of 86 individuals tried by court-martial for rape or various rape-type charges (i.e., attempted rape, sodomy, statutory rape), and 50 convicted between the period January 1, 1965, and January 31, 1973. Within these figures there were 24 convictions for rape and 4 convictions for assault with intent to commit rape. By contrast, during the period May 31, 1951, to May 30, 1953 (the Korean War), army records reveal that 23 persons were convicted for rape, and 9 were convicted for assault with attempt to commit rape. The peak U.S. troop strength in Korea was 394,000, while in Vietnam it reached as high as 543,400. Thus from court-martial conviction records it appears that there were slightly more convictions for rape-related charges during this two-year period of the Korean War than in eight years of the Vietnamese War. There is little reason to believe that the rape rate for soldiers was higher in Korea than in Vietnam. Rather, it is likely that in Vietnam the "investigatory and court-martial procedures for rape-related charges" were simply more lax (Brownmiller 1975:99). In civilian life the arrest and conviction rate for rape is a very small fraction of the estimated actual incidence of rape. Within the context of a military population, a war, and a civilian population that "knew no English, [and] had little or no recourse to the law" (Brownmiller 1975:101), the actual incidence of rape must have been enormous compared with the reported conviction rate.

Rape simply became a relatively routine activity with many U.S. military units, especially out in the rural areas, where the troops were going on patrols and making sweeps through peasant villages. In the view of CBS correspondent Dan Rather (quoted in Brownmiller 1975:92):

> Everywhere you looked there was a horror and a brutality. Rape may have been mentioned to me several dozen times while I was in Vietnam. When you see women crying, and you see that universal look of bitterness and anger, you find out about rape. My own limited experience led me to conclude that everybody who passed through a village did it—steal a chicken and grab a quick piece of ass, that sort of thing.

Rape in Vietnam was not infrequently followed by the murder of the victim. One GI told of being with three other soldiers in a field of elephant grass on a patrol in Vietnam and coming across four Vietnamese females whom they subsequently raped and killed. As the soldier describes it (Brownmiller 1975:107):

> We balled these chicks. They were forcibly willing—they'd rather do that then get shot. Then one of the girls yelled some derogatory thing at the guy who'd balled her. . . . He just reached down for his weapon and blew her away. Well, right away the three other guys, including myself, picked up our weapons and blew away the other three chicks. Just like that. . . .

A marine sergeant told of a squad of nine men that went into Chu Lai seeking a "Vietcong whore." They found her and, rather than simply capture her, they raped her. All of the men in the squad raped the woman except the sergeant, who apparently didn't have the stomach for it. He just went to the other side of the village and waited. As the informant related it, "But at any rate, they raped the girl, and then, the last man to make love to her, shot her in the head" (Vietnam Veterans Against the War 1972:29). Rape, even followed by the murder of the victim, became something of a casual diversion, or entertainment in passing. It was reported, for example, that a peasant woman, working in a field with her baby nearby, was seized, gang-raped, and murdered by a group of GI's. While this was going on, one of the participants photographed it step by step with his Instamatic camera (Brownmiller 1975:103).

In some instances, U.S. military personnel acted with a sadistic zeal toward Vietnamese civilians, moving beyond mere brutalism. One marine told of a civilian female who was shot by a sniper in his unit. When the marines approached the wounded woman she was asking for water. The lieutenant in charge said to kill her. As the marine described it (Vietnam Veterans Against the War 1972:14):

> So he ripped off her clothes, they stabbed her in both breasts, they spread-eagled her and shoved an E tool up her vagina, an entrenching tool, and she was still asking for water. And they took that out and they used a tree limb and then she was shot.

A helicopter door gunner told of spotting a woman's body on the ground below while flying a routine patrol. The pilot flew down for a closer look. As the soldier put it (quoted in Brownmiller, 1975:105), "She was spread-eagled, as if on display. She had an 11th Brigade patch between her legs—as if it were some type of display, some badge of honor."

A GI from the Americal Division told of seeing the interrogation of a civilian female whose pubic hair was set on fire (Vietnam Veterans Against the War, 1972:118). Even mutilation of civilian bodies was practiced on occasion. One marine told of a civilian female who was rounded up and because she had bandages she was assumed to be a Viet Cong suspect. She was questioned, shot about 20 times, then her body was slit open from "her vagina almost all the way up, just about up to her breasts," and her internal organs were pulled out and thrown away. Finally all of her skin was peeled off and she was left as a "sign for something or other."

Violence directed toward Vietnamese civilians by U.S. military personnel had a decided racial dimension. Studies of the incidence and type of crime committed by servicemen in Vietnam (Kroll 1976:53) underscores this racial element. The incarceration rate of black servicemen in Vietnam was from two to nine times higher than that of white soldiers, depending on the type of crime (except for violent offenses against Vietnamese nationals, in which there was no significant difference). The black servicemen were more prone to direct their violent offenses toward other members of the military, such as officers and noncommissioned officers who were hated authority figures and thus symbolic of black oppression, or simply other servicemen who were white. Black servicemen apparently could identify with the Vietnamese as a nonwhite race and felt a kind of racial kinship rather than racial hostility toward them. Some black soldiers who went AWOL in Vietnam lived in native villages with Vietnamese or Cambodian families.

Some white servicemen, on the other hand, developed a near-racial hatred of the Vietnamese for whom they were fighting to save from Communist enslavement. Even the military training of the servicemen tended to exagerate or exacerbate their racial hostility. According to one infantry sergeant (Vietnam Veterans Against the War 1972:45), "You are trained, 'gook, gook, gook,' and once the military has got the idea implanted in your mind that these people are not humans, they are subhuman, it makes it a little bit easier to kill 'em. . . ." Even the members of the South Vietnamese military—the ARVN—were disliked by U.S. servicemen. The ARVN were small in stature, effeminate in behavior (according to U.S. stereotypical standards of masculinity), and, by U.S. military standards, not good fighters, and were accordingly characterized by U.S. GI's as "faggots" or homosexuals, and treated accordingly (Levy 1971).

The fact that the enemy and the allies were both Vietnamese and thus "gooks" was unfortunate for the allies. As part of the racial inferiority ideology there was also the concept of the oriental mentality and perspective being different. One officer, for example indicated that "Only the fear of force gets results. It's the Asian mind. It's completely different from what we know as the Western mind, and it's hard for us to understand." (Schell 1967:56).

Thus, as subhumans who only understood force, the Vietnamese could be treated accordingly. The Vietnam War was frustrating because it was a guerrilla war, and the Americans were not used to guerrilla wars or prepared to fight them. The enemy was often unseen when he struck, and many U.S. casualties were from mines and booby traps. The enemy would only occasionally come out into the open for fire-fights and battles. In addition, the enemy and the allies looked alike. The U.S. serviceman therefore tended to take out his frustrations on the Vietnamese civilians, his allies, with both overt brutality and an insensitivity to human suffering. One officer, when asked if civilians were not occasionally killed in the bombings, replied, "What does it matter? They're all Vietnamese" (Schell 1967:104). As the war moved on and the "free fire zones" permitted the soldiers to shoot and kill anything that moved, the pressure for higher "body counts" made it a point of indifference whether one shot and killed a civilian or a Vietcong. In way of illustration, a warrant officer was instructed in how to tell a Vietcong from a civilian (Vietnam Veterans Against the War 1972:74). If the person sighted on the ground "were running, they were Viet Cong. If they were standing there, they were well-disciplined Viet Cong, and shoot 'em anyhow." In this same vein, some popular slogans were "If its human, dead, and not white, it's Vietcong," and "M.G.R.—the mere gook rule."

The enormity of the crimes committed against enemy troops and allied civilians in Vietnam was such that an enormous literature has emerged to document the offenses, and to address crimes of war in general. A few interesting references will serve as examples. Lane (1970) interviewed both military veterans and deserters from Vietnam concerning their experiences in training and in combat. Emerson (1972) has written a detailed journalistic account of the Vietnam War, the era, and its participants, including offenses against civilians. Other similar expositions include McGrady's (1968) observations on the war, and Lifton's (1973) account of the Vietnam veterans and their "search for reconnection and continuity." More general treatments of war crimes, including those in Vietnam, include Knoll and McFadden (1970), and Falk, Kolko, and Lifton (1971). Some particularly critical treatments of the war were "Two, Three—Many Vietnams" (*Ramparts* 1971) and *Nuremburg and Vietnam: An American Tragedy* (Taylor: 1971).

Many of the offenses against Vietnamese civilians committed by members of the U.S. military were individual, or involved small groups of servicemen, and were often impulsive or spontaneous. Most important, they were in violation of military regulation and international law. Regardless of the laxity of enforcement and sanction, they still represented extra-occupational crimes against person. In other instances, however, there were some broad-scale activities that had their origin in military strategic and tactical policy, were implemented by the larger military entity against Vietnamese civilians, and had the effect of victimizing the civilians. Although such activities were approved by military authorities as being necessary expedients, and clearly were recognized as posing residual hardships for the civilians, they were not viewed as offenses against the civilians, although many critics both here and abroad did label such activities as "war crimes." One such activity was the vast effort to defoliate large areas of the countryside as a means of denying concealment to the Vietcong. Agent orange and other highly toxic chemicals were sprayed over tens of thousands of acres of land, with the result that significant forest areas were destroyed, some farm land was rendered unproductive or useless, some livestock was sickened or killed, and fish in the canals and rice fields died, depriving the Vietnamese peasants of an important source of food. The natural plant and animal ecology of large areas of Vietnam was effectively altered, and in some areas, such as those in which a "lunarization" program was implemented, destroyed (60-ton bulldozers would simply level a forested area and reduce it to a lunar-like landscape [Lewallen 1971:104]). There has been some suggestion that the defoliant agents dropped on Vietnam may even cause genetic defects in the Vietnamese people over a period of time.

Another military policy that has been criticized as constituting an offense against Vietnamese civilians was the resettlement program. Where the military could not deal effectively with the guerrilla activity in a given area, it would forcibly remove and resettle all of the peasants living there to another part of the country. The villages could then be destroyed and the area declared a "free fire zone"; presumably, anybody still there would be Vietcong. The relocation of peasant villages also meant that the Vietcong could be deprived of sympathizers and some food and supplies that they normally obtained from the peasants. For the peasants, however, it meant giving up their land, their crops, their houses, and in some instances their livestock and belongings. The former villagers became, in effect, refugees resettled in concentration camps in "secure" areas where they could be watched, where they lived in tents and huts behind barbed wire and sometimes received only a few piastres a day with which to buy rice, if it was available. There were approximately two million such refugees.

Of all the various mistreatments, offenses, crimes, or attrocities committed against Vietnamese civilians who were supposed to be allies, none exemplify the general posture toward civilians in the Vietnam War more than the incidents of the squad patrol near Cat Tuong in the Central Highlands and the subsequent rape murder of a young female, and the My Lai 4 massacre.

In the Cat Tuong incident a squad of five infantrymen was assigned to undertake a reconnaissance patrol of several days duration, to comb a section of the Central Highlands, and look for signs of Vietcong activity. The sergeant in charge of the patrol told the men before starting out that "he was going to see to it that they found themselves a girl and took her along 'for the morale of the squad.' " The sergeant indicated that they would use the girl for "boom boom" or sexual intercourse while on patrol and would dispose of her before returning so that she could not accuse them of abduction and rape (Lang 1969:25–26). Before the men struck out on patrol they took time to go to the hamlet of Cat Tuong, where they found Phan Thi Mao, a young female of 20, who apparently suited their purposes. They tied her hands behind her and marched her off at gunpoint. Her mother ran after them to give them Mao's scarf. Rather than putting it around the girl's neck, however, they stuffed it in her mouth to gag her. Later they found an abandoned hut that they used as a command post, where four of the five men raped her. One refused to participate. The girl was apparently ill and by the next day, as the men continued their patrol activity with her in tow, her condition had worsened. When they heard helicopter gunships approaching they decided to go ahead and kill her. One of the men dragged her behind a bush and stabbed her, but she managed to crawl away. Several of the men then shot and killed her. The girl had a gold tooth, and one of the men asked if anyone wanted it. When they got close to the girl, however, her head was partially blown away. The sergeant reported by radio to his platoon leader, "One V.C., K.I.A."

The reluctant member of the partol who had not participated in the rape reported the incident to his platoon leader when he returned from patrol and, after a difficult time in getting the authorities to act, testified against the other men at their court-martial. The four men were convicted, the heaviest sentence being dishonorable discharge and life imprisonment (although this was later cut to eight years after review), with the others receiving various prison sentences and dishonorable discharges. In time one of the men on appeal was retried and acquitted, while the sentences of the other three ultimately were reduced considerably.

The epitome of the treatment of civilians in the Vietnam, however, was the My Lai 4 episode, which has been thoroughly documented (see, for example, Hersh 1970, 1972). My Lai was to have been a relatively simple military mission. For some time, members of the American Division had been encountering mines, booby traps, and snipers in the area around the village of My Lai.

It was believed that the crack 48th Vietcong Battalion was encamped in the vicinity of the village. Task Force Barker was formed from elements of the Eleventh Brigade of the Americal Division to attack the village complex. Charlie Company, commanded by Capt. Ernest Medina, was to go into My Lai, and the first platoon of the company, led by Lt. William L. Calley, Jr., was to enter the village first, from the south. The platoon was ferried in by helicopter and began their attack. They encountered no Vietcong, only civilians—mostly women, children, and old men. Lieutenant Calley and many of his men (often under orders from Calley) simply redefined the civilians as enemy and shot them down. Civilians were, in some instances, gathered up, pushed in a ditch in piles, and murdered. Some men killed spontaneously, while others were alleged to have been ordered by Calley to "waste 'em" or "take care of them." Civilians were beaten and brutalized, and some of the younger women and girls were raped and then murdered. It was officially reported at the time that 128 Vietcong were killed. It was later estimated (Hersh 1972:7), however, that 347 Vietnamese men, women, and children were slain.

My Lai has been accurately described as a "massacre." Incredibly, the incident was successfully covered up by various individuals in the chain of command for almost a year and a half (see Hersh 1972). Ultimately it became front-page news, precipitated a Department of the Army investigation, and was to lead to the recommendation that court-martialed charges be filed against 15 persons. Only two, however, ever faced court-martial—the brigade commander, who was tried and found not guilty, and Lieutenant Calley, who was found guilty and sentenced to life imprisonment. Lieutenant Calley had become the symbolic defendant for My Lai. Interestingly, he had very broad-based public support, including some critics of the war who felt that My Lai was not an unusual incident, and that Calley had become a scapegoat (see DiMona 1972; Hammer 1971; Hersh 1970). In time, after much legal maneuvering, Calley managed to escape his sentence and was discharged, a free man. My Lai, however, remains in the public's mind as one of the more infamous military crimes of all time—an extra-occupational crime against allied civilians.

My Lai, the entire Vietnam War, and the endemic crimes against Vietnamese civilians who were theoretically the allies of the U.S. military were all unusual occurrences of war. Historically, and in general, many armies have committed atrocities against conquered enemy civilians, but friendly, allied civilians were usually treated in a civilized manner. There have been a few exceptions in our history, of course. At the turn of the century, U.S. troops were fighting Filipino nationalist insurgents. Inasmuch as the United States had freed the Philippines from Spain, the citizens were theoretically our allies. As in Vietnam, the U.S. troops were frustrated by the guerrilla tactics of the insurgents. In addition, because many of the civilians were sympathetic to the insurgents, they were often uncooperative with the U.S. forces. As in Vietnam, the U.S. troops soon began using brutal methods against the Philippine civilians (see Miller 1970). Captured suspects were tortured, civilians were into "camps of instruction and sanitation," retaliatory shootings of civilians were implemented, villages were burned, and civilians were raped and shot. Again there were racial overtones, and the Filipinos were referred to comtemptously as "goo goos" and "Filipino niggers" (Miller 1970:26). After the massacre of a company of U.S. infantry on one island, the military was moved to excessive methods, including relocation of the population of the island on the coast, destruction of livestocks, crops, and villages, and the killing of men, women, and children who remained behind in what had become, in effect, a "free fire zone." Other oppressive measures were to follow. In time there were courts-martial but, as with Calley, the defendants received only minor sanctions. The military saw their actions as military expediency, but critics of such behavior, such as Teddy Roosevelt, viewed the brutal treatment of civilians as "the cruelty, treachery, and total disregard of the rules and customs of civilized warfare" (Miller 1970:28). From the standpoint of the soldier in the field, however, the friendly allied civilians simply did not act as allies were supposed to act and, as in Vietnam years later, their own attendant treatment of civilians was accordingly a justified act toward a treacherous enemy.

CRIMES AGAINST PERFORMANCE

The military's relationship to an allied civilian population is, in theory, not unlike its relationship to its own civilian population. In either case, the civilian population, in effect, suffers the presence of the military. It is to the advantage of the military, therefore, to insist on relatively circumspect behavior on the part of its members. Ideally they should present an image that inspires confidence and respect, and behave in a fashion that promotes cooperation and goodwill. Dress norms are frequently seen as very important in this respect, and are often vigorously enforced. The military is often particularly concerned about actions by its members that precipitate contempt or outrage among the civilians, such as drunkenness or uncouth or offensive behavior. Foreign friendly civilians are not to be abused or insulted, and their customs and values are not to be ridiculed or belittled. Brawling and fighting could well generate antagonisms and tensions between civilians and members of the military and, accordingly, such behaviors are frequently dealt with severely by military authorities. Altercations of this type could provide a stepping-stone to an international incident.

Competition for available allied civilian females may be keen, and the fact that members of the military may date and fornicate with civilian females may be especially irritating to the civilian population. This situation may be exacerbated if the pay of the military is higher than the prevailing civilian pay scale, or if the members of the military have access to scarce goods not normally available to the civilians. In either instance the servicemen have an unfair economic advantage in wooing and winning the local females.

Even an economic style of consumption by members of the military may invite invidious comparison by the civilian population and create envy and hostility. During World War II millions of U.S. servicemen were stationed in England, and while the English were glad to have America as an ally they were not always overjoyed to have the servicemen in their country. A popular saying of the day was that the U.S. servicemen were "overpaid, oversexed, and over here." Like members of any military, U.S. servicemen violate military norms and regulations and commit crimes against performance in regard to a friendly foreign population. They often insult and antagonize civilians and pursue their women to the point of molestation. Fighting and brawling with allied civilians is not infrequent and is sometimes overlooked and tacitly tolerated, if not encouraged, by military authorities. One writer (Weltner 1947: 83), of the World War II era for example, has observed that:

> The official army line was that the perpetual gripping and "bitching" of the average soldier was a healthy sign was belied by the fact that, quite apart from combat, some of the fury *was*

released in action—not against the army but against civilians, both here and abroad. And the fact that the army was generally indulgent of such depredations suggests an implicit recognition of the rebellion these acts expressed. Better let the men wreck dance halls, beat up civilians, and rape women than run the risk of their rebelling directly against the authority of the army.

The military usually tries diligently to prevent, or at least discourage, its members from trafficking on the black market. The black market often is severely damaging to the local allied civilian population, and servicemen may well divert badly needed military supplies into illicit civilian channels. It may also, on occasion, be a conduit for stolen civilian goods with the servicemen as an unwitting participant.[12] Black marketeering may involve a criminal element and could erode the positive image of the military. Few militaries, however, have ever been very successful at controlling the black market activities of their members, and in some instances have exerted only the feeblest efforts to do so.

Finally, the military may in some instances attempt to control or minimize the fraternization of its members with the civilian population. The military has sometimes not permitted its members to leave the camp or post in a foreign country, thus effectively forestalling interaction with civilians. In other instances, such as when the U.S. military was in Korea during the war, there have been efforts to minimize the number of marriages between American servicemen and local civilians. Permission was required to marry a foreign civilian, and marriage without such permission was a punishable offense. Obtaining permission was often a lengthy and tedious process, with the military taking the position that such a policy tended to protect the serviceman against his own immature judgment, that such marriages were not sound ones, and, perhaps most important, that marriage between U.S. servicemen and Korean females were not in the best interest of either the military or American society.[13] American servicemen, like ser-

[12] It was reported in *Life* magazine some years ago that an American GI in Korea had acquired an enormous rug of Siberian tiger skins on the black market for the equivalent of $200 (American). The rug, it turned out, had come from a royal palace in Korea and was a national treasure. The authorities ultimately tracked it down in New York City where the soldier had sent it to his family.

[13] In Korea in the early 1950s it was official army policy to discourage marriages with Korean nationals. The individual's commanding officer and chaplain would try and dissuade the serviceman. If this failed, the serviceman had to wait for a lengthy CID investigation of the girl's moral character and history before he was free to marry her. In the stateside army company that I commanded in

vicemen of all countries, have frequently found ways of evading
the rules or overcoming the obstacles and marrying their "war
bride."

Enemy Civilian Social System

In theory, an enemy population is more apt to be surrendered
(and subsequently peacefully occupied) if the enemy believe that
their peoples are safe from plunder, murder, and rapine.[14] In this
connection, and especially in recent times, it is the policy of many
militaries, in the interests of military expediency and in response to
international expectations of humane treatment, to effect a civilized and regulated posture toward conquered civilian populations.
The U.S. military has been among the strictest in its formal enforcement of regulations covering the treatment of civilian populations and property in occuped countries. However, no set of
military regulations, no matter how strict or how severely sanctioned, can effectively separate for long the victor from his spoils.
In this regard members of the U.S. military have, on many occasions, been flagrant in their violations of the rules, laws, and norms
that proscribe the various types of offense against enemy civilians.

---

those days was a young sergeant who wanted to marry a Korean girl, with
whom he had lived when he was stationed in Korea. He was forced to wait for
the investigation of the girl, however, and had been sent back to the United
States in the meanwhile. To care for the girl while they awaited permission to
marry, he had left her money and bought her a sewing machine in order that she
might earn a living as a seamstress. When the CID report on the girl came in, it
was my unpleasant duty to inform him that the report indicated that as soon as
he had left Korea, his girlfriend had sold the sewing machine and set up a
whorehouse of which she was the Madame! Permission to marry the girl was
naturally denied.

Moscos (1970:95–96) in discussing American servicemen marrying foreign
women, observes that, "In any event, whatever the circumstances of the couple's
meeting, a serviceman who decides to marry a foreign woman finds formidable
obstacles in his way." He articulates a series of ten bureaucratic steps that must
be taken by the serviceman before the marriage can take place. Moscos concludes that, "The intended purpose of this bureaucratic labyrinth is to
discourage hastily formed marriage plans."

[14] For a fuller documentation of the military and political considerations involved
in tactical and strategic surrender, see Kecskemeti (1957:esp. chap. 2). At the
end of World War II, the Germans were fearful concerning possible occupation
by the Russian armies and their troops fought to the last to hold off the Russians
as long as possible in the hopes that the allied armies would be able to occupy
their territory first.

CRIMES AGAINST PROPERTY

Although soldiers have always fought for booty and plunder, such behavior traditionally was essentially economic in motive, inasmuch as warriors received little or no remuneration other than the spoils of war. Thus vast armies frequently were raised on little more than the promise of booty. The Asiatic armed hordes fought their way across Asia and Europe for the residual economic benefits of sacking cities for loot, prisoners to enslave, and agricultural lands for foodstuffs and livestock. The king of Poland might gather an army of 10,000 Cossack horsemen with which to invade a neighboring state, and reward them simply by affording them looting privileges. The Mongals, the Huns, the Goths and Visigoths, the Arabs, the Turks, and all the various European and Eurasian armies throughout history sacked cities, looted, and plundered the civilian populations they conquered as a victorious warrior's right. The privilege of looting and plunder was not without hazard. To allow uncontrolled pillage was, in effect, to lose control of the army. In chronicling the sack of Rome in 1527, for example, Hook (1972:157–58) speaks of the dilemma of the duke of Bourbon, who led the besieging army:

> Even if all the defenses were broken through Bourbon must have been aware of one other overriding consideration; in the circumstances he would find it impossible to forbid the sack of a city which he had been promising his troops for months. But in the sixteenth century a sack meant the certain disintegration of any army and all experienced military commanders therefore went to extraordinary lengths to prevent their soldiers embarking on the systematic sacking of towns.

In addition to providing economic motivation for warriors or soldiers, looting and pillaging has served other historic functions. In some instances, looting and pillaging was permitted as a retaliatory gesture, as a means of wreaking vengeance on a conquered people, or to demoralize and thus weaken them. Whatever the reason for looting and plundering, for much of history there have been rules, laws, and customs regarding looting and prescribing what can be looted, by whom, under what circumstances, and in general rigorously circumscribing such activities. Karsten (1978), in his detailed exposition on the history of military law and its violation, points out that even in ancient times the limits of treatment of conquered people were often prescribed by custom

and norm. Moses instructed the Isralites not to cut down certain of
the enemy's fruit trees because of their importance to the economy.
In addition, attractive captive women were to be wed before they
were raped. In 400 B.C. the Athenian general Xenophon had his
men behave with moderation and refrain from plundering on their
retreat through Asia Minor (Karsten 1978:7). On several occasions
Roman troops sacked cities against the orders of their commanders.
When the commanders regained control of their troops, they
punished those chiefly at fault, had the loot returned to the victims, and offered public attonement (Karsten 1978:xiii). In the
early Muslim *jihad* (holy war) armies were contrained not to do
"unnecessary harm to fruit trees, bee hives, wells, camels, noncombatants, and religious persons and places" (Karsten 1978:9). On
into the middle ages and even until modern times there was a
customary law of warfare that addressed and prescribed the treatment of conquered peoples and their property, for reasons of
reciprocity, humanity, tradition, and practicality.

By modern times, military leaders had gained relatively complete control over the mass actions of their men and could generally
prohibit looting and pillaging on a mass scale, such as the sacking
of a city. They have been less successful in checking or even greatly
minimizing individualized looting.

Today's wars are obstensibly political in motive and the armed
forces involved are often well paid, especially the American
military. Booty and plunder have taken on more of a symbolic and
souvenir nature not unlike the practice of scalp taking among the
American Indian tribes or head hunting among various primitive
peoples. In actual practice, however, American servicemen may be
among the worst offenders in the violation of such military regulations. With their cultural preoccupation with material goods, it is
perhaps not surprising that our servicemen often were (and still
are) flagrant looters, military regulations to the contrary notwithstanding.

In World War II, especially in Europe, perhaps because of the
"better pickings," looting tended to be endemic among many combat units. From his personal observations, McCallum (1946:481),
for example, reported that:

> Basic to our way of life in a capitalistic economy is the deeply
> ingrained respect for the sanctity of private property. That at-
> titude may have been, at the least, weakened by the widespread
> looting of private property which went on not only in enemy Ger-

many but in friendly France. "How was the looting?" was the first question by a newcomer to a town that our troops had just occupied. Although looting was officially frowned upon, it had powerful group sanction, and approximately 80% of my company engaged in it in one form or another. (This looting continued for extended periods after order ostensibly had been restored.) To be an expert looter was a term of social approbation.

Regardless of the values held by the individual serviceman concerning theft prior to joining the military, the situation can be adequately redefined by both the informal peer group and at times by military authorities themselves so as to permit looting with little or no personal discomfort. American servicemen do not loot, they "liberate" or "appropriate."

Much enemy civilian property is found "abandoned" and is gathered up for use by our troops as a "military expedience." Most such property is of modest value and the original owners have, in fact, fled, leaving only items of little value behind. American troops frequently picked up household or decorative items as they passed through villages and towns.[15]

As a general rule, American military personnel in World War II found little of any real value to loot during hostilities, or else were sufficiently unknowledgeable about the value of items and property that they encountered. By the same token, years of war had depleted the amount of goods and property in the hands of enemy civilians. It was after hostilites or during the occupation period that the greatest amount of looting took place. A small number of individuals were apparently knowledgeable about valuable items and made efforts to steal particular kinds of things.[16] One such instance was the well-known World War II case of the American of-

---

[15] One newspaper account in World War II told of a GI who "found" a mirror with an ornate frame and carried it through several battles. Before each battle he would carefully bury the mirror and dig it up later, always hoping to get it back home to America as a gift to his wife. Unfortunately, the mirror was ultimately destroyed after surviving several battles safely.

[16] When in Military Police Officers School during the Korean conflict, the author studied an actual case that concerned an American army colonel in the military occupation of Japan who stole so much material during his tour of duty that it required ten 2 1/2 ton trucks to transport it all to the docks as he was preparing to leave for the states, intending to ship his loot back as "household belongings." We once met an army major who had acquired so much material in Germany that his home looked like a museum and his living room was filled with "do not touch" signs.

ficer and his WAC accomplice who attempted to steal the crown jewels of the House of Hesse. However, most efforts at looting were apparently spontaneous or done more as a lark rather than as a serious monetary exercise.[17] After hostilities there was more time to loot; one could be more systematic in locating items of value. It was usually then that the enemy population brought out of hiding such items of value as they might still retain after the fighting had stopped. In a hunting journal some years ago (Sipe 1959:139–40), a firearms collector told of a fine German drilling [three-barrel gun] that he acquired from a serviceman who had been in World War II:

> I found that he [the serviceman] had been in army in- telligence in Germany and had, one evening, learned that a wealthy German (a retired colonel who was posing as his own gamekeeper) had a beautiful gun hidden in the walls of his cot- tage. With a squad of men, this GI searched and found the Kuchenreuter [the gun]. The fortunes of war, ja?

The U.S. military, anticipating the problem of looting, established special teams of men with appropriate training and expertise who moved into enemy areas right behind the infantry for the purpose of locating and protecting known works of art, monuments, and items of artistic value. For this reason looting of items of real value was limited and most of what took place was for "souvenir" pur- poses.

With few exceptions, Korea offered rather limited oppor- tunities for looting. Similarly, the poverty of the rural peasants in Vietnam has not provided very fertile opportunities for looting civilian goods and belongings, with the exception of the acquisition of some small household items, such as an occasional transistor radio.

Looting of property from enemy civilians is perhaps the most prevalent of all military crimes. After Peking was relieved by troops from the outside world from its besiegement by the Boxers, even the well-trained troops who had held off the Boxers for so long turned their attention to looting. Men and officers of all the foreign military contingents, and even many high-ranking diplomats, were

---

[17] One informant told us that his men looted "for the fun of it," usually taking some worthless items as a kind of joke and discarding them later. He did say that he himself had looted a box of dental burrs from a German dentist's office and gave them to his own battalion dentist, who was able to put them to use.

active looters. It was reported that one Russian lieutenant general, for example, returned to his post in Russia with "ten trunks of valuables from the looted Peking palaces" (O'Connor 1973:292). Literally anything and everything of any value was stolen if the troops could find it. The looted items ranged from silver bullion to grain, from fabulous fabrics to hens, and from bronze astronomical instruments at the Peking Observatory to antique porcelain vases. In some instances the foreign military units actually took away whole pack trains and convoys of army wagons loaded with loot. President McKinley had specifically forbidden the U.S. troops to loot and they had been prohibited from taking the Forbidden City (O'Connor 1973:288–89). Some U.S. troops did manage to get in on the action, however. The military authorities made only minimal efforts to stop the pillage and rape, viewing the actions of the troops as giving the Chinese what they justly deserved. As O'Connor (1973:293) commented: "Nor was any effort made to control what many of their commanding officers regarded as a just retribution. Almost as rare was the missionary who spoke out against vengeance."

Involvement of the U.S. military in the looting of civilian goods is apparent throughout history. Ward (1952:750), in his account of the American Revolution, relates that when Nathanael Greene took command of the armies in the southern department he undertook to reestablish order among his troops. In a letter to a friend, Greene wrote that his troops had lost "all their discipline" and were "so addicted to plundering that they were a terror to the inhabitants." Presumably the troops had been plundering from Tory civilians, but they probably were also plundering from their own civilians as well. Washington's troops were in such miserable straits while wintering at Morristown that they were reduced to plunder to obtain subsistence (Ward 1952:613). Again it is to be presumed that Tory civilians were the most likely to be so victimized. When Ethen Allen and Benedict Arnold captured Fort Ticonderoga, the approximately 100 men with them behaved with "uncommon ranker," in "destroying and plundering private property, committing every enormity and paying no attention to publick service." There was a group of British and Tory civilians at Ticonderoga and the men looted their belongings along with military items and supplies (Ward 1952:69). It appears that Continental military authorities such as Washington were concerned about the looting, not so much because it constituted theft, as because of the fact that when the troops were "continually rambling about" plundering, they were away from their "quarters and encampments" and thus were "not to be able to oppose the enemy in any sudden approach" (Ward 1952:238). The British and Tory troops, it should be noted, were equally vigorous in their efforts at looting and plundering the homes and belongings of Continental civilians (Ward 1952:708, 740, 744).

It may well have been, as Winston Churchhill once observed, that "the Civil War was the last war fought between gentlemen." Even so, gentlemen on both sides looted. In that era, however, the euphemism "foraging" indicated an expediency to obtain needed supplies, while looting and pillaging was seen as senseless. In actual practice the difference became blurred. Troops from both the Union and the Confederacy would use split-rail fences from a civilian farm for firewood rather than bother to chop down trees. Not infrequently they would plunder homes while no one was there. They would steal livestock and poultry to break the monotony of their army rations. One Union soldier observed that "every hog seen is a 'wild hog' of course," and a rebel soldier commented that "fowls and pigs and eatables don't stand much chance." From a commander's standpoint, William Tecumseh Sherman, reminiscing about his march to the sea, stated that "The skill and success of the men in collecting forage was one of the features of this march" (American Heritage 1960:372–73). There was also a considerable amount of looting committed by "bummers," stragglers, deserters, men who were AWOL from their units, and nonsoldiers, all of whom "preceded, surrounded and followed" an army on the march. They were marauders, out from under anyone's control, and robbed, pillaged, looted, and burned at will (American Heritage 1960:547). Sherman's army in Georgia, perhaps because of its destructive mission, tended to attract an inordinate number of "bummers" who looted everywhere they passed. A Union lieutenant with Sherman in Georgia described one of these "bummers" loaded with, "first, a bundle of fodder for his mule; second, three hams, a sack of meal, a peck of potatoes; third, a fresh bed quilt, the old mother's coffee pot, a jug of venegar. . ." (American Heritage 1960:547). Armies sometimes simply destroyed civilian property to demoralize the enemy and weaken their ability to fight or resist. When Sherman reached the sea, he had confiscated, among other things, 40,000 bales of cotton, and estimated that his army had caused damages along the route of almost $100 million. He contended that $80 million worth of these damages were "simply waste and destruction" (*American Heritage* 1960:561).

Throughout history, no matter how well disciplined the army, members of the military are usually disposed to and preoccupied with looting from enemy civilians. Looting has sometimes taken strange forms, and operates at various levels of utility. After the Russians took Berlin and occupied part of Germany in World War II, it was not unusual to see trucks or even horsedrawn wagons headed eastward, loaded with bathtubs and toilets. Plumbing fixtures were almost impossible to obtain in Russia, and many high-ranking Russian officers looted fixtures out of German homes and transported them back to Russia for use in their own homes or future homes. Ryan (1974:22–23), in his account of the battle of Arnhem, recounts how, as discipline broke down in the German army as it retreated from Holland, the soldiers stole all sorts of transportation from the Dutch civilians, including horses, wagons, trucks, bicycles, cars, and even perambulators. All these they loaded up with loot "filched from France, Belgium and Luxembourg." The loot, Ryan says, "ranged from statuary and furniture to lingerie. In Nijmegen soldiers tried to sell sewing machines, rolls of cloth, paintings, typewriters—and one soldier even offered a parrot in a large cage." As the Germans hurriedly left, they tried to sell some of their loot, and also tried to get some of it back to Germany. Many officers tried to go home carrying their mistresses and "large quantities of champagne and brandy." Ryan mentions one Dutch woman who recalls seeing a retreating German truck carrying a large double bed in which was reclining a woman, presumably the mistress of a German officer. The German military took a dim view of such activity and stopped many such loot-laden officers at the Rhineland, where they "set up special courts-martial to deal with such cases." Looting may be the large-scale pilferage of a mass of goods or it may be simple straightforward theft of a civilian's personnel belongings. In one account of American troops in Germany in World War II, for example, a German girl is leading a young man with two artificial legs. An American lieutenant walks over to the couple as if to help. According to the author (Atwell 1958:421): "The girl turned to him gladly in entreaty, but instead of helping her, he snatched the watch from her wrist and returned to the sidewalk, holding it up to the sunlight, swaggering before a laughing audience."

CRIMES AGAINST PERSON

In wartime the civilian population of an enemy nation may sometimes suffer worse than the members of its military. When a nation is conquered it is the civilian population that may feel the wrath of the conqueror. In ancient times, a victorious military might destroy a vanquished people. Towns might be burned, crops destroyed, and the people themselves killed or enslaved. The Mongols and Tatars would sometimes behead the entire population of cities they captured and catapult the heads over the walls of the next city they besieged as a means of terrorizing the defenders. Whole populations might be ruthlessly butchered, or selective segments of the population, such as the children, might be systematically murdered. The civilian population might expect rape, mutilation, murder, enslavement, or at best physical abuse at the hands of conquering or occupying troops.[18]

The physical mistreatment of enemy civilians by a military might occur for several reasons. It might take the form of revenge for crimes committed against their own civilians. The rape and mistreatment of German civilians by the Russians when they invaded Germany in World War II was rationalized as being the repayment for what Germans had done in Russia. One German girl, for example, raped by a Soviet trooper, was told by the trooper afterward, "That's what the Germans did in Russia" (Brownmiller 1975:67). After the various foreign and U.S. diplomatic legation personnel and military were rescued from the Boxer siege at Peking, the surviving troops and the rescuing troops went on a rampage, looting, murdering, and raping Chinese civilians, often in the name of vengeance and as a "punitive" lesson. The German rescue military claimed they had been so ordered. According to O'Connor (1973:298), "they say that the Kaiser, in his farewell speech to his first contingent, told the men to act in this way. They are strictly obeying orders." The U.S. military, of course, was often quite brutal in its treatment of Indian noncombatants in the Indian "wars" of the late 1800s.[19] "The

---

[18] For a fuller discussion of atrocities against civilians committed by conquering troops in war see Karsten (1978).

[19] Perhaps the most infamous incident of an atrocity against Indian civilians was the "fight" at Wounded Knee on December 29, 1890. The "fight" has been better described as a "massacre" inasmuch as approximately 200 Indians, including men, women, and children, were killed or mortally wounded. (For a detailed

only good Indian is a dead Indian." so the saying went, and the army, in effect, embarked on a determined campaign that bordered on extermination.

During World War II, when Hitler's Panzer divisions invaded southern Russia, especially the Ukraine, the local inhabitants initially treated the invading German troops as liberators. Hitler allowed his personal biases to cloud his military judgement, however. Feelings that all Russians, even Ukrainians, were "inferior Eastern peoples," if not *"untermensch,"* he issued an infamous field order to his combat troops on the Russian front, which stated in essence that no crime committed by a soldier against a Russian civilian would be punished. German soldiers were thus free to steal, murder, and rape as they wished. Some unit commanders at various levels did try to control their men's behavior but, in general, offenses against Russian civilians were widespread and unsanctioned. Although some Ukrainians, especially various Cossack groups, did fight alongside the German army, Hitler's orders understandably stiffened Russian resistance and precipitated Russian partisan activity. In addition to the usual range of offenses and brutalities committed against civilians, the Germans in some instances had mobile vans that followed the front-line troops and gassed to death sizable numbers of Polish and Russian civilians, especially Jewish populations. Hitler's invasion of Russia cost 25 million casualties, the majority of whom were civilian (Morris 1973:55). It is perhaps, understandable that the Russians would want to retaliate with crimes against German civilians as well as the German military. The Germans were particularly brutal in their treatment of Jewish, Polish, and Russian civilians. Jewish girls were kidnapped and forced into military brothels. There were also mass beatings and rapes of Jewish females, as well as all manner of indignities. The Germans used rape as a reprisal weapon on

---

"official" version of the incident see Secretary of War 1892). Since the massacre there have been attempts to have the government pay indemnities to the heirs of those Indians killed at Wounded Knee for the crimes against person committed against their ancestors.

Considerable public attention has been focused on the Wounded Knee incident as a result of a popularized history of the various Indian "wars," entitled *Bury my Heart at Wounded Knee* (Brown 1970). The volume includes an account of the shooting at Wounded Knee, and as might be expected, portrays the Army in a somewhat more villainous light than did the nineteenth century "official" account. Brown indicated that perhaps as many as 300 Indian men, women, and children were killed by the Army troops (1970:444).

many occasions. In one such instance in France, the Germans raided a French village known to be a Maquis (resistance fighter) stronghole. The Maquis had fled and the Germans, in their frustration, carried out a mass rape of civilian females in retaliation.

When the Russians advanced into Germany and Austria at the close of World War II, the civilian population had to endure beatings, rapes, and murder at the hands of Russian military personnel. In Vienna, for example, it was reported that the invading Russian soldiers raped the majority of all women in the city between the ages of 16 and 60. The fall of Berlin and its occupation by Russian troops perhaps stands as the epitome of rapine. (For a most detailed expositon on the Russian capture of Berlin and subsequent rape of the city, see Ryan 1966). Berlin was largely a city of females, the males being away at war. The Russian soldiers simply raped as they pleased. The doors to homes and apartments were battered down and the women raped, often in front of their children or elderly relatives. Many women were gang raped, and others were raped numerous times during a single night. Not infrequently, women were murdered after they were raped. Even German women in maternity hospitals who were pregnant or had just given birth were raped by Russian soldiers. After the first wave of occupying troops passed on and the civilian routine returned to some degree of normality, the Russian soldiers still broke in almost nightly to rape women. One German women recalls that the Russians would break in and rape them in bed by the light of a flashlight. She bitterly commented, "During the day we had to work hard, and at night the Russians left us no peace" (quoted in Brownmiller 1975:69). Some Russian officers, on an individual basis, tried to control their men and stop the rapes. Few succeeded, however, and the official posture of the Soviet military was to ignore the atrocities. The Germans were simply getting what they deserved.

The French Moroccan troops in Italy during World War II had a particularly bad reputation for rape and brutal treatment of civilians (Brownmiller 1975:73). The American army in World War II was not without guilt either. In the Oise-Aisne military cemetary at Fire-en-Tardenois are the graves of 95 American soldiers hanged for the crimes of murder and/or rape against unarmed civilians (Huie 1954:8). The atrocities committed by members of a military against enemy civilians have in some instances been of such enormity that the name of the city involved has become synonymous with rape and brutality. Nanking was such a city. When the Japanese military occupied Nanking, China, in 1937, they burned, looted, destoyed, killed livestock, brutalized the population, murdered, and raped. It was estimated that there were 1,000 cases of rape a night—20,000 case in the first month of occupation. Perhaps as many as 65 percent of the females between 15 and 29 were raped (Brownmiller 1975:58). The same pattern emerges as in other wars. Females were often raped in front of their husbands and families. They were frequently gang raped and many times were mutilated or murdered after they were raped. As Brownmiller (1975:59) relates: "When a group of soldiers was finished with a captured woman, a stick was sometimes pushed up into her vagina; in some cases the woman's head was severed."

The Japanese military apparently made little or no effort to control the troops or to prevent the looting, rape, and murder, and may have tacitly encouraged such behavior. In the opinion of the Tokyo Military War Crimes tribunal the "sack of the city had been 'either secretly ordered or willfully committed' " (Brownmiller 1975:61). The Chinese people were seen as inferior and the Japanese military wanted to terrorize and crush the will of the Chinese to resist. Crimes against civilians were simply viewed as another military weapon. In World War I, when the Germans invaded Belgium, crimes against civilians were widespread, and alleged to have been tacitly tolerated, if not encouraged, by military authorities as a weapon of terrorism against Belgium. Burnings, looting, rape, and murder were common. Such atrocities triggered a propaganda campaign in England and the United States, and probably hastened our entry into the war. Later in the war, the German military authorities tightened their control over their troops, and crimes against civilians diminished dramatically.

In addition to a weapon of terrorism, the rape of enemy civilians has historically been conceptualized as a prize of war—booty, as it were. Enemy women were simply the "spoils of war," and the victorious soldiers were entitled to the spoils. When the Byzantine emperor Alexius was recruiting men for the First Crusade, he is said to have extolled the beauty of Greek women who could be raped by their conquerors (Brownmiller 1975:35).

One of the most extensive instances of the murder or rape of enemy civilians by members of a military was the Pakistani military action in Bangladesh in 1971. When East Pakistan (Bengal) declared its independence and called itself Bangladesh, a sizable number of West Pakistani troops were flown in to put down the rebellion. Over the nine-month period of the war, it has been estimated that as many as 3,000,000 persons were killed, 10,000,000 fled to India, and between 200,000 and 400,000 Bangladesh women were raped (Brownmiller 1975:80). Women were beaten, often gang raped, and sometimes forced into service in Pakistani military brothels. Most of the victims contracted veneral disease, and more than 25,000 became pregnant. Traditionally in Bengal, raped women have been ostracized. Most of the raped women had been Moslems, and by Moslem tradition, once a woman has experienced sex with another male, even if forced, no husband would stay with a wife, and no man would marry a fiancee. Thus the rape victims became castouts or pariahs, often with no home or place to turn. Those that were pregnant would bear half-Pakistani children who would probably be taller and lighter-skinned than the Bengalis, and would thus never be accepted. The Bangladesh government tried unsuccessfully to portray the rape victims as martyrs or national heriones, and thus validate their social acceptability. The Pakistani military made little real effort to control their troops or stop the bruality and rape. Rather, it has been suggested that crimes against civilians were simply another type of military weapon, and that the rapes were part of a "conscious army policy" and were " 'planned by the West Pakistanis in a deliberate effort to create a new race' or to dilute Bengali nationalism" (quoted in Brownmiller 1975:85). It was even reported that in some Pakistani military camps (where Bengali women prisoners were forced to serve as prostitutes) pornographic movies were shown to "work the men up."

Crimes against the person of enemy civilians must first be viewed as a matter of opportunity structure. The civilians are there, they are the enemy, frequently they have no protection, and the troops have almost complete power over them. Sanctions against members of the military may be enforced laxly, if at all. The troops may have endured an inordinate amount of stress or frustration because of combat or boredom, and this may manifest itself as violence directed toward civilians. There may be a deliberate or at least tacit military policy of terrorism, including rape and murder, as a means of subjugating the enemy. Members of the military may be seeking revenge and committing crimes against civilians to reciprocate for the death and violence their fellow soldiers or their own civilians may have experienced. There is frequently a situation of anomie or breakdown of norms when troops initially encounter enemy civilians, and the individuals may simply act out their aggressions in a primal manner. Finally, the supportive and facilitative value system of the military helps the individual member of the military to reconceptualize the offense against a civilian in a more acceptable light. The extant value system lets him see the civilian as enemy and himself as conquering warrior entitled to the fruits of victory, including the rape and murder of his subjugated.

The militaty normally tries to prevent or minimize military crimes committed against enemy civilians, especially crimes against person. It does so in the belief that enemy territory will be easier to occupy and its population easier to control if they feel secure against harm from the invading army. In some instances military leaders have failed to follow this reasoning and have experienced resistance in occupying the area, and handicaps in accomplishing their further combat and logistic missions.

In the final analysis, it is often difficult for military commanders to restrain their troops from availing themselves of the aggressive privilege of the victors, and troublesome, if not impossible, to convert finely honed combat soldiers into nonaggressive occupation troops.[20]

CRIMES AGAINST PERFORMANCE

Perhaps far more prevelant than looting property, black marketeering has constituted the largest incidence of economic crime against an enemy (or foreign friendly) civilian population. Black marketeering means involvement in a criminal economic system and involves civilian collusion to subvert or circumvent the economic norms of the military and the military government. It also erodes whatever positive image the military may have (since the individuals involved appear as criminal participants in the black market) and thus brings discredit to the military, which may cause damage to its authority. Accordingly, black marketeering is a military crime against performance vis-à-vis civilians. Even though

[20] As a general rule, the "tougher" combat units make poor occupation troops because of their aggressiveness. After World War II, for example, the Eleventh Airborne Division occupied Yokohama, Japan, but had to be removed soon thereafter because of several rapes and robberies and a few murders allegedly committed by the paratroops (Bowers 1970).

military authorities may be diligent in trying to minimize or prevent servicemen from becoming involved in black marketeering,
and vigorous in their sanctioning of offenders. violations of the proscriptions against such activity are endemic in most militaries in
most wars.

In World War II, for example, the economies of conquered
countries like Germany were devastated and the people desperate
for food, clothing, and other goods. "Luxury" items like cigarettes
and coffee were simply unavailable on the local economy. The U.S.
military authorities were naturally anxious to restore equilibrium
to the economy and, accordingly, attempted to enforce regulations
preventing black marketeering and currency manipulation. The
GI's were on familiar ground, however, when it came to trafficking and trading, and many, with typical Yankee (and southern) enthusiasm, became extensively involved in selling American goods to
the German civilians at fantastic prices (Weltner 1947).[21] Mc-
Callum (1946:482) relates, for example:

> Another incentive to deviate behavior was the existence in the
> war-torn economies of France and Germany of thriving black
> markets in which fantastic prices were offered for many articles
> that the soldier could easily lay his hands on. Cigarettes, for in-
> stance, brought $2.40 a package, a chocolate D bar brought a
> dollar, a pair of GI shoes $30.00, a khaki shirt, $20.00. Participa-
> tion in this black market was widespread in the army, although
> confined in general to the selling of articles which actually
> belonged to the soldier rather than to the actual misappropriation
> of government property. . . . While returning to the United
> States, I often heard the remark made that a man was a fool if he
> didn't leave the port of Le Havre with at least $1,000 in his
> pocket—and this money could be obtained only through black
> market operations.

The civilian populations in the conquered countries in World
War II were reduced to such desperate straits that a significant
number of females turned to prostitution, or at least offered their
sexual favors to particular servicemen for gifts of food, cigarettes,

---

[21] Goods were equally scarce in the Pacific theater of war. One enterprising GI
landed in the Philippines with MacArthur's returning forces. He took with him a
whole duffel bag of *needles*, which he knew would be nonexistent after several
years of Japanese occupation but eagerly sought after, since clothing could be
sewn from army cloth, such as abandoned parachutes and uniforms. Needless to
say, he made a small fortune from his needles.

and other needed items. Servicemen were not slow in learning that such merchandise was easily negotiable for sex in the occupied countries. Elkin (1946:413) observed that:

> The populations of North Africa and Europe quickly became familiar with the mercantile ways of their democratic liberators who went about offering specific quantities of cigarettes, chocolate, C-rations, etc., not only for money but "in trade." Such methods were particularly effective in famine-stricken areas, such as the Naples region in 1943–44, and invariably brought results to those hardheaded and enterprising GI's who operated on the basis of statistical probability. Soldiers were made keenly resentful by reports that Negro troops, by virtue of belonging to the Quartermaster Corps, enjoyed an often prodigious advantage in such "trade."

In some instances where black marketeering took on a professional volume, the military usually stepped in and took stern action. In a number of cases whole units were involved in a combination theft and black marketeering ring. McCallum (1946:484) tells of one such incidence:

> The latter [theft and black marketeering], however, was going on all the time; a railroad battalion was actually caught red-handed, with the result that 6 officers and 182 enlisted men of the organization were court-martialed. But the pilfering of government supplies in this railroad battalion took on a quasi-legitimate character because it had the sanction of the group behind it.

Black marketeering was also common in postwar occupied Japan, where it was common for many servicemen to acquire a Japanese mistress and set up housekeeping. To finance the original furnishings and the weekly expenses, the servicemen would often give a quantity of cigarettes and other PX goods to their Japanese mistresses, who would sell them on the black market and buy food and other household needs.[22] Occasionally a GI might even "buy" his mistress out of a brothel by paying the "momma-san" a substan-

---

[22] In occupied Germany, particularly in the period immediately after the war, "there was no employment available in any recognizable sense of the word, except for that connected with the physical needs of a large male population of occupying forces" (Morris 1973:67). Many females, married and single, became the "breadwinners," as it were, by entering into a "liaison" with an occupying soldier. By becoming kept mistresses, paid with food and cigarettes, the females could survive, and in many instances support their children or families, by selling some of the food and cigarettes on the black market.

tial number of cigarettes or other goods easily negotiable on the black market.

Black marketeering was also a military problem in the Korean conflict, and continued to be one in Vietnam. Often in Vietnam, medical supplies and narcotics were prime black market items (see, for example, Adams 1970). Where military personnel have access to negotiable goods and the local population has money, items of value, or services to render, there will likely be black marketeering.

Often in occupied enemy countries, U.S. servicemen (or the members of any conquering military) have been forbidden to fraternize with the civilian population. Appropriate social distance must be maintained between conqueror and conquered. The military often takes the position that fraternization breeds familiarity, and familiarity erodes respect and authority. In some instances the military has felt that to fraternize with the enemy is to run the risk of compromising the military mission, inasmuch as the enemy civilian might be cooperating with the enemy military. To insure that social distance is maintained, our military, as do others, has sometimes had formal regulations proscribing fraternization with enemy civilians, and violators of such norms were sanctioned. However, members of the military have routinely violated these norms. In one account (Atwell 1958:347) of a group of U.S. infantrymen moving into Germany in World War II, mention is made of this regulation. Some of the men are spending the night in a German farmhouse, sharing their combat rations with some women in the house. The supper has become festive with talk and laughter:

> The small house took on the air of a family party. Everyone milled about, talking and smiling affably. Phil started to laugh. "Good God," he said, "*look* at us getting ready to cross the historic Rhine! Do you realize every one of us could be fined sixty-five dollars for fraternizing with these people?"

Sometimes the military mandate for social distance between conqueror and conquered assumes quite different dimensions. In Nazi Germany it was technically forbidden for a German to have sexual relations, including rape, with a Jew, because the German would be "racially defiled," in that Aryan "blood" would be contaminated. This proscription, which had its genesis in the 1935 Nuremberg race laws, was especially frustrating to some members of the German military and Gestapo, who were otherwise generally free to brutalize conquered civilians, especially in the Eastern countries like Poland and Russia. Brownmiller (1975:51) relates the account of a Jewish woman in occupied Poland who was taken to the local Gestapo on some minor pretext. She was forced to strip before the Gestapo men at the station, slapped about, and then carried into an adjoining room where she feared she would be raped. Instead:

> I was in a small office and the German had a long heavy whip in his hand. "You don't know how to obey . . . I'll show you. *But I can't have you, scum, because you're Jewish, and filthy* [italics added] What a shame!" He swung the whip across my breasts. "Here's what you can have for being a dirty Jew—instead of me—this!" He lashed the whip again and again and I fainted.

Servicemen are sometimes directed not to fraternize with prostitutes or black marketeers, but the servicemen have routinely ignored such directives and both the local black market and prostitution thrive on a GI economy.[23] Servicemen are, of course, heavy users of prostitutes' services in this country as well as in foreign occupied countries (see Winick and Kinsie 1972). In addition, servicemen also frequently become emotionally involved with females in these countries and sometimes marry them without permission, in violation of military regulation. In consorting with the local civilians, servicemen also commit other crimes against performance, such as going AWOL, using drugs, and incapacitating themselves for duty.

Summary

Civilians, friendly and enemy, are frequently the victims of military crime. The sheer numbers of young males concentrated in

[23] Prostitution and black marketeering are often the backbone of the economy in many war-torn areas occupied by the Americans. When the Americans leave, or reduce the size of their forces, as has happened in Vietnam, the economy is often thrown into a tailspin.

According to some accounts (see Randal, 1972:B4), the girls were left with practically no income and few if any other vocational skills than those of a prostitute. In some cases they had children fathered by Americans, who will likely never be fully accepted by other Vietnamese, and the girls themselves were politically vulnerable when the Viet Cong took over because they could be accused of consorting with the enemy.

military camps and installations may be a disruptive element in local community life, and certain frictions and hostilities may accordingly develop between members of the military and the civilian population. The military, sensitive to civilian political influence and the possibility of military-civilian conflict, generally attempts to maintain some degree of segregation in regard to its personnel. The segregation of military personnel also tends to expedite the socialization and control of its members. The behavior of servicemen is carefully monitored by military authorities, and strong social controls are evoked to mandate circumspect behavior on the part of individuals in the military. In spite of such efforts, members of the military do commit offenses against local civilians. In general, crimes against property are minimized, except perhaps for damage to civilian property resulting from altercations with civilians, or economic offenses involving violations of trust, such as cashing bad checks and defaulting on debts.

Members of the military are somewhat more likely to commit crimes against the person of civilians. Fights and brawls with civilians are not uncommon, and assaults and aggressive behavior toward civilians occur with significant frequency in some circumstances. Members of the military may also molest or assault females, and in this connection sex-related offenses against females are among the more endemic forms of military crime. Because of its concern with the civilian image of itself and its members, the military prescribes especially circumspect comportment of servicemen in their public behavior. Such norms may regulate appearance and demeanor, and violations may elicit punitive sanctions.

Where the military has units stationed in a foreign friendly country, the problem of military-civilian conflict may be exacerbated and offenses against civilians committed by members of the military may increase. Again crimes against property are, in general, infrequent, with the exception of damage to civilian property growing out of brawls and violations of economic trust. Members of the military have on occasion, however, undertaken to cheat or swindle allied civilians, particularly if they tended to be relatively unsophisticated. Hostility between allied civilians and members of the military may be such that fights and assaults are frequent. Sometimes members of the military may view the allied civilians as "inferior" and act in a contemptuous and abusive fashion toward them. The civilians may be resentful of the military intrusion in their life, and jealous of the pay or supply affluence of the members of the military. Competition for females may also be a factor in military-civilian conflict, and resulting altercations occur with some frequency. Sexual offenses against allied civilian females may also be relatively common. In some situations, such as the American involvement in Vietnam, many U.S. servicemen tended to reconceptualize the South Vietnamese civilian population as enemies rather than as allied civilians. As a result, many civilians were robbed, beaten, tortured, raped, and killed with an almost casual indifference. The civilians not only became enemy, they became a subhuman enemy. As with their own civilians, the military attempts to enforce circumspect and appropriate behavior on the part of its members vis-à-vis foreign allied civilians, including the prohibition or minimization of fraternizing. The foreign context not infrequently tends to erode the mechanisms of social control, and stresses and strains of military existence may prove to be a frustrating factor. This, plus the constituent informal military value system, may well precipitate inappropriate and offensive behavior on the part of servicemen, and generate crimes against performance.

For reasons of pragmatism and military expedience, as well as humanitarian concerns, the behavior of members of the military toward the enemy civilian population is normally proscribed and offenses directed at such civilians are prohibited and sanctioned. Tradition dictates that to the victor belongs the spoils, however, and historically members of the military have robbed and looted. Loot may have real economic value or, as is more often the case in recent times, may be essentially a symbolic object that commemorates or celebrates the military experience and the victory. In some instances civilian property is stolen for the mere comfort and convenience of the military personnel involved. Civilian property may also simply be destroyed as an act of retribution or vengeance.

The dictates of international treaty and the norms of "civilized" warfare require that the enemy civilian population be treated with dignity and humaneness. Systematic mistreatment of enemy civilians has always been, and remains, a kind of military weapon or tactic. Sometimes an enemy nation can be terrorized and demoralized to the point of loosing its will to fight. The enemy civilian population can be an instrument in this process of terrorization. Historically, conquerors have brutalized their vanquished enemies. Enemy civilian populations have experienced rape, mutilation, murder, enslavement, and physical abuse at the hands of conquering or occupying troops. Such offenses have sometimes occurred as revenge for similar acts committed by the enemy military. In other instances atrocities against enemy civilians are simply seen as the conqueror's right to kill or rape at will. In some wars the rape or murder of enemy civilians reached an almost unbelievable level; whole populations have been exterminated. Courts-martial and postwar tribunals have punished violators for war crimes, but the vast majority of offenses committed against enemy civilians go unpunished, if not undetected.

When an enemy country is occupied by the victorious military, its members may be further constrained in their behavior in regard to the civilian population, even to the extent of being prohibited from fraternizing with enemy civilians or engaging in certain kinds of economic activity. As with other military norms, however, servicemen soon find ways of subverting or circumventing the rules and regulations, often becoming active in the black market and indulging themselves in advantageous relationships with enemy civilians, especially females.

PART FOUR

Inter-
Occupational
Crime

War consists largely of acts that would be criminal if performed in time of peace. Accordingly, the whole notion of reducing crime in war was always rather preposterous.

Alastair Revie, *The Bomber Command*

CHAPTER
EIGHT

Crimes Against Property

Only the trappings of war change. Only these distinguish the Marine souvenir hunter, bending over the fallen Jap, from Hector denuding slain Patroclus of the borrowed armor of Achilles.

Robert Leckie, *Helmet for My Pillow*

War has almost always been motivated primarily by political considerations. There are, of course, a few primitive and pastoral societies for whom raiding and counterraiding of herds and flocks have become institutionalized patterns of economic exigency, and where the political overtones of the conflict developed subsequent to the economic necessity.[1] Sometimes a necessary distribution of goods such as livestock, and thus survival, can only be insured by the forced redistribution of livestock through raiding and war. Such tribal groups are relatively rare, however. On the other hand, no warfare is without some element of economic consideration. Countries have sometimes had to wage war on other countries in order to obtain some scarce and needed resource. In general, the cost of waging war usually exceeds the value of the resource that is sought through conflict.[2] Thus, in effect, it would likely have been

[1] There are some primitive and folk societies where war or warlike activities have become essentially an economic way of life. Survival, in effect, depends on limited war. Such an example might be the perpetual camel raiding of some Arabic Bedouin groups (see Sweet 1965.)

[2] For an exhaustive and definitive exposition on the costs and other facts and figures of war, see Singer and Small (1972).

245

economically advantageous to obtain the needed resources through trade rather than through war.

For the individual soldier, however, political considerations have represented only a modest dimension of the motivation to fight. It is true that in many countries the male citizenry has tended to rally to the flag in time of war. Until the time of Vietnam, Americans have often been enthusiastic in volunteering to fight in behalf of their country. Prior to World War II, many young men in Germany and Italy were swept up in the political causes and military zeal of the times. So, too, the British, in many of their wars, were converts to the political cause of the day. It is likely, however, that throughout history more soldiers have been motivated by concerns other than political or patriotic zeal, not the least of which is forced conscription and legal coercion. Such concerns have included economic rewards and the intrinsic challenge of combat itself.

Warriors universally and traditionally have fought for booty and loot, derived both from the enemy civilian population and one's military opponents. In medieval times and earlier, armies were sometimes raised primarily on the promise of loot and booty. As discussed in the preceding chapter, the opportunity to engage in civilian looting often seemed potentially lucrative. In the absence of civilian booty, there were still economically attractive opportunities to profit from one's enemies. In those times, as earlier, the knight or warrior usually owned his own mount, weapons, and equipment. Such accoutrements and belongings were relatively costly and represented a considerable investment for the individual. To kill an enemy in battle generally entitled one to confiscate his armor, weapons, equipment, and horse, which could then be utilized personally or sold. The slain enemy might have a purse of money or precious metals, or perhaps jewelry. Even a captured enemy of uncommon rank might be ransomed for profit. There was profit even in the simulation of war. In the tournaments of the day, and in other forms of simulated combat, "it was common practice for the loser to forfeit arms and weapons to his victor" (Wilkinson 1971:34). In actual time of war, in addition to the possibility of taking booty from a killed or vanquished enemy, there was also much in the way of weapons, armor, and equipment, not to mention stray horses, to be gleaned from the debris of battle. As the physical dimensions of combat and warfare enlarged at a geometric rate to keep pace with accelerating technology, the ransoming of prisoners as an economic enterprise gave way to the simpler expedient of robbing the dead and wounded on the battlefield.

Gleaning in the Fields of War

There is little doubt that in medieval times the prospect of loot was an extremely important factor in the "will to combat." The ordinary archers, soldiers, and men-at-arms of the military forces of the time were all men of very modest economic means, with few opportunities to enhance their economic possessions. War, with its possibilities for capturing and ransoming prisoners, and for robbing the dead enemy, gave them these opportunities. Even the armor and weapons taken from a vanquished enemy represented a consequential sum of money when sold, and made possible the rapid accumulation of relative wealth. There was, at the time of the Battle of Agincourt in 1415, a rather elaborate implicit code concerning the treatment of a captured prisoner, but looting of the dead was simply the prerogative of the victor. In regard to looting at the time of Agincourt, Keegan (1976:115) has cogently observed:

> Medieval warfare, like all warfare, was about many things, but medieval battle, at the personal level was about only three: victory first, of course, because the personal consequences of defeat could be so disagreeable; personal distinction in single combat—something of which the man-at-arms would think a great deal more than the bowman; but ultimately and most important, ransom and loot.

With time, however, war changed and the size of armies increased. The weapons of war also changed and the personalized single combat of swordsman against swordsman gave way to the totally depersonalized combat of massed musket volleys and artillery fire directed at a collective enemy. The personal consequences of defeat in battle remained equally disagreeable, but became perhaps even more ignominious. There was certainly little opportunity for personal distinction in single combat, although suicidal bravery in mass battle remained until today as a means of achieving formalized recognition for courage and "gallantry." Mass warfare rendered obsolete the concept of ransoming prisoners. The size of the armies on the battlefield made it effectively impossible to sift out the valuable enemy from the less valuable. Furthermore, the speed and confusion of mass warfare would have made the communications and negotiations of ransoming extremely difficult. The opportunity for economic benefit through looting, however, may well have increased, because the greater number of men involved, plus the advanced technology of warfare, made for a greater number of dead and wounded bodies from which to steal personal belongings. While the mass battles of the eighteenth and nineteenth centuries rendered the selective taking of prisoners an unviable process, they also afforded an enormous number of casualties. After a battle, the dead and wounded lay in profusion about the area, and the corpses and those alive but weak or helpless—whether friend or foe—could expeditiously be robbed. Keegan (1976:180–81) discusses the historical phenomena of looting:

> Soldiers have always looted; indeed, the robbing of the enemy, particularly an enemy killed in single combat, and, for preference, of an object worthy of display for its intrinsic or symbolic value—the finery or weapons of the vanquished—has provided an important motive for fighting. But an economic motive operates too. The capture of a ransomable captive had offered the medieval warrior one of the few chances than available of making a sudden fortune. Ransom had long since lapsed as a practice and its institutionalized substitute, prize money, offered nothing like the same rewards, even though it accrued by right and not by hazard: Waterloo prize money for privates amounted to £ 2.11s.4d. Very much larger sums than that—which equaled forty day's pay—were to be found, however, on the bodies of the dead and wounded, for the only safe storage for valuables in an army without bankers was about the person.

At the Battle of Waterloo there was considerable looting of the dead and wounded by enlisted men on both sides. According to one account (Keegan 1976:194):

> Most of Wellington's men were too tired, as much by the nervous as physical strain of the day to do anything but slump down to sleep. Many of the private soldiers, like Lieutenant Keowan's servant, slunk away to loot—there are several accounts by wounded British officers of their being plundered, and might be more if the looters had not killed a number of their victims; but sleep was what the survivors wanted most, more often than food.

Looting was widespread and often a significant factor in motivating the soldiers to individual acts of aggressiveness as well as to a collective inattentiveness to the battle and the mission at hand. In regard to the former, Keegan (1976:180) relates the account of a French straggler charging the 44th Regiment [British] from the rear in the Battle of Waterloo, whereupon "one of the privates unhorsed him with a single shot in front of the regiment, ran forward to kill him and swiftly robbed his body before rejoining the ranks." In speaking to the latter consequence, Keegan (1976:180) tells of a British officer at the Battle of Waterloo who said: "At the height of the battle an officer of Picton's division 'saw (the truth must be told) a greater number of our soldiers busy rifling the pockets of the dead, and perhaps the wounded, than I could wish . . . with some exertion we got them in. . . .' "

In some instances a wounded individual would barely hit the ground before someone (an enemy soldier or one of his own comrades) would be trying to steal his purse, his spectacles, or other personal belongings. The prospect of looting the dead and wounded often made it difficult to maintain disciplined formations in combat, inasmuch as the men were prone to break ranks or straggle in order to take advantage of opportunity corpses, especially those of officers. On the other hand, the prospect of loot may well have been a factor in keeping men in the attack, rather than retreating or deserting to the rear. In the final analysis, however, the real profit to be made from looting was probably not as great as anticipated. After the Battle of Waterloo, as with other battles, the plunder of gold and silver watches, rings, and keepsakes was sold back and forth "in great quantities." The price, however, tended to be relatively low, perhaps for pragmatic reasons. As one British officer at Waterloo described the market for plunder (Keegan 1976:181):

> I might have bought a dozen [watches or rings] for a dollar a piece (but) I do not think any officer bought . . . probably reflecting (as I did) that in a few days [they expected another battle] "our pockets would be rifled of them as quickly as those of the French had been!"

By the time of World War II there was little economic motivational basis for looting from one's military enemies. Modern mass warfare, and the enormous expense attendant to the constituent technology and weapons, had all but completely eroded the historical practice of owning one's own weapons and equipment. The fighting man, in effect, had been separated from the means of production (or, rather, means of destruction). Furthermore, new systems of safeguarding money and valuables left the average soldier less vulnerable to looting. The enemy had nothing of real value to loot. As Keegan (1976:276–77) has put it:

> The hope of plunder as a motive may be discounted. Soldiers of 1914–18 could leave their money as credits with the pay-master, while trinkets had declined in relative value, so that there was little for which life was worth risking to be found across no man's land. Compulsion, on the other hand, was as important an agent in impelling men into the fight as ever. . . .

He goes on to detail that it was necessary to have "battle police" to round up stragglers and send them back into battle. Officers sometimes had to shoot a retreater as an example to others retreating with him, who would then frequently turn back to the front. The lure of military looting was simply not enough inducement to motivate soldiers in combat.

Looting from the enemy has moved from a largely economic enterprise, originally of serious monetary import and later of more petty value, to a pursuit of military trophies of essentially symbolic value, or for pragmatic concerns of health and comfort. This change in the function of, and motivation for, looting grew out of the advances in military technology that required the enormous increase in the size of opposing armies and the physical parameters of battle. Much military equipment became too complex and expensive for the individual soldier to own, but had little economic value outside the military context. The subsequent value of equipment issued on a mass scale in large armies was diluted to the point where there was only minimal economic benefit to be derived from looting such arms and equipment. The professional mercenary soldier of medieval times who fought for booty and plunder gave way to a professional wage-earning soldier of later centuries who infrequently possessed anything worthy of stealing. The professional British soldier of the Victorian era earned only a few shillings a day, primarily fought colonial natives even poorer than himself, and seldom had any possession of sufficient economic value to motivate a civilized enemy soldier to loot from him. By the time of modern mass warfare in World War I, the conscript soldiers of the United States would have little interest in looting the enemy for economic purposes. But as a temporary soldier—an emphemeral warrior, as it were—the conscript (or even volunteer) soldier might seek some symbolic trophy to commemorate and legitimate his sojourn as a warrior. The war souvenir would attest to his trial by ordeal and undergird his claim to manliness and courage. Enemy souvenir hunting in this context appears to have developed in the late nineteenth and early twentieth centuries, and reached full bloom in World War II. In this regard, robbing the dead for objects of symbolic value became a process endemic to the military forces of all countries, but flourished especially in the U.S. military.

From the standpoint of military norms attendant to looting from the enemy, those codes of medieval times appear to have been concerned primarily with regularizing the relationships between captor and captured so as to maximize the opportunity for obtaining ransom for prisoners. Robbing the dead was an optional and largely unregulated activity. Several hundred years later, the process of ransoming prisoners was largely impractical (except for large-scale prisoner exchanges), but looting the dead for economic gain was rampant. Most militaries opposed it because it was a practice that was disruptive to appropriate battlefield conduct and prejudicial to good military order and discipline. Officers in a battle might literally have to beat their men with the flat of their swords to restrain them from looting. Looting also posed a morale problem inasmuch as almost all members of the military feared the prospect of being wounded and then robbed of their belongings, perhaps being killed in the process by the enemy or even one's own men. Even the thought of being looted if killed was distasteful. In modern times, looting personal property from captured enemy troops is prohibited by military regulation because of international agreements on the humane treatment of prisoners. In the face of such constraints (although seldom observed), robbing the dead enemy soldier has become the prevalent means of obtaining the desired symbolic military souvenir.

Robbing the Dead Enemy

There is no formalized military proscription against robbing the dead enemy. In theory, the dead, having no use for weapons or personal property, cannot therefore be robbed as such. Still, the act of confiscating arms or items of property from a dead enemy serviceman is not without some aspect of crime, even if the act only violates some informal and generalized norm in the process of conforming to other informal and more localized norms.[3]

Whether the enemy is dead or alive, swords, weapons, or equipment taken from him are, in theory, the property of the military service, not the individual serviceman. Captured weapons and equipment are supposed to be turned in to appropriate quartermaster and/or ordnance channels. To retain such weapons or equipment for personal souvenirs subverts the military intention in regard to such captured items.[4]

Beyond the concern with the appropriate disposition of captured enemy weapons and equipment, there is the further official military disaffection for the servicemen's preoccupation with souvenir hunting because of the hazard involved. In various wars, enemy forces cognizant of the American predilection for souvenir hunting have often turned this pathology against U.S. troops by setting up ambushes and booby traps, baiting them, in effect, with an officer's sword or pistol. Many American servicemen have died or become casualties because of an enemy-contrived souvenir trap. Another related military concern is that servicemen preoccupied with obtaining souvenirs do not make the best combat troops. They are reckless, careless, lack discipline, are often inattentive to their mission, and lack objective judgment in making decisions. Accordingly, the official U.S. military posture is to discourage souvenir hunting, especially from dead bodies, on very pragmatic grounds.

Aside from the pragmatic military hazard engendered by robb-

---

[3] Not infrequently, the dead have to be buried or loaded by captured enemy soldiers. It is considered to be a particularly offensive indignity to have a POW rob the dead body of a fellow serviceman, and sanctions for such behavior are often severe. In World War II, the Germans used Russian POW's to bury their dead. If a prisoner was caught robbing a German body, he was generally shot immediately by an officer. Sajer (1972:143) relates that he once observed three Russian prisoners have their hands tied to the bars of a gate as a result of their having robbed the body of a dead German. A German soldier then stuck a grenade in the coat pocket of one of the prisoners, pulled the pin, and ran for shelter. According to Sajer, "The three Russians, whose guts were blown out, screamed for mercy until the last moment."

[4] In World War II, Korea, and Vietnam, there were some instances of military commands actually distributing captured enemy weapons to individual servicemen in order that everyone might have an enemy souvenir to take home. In other cases, regulations were sometimes instituted that authorized individual servicemen to retain their trophies of war. Such enabling rules and regulations were not universal, however, and some GI's had their trophies confiscated. Others had to sneak them home in their luggage, or ship them disguised as something else. The policy addressing the disposition of captured enemy weapons has always been erratic, vague, or confusing, and selectively enforced.

ing the bodies of dead enemy soldiers, there are humane, aesthetic, and chivalrous proscriptions against robbing the dead that are routinely violated in wartime by almost all armed forces. If an armed service has respect for the military abilities of an enemy in life, it would presumeably maintain respect for the enemy in death. In World War I, when the German ace Baron von Richthofen was shot down and killed over Allied territory, the Allied military forces gave him an appropriate burial with full military honors. They did so out of a sense of respect, chivalry, and military honor. The Allies could have permitted his body to be mutilated in order that numerous servicemen might retain a piece of the famous warrior for a souvenir, but instead chose to treat a gallant enemy with dignity and ceremony. There is ignominy in treating the fallen enemy to a mass or unmarked grave, as was the case with the dead Indians at Wounded Knee. Similarly, to strip the body of a dead enemy officer is to defile the dead, as well as to treat a fellow warrior with contempt and disrespect.

At a practical level, if the body of a dead soldier is stripped of insignias of rank, unit, and other identifying items, it may be impossible to determine who he was, and thus friends and family cannot be notified of his death. His body may not be able to be shipped to his homeland for appropriate burial, and he cannot even be mourned, inasmuch as he will remain in the limbo of "missing in action."[5] To strip a body of personal items and mementos (such as pictures, watches, wallets) would prevent such things from being collected and sent to the nearest of kin, who might derive some serenity from having the keepsakes of their deceased loved ones. Stripping the dead is one of the final indignities of war that can be heaped on an enemy, and such behavior, at least at the level of humane dignity and proprietous action, represents a crime of sorts against the person of the enemy.

According to Keegan (1976:191):

> The facts of death in battle are invested, by those who recount what they witnessed, or even perpetrated, with a tinge of romantic regret caught at goodness knows how many removes from *Young Werther* and the poetry of Schiller; while on the acquisition of trophies, which meant the personal possessions of the dead, there was something approaching a taboo.

---

[5] Even today, bodies of soldiers from various nations, killed in World War II, are found occasionally in jungles or on remote islands. Every effort is made to identify the body so that the remains can be shipped home for interment.

Members of the military everywhere, however, strip the dead for souvenirs, with differing degrees of zeal and purpose. The penchant for acquiring trophies infects persons of all nationalities and of various levels of professional bent. Neumann (1958:182), an officer in the coldly efficient Waffen SS in World War II, describes how he and his unit ambushed a Russian Cossack unit and killed a number of the enemy troops. He approached the dead Cossacks, and as he relates it:

> I bend and turn over the body of an officer, easily recognizable by his two metal stars. There are broad straps of gold braid on the shoulders of his uniform against a royal blue background. The IO was quite right. They are defintely Cossacks. The man has a white stripe bordered with red on his left pocket. I believe this is the order of the Suvarov, platinum star. In any case it's a splendid souvenir, and I tear it from the dead man's tunic.

American troops who fought the Japanese in the South Pacific during World War II appeared to be particularly prone to collecting souvenirs from the bodies of dead Japanese soldiers. This probably resulted from several factors. The American troops uniformly had a low opinion of the Japanese. They respected their fighting ability, but harbored great hostility against them because of their behavior in the war, real (e.g., the "sneak" attack on Pearl Harbor, the Bataan Death March) and imagined (the stereotype of the Japanese fighting man was essentially one of an amoral, barbarous butcher). They also viewed the Japanese as essentially a subhuman, and this attitude shows up in the pejorative terms that American GI's often applied to the Japanese (e.g., Japs, Gooks, Nips, slant-eyes). In addition, the Americans fighting the Japanese often did so in a relatively confined space, such as a small and isolated island, and thus after a battle they were surrounded by the enemy dead for some time. American troops in Europe were somewhat more mobile, often moving considerable distances immediately after a battle. Then, too, the military in the European theatre was usually more prompt in removing or burying dead after a battle. Matthews' (1947) chronicle of marines fighting the Japanese on Iwo Jima in World War II contains a number of references to robbing the bodies of dead enemy soldiers. In one firefight, the marines wounded a single Japanese soldier who then killed himself with a grenade. According to Matthews (1947:75):

Two other Marines walked up and stood over the Jap. One of them put the toe of his boot under the body and turned it over and they explored his pockets. One found a small battle flag and the other, with his combat knife, severed the leather belt to which hung the Jap's bayonet.

Matthews (1947:152) also mentions a marine who captured an enemy soldier's rifle and later carved his own initials into the rifle stock. Japanese sabers were particularly sought-after war souvenirs. Matthews (1947:176) relates that when his platoon killed eight Japanese soldiers in an attack, "six wore sabers which found their way to new owners." Once GI's took possession of a coveted saber or pistol, they were tenacious in hanging on to their souvenirs. Again Matthews (1947:202) mentions a company runner who calmly "strolled" across an open field to see if he would draw enemy fire. Ideally he would be as unemcumbered with equipment as possible, but in this instance he had "a huge Japanese saber dangling from his back." In another instance Mattews (1947:197) describes a wounded marine's attachment to a souvenir:

An ambulance came and stretcher bearers moved toward it with the man with the wound in his hip. He had been stripped of all his gear and, now composed but pale and unspeaking, he clutched tightly to him the Jap saber which he had captured two days before.

Servicemen would often take extraordinary risks to obtain souvenirs. In Leckie's (1957:87) autobiographical account of the Guadalcanal campaign in World War II, he reminisces about a time when he shot a Japanese soldier in a grove from across a river, and thought he saw something silver flash from the sun's reflection. Thinking that the silver object might be an officer's insignia, and that a dead officer would be armed with a saber, the "most precious prize of all the war," he went down to the river, stripped, and, with his bayonet in this teeth, swam across to where the bodies of Japanese soldiers were strewn about the grove. The bodies were rotting, and the air was thick with flies. As he describes it:

Holding myself stiffly, as though fending off panic with a straight arm, I returned to the river bank and slipped into the water. But not before I had stripped one of my victims of his bayonet and field glasses, both of which I slung across my chest, criss-cross like a grenadier. I had found no saber. None of the dead men was an officer.

After he returned to the other shore, he and his comrades saw a crocodile begin feeding on the bodies of the dead Japanese. Leckie wrote that his "knees went weak" when he realized that the Tenaru River, which he had swum, was infested with crocodiles.

In some instances, servicemen were just as delighted to take enemy souvenirs of pragmatic utility as they were to secure weapons. In one such case on Iwo Jima in World War II, the owner of a newly acquired souvenir from a dead enemy soldier liked his acquisition, but was even more taken with the souvenir acquired by a friend (Matthews 1947:152):

> Leiden, beaming, joined us and displayed a small wrist watch he had taken from the body of a Japanese ahead of our lines. It was a small steel instrument enclosed in a larger weather-proof casing. I admired it and he said: "You ought to see the one Degliequi got. It's a combination regular pocket watch and stop watch and a beauty. He got it off a Gook he and Mikell killed last night."

Robbing dead enemy soldiers was not always a solitary activity. Sometimes a number of GI's were involved. Leckie (1957:86) tells of a time on Guadalcanal when one regiment killed approximately 900 Japanese troops in a battle. The dead soldiers were literally piled up in "clusters and heaps" in front of the marine gun enplacements. According to Leckie, "Moving among them were the souvenir hunters, picking their way delicately as though fearful of booby traps, while stripping the bodies of their possessions."

Sometimes robbing the dead goes beyond mere souvenir hunting. Leckie (1957:86, 238) relates that in some instances marines would take the gold fillings and gold teeth from the bodies of dead Japanese soldiers. One such marine, nicknamed "Souvenirs" by his comrades, had even purchased dental equipment by way of planning his gold-mining activities. Leckie recounts that:

> The Japanese dead lay in heaps on the hillside, and they filled the trench where Obie's gun had been located. The souvenir-hunters were prowling among them, carefully ripping insignia off tunics, slipping rings off fingers or pistols off belts. There was Souvenirs himself, stepping gingerly from corpse to corpse, armed with his pliars and a dentist's flashlight that he had had the forethought to purchase in Melbourne.

Robbing captured enemy soldiers of their personal belongings and mementos violates the international Rules of Land Warfare, and also represents a departure from civility. Robbing the dead may violate no law as such, but is the final indignity to the dead, and reduces the perpetrator to a kind of military ghoul or scavenger. The warrior earns and deserves the trophy of war, however, and the taking of "souvenirs" from the enemy is thus universally tolerated and permitted, if not encouraged, by military authorities. Where the victim is a wounded enemy soldier and thus even more helpless and vulnerable than the able-bodied prisoner, the offense is perhaps more despicable and the looter even more degraded by his actions. Such behavior is, and always has been, common in war. Reinhold Pabel, a German sergeant captured by the Americans in Italy in World War II, tells of being seriously wounded and robbed of personal belongings in an American field hospital (1955:131–32):

> At the collecting station I got my first bitter taste of being a prisoner. As soon as the stretcher had been placed on the floor, a bunch of souvenir hunters ripped some of my decorations off my blouse. After they had done so, they asked me if I had any objections. I kept my mouth shut. . . .

Robbing the enemy wounded is by no means a recent phenomenon, nor are the victims confined to the enlisted ranks. During the American Revolution, in the Battle of Camden, the French General DeKalb, who was leading American Colonial troops, was wounded and robbed by enemy soldiers. In Ward's account (1952:730) of the incident, he details that:

> Prostrate in the field lay DeKalb. It was only when the Chevalier du Buysson, his aide, threw himself on his general's body, crying out his name and rank, that the thirsty bayonets were withheld from further thrusts into his body. Some of the enemy, British or Troy, carried him off and propped him against a wagon so that they might easily appropriate his gold-laced coat.

Only the intervention of the British General Cornwallis himself accomplished the rescue of DeKalb from "the despoilers."

In earlier times robbing prisoners—well, wounded, or dead—had more of a pragmatic or economic basis, rather than the symbolic motive of trophy hunting in World War II and later in Korea and Vietnam. Throughout recorded history, and undoubtedly even before, the warrior who survives the fight has sought to bring away with him some residual element of the foe as tangible evidence of his success in vanquishing the enemy.[6]

As Keegan (1961:191) phrased it:

> For the Homeric hero, there could be no honour without public proclamation, there could be no publicity without the evidence of a trophy! Worthwhile trophies could be won only in single combat, and single combat could be concluded only by violent death—and a death in which the victor exulted.

Personal Property of Enemy Military Personnel

The treatment of enemy military personnel and the disposition of their equipment is rigidly specified by U.S. military regulations and international treaties, such as the articles of the Geneva and Hague Conventions. The Rules of Land Warfare (War Department 1940:19) are specific in indicating that a prisoner of war shall retain "all effects and objects of personal use." This does not include "arms, horses, military equipment, and military papers." It does, however, include metal helmets and gas masks (presumably these two items would serve to protect the prisoner in case of attack and thus he should not be deprived of them). The prisoner is also not to be deprived of "identification tags and cards, insignia of rank, decorations, and objects of value." Money in his possession cannot be taken away from him except by order of an officer and after the amount is determined. In such instances, a receipt will be given and the money deposited to the prisoner's account. Violations of these laws and regulations may be severely sanctioned, with punishment emanating from U.S. military authorities or the belligerent military authorities, if the offender is captured. Just as looting from friendly or enemy civilian populations is forbidden by military regulations, so, too, is the appropriation of enemy property by the individual soldier. According to military rule and tradition, captured military personnel are supposed to retain certain personal items, such as watches, medals, and keepsakes. In

[6] An interesting exception to such a practice was the tradition of the Cheyenne Indians (and some other Plains tribes) to *count coup* in battle. Here the indian brave would ride into battle using only a stick or whip as a weapon. The intention was to strike the enemy but manage to escape without injury. Thereafter the individual would proclaim his courage by recounting the number of times he had bravely struck an enemy and survived—*counted coup*. Such bragging said, in effect, look how brave I am, I used no weapon but a stick, but actually struck the enemy and received no injury.

actual practice, however, military personnel of almost all nations have been quick to dispossess the captured enemy troops of such "souvenir" material, even if military crimes against property are committed in the process.[7]

Sometimes misappropriation of the personal property of captured enemy personnel is essentially more pragmatic then symbolic. The capturing troops may have been deprived of some items, such as food, coffee, or cigarettes, that the captured prisoners may possess. To the victor belongs the spoils! American GI's in World War II were almost always better supplied with food and cigarettes than the enemy troops. The German troops especially had a penchant for American cigarettes and, when they captured American troops, frequently undertook to relieve the prisoners of their cigarettes. Toland (1959:135) relates such an incident during the Battle of the Bulge in World War II. An American infantry regiment found itself surrounded by German troops; with many wounded and almost no food, water, or ammunition, the situation looked hopeless. The regimental commander ordered his unit to surrender and sent out an officer with a white flag to find the Germans. As Toland describes what followed:

> Soon a young German lieutenant and several grenadiers returned with Nagle. He explained in French what he wanted. Descheneaux, a French-Canadian, replied in French. He saw the grenadiers relieving some of his men of cigarettes and watches. "Let my men keep one pack apiece," he insisted.
> The German lieutenant nodded. "Everything will be correct, Colonel."

The Germans in World War II were usually quite prone to strip personal objects from captured Allied personnel. In Ryan's (1974:481–82) account of the battle for Arnhem in World War II, he recounts how a British paratroop officer was captured by German troops. The officer's pistol was empty and just as the Germans surrounded him, he "contemptuously" threw his pistol over a garden wall "so they couldn't get it as a souvenir." The Germans searched the captain:

> His watch and an empty silver flask that had been his father's were taken from him, but an escape map in his breast pocket was

[7] One informant told me that in his army outfit in Europe in World War II, his men tended to observe the rules of land warfare and did not confiscate the watches of captured German enlisted men, but, in the instance of captured German officers, did not hesitate to take their watches (or anything else).

overlooked. An officer returned the flask. When Mackay asked about his watch, he was told, "You won't need it where you're going, and we're rather short on watches."

In this situation the German officer displayed a curious, but not infrequent, ambiguity in observing the treatment of captured prisoners under the Rules of Land Warfare. The German correctly returned the silver flask inasmuch as it was a keepsake. On the other hand, he violated the rule about personal property by retaining the British officer's watch. It may well have been, however, just as he said, that the Germans needed the watch and, in the interest of military expediency, kept it in open violation of the norm.

Sometimes captured soldiers take umbrage at being robbed by their captors of personal belongings and keepsakes. As an instance in point, one American veteran of the Italian campaign in World War II recalls (Adleman and Walton 1966:189):

> I'll never forget the night we made a company raid on one of the towns at Anzio. Dave Woon and myself took a prisoner and Dave searched this prisoner and came upon the picture of a pretty woman. When Dave threw the picture on the ground the German, who was a fair-sized boy, become quite violent and offered to take Dave on in a boxing match. So there and then Dave put down his Thompson and they proceeded to have one hell of a good scrap while I leaned against the building and looked on.

It is to be admitted that in many instances the taking of personal property, keepsakes, or mementos, whether from a live enemy prisoner or from a dead enemy soldier, is not necessarily motivated by a desire to acquire souvenirs. It might well be that the personal property of an enemy soldier is confiscated for intelligence purposes. In way of illustration, Matthews (1947:184) relates an incident on Iwo Jima during World War II:

> Already in the ruined shelter were two Marines, one of whom had uncovered a batch of Japanese letters and a note book whose pages looked as if the former owner had been a correspondence student in geometry. *The Marine stuffed the letters into his pocket for delivery to his platoon leader* [italics added].

Few war souvenirs are more desired or sought after than a pistol or sword, especially if they belonged to an officer. In World Wars I and II, a German Lugar pistol was considered particularly desirable. In theory, such captured weapons are supposed to be turned in to ordnance, but in actual practice, they almost never are. In various of our wars, the enemy, knowing the value which our troops put on captured weapons, have often left pistols or swords where our troops could find them and then booby-trapped them. Inasmuch as military personnel in the rear echelons seldom had a chance to acquire souvenirs directly from either live or dead enemy soldiers, they would frequently pay extremely high prices to purchase them from front-line troops. Leckie (1957:267, 273, 278) in his account of combat in the South Pacific with the marines during World War II, relates the story of a marine enlisted man who had obtained a pistol from a Japanese major at Galasea who had killed himself with it. The marine's company commander subsequently "pulled rank" and took the pistol for himself. The enlisted man, in turn, stole it back from the company commander. Fearing that the pistol might be found in the next shakedown inspection, the marine asked a friend who was going into the hospital to keep it for him. The friend intended to keep it in the hospital storeroom, but one of the doctors took it into custody and said to the friend:

> "Oh, by the way, . . . I have that gun of yours. How would you like to sell it to me? I'd like to send it home as a souvenir."
> "Sorry, sir, but I can't, It's not mine."
> "Too bad," he said, rising, "but if you should change your mind let me know. The folks back in Atlanta'd get a kick out of it."

When the marine left the hospital the doctor returned his pistol, although he again tried to buy it for himself.

Perhaps more than members of any other military in the world, or in history, Americans have tended to be inveterate, compulsive, and almost pathological souvenir seekers.[8] Similarly, many servicemen became particularly adroit at, and inured to, killing in their efforts to obtain an enemy pistol or saber.[9] Adleman and Walton (1966:217) quote a member of the First Special Service

---

[8] This pathology was widely recognized during World War II. There was a saying to the effect that the German soldier fought and died for the fatherland, the Third Reich, and the Führer; the Italian soldier fought and died for Italy, Mussolini, and "the glory that once was Rome's"; the Japanese soldier fought and died for the land of the rising sun, the Japanese empire, and the emperor; and the American soldier fought and died (if necessary) for souvenirs!

[9] While I was in the service some years ago, a sergeant related the story of a friend of his in World War II. The friend was in an American unit that linked up with a Russian unit in Germany. Men from both units took the occasion to trade souvenirs. The friend had gone off to an isolated area with a Russian soldier and was trading cigarettes for items that the Russian soldier had. The American

Force, a joint U.S.-Canadian ranger-type unit that fought in Italy
and France in World War II:

> You know, I been reading how the F.B.I. is organizing special
> squads to take care of us boys when we get home. I got an idea it
> will be needed all right. See this pistol? I killed a man this morn-
> ing just to get it. Ran into a German officer in a hotel near the
> edge of town. He surrendered, but he wouldn't give me his pistol.
> You know, it kind of scares me. It's so easy to kill. It solves all of
> your problems, and there's no questions asked. I think I'm getting
> the habit.

Many men have risked their lives for enemy souvenirs. Soldiers
sometimes became so preoccupied with souvenir hunting that the
war and the immediate combat mission paled into insignificance.
One U.S. soldier who fought the Germans in Italy in World War II
provides a vivid and humourous example (Adleman and Walton
1966:187):

> I remember about six of us making a raid on a farmhouse one
> day. We saw a white flag, so we stopped shooting. The krauts
> came out with their hands up. The first thing I knew, I was
> standing there by myself. The rest of my gang had gone in the
> house for souvenirs.

Those who could not get them directly, like the doctor, would
pay almost any price to get souvenirs. Taking souvenirs back home
has always been something of a status symbol to Americans. The
souvenir is a visible symbol of a vanquished enemy. So desperate to
buy souvenirs were the rear-echelon troops that some enterprising
GI's in both World War II and Korea engaged in "manufacturing"
enemy souvenirs. During World War II small Japanese "meatball"
flags, for example, were easily mass produced and brought a handsome price from service troops and other noncombatant personnel
who did not get the chance to "liberate" souvenirs directly from the
enemy. Obviously the mark-up in real souvenirs like enemy
officer's cameras, binoculars, and pistols was considerable, and
many U.S. servicemen became "wholesalers" of the first magnitude. Not only are the belongings of individual POW's supposed to
be left in their possession or turned in to the proper authorities, but
captured enemy equipment and stocks of supplies are also to be

---

wanted the Russian's fur hat, but the Russian would not trade. Finally the
American lost patience, took up his rifle, and shot the Russian soldier dead. He
then took the coveted fur cap and escaped.

disposed of in a carefully regulated manner, usually through appropriate quartermaster and ordnance channels. American troops for a number of wars have had the reputation of being ingenious and pragmatic when it came to diverting captured enemy supplies and equipment to their own needs. Military folklore is full of tales and legends, facts and fiction, of individuals and units that were able to subvert captured equipment to their own comfort and luxury.[10]

Corporate Property of the Enemy Military

In the course of combat, military forces capture enemy troops and confiscate various kinds of corporate property and equipment. In some instances they may even capture the corporate property of the enemy without bothering to take the enemy troops as prisoners. In taking such equipment and property as military booty and misappropiating it for personal or unit use, the offenders may be in violation of international law in some situations, and/or be in violation of the regulations of the parent military service itself. Sometimes such behavior may constitute a serious violation of the norms; in other cases it may represent an exemplary instance of military ingenuity and expedience.

CAPTURED ENEMY ORDNANCE AND VEHICLES

When enemy vehicles, ordnance, or stocks of equipment are captured, they are to be turned over to the appropriate military branch or unit, such as Quartermaster, Ordnance, Medical Service, and so on. In theory, they are not to be commandeered by the

---

[10] A relative of mine who served with the U.S. Army Quartermaster Corps in World War II related the story of how his unit took control of a Japanese weapons and supply depot in occupied Japan. Knowing that such things had enormous value to navy personnel who seldom had the opportunity to acquire souvenirs, his unit took a small truck convoy of Japanese weapons and other equipment to the coast and worked a deal with some navy chief petty officers on a naval supply ship. The outcome was that the navy, without knowing it, swapped a sizable supply of frozen beef carcasses, which were in short supply, for a load of Japanese guns, swords, and uniforms. This transaction, while clearly illegal by military standards, had the tacit approval of the quartermaster commanding officer. The army personnel, needless to say, ate quite well for some time.

capturing troops for personal use. Not infrequently, however, this does happen. In one autobiographical account of combat in Europe during World War II, the author recounts how he acquired a captured MK-5 German tank for his own use and gave joyrides to various men and officers in his unit (Giles 1965:70–71). When the tank stuck in a hole and he could not extricate it, he confiscated a V-8 motored German halftrack and ran around in that. He went on a short trip and, on his return, discovered to his annoyance that a friend had given his halftrack to an ordnance outfit that had been seeking operational German military vehicles and transporting them to supply depots.

In the Kiska invasion in the Aleutian Islands during World War II, members of the First Special Service Force indulged in the acquisition of enemy vehicles along with their other souvenir collecting. According to Adleman and Walton (1966:109), the members of the Allied unit "faced the rest of the day in high good humor, zooming around the beaches in the Japanese motorcycles and trucks which were among the hoard of souvenirs they quickly amassed." Members of this same unit had occasion in later campaigns to steal American military vehicles, including jeeps and ambulances (Adleman and Walton 1966:169, 220). The men of the unit were so prone to steal any unattended vehicle that it turned out that the First Special Service Force "had almost twice as many jeeps as it was authorized." Such thefts, including the misappropriation of captured enemy vehicles for personal use, generally represent a crime against the parent military service more than a crime against the enemy. In some instances, however, the victorious troops may confiscate various kinds of corporate equipment and property, such as medical or dental supplies, rations and foodstuffs, and tents and other supplies, from enemy personnel, thereby depriving them of the means of survival as POW's Sometimes such dispossessions occur because of misunderstandings or cultural differences between the two opposing militaries. At the surrender conference at Appomattox at the end of the Civil War, for example, such a misunderstanding almost occurred. In proposing terms of surrender to General Lee, Grant initially indicated that Confederate troops surrender all ordnance, rifles, and horses to the Union forces. Only Confederate officers could retain their sidearms. Lee had to point out to Grant that members of the calvary and the artillery in the Confederate army owned their own mounts and would need to keep them in order to return home and accomplish the spring planting. Grant graciously consented to such an arrangement. Not doing so would have meant extreme hardship for many of the Confederate soldiers. Had Grant not been so accommodating in his surrender terms, the Union army, in a corporate fashion, would have taken the personal property of many of the Confederates, thus committing a crime against property from the Confederate perspective, but not in the Union view.

Perhaps one of the more heinous offenses involving corporate property of enemy prisoners is the confiscation of Red Cross supplies. Although in theory the Red Cross parcels are supposed to be issued to individual prisoners, in actual practice the contents of the packages are often pooled by the inmates of POW camps and particular items, such as medicine or vitamins, issued to particular prisoners most in need of them. During World War II the Allies were scrupulous in seeing that their POW's actually received the parcels. So, too, were the Germans in most instances. The Japanese, however, were frequent offenders in confiscating Red Cross parcels and using the contents for themselves. Caffrey (1973:226) provides one account of such offenses, in this instance involving British and Commonwealth troops captured at Singapore and imprisoned in Japanese camps in Siam:

> The Japanese were often unable to keep the rations up to the ungenerous amount authorized by their own High Command, though opinions vary about how hard they tried. And they invariably appropriated any Red Cross food parcels or medical supplies, few as there were of these that got through.

In some cases captured military prisoners have retaliated and stolen both the personal and corporate property of their captors, even though this is clearly a violation of military rule. Caffrey (1973:226) also tells of a British POW who was sick, swollen, and dropsical with beriberi, who stole a bottle of Vitamin B tablets from the haversack of a Japanese officer and ate all the tablets, subsequently curing himself.

In a similar kind of occurrence, Toland (1959:266) relates an amusing situation involving U.S. GI's, captured by the Germans, stealing from a German officer. A number of American troops were captured by the Germans in the Battle of the Bulge during World War II. The Germans were marching the American POW's, led by a colonel, through the woods. A German major handed a suitcase to an American soldier in the front of line. As the march

continued, the suitcase was passed back from prisoner to prisoner
and wound up at the end of the line. In time a German guard
noticed that the suitcase being carried by the GI at the end of the
line was hanging open and empty. The guard took the soldier and
the suitcase to the German major who, seeing the open suitcase,
struck the American in the face with his riding crop. The American
colonel interceded and the German officer responded:

> "He claims the American soldier stole everything," said the in-
> terpreter.
> "What was in the suitcase?" asked Fuller [the American colo-
> nel]. "Cheese and butter." Fuller laughed.
> The major's face turned red. He raised the riding crop as if to
> strike Fuller, then suddenly burst out laughing and threw the
> empty suitcase into a snowbank.

Sometimes the corporate property of the enemy assumes interesting variety. The U.S./Canadian First Special Service Force
was prone to rob the Germans, prisoner or still fighting, of all sorts
of unusual things. Adleman and Walton (1966:177, 180, 191) mention that among the things members of this unit stole from the Germans at one time or another were a herd of cattle and the contents
of several wine cellars; crates of chickens, a bed and mattress, and
a baby carriage full of potatoes; a sewing machine and a cow and
assorted other livestock and farm implements. Members of the First
Special Service Force were reported to have gone in for farming
during lulls in the fighting. They milked the cows they stole,
planted gardens, slaughtered hogs, and harvested German fields.
One officer of the unit remembers that "It was not unusual to see a
soldier in a trench made large enough for himself and a cow"
(Adleman and Walton 1966:190). Some members of this unit even
stole a town. A night patrol discovered a small deserted Italian
village called Borgo Sabotino behind German lines. They decided
to "keep" it and "elected" one of their comrades, nicknamed
"Gus," as mayor. Then they renamed the village "Gusville." Even
though the Germans periodically sent tanks into the village, the
American troops stayed on and foraged deeper behind German
lines to steal food and livestock. They also raided German-held
wine cellars and used their loot to stock a bar in Gusville. The
"mayor" even tried to impose a toll or levy on other U.S. units passing through the town on patrol (Adleman and Walton
1966:174-77). Later, in the advance on Rome, some members of

the Force raided a German OP and "hit them for fifteen cases of cognac and three hams." This sustained them on the way to Rome (Adleman and Walton 1966:215).

The spirited highjinks of the men of the First Special Service Force did not exactly represent a true crime vis-à-vis the enemy. There is, however, a certain element of chicanery, if not treachery, in stealing the belongings of the enemy without first fighting him. Furthermore, these men were often in violation of at least the spirit, if not the letter, of U.S. military regulation. The army did not authorize the taking of Borgo Sabotino, or raids to capture cows, cabbages, or wine. From the standpoint of military authorities, such "grandstanding" or theatrical heroics are inappropriate because they entail unnecessary risks, and could possibly jeopardize more legitimate combat activities of other units. Then, too, in theory, all captured enemy stores or equipment belongs to the larger military entity, and not to the individual soldier or small unit. Thus all of these activities constitute a crime against property, albeit a particularly bizarre mode of offense, and could be punished if detected by higher military authority.

CAPTURED ENEMY MONEY

There are occasions in the course of combat when military units capture large sums of money or other forms of wealth when they capture or kill enemy troops. The most frequent such incidence is when an enemy finance or payroll unit is killed or captured. Again the First Special Service Force appears to have had such an experience in the Italian campaign during World War II. Adleman and Walton (1966:195) relate that:

> There were several occasions, however, when the extracurricular activities of the Force seriously embarrassed higher commands. One of them involved two German finance officers who were riding out to their troops in order to conduct payday. They made a wrong turn and landed in the Force's lines. Possessing thousands of Italian lire, they represented too fine a haul to the Force to be sent further back for normal prisoner of war interrogation.

The members of the Force apparently enjoyed their newfound wealth, but became too obvious in their ostentation. Higher military authorities began to hear tales of men in the unit lighting

their cigars with 1,000-lire notes. At this point they demanded that
the money and/or the paymasters be turned over to proper
authorities. As the authors put it, "Despite repeated and stringently worded orders, they never got either one."[11]

Summary

The treatment of enemy military personnel and the disposition
of their equipment is rigidly specified by U.S. military regulations
and international treaties such as the articles of the Geneva and
Hague Conventions. Violations of these laws and regulations are
severely sanctioned and punishment may emanate from either U.S.
military authorities or the belligerent military authorities, if the offender is captured. Just as looting from friendly or enemy civilian
populations is forbidden by military regulation, so, too, is the appropriation of enemy military property by the individual soldier.
When enemy military personnel are captured, according to regulations, certain personal items, such as watches, medals, and keepsakes, may be retained by the POW's. In actual practice, American
servicemen have often been quick to dispossess the captured enemy
troops of such "souvenir" material. In the quest for souvenirs, GI's
have been known to take everything, including the uniform, from
a captured enemy. The weapons and equipment of the captured
personnel are supposed to be turned over to appropriate units in
our military establishment, such as Ordnance or Quartermaster.
Captured enemy military property often has significant economic
and political value as well as import for subsequent combat
engagements.

The most desired souvenir of all is an officer's pistol (in World
Wars I and II a German Luger was considered particularly
desirable). Accordingly, few such captured weapons are ever
turned in to Ordnance. In several wars the enemy, knowing the

[11] An informant who was in the U.S. Army in World War II has shared a similar
experience with me. While fighting in France, some men in his unit ambushed
and shot up a German payroll truck, killing the German crew. They confiscated
a very large amount of enemy currency (which was redeemable for Allied currency) and, rather than turn the money over to proper authorities, hid it for a
time in the headlights of the unit vehicles and later divided it among members of
the entire unit.

value our troops put on captured weapons, have often left booby-trapped pistols where our troops could find them.

Winston Churchill once called the American Civil War "the last war fought between gentlemen," referring to the remnants of chivalry and gentlemanly conduct between combatants. At Appomattox, for example, when Lee pointed out that artillerymen and cavalrymen in the Confederate army owned their own mounts, Grant graciously allowed them to retain their horses for "spring plowing," along with the officers who could retain their swords and sidearms. There were traces of such conduct even in World War I, especially among the aviators and other elite troops. By World War II, however, American troops were often free-booters rather than freedom defenders, and there are few ex-combat servicemen who cannot sport some kind of captured memento obtained from an enemy POW.

Military folklore is full of stories, many true, of instances where small groups of GI's or whole units undertook to "confiscate" every imaginable kind of enemy material, from German "jeeps" for joyriding to captured stores of Japanese saki, all in express violation of military regulations. Combat units, such as infantry, marines, rangers, and paratroopers, were supposed to be particularly cavalier in their disposition of such equipment.

War may not be fun, but some servicemen attempt to make it at least more bearable in terms of all the comfort and luxury that can be effected under the circumstances, if not profitable in the sense of looted booty, black-market earnings, or captured souvenirs that provide the basis for richly embellished "war stories" with which to regale the "folks back home."

CHAPTER NINE

Crimes Against Person

*Thus, there is a time to take prisoners and a time
to dispose of them—and the opposite is just as true. . . .*
Special Forces instructor, quoted in Donald Duncan,
The New Legions

The object of war is to impose the political will of one society or
group upon another society or group.[1] The killing of the enemy
military is attendant to this process but, in theory, incidental.
Total annihilation of the enemy military is generally not considered
necessary or even altogether desirable. In this vein, the norms of
warfare have traditionally proscribed and prescribed the conditions, circumstances, and techniques of combat, means of assailing
the enemy, and treatment of the enemy if taken prisoner, among
other considerations. These norms have operated at various levels,
including those specified and agreed upon by mutual treaty, those
determined appropriate by the military entity itself, the norms of
behavior presumably constituent to a humane and civilized posture
and perspective, the norms implicit in a kind of universal warrior's
code of chivalry, and those norms that operate at a more or less informal level and spontaneous basis and basically involve a

[1] The U.S. military defines this function in this way: "The object of war is to bring
about the complete submission of the enemy as soon as possible by means of
regulated violence" [italics added] (War Department 1940:7).

reciprocity in regard to survival. Thus the concept of the military entity that asks no quarter and gives none is largely myth, for all military units subscribe to, and fight in, a context of normative regulation and patterning of behavior. Almost all militaries proceed on the basis of disabling, neutralizing, or conquering, but not necessarily annihilating, the enemy. There have, of course, been exceptions to this principle. In 1874 the Texas legislature established and appropriated money to fund two military Ranger forces: the Special Forces, which would operate in southwestern Texas against *bandidos* and other outlaws, and the Frontier Battalion, which was to consist of six companies of Rangers, each with 75 men. The function of the Frontier Battalion was simple and direct. They were to serve as "Indian exterminators" (Haley 1976:85). Obviously, the Frontier Battalion was created with an explicit mission of annihilation.

It should not be assumed that if warfare involves a preliterate society there is an absence of norms and rules governing the combat, at least on the part of the primitive group. On the contrary, anthropologists who have studied warfare among primitive groups have pointed out that even among the most rudimentary societies there are well-defined normative configurations to the pattern of combat and military behavior, and that these rules and customs are scrupulously adhered to (Bohannan 1967; American Anthropological Association 1967). Furthermore, it has been recorded that it is particularly vexing to these preliterate groups when an opponent of more cultural advancement fails to observe the appropriate norms of war. Haley (1976:3-4), for example, reports that in the nineteenth century the Mexicans were extremely unpredictable in their dealings with some of the Indian tribes of the southwest American Plains, such as the Kiowas and Comanches. The Mexicans would, in their military policy toward the Indians, veer back and forth between "mustache-twirling sweet talk" and "inquisitorial butchery." As Haley puts it:

To the Indians the Mexican manner was detestable; the Indians themselves observed rigid rules of war, and once an expression of friendship or hospitality was made it might not be dishonored. As Thomas Battery observed, even when an avowed enemy came to one's tipi and asked for food and a night's lodging, they were given, and safe passage accorded. Hence, the Mexican's sometime practice of luring the Indians into settlements with promises of food and talk, then sealing them off and murdering them, was eminently hateful.

Just because preliterate people wage war within a framework of specified expectations and norms, it should also not be assumed that they are uniformly dedicated merely to imposing their political will on their opponent, and accordingly interested only in neutralizing or conquering their military enemies. Indeed, they are often direct and pragmatic on this point. The Maoris, as cannibals, often ate their vanquished enemy. As one old Maori sagely explained such logic (Vayda 1967:372–73):

> You ask . . . if it is not better to save the life of an enemy, when you have rendered him helpless, than to kill him? No, it is not better; neither is it wise. What is the use of getting a man down, if you are fighting with him during wartime, or wounding him, unless you finish your work by killing him? Never, even, let him get up again; that would be wrong, and wasting all the advantage your strength and education had given to you, a wasteful expenditure of strength and *matawranga* (science), and a future source of trouble; think, too, of your cartridges wasted . . . So always kill your enemy, if you once get him under and make him fit for food. . . .

Furthermore, no matter how slavishly a preliterate group might tend to adhere to the customary rules of war, there are universal instances of individuals or groups that violate such rules, even if only in extraordinary or mitigating circumstances. To violate the rules and customs of war is a vagrancy of social conformity and constitutes deviancy just as any other normative violation in a given society. One modality of such offense is the violation of those military norms that address the treatment of the enemy's person either as combat opponent or as captive of war. Offenses against the person of the enemy represent a particularly reprehensible pattern of inter-occupational crime and may elicit sanction from the enemy military, if not one's own military.

The exact pattern of behavior defined as a military offense and the particular configuration of sanction, as well as the source of the sanction, are all a function of the definitional contextual setting in which the offense occurs, and the level of normative dictate and specificity.

The Norms of International Military Agreement

War has always been fought according to rules. Frequently these rules originated in the mutual negotiations and agreements between opponents. In some cases the rules have evolved on a unilateral basis and have grown out of the ideological conviction of a particular society.[2] In the Hindu *Book of Manu,* written 30 centuries ago, there are various proscriptions and prescriptions pertaining to the conduct of land warfare (Friedman 1972:3). Similarly, at the time of the Egyptian and Sumerian Wars of the second millenium B.C., there were rules defining the circumstances under which war might be initiated. In ancient China there were also rules circumscribing hostilities, including the prohibition of war during the planting and harvesting seasons. A formal exchange of letters generally preceded hostilities among the Hittites of the fourteenth century B.C. There were also numerous instances of norms regarding the humane treatment of prisoners of war. Sun Tzu, in his military classic *The Art of War,* written in the fourth century B.C., counseled that "all of the soldiers taken must be cared for with magnanimity and sincerely so that they may be used for us." The Babylonians of the seventh century B.C. also treated prisoners in accordance with well-established rules. The rules governing war observed by the ancient Hebrews are laid out in Deuteronomy 20. Innumerable agreements and treaties were established between and among nations and societies over the span of history, and have addressed every minute facet of war and the conduct of its participants. Often these bodies of rules and laws concerning warfare grew out of encyclopedic efforts at documenting the history of the laws of war. One such famous treatise was Hugo Grotius's monumental three-volume work, *On the Law of War and Peace,* written in 1625 (see Friedman 1972:3–146). Grotius's definitive book of legal precedents was no doubt the basis for many later legal treaties and agreements concerning the conduct of war.

Some of the earlier international treaties of the past few centuries seemed to concern themselves primarily with economic concerns, such as appropriate rules on the maritime law of capture. More recently, however, the various international treaties have

[2] Our discussion in this subsection draws heavily on Friedman (1972).

tended to address the treatment of combatants and the proper instruments of war. In 1864 the Geneva Conference "established protective principles for Red Cross personnel and others engaged in helping the wounded" (Friedman 1972:151). About this time explosive bullets were developed, and the leading military powers, thinking that this weapon caused unnecessary suffering while not adding that much to their weapons capability, met at St. Petersburg in 1868 and agreed to ban the explosive bullet as an instrument of war. As military technology rapidly advanced and the small-bore rifle, the Maxim machine gun, submarines, balloons, and rapid-fire artillery pieces appeared, some nations feared that their own military parity was being eroded. Tsar Nicholas II of Russia, for example, realized that his country was not economically able to stay up with other nations in the arms technology race. In 1898 he called for all nations of the world to join in a conference to limit armaments. Representatives from 26 nations met at The Hague in 1899. The stronger nations managed to prevent the imposition of any serious limitation on the conduct of war. The United States opposed a ban on poisonous gas and England and the United States opposed a ban on dum-dum bullets.[3] Ultimately, agreements were reached on such issues as treatment of prisoners of war and the wounded. Proposals to ban poisonous gas, dum-dum bullets, and the dropping of bombs from balloons (for five years) were adopted. Other international agreements were reached in 1904 and 1906, and in 1907 a second international conference was called to refine and extend the rules of war. A third international

[3] The term "dum-dum bullet" refers to hollow-point or other forms of expanding bullets fired from rifles and handguns. The term derives from the fact of one Capt. Bertie Clay, a British officer attached to the munitions works at Dum Dum, near Calcutta, discovering in the late nineteenth century that certain configurations of soft-nosed bullets tended to expand on impact, making them more effective. At that time the British were fighting the tribesmen along India's northwest frontier and the expanding projectiles tended to inflict a more severe and thus more potentially lethal wound. Because such bullets were subsequently outlawed by the Hague Conference, the U.S. military has traditionally used full copper-jacketed bullets. In recent years, however, our adoption of the M-16 rifle and its .223 ammunition as one of our standard service calibers has, in effect, subverted the Hague prohibition on dum-dums. The .223 bullet is a high-velocity projectile and is not well stablized when fired. When it hits a target such as an enemy soldier, it tends to tumble and act as a buzz saw, doing more tissue damage than larger full-jacketed caliber bullets. Many police and other law-enforcement departments are now beginning to use hollow-point, dum-dum bullets, and this practice is creating something of a public controversy inasmuch as some feel such bullets to be "inhuman" and "totally at odds with any sense of rehabilitation" (Newsweek 1974b:53).

conference was planned for 1915, but World War I intervened. In 1922 there was another conference on the rules of war at the Hague, and additional agreements were reached in 1922 and 1925, including a ban on the use of asphyxiating gases and bacteriological agents.[4] The subsequent conference at Geneva at the end of the decade produced a far more comprehensive code concerning the treatment of prisoners of war and the sick and the wounded. The Kellog-Briand Pact signed in Paris in 1928 made war itself illegal, and in theory did away with the need for elaborate rules of war. The 1930 Treaty of London mandated that submarines attempt to save the crew and passengers of all ships they torpedoed.[5] World War II demonstrated that the various treaties and agreements concerning the treatment of prisoners of war and captured enemy civilian populations were inadequate, and again Geneva was chosen as the site for an international conference in 1949. At present, 110 nations have agreed to the rules that grew out of that conference. Since then, the United Nations has issued various resolutions on certain aspects of warfare, such as the 1961 resolution condemning the use of nuclear weapons.

Violations of the various international treaties have been widespread in all of the wars that have intervened since the conventions produced the rules. Not infrequently, these violations occur with the tacit, if not the deliberate, assent of the military or militaries involved. At the time of the Italo-Ethiopian War in 1935–36, gas warfare was theoretically prohibited by international treaty. The Italian army, however, used it with great effectiveness against the ill-equipped Ethiopian tribesmen. Dugan and Lafore (1973:246) state that in one battle the Ethiopian commander had to retreat because of the gas:

> His retreat, he wrote, was decided by his own refusal to expose his men to the horrors of poison gas, which he said was used very lavishly by the enemy. It contaminated the whole countryside, he said, killed more than 2,000 animals, as well as uncounted men, and made further offensive operations impossible.

[4] Although the 1925 international agreement barred the use of all gases and bacteriological agents, the U.S. Senate never ratified the treaty. The U.S. military voluntarily refrained from using gas warfare in World War II, both because of humanitarian reasons and perhaps because of fear of retaliation by the enemy. In Korea and Vietnam, however, the U.S. military did make use of tear gas and other forms of nonlethal gases, even though we were widely critized for doing so.

[5] This norm was violated by every nation with submarines during World War II (Friedman 1972:154).

The authors go on to cite another authority who reported: "I can state with *absolute certainty* that . . . the lower regions of Tembien were drenched with yperite [mustard gas] on several occasions." There was worldwide indignation and strong criticism of the Italians for using gas, and also for their indiscriminate air attacks. The Italians tried to counter this bad image by claiming that the Ethiopians were using dum-dum bullets supplied by England (Dugan and Lafore 1973:255). In the Sino-Japanese war there were reports of isolated use of gas by the Japanese.

Shotguns were not prohibited by treaty in World War I and were used, especially by the Americans. Winchester model 97 pump shotguns with sawed-off barrels and fitted bayonets were used as "trench" weapons to assault enemy emplacements. Although they were outlawed in World War II and subsequent wars, the Americans occasionally still used them. They were issued to MP's and used in guarding POW camps. They also were issued in some instances as Special Services equipment for entertainment and recreation purposes to hunt and shoot skeet. Occasionally in World War II and in the Korean campaign, they would be subverted into offensive use. In the early stages of Vietnam the offensive use of shotguns by U.S. troops was not infrequent.

Most violations of international treaty norms, however, have involved the treatment of prisoners. Every war and conflict has seen such violations and every military of every country has been guilty at one time or another of violating both the letter and the spirit of treaty norms. Where the individual violates such a norm on his own, he might well be sanctioned by his own superiors. If he were to be caught by the enemy who had evidence of his offenses, he might be executed. A captured soldier with dum-dum bullets in his possession, or who had been seen mistreating or killing prisoners, might well be killed on the spot himself. After a war, the victors have often punished members of the enemy military for their offenses and transgressions against the international treaty norms of warfare. The various war-crimes trials following World War II represent signal examples of such military justice.

In general, unless forced into violating the international rules of war by military exigency, or unless the enemy failed to observe the rules, most militaries in contemporary times have attempted to observe such norms. In World War II the German Panzer Col. Jochen Peiper captured an American battalion commander, Hal McCown, during the Ardennes offensive. McCown had a lengthy discussion with the German officer and finally asked (Whiting 1971:150): " 'Colonel Peiper,' he said, 'will you give your personal assurance that you'll abide by the rules of Land Warfare?' Peiper looked at him solemnly: 'You have my word,' he answered." McCown further indicated that in several days of captivity he observed only one breach of the Geneva Convention, when Peiper ordered some American POW's to load some trucks under fire. Peiper's endorsement of the Rules of Land Warfare was apparently situational, however, and dependent on his perception of the enemy. When McCown asked him about the "notoriously ruthless" treatment of Russian prisoners taken by the Germans, Peiper replied in this manner.(Whiting 1971:149–50):

> Peiper smiled: "I'd like to take you to the Eastern Front," he said enthusiastically. "Then you'd see why we've had to violate all of the rules of warfare. The Russians have no idea what the Geneva Convention means. Some day, perhaps, you Americans will find out for yourselves, and you'll have to admit our behavior on the Western Front has been very correct."

It would appear that international treaties and agreements concerning the conduct of war are often highly idealized and not always based on humane rationale, but sometimes reflect more of a concern with military parity and thwarting of retaliation. In any event, the rules emerging from such treaties and agreements are sufficiently abstract and impractical within the context of modern mass warfare. Definition and implementation of the rules is often largely a matter of individual military entities' and units' interpreting the requirements for combat behavior and dictating the appropriate posture and mode of warfare.

The Combat Norms of Individual Units

The rules and laws of warfare established by international treaty or mutual agreement may establish the broad parameters of military behavior toward the enemy, but the more specific combat configurations and the individual posture in regard to the appropriate degree of violence to be visited upon the enemy is largely a matter of definition by particular military entities or units. All of the subunits of a given armed force share the overall mission of defeating the enemy, including killing enemy troops, if necessary.

Certain units, and especially elite units, may be more intense in pursuing that mission. Such elite units are frequently shock troops committed to battle in the vanguard of the assault, or where enemy resistance is expected to be the stiffest. The shock troops are expected , in effect, to absorb more violence from the enemy as well as to carry more violence to the enemy. They must be overachievers in terms of combat effectiveness. To accomplish this degree of combat effectiveness, these elite troops must go beyond the limits of prescribed warfare behavior. They must be more efficient at destroying the enemy, they must be more aggressive, they must be more inured to death and violence, and they must be ruthless in dealing with the enemy. In this regard, they may, in a sense, have to disregard some rules of warfare established by treaty. Blake (1970:339) has commented on this and points out that:

> In some units a certain amount of fighting spirit (lack of discipline) is encouraged as a characteristic. The foremost sign of achievement is combat experience, and the actor is encouraged to look forward to combat.

This particular frame of mind is produced through an intensive and rigorous training process in which the individual soldier is "hardened" and effectively socialized into violence (see Blake 1970). Elite units such as the U.S. Marine Corps, U.S. Special Forces, British Commandos, the German Waffen SS of World War II, and U.S. Airborne Forces, to name some examples, institutionalized such a regime of training and indoctrination (see Stack 1975; Neumann 1960; Weiss 1967; Levy 1971; Mares 1971).

Excessive ruthlessness toward the enemy that may exceed the limits established by international treaty is often manifested in acts of "not taking prisoners" (i.e., not allowing enemy soldiers to surrender, shooting them as they surrender, or even killing them after they have been captured). Such behavior is proscribed by military regulation in the U.S. military as well as many other foreign armed forces, in addition to being prohibited by international treaty. The killing of military prisoners would then represent a serious mode of military crime. Blake (1970:342) points out that "the general rule in use by modern armies is that killing prisoners of war is unnecessary and unjustified." He goes on to report, however, that his analysis of numerous sources pertaining to ground combat suggests that the killing of prisoners is not infrequent. He concludes that, "to the higher organizational authorities, the norm is virtually never officially suspended."

Elite troops, because of the aggressiveness component in their "fighting spirit," may be more prone than other units "not to take prisoners." As Adleman and Walton (1966:131) put it, "most shock troops are rarely prepared to take prisoners," since not doing so would in effect be living up to their reputation and self-image of asking and giving no quarter. Shooting enemy personnel who are trying to surrender may occur on occasion among all kinds of military unit, if the men in the unit are of such a mind. Parks (1968:112–13) gives an account of a firefight between an American unit and some Vietcong in Vietnam. One of the U.S. soldiers shot a Vietcong hiding under water and, as the wounded enemy soldier stood up and tried to surrender, begging for his life, the U.S. soldier emptied another clip of ammunition into him. Another U.S. soldier in the same fight shot a wounded Vietcong soldier who had one of his legs blown off. Toland (1959:338), in his history of the Battle of the Bulge in World War II, tells of a group of American paratroopers who charged a row of German foxholes. As the Americans drew near the enemy positions, "twenty-five Germans popped out of foxholes, hands over head, shouting, 'Kamerad.' " In the heat of the attack, however, some of the Americans were not disposed to take prisoners. As Toland describes it: "Several paratroopers thrust their bayonets into the surrendering prisoners. One trooper, trying vainly to pull out his bayonet, finally released the flip and left his bayonet in the dead man's chest."

Some military units and some nationalities have developed particularly fearsome reputations because of their ruthlessness. In the Korean War the Turkish and Ethiopian units became almost the object of legend because of their alleged fearlessness and merciless behavior toward the enemy.[6] In World War I the French Senegalese troops enjoyed a similar reputation, especially with the Germans. In World War II the Tatar and Mongol units of the Russian army were reputed to be particularly tough and vicious fighters. Of course, such units with distinctive racial or nationality characteristics had a high degree of group solidarity and morale. In most cases the personnel in these units have come from peasant or even preliterate backgrounds and were, in a sense, inured to deprivation and the rigors of military existence. They were, in most instances,

[6] A popular story told about the Turkish Brigade in the Korean War was that if they caught a Korean attempting to steal supplies from their compound, they killed the culprit by jamming a rifle cleaning rod in one of his ears and out the other. They then hung the body up on the perimeter wire. A number of persons have told me this story and I am inclined to believe it to be valid.

also inured to violence and death. Some had tribal backgrounds with a warrior tradition, and thus made particularly fearsome combat soldiers. During the Spanish civil war the "Moors" or Moroccans, who fought in the Army of Africa on the side of the Nationalists, were warriors by birth and tradition, and made exceptionally aggressive and tenacious soldiers. These characteristics, plus the fact of their cultural background, which provided them with a perspective of appropriate behavior in war and combat different from that held by most of the European combatants, tended to also make them more prone to atrocities and violations of the accepted rules of warfare. In Thomas's (1961:375–76) definitive account of the Spanish civil war, he relates that in the battle of the Jarama the Nationalist forces managed to force their way across the Jarama River. Some Moroccans managed to knife the sentries of the French André Marty battalion, permitting elements of the Nationalist cavalry to cross the river and subsequently surround this Loyalists battalion, members of which fought until their ammunition was exhausted. At this point, according to Thomas, "the Moroccan cavalry charged and killed most of the survivors."

In the siege of the Alcazar, the Nationalists succeeded in relieving the citadel when the Loyalists militia fled in the face of the Moorish attack. As Thomas (1961:284) put it:

> Once again, *the violence and training* [italics added] of the Army of Africa told immediately, although Toledo is easy to defend. . . . There remained only the usual bloodbath that always attended a Nationalist capture of a town.

As the Nationalist troops enterd the town, the mutilated bodies of two Nationalist airmen were discovered. As a result of this, no prisoners were taken. As usual, the Moors were particularly brutal in their assault. Thomas tells that "Moroccans killed the doctor and a number of wounded militiamen in their beds at the San Juan hospital." The Moroccans operated throughout the war according to their own traditional concepts and perceptions of appropriate battle, even though this often tended to violate the European military norms at both formal and informal levels. Thus we have an instance of military culture clash where combatants on both sides may be adhering to their respective normative structure, but where there is a lack of convergence of the two normative structures. In this instance, of course, the Moroccans were fighting in the Spanish Nationalist Army and, in theory, were subject to the norms of that military entity. Spanish Nationalist military authorities, however, tended to accommodate the Moorish fighting customs so as not to alienate or constrict the combat capability of the Army of Africa. They even encouraged the Moorish military ruthlessness in many instances as a means of undermining the morale of the Republican forces. As time went on, the Nationalist military leaders did take steps to curb and control the excesses of the Moorish troops. In the instance of the mutilated bodies of the Nationalist airmen found in Toledo, the Nationalist forces viewed this as a violation of the norms of war—a military crime—and thus permitted military crimes in the form of taking no prisoners, and the shooting of the Republican wounded in the hospital.

The killing of enemy wounded has not been an uncommon practice in any war. Keegan (1976:200), for example, reports that in the Battle of Waterloo the Prussians bayoneted the French wounded, French lancers routinely speared British wounded, and the British cavalry, in turn, "were guilty of cutting at the French wounded." In World War I, in the Battle of the Somme, both the British and the Germans fired at prisoners as they were being taken to the rear, and shot at wounded men as well (Keegan 1976:278).

It is not only constituent units comprised of aliens in a given armed force that develop fearsome reputations. Many elite units develop deservedly ferocious reputations, and often try to live up to their legends, even to the extent of violating various norms and rules of war. In World War II the Germans labeled our airborne troops as "those devils in baggy pants." The joint U.S./Canadian First Special Service Force was called "The Black Devil's Brigade" (Adleman and Walton 1966:178–79) by the Germans, who feared them as much as any other Allied unit. To embellish this rumor, the commander of the unit, Gen. Robert T. Frederick, had printed up a supply of stickers that contained the unit's insignia and the inscription, "The Worst Is Yet to Come." When a member of the Force killed a German, he would paste one of the stickers on the helmet or the forehead of the dead enemy soldier. The Force had the motto, "Killing Is Our Business." The Germans believed that this unit took no prisoners (which it did), that many of the men were ex-convicts (which some of them were), and that they would show them no mercy (which they sometimes did.)[7] In any event,

---

[7] Although the First Special Service Force had a particularly bloodthirsty reputation, and did not, as a general rule, take prisoners unless they were needed for intelligence purposes, there was a streak of humanity in some of them. Adleman

they did kill or capture more than their share of enemy personnel, often using techniques and behavior that violated traditional military norms in regard to battle and combat.

All such elite units tend to have a fanatical fighting spirit and an ideology of combat ruthlessness that seeks to annihilate the enemy without necessarily observing the niceties of war. Some indication of the intensity of the dedication to combat held by some military units can perhaps be deduced from the practice of members of the Spanish Foreigh Legion to speak of themselves as being married symbolically to death. For such troops, death, given or received, is their raison d'être, and it might be expected that for them the object of combat is to kill, regardless of the technicalities of the formal military laws of war and combat. In this regard, Thomas (1961:247) provides an excellent example in describing an attack of the Spanish Foreign Legion on Republican forces during the Spanish civil war: He writes:

> A *bandera* of the Legion stormed the Puerta de la Trinidad singing, at the moment of the advance, their regimental hymn proclaiming their bride to be death.[8] At the first assault, they were driven back by the militia's machine guns. At the next, the

---

and Walton (1966:157) relate the poignant story of one of their patrols capturing a German prisoner on a particularly bitter cold night. The miserable prisoner was turned over to one of the "large, hard-boiled sergeants." There was concern lest the sergeant might shoot the prisoner. "Instead the sergeant took off a woolen scarf he was wearing and offered it to the prisoner. . . ." The prisoner did not understand the gesture and bent down and began tying the scarf around the sergeant's ankles. The sergeant took the scarf from the prisoner and tucked it around the German's neck for him.

[8] It is difficult to determine whether this unit's practice of using a hymn to death as a regimental song represents a serious ideological posture of morbidity or is simply a mechanism for handling fear and anxiety. Many military units have songs for such purposes. In some U.S. airborne units there is even a paratroop song that is morbid to the extreme (Weiss 1967:26). This song, sung to the tune of the "Battle Hymn of the Republic," contains such gory stanzas as:

> There was blood upon the risers,
>   there were brains upon the chute,
> His intestines were a dangling
>   from his paratrooper boots;
> They picked him up still in his chute
>   and poured him from his boots;
> O he ain't gonna jump no more!

And it goes on to conclude in the chorus that: "Glory gory what a helluva way to die!" Such lyrics serve as a means of reducing tension and ameliorating fear by externalizing it and subjecting it to ridicule in a manner not unlike "gallows humor."

legionnaires forced their way through, stabbing their enemies with knives. . . . The legionnaires killed anyone with arms, including two militiamen who were killed on the steps of the high altar of the cathedral. Many militiamen, who though disarmed could hardly be said to have surrendered, were shot in the bull-ring.[9]

Particular military units might undertake to commit crimes against the person of enemy soldiers, such as shooting individuals trying to surrender, for a number of reasons, including the intensity of the attack, or because the enemy committed some such crime initially and thus a reciprocity is invoked. In one attack by the First Special Service Force in the Italian campaign in World War II, one of the unit officers and his squad "flushed out" a group of German soldiers from a hidden enplacement (Adleman and Walton 1966:131). The first German raised a white flag and the officer went forward to grab him. As he did, one of the enemy soldiers shot the officer in the face, killing him. The men of the American squad opened fire on the rest of the Germans, killing them all. Angered by what they perceived as treachery and a violation of the norms of battle, members of the Force "never took prisoners, unless specifically ordered to," when prisoners were needed for intelligence interrogation purposes.

Blake (1970:342–43) has articulated several factors "which lead to the definition of killing prisoners as necessary or justified." He mentions the factor of "reprehensible conduct" by enemy personnel who have been captured, or by their compatriots. In some instances the enemy may have the reputation of routinely committing "reprehensible acts" and may suffer accordingly, whether or not there is any validity to the labeling. Ware (1960:2–3), for example, relates that in the latter part of the Civil War, the Confederacy recruited a number of Indians to fight in its ranks. Word of this spread to the northern newspapers and, because of their fearsome reputation, these Indians were marked for execution, in spite of the fact that they were to be soldiers and should be treated accordingly. As Ware summarizes it:

> As the methods of Indian warfare were known, and no one expected any quarter from Indians, the sentiment prevailed that every Indian caught in hostility to the Government should be

---

9   Estimates of the number of militiamen killed in the bull-ring vary from 200 to 2,000 (Thomas 1961:247).

summarily killed, and no feelings of humanity or sentiment seemed to oppose it.

Reprehensible conduct might include such things as being a sniper. Enemy snipers, especially if they have recently killed a member of the unit, are often viewed as being guilty of reprehensible conduct. Atwell (1958:298–99, 393, 495) relates several instances during World War II when captured snipers were shot out of hand. In one case an American general took a German sniper out of a POW cage, had him marched out of town and made to dig his own grave, then executed him. Bloem (1967:40), in his account of a German unit in World War I, relates that when a patrol of German Hussars rode into a Belgian village, one of the men was shot dead from ambush. The other Hussars dismounted, entered a house, and found two peasants with rifles. The peasants were promptly shot, and the village was burned for revenge.

Reprehensible conduct might also mean the act of being a partisan (Bloem 1967:40–41; Pabel 1955:100; Neumann 1958:159–62). Where partisans had ambushed a military unit, or used some other guile or deception to kill soldiers, the victimized military unit may be particularly ruthless in extracting their vengence. Neumann (1958:192–205) tells of a German Waffen SS unit, moving by train through Russia during World War II, whose train was attacked by a band of Russian partisans. The partisans managed to kill several of the Germans in their ambush, but ultimately the Germans killed or captured the partisans. The partisans were interrogated, beaten, stripped naked, and thrown in the snow. One was stabbed in the throat, but the others still refused to divulge the location of other partisans. Finally, the SS officer doing the interrogating ordered up a flame-thrower unit and had the flame-thrower operator douse one of the partisans with a burst of flaming fuel. The Russian partisan died in agony, and even the hardened SS troops were stunned and sickened. The other partisans, including two women, were then mercifully machine gunned. Prior to the use of the flame thrower, members of the SS unit had seen the death of the partisans (both in the attack and the one stabbed in the interrogation) as being justified in view of their ambush, which killed members of the SS unit. Neumann (1958:200) succinctly sums up this feeling when he says:

> Personally, I am unable to feel the slightest pity for either the men or the women. Their sufferings are a matter of complete indifference to me. They even provide a sort of balm to ease my

own grief. They relieve, momentarily, the insatiable thirst for vengeance which is devouring me. *They have killed, like cowards, in the dark* [italics added]. For their country? Perhaps. But for our own country's sake, I fully accept Stressling's decision: death to them.

During World War II the German Waffen SS had specific orders to shoot, without trial, all Russian People's Commissars and Jewish functionaries, civil or military (Neumann 1958:126). The Russian high command conversely urged their soldiers and their partisans to shoot, without a trial, any SS personnel captured in action (Neumann 1958:212). The red troops did exactly that, shooting "without trial all men captured wearing SS uniforms" (Neumann 1958:269).

In some cases, enemy prisoners are not killed out of a lust for killing, but rather as a simple military expediency. When a unit is on the move, prisoners are a decided liability. Sometimes it is necessary, or at least simpler, to kill them than to attempt to carry them along. MacDonald (1947:155, 157), in his account of combat with the 23rd Infantry of the Second Infantry Division during World War II, describes such a situation. MacDonald, the company commander, called one of his platoons on the radio, and a Sergeant Patton replied:

> "We've got three prisoners in the basement of a house," Patton said, "and we have to cross a hundred yards of open field to get back out. We'll never make it with the prisoners."
> "Roger," I answered, "Do what you can."

Later the company commander reflected:

> Sergeant Patton's platoon arrived, tired and dusty from the tiring uphill walk from Bendorf-Sayn. The prisoners were not with them.
> *Company G today committed a war crime. They are going to win the war, however, so I don't suppose it really matters.*

Military expediency, requiring the killing of prisoners, might also occur in other contexts. In the Battle of Agincourt in 1415, Henry V, king of England, had invaded France and was locked in combat with a formidable French army. The English had taken a number of French prisoners, and were keeping them to the rear of their forces. Facing the possibility of an attack by the French cavalry, and the further possibility, in this event, of the French prisoners in the rear rearming themselves from the "jetsam of battle" and attacking the English rear, Henry ordered 200 of his archers to kill the prisoners. The lives of some of the more valuable prisoners were spared, but the archers began the execution, only to have Henry order the killings stopped when he saw the French third division retiring from their attack position and preparing to leave the field of battle (Keegan 1976:107-12). Henry was well aware that such behavior on his part was a gross violation of the extant international rules "governing relations between a prisoner and his captor." Furthermore, he also knew that his order outraged his knights and subordinates almost to the point of refusing to obey. After all, the prisoners really belonged to the knights and soldiers who had captured them. Prisoners could be ramsoned, and thus had a value. In the interest of military expediency, Henry nevertheless elected to be a military offender in order to survive the battle.

Blake (1970:343) points out that where the enemy commits atrocities, there is more of a tendency for military units to seek revenge through the killing of prisoners, especially in the period immediately after members of the unit have seen the atrocities. Keegan (1976:49), for example, relates the story of some Australian troops in World War I who were surrendered to by some Germans in a pillbox. The Australians relaxed as the surrendering Germans came out, but then a German sniper in the top of the pillbox shot an Australian soldier. Another Australian, in anger, was about to bayonet one of the surrendered German soldiers when he realized that his bayonet was not on his rifle. "While the wretched man implored him for mercy, he grimly fixed it and then bayoneted the man."

Although the highly propagandistic war movies in the United States during World War II always portrayed the Nazi, and especially the Japanese pilot, as the villain who would strafe a helpless enemy, in actual practice, the Americans were often prone to strafe helpless enemy troops. At one point in the war, a Japanese troop convoy was traveling through the Bismarck Sea when it was attacked by bombers of the U.S. Fifth Air Force. Some of the B-25's had been equipped with eight .50-caliber machine guns in the nose, and when the B-25's came in at wavetop for their bomb run, they were able to spray the Japanese troops crowded on the decks with machine-gun fire. According to Toland's account (1971:497), "It was slaughter." Several ships went down as the planes continued to bomb and strafe. The American planes were determined to destroy the Japanese troops and, as Toland describes it:

> The attack continued through the afternoon. The damaged ships were finished off, and the survivors in rafts and lifeboats ruthlessly strafed. The attackers were in no mood to fight a gentleman's war. They had heard too many stories from Australians whose buddies had been bayoneted after capture and left to perish with placards reading: "It took them a long time to die."

It was later rationalized that inasmuch as "Japanese soldiers do not surrender," they might have swum to shore and joined Japanese forces there. Thus the strafing "was a grisly task, but a *military necessity*" [italics added.]. Several hundred Japanese troops did manage to swim ashore to New Guinea, but there they faced Papuan natives who tracked most of them down "as in the old head-hunting days." Needless to say, after the strafing by the Americans, the Japanese resented being labeled as inhuman for sometimes strafing parachuting American pilots.

Later in the campaign for the Philippines, 200 American carrier planes from Task Force 38 caught a Japanese troop convoy and bombed it, sinking every transport and four destroyers (Toland 1971:667–68). The American planes busied themselves in "strafing the men struggling in the water. The slaughter was frightful." Of the 10,000 troops, only a few managed to swim ashore through the "crimson sea." The Japanese were sometimes more humane than the Americans in regard to this kind of behavior. When Japanese planes bombed and sank the British battlehsip *Repulse*, hundreds of British sailors were in the water. The leader of the last wing of Japanese bombers, Lieutenant Iki, could see British destroyers picking up survivors. He did not attack the men in the water, inasmuch as "It never occurred to Iki to strafe them. The British had fought gallantly, in the tradition of *bushido*. He had yet to learn that an enemy spared today may kill you tomorrow" (Toland 1971:276). The next day Lieutenant Iki flew over the spot where *Repulse* and another battleship *Prince of Wales*, had been sunk and dropped bunches of flowers.

The American penchant for destroying the enemy was not confined to the naval context. Toland (1971:661–63) tells of a battle in the Philippines where an American infantry unit overran a string of Japanese enplacements after a devastating mortar barrage. All of the Japanese soldiers were dead or wounded. The Americans went from hole to hole, machine gunning the dead and wounded occupants. Many American GI's in the Philippines were angered by the Japanese treatment of the American and Filipino prisoners of war that they liberated, and undertook to annihilate the Japanese troops with "vehemence" (Toland 1971:766). Posters exhorted the Americans "to have no mercy on the 'yellow bastards.' " Excesses toward the Japanese military personnel were not at all uncommon. Toland cites Charles Lindbergh, who, after touring the Pacific, wrote cogently:

> Our men think nothing of shooting a Japanese prisoner or a soldier attempting to surrender. They treat the Japs with less respect than they would give an animal, and these acts are condoned by almost everyone. We claim to be fighting for civilization, but the more I see of this war in the Pacific, the less right I think we have to claim to be civilized. In fact, I am not sure that our record in this respect stands so much higher than the Japs.

There is a thin line between the aggressive fighting spirit displayed by some units and their group-defined ruthlessness as military necessity, and the inhumanity of indiscriminate slaughter as reprisal or butchery as military expediency.

Violations of the Norms of Humanity

Regardless of the particular posture of a given military unit in regard to treatment of the enemy, there is usually a point of violence and ruthlessness beyond which they are not inured. This is to say, even for elite shock troops who may be hardened to give and expect no quarter, there are limits to their toleration of violence. Seeing combat deaths, not taking prisoners, and even engaging in isolated incidences of shooting prisoners either for revenge or for the sake of expedience, or having the enemy act in a similar fashion, may represent acceptable and appropriate military behavior and be viewed as merely the exigencies of war. Some actions on the part of the enemy may exceed this threshold of toleration, and such atrocities may precipitate similar atrocities or even acts of greater cruelty in retaliation. Giles (1965:200–201) tells of an American unit during World War II that entered a small European town formerly occupied by German tanks. They discovered that a number of civilians had been butchered by the Germans before leaving. As Giles describes the scene:

> We were shown what had happened in a cellar of one of the houses. Apparently the Germans had gathered all of the people left in the town into the cellar of one of the houses and there they proceeded to punish them for befriending the Americans. Two small children actually had their heads smashed in. Men were dismembered and shot. One pregnant woman had been cut open and left to die. The scene was viewed by hundreds of GI's. . . .

In response to this atrocity, the American troops undertook to commit a reprisal atrocity. Giles goes on to describe this action:

> Prisoners were . . . rounded up and brought to the bridge . . . and marched, some practically naked, most without shoes, to that particular cellar and forced to view the awful scene in it. From there, they were marched through the town into a wooded section, from whence shortly came the sounds of much shooting. . . . I have always been glad the 291st had no part in the executions.

Where a unit might, with the assent of the commanding officer, adapt a policy of not taking prisoners, and perhaps have the unanimous support of the troops, atrocities such as the one described above seldom enjoy the approval of higher authority or the uniform support of all the men in the unit. Frequently there is conflict concerning the commission of such as act, and some members of the unit may attempt to prevent it. Blake (1970:343–44), in his discussion of the killing of prisoners, discusses several illustrations of individuals intervening to prevent the killing of prisoners. Two of these were reported by Toland (1959:71, 225–26). The first was an instance of a German Panzer unit that captured some American soldiers. A German officer ordered a sergeant to "shoot them all" (eight had previously been shot), but another officer wearing SS insignia came over and said, "Leave them alone, sergeant." Consoling a civilian who had tried to intercede in the execution, the officer put his hand on the man's back and remarked, "You're right, mein herr. It's a shame how some people treat prisoners." The officer then turned to the sergeant and ordered, "put these men in that room and treat them as you'd want the Amis to treat you." In the other incident, five Germans ran from a blazing armored car toward cover in a ditch. An American lieutenant saw them, ran up, and shot one of the Germans in the back of the head with his

.45 automatic. An American colonel observing him shouted at the lieutenant to stop, but the lieutenant murdered another helpless German. As he was about to kill a third, another American knocked the gun out of his hand. The colonel gave the lieutenant a dressing down, and then left the scene. No doubt distrubed by the cruelty and inhumanity of the lieutenant's behavior, he also had some pragmatic concerns about the incident. As Toland puts it, "A likely prospect for imminent capture, he now had two Germans, shot in the back of the head."

In both cases another officer intervened in the killing and took issue with such action. As Blake (1970:344) has cogently observed, "It should be apparent, then, that a definite conflict exists regarding the utilization or suspension of the rule concerning the treatment of prisoners." When military expediency and the impedus of combat give way to deliberate atrocity and massacre, the solidity of collective ideology becomes much diluted. The conflict of values attendant to war and combat becomes compounded and evident in the face of excessive cruelty and inhumane behavior. Official military doctrine, supported by international treaty, may proscribe the shooting of enemy troops attempting to surrender. Individual unit ideology, however, may normatively dictate such action, especially in the heat of battle and the intensity of attack, or in retaliation for some enemy offense. Combat excesses, such as systematically killing numbers of prisoners, transgresses both sets of norms as well as a more generalized set of normative expectations in regard to the behavior of a civilized individual. Such behavior transmutes the role of the soldier to that of butcher and barbarian.

Where such acts of excessive inhumanity occur, the conquering military may undertake to seek out and punish the offenders. Many of the war crimes trials after World War II, such as the Nuremberg trials, addressed crimes of enemy military personnel directed at military personnel in the Allied armies. One of the most widely publicized and infamous incidents of inter-occupational crime against person was the so-called "Malmédy massacre" (see Whiting 1971). During World War II, when German units attacked the American line through the Ardennes, large numbers of American troops were captured by the fast-moving Panzer columns. One of these—Battlegroup Peiper—commanded by a young SS colonel, Jochen Peiper, overran some American units and took a number of prisoners. The prisoners were a burden to the German Panzer unit in that they could not easily be carried along on their advance. Approximately 150 American prisoners were gathered together in a field at the Baugnez crossroads near the town of Malmédy. Suddenly two German armored vehicles pulled up to the group of prisoners, and a German soldier in one of the vehicles took out his pistol and began to shoot the Americans one by one. At this point, other German troops in other tanks and vehicles opened up on the helpless prisoners with machine guns. Some tried to run for cover and were cut down by gunfire. As they all lay dead or dying, some of the SS troops walked among the prostrate bodies, kicking them to see if any were alive. As some moved or flinched, the Germans shot them. At this point, 84 Americans were dead and the rest badly wounded.

As the Germans moved on, some wounded Americans did manage to get up and run into the woods. Some found their way to the town of Malmédy and were picked up by American units holding the town. Word of the massacre reached higher command, and the decision was made to give maximum publicity to the story. News of the incident quickly reached even front-line divisions. Everywhere along the American line, commanders were giving orders such as Whiting (1971:61) cites: "We're not taking any Krauts prisoner this time, fellers. Specially if they're SS." In some instances even written orders to this effect were issued, presumably with the tacit approval of higher command. The 328th Infantry Rgiment, in giving written instructions for an attack the next day, included the order, "No SS troops or paratroopers will be taken prisoner, but will be shot on sight. . . ."

After the end of the war, the U.S. military undertook to try those persons in the enemy military for crimes perpetrated against its own personnel. Colonel Peiper, his superior General Dietrich, other officers, and various individuals who had actively participated in the shooting—a total of 74 persons—were tried by an Allied war crimes commission for the crime against person that the Malmédy massacre represented. After the lenghty trial, all of the defendants, including Peiper, were found guilty of the Malmédy shootings, as well as some other incidents, and sentenced to death by hanging. There were stays of execution, however, and other legal efforts to change the sentence.[10] None of the defendants were

---

[10] At one point Peiper received a new trial because of the initiative of a young senator, Joe McCarthy. The new trial revealed that Peiper had been tortured by U.S. Intelligence to obtain his confessions. As a result, his death sentence was commuted to 12 years imprisonment (Whiting 1971: front flap).

ever hanged and, after 13 years in jail, Colonel Peiper was released.

Inappropriate violent behavior against the enemy, to the point of atrocity, is perhaps most likely where there is a widely held perception of the enemy as inhuman, subhuman, or racially inferior to the opposing military force. Certainly there has been a persistent trend in this regard with American forces. On December 29, 1890, a band of Minneconjou Indians led by Chief Big Foot was involved in a brief battle at the Cavalry Camp at Wounded Knee (see War Department 1892). U.S. cavalry troops disarmed some of the Indians, but, when an attempt was made to take a rifle from a young brave, the brave discharged the gun, and this was returned by fire from the troops. There was close fighting with knives, clubs, and pistols, but as the Indians began to spread out, several Hotchkiss guns overlooking the area opened fire. Ultimately 25 calvary troops were killed and 33 wounded, but approximately 200 Indian men, women, and children were killed or wounded. The military, even at the time, conceded that the response of the cavalry was excessive and exceeded the norms of war, but also maintained that the incident was provoked by the Indians' behavior.

During the Philippine insurrection in 1900, there were numerous incidents of military crimes against person perpetrated against the enemy, many reaching the point of atrocity. U.S. troops allegedly used dum-dum bullets, frequently shot prisoners after they had surrendered, shot prisoners as retaliation or reprisals for other acts committed by the enemy, and tortured prisoners (Miller 1970:23). The "water cure" was reported to be a favorite method of torture. The prisoner was made to drink large amounts of water, often salted. Then a soldier would jump on the victim's distended stomach and the process started over again. Homes and villages were burned, and their populations beaten and abused. The Filipinos admittedly committed some atrocities themselves, such as beheading a captured American soldier on one occasion. Many members of the military were "Old Indian fighters" and simply viewed the Filipino insurrectionists as "savages." Inasmuch as the insurrectionists were waging a guerilla-type war, U.S. military authorities saw them as deviants in regard to the traditional rules of war. General J.F. Bell said the Filipinos were carrying out "a reign of terror" that was "in direct violation of the well-known laws and usages of war" (Miller 1970:25). The Americans retaliated drastically against such acts as the Filipinos' use of booby traps and pits lined with bamboo spears. The insurrectionists were labeled as "goo goos," "Filipino niggers," "bandits," "criminals," and "veritable children" who had all "the weaknesses and the vices of the resourceless and unmoral human infant." President McKinley called the process of subduing the insurrectionists a process of "benign assimilation." Military commanders ordered their troops not to accord captured enemy soldiers the "privileges of war." General Chaffee said that "If you should hear of a few Filipinos more or less being put out of the way, don't grow too sentimental over it" (Miller 1970:25). The army simply attempted to exterminate the enemy, if it could not terrorize them into submission.

In time the full story of the atrocities and barbarous acts of the military came to the attention of the American public, and the general outrage, not unlike the reaction to atrocities in Vietnam, was too vocal to silence, and the crimes too heinous to cover up. There were U.S. Senate hearings and courts-martial. Included in the trials were officers like Brig. Gen. Jacob H. Smith, who ordered excessive retaliatory violence against the enemy military and civilians of Samar and ordered that no prisoners be taken. The court-martial found him guilty but, because of his military record, was lenient and only suspended him from command for one month and fined him $50.00 (Friedman 1972:819). There were other courts-martial, many resulting in lenient punishments. Lieutenant Preston Brown, who was accused of shooting an unarmed Filipino with a pistol, was originally found guilty and sentenced to be dismissed from military service and sent to prison for five years. Ultimately, however, his sentence was reduced to only a reduction of "thirty files in lineal rank on the list of first lieutenants of infantry" and to a forfeiture of one-half monthly pay for nine months (Friedman 1972:829). Crimes against the person of the enemy in the Philippine insurrection may have been formally sanctioned, but the sanctions were diluted or subverted because the enemy simply had not played the game of war according to traditional rules, and were an inferior race in addition.

Even in the Philippine insurrection or American Indian wars, U.S. military personnel did not act toward their enemies with the degree of brutality and inhumanity that they did in the Vietnamese conflict. Many of the atrocities committed by American troops were admittedly directed at civilians, and it is these that were most widely reported. Americans also frequently acted in a brutish fashion toward their allied troops, the ARVN. Where the enemy was concerned, there were, in many instances, simply no limits to what a U.S. or allied soldier could do. When enemy troops were captured, they might be routinely tortured and brutalized. The "telephone" hour, where captured enemy personnel would be shocked with a telephone magneto, was a popular mode of torture, as was the "water treatment," where the POW's were tied and water poured down their noses and mouths to make them strangle. There were instances of prisoners having fingers or toes cut off with a knife, joint by joint. Sometimes a Vietcong prisoner would be pushed out of a helicopter from a great height in order to "loosen the tongues" of the other prisoners who observed his fate. Mutilating, beating, and shooting Vietcong prisoners appear to have been endemic practices in almost all American military units.

The ARVN troops were perhaps even more brutal to captured Vietcong than were the Americans. Duncan (1967:162–70) tells of an attack on a Vietcong village by a unit of ARVN troops accompanied by American advisors. The ARVN troops fired the village and shot both civilians and suspected Vietcong. One captured Vietcong was brought out for interrogation, his hands tied behind his back with wire. He had multiple wounds, including a leg broken below the knee by a bullet. The ARVN poured water down the prisoner's nose and mouth, and they kicked his broken leg several times. The prisoner still refused to talk. An ARVN officer held him up by the hair and stuck a knife into his abdomen. Another ARVN officer took a knife and slashed the prisoner's gut open, striking him in the face as the prisoner screamed in agony. Then, according to Duncan:

> The body gives a few jerks, quivers, is still. Mon [the ARVN officer] shoves his hand into the stinking hole and brings out the gall bladder. Grinning triumphantly, he holds his gory trophy overhead for all to see.

An American NCO advisor, exposed for the first time to such butchery, tells his lieutenant that this has to be reported. The lieutenant replies: "Damn it Dick, calm down before they hear you. This is your first time out—it's always a shock the first time, I suppose, *but you get used to it* [italics added]. Relax."

Duncan (1967:156–61) notes that as a member of the Special Forces he received training in "interrogation," including torture techniques. In this connection, one of his instructors cogently points out: "Even if a trained interrogator is on hand, if the prisoner is not disposed to talk voluntarily, it is hardly the time or place to be concerned with the Geneva Conventions." On the whole, however, there would seem to be moral revulsion at the mistreatment of captured enemy personnel once they have actually been processed as POW's. A POW, in effect, takes on a different status than that of a soldier, even a recently captured soldier, and as such is in theory entitled to special treatment.[11] Failure to afford this treatment is a gross violation of the rules of war, and is often viewed as a crime against humanity as well as a military crime against person, and is severely sanctioned by both the military authority holding the prisoner and the enemy, should they ever have control of the violator. Following the Doolittle raid on Tokyo in World War II, the Japanese captured eight of the crewmen of the planes. After they were officially POW's they were starved, tortured, and made to sign "confessions" of war crimes. They were tried and found guilty of the crimes. Three of them were executed (Jablonski 1971:70). The people of the United States were horrified and enraged at this inhumanity and their resolve to destroy the Japanese military machine was strengthened.[12]

In general, in World War II, captured American soldiers processed as POW's were accorded relatively humane treatment by the Germans. There were other instances of Japanese brutality to POW's, however. There were numerous reports of American POW's being starved, subjected to freezing weather, and left to die of wounds and illness. Of 1,619 American POW's transported by ships from Manila to Japan, only 450 survived the trip (Toland 1971:711–15). One of the most infamous instances of the inhumane treatment of POW's was the "Bataan Death March" of World War II. Seventy-six thousand Filipino and U.S. servicemen were to be moved to POW camps. Between 7,000 and 10,000 soldiers died on this trip to Camp O'Donnell alone. Some of the POW's in the march encountered acts of kindness from their Japanese captors (Toland 1971:336). Many others, however, experienced beatings,

[11] A German prisoner in a POW camp in the U.S. in World War II has told how, when a guard cursed and verbally abused him, he filed a formal written complaint with the camp commander, as per the Geneva Convention provision that a prisoner must be protected against insults (Pabel 1955:158).

[12] Perhaps the public outrage at this atrocity was exacerbated by the publicity it received in America, including a film, *The Purple Heart*, which was obviously intended to make the act appear even more monstrous and inhumane.

kickings, bayoneting, starvation, slashings, and shootings. Some wounded Americans were buried alive, and others executed simply for falling down. Japanese soldiers driving past the marching prisoners in trucks would sometimes try to hit the men in the head with long bamboo poles. Allied forces in the Pacific theater, having learned of such atrocities, tended not to forget throughout the war when fighting the Japanese. The Japanese were equally ruthless in some instances in dealing with British POW's. To the Japanese, however, surrender meant disgrace, and thus they had little "forbearance" for Allied soldiers who did surrender (Caffrey, 1973:185). They simply could not muster the requisite sympathy or empathy for Allied POW's or the conditions of their captivity. Many Japanese officers and NCO's paid with their lives, or their own freedom, when they were tried by the Allies after the war and found guilty of war crimes. Even though Japan had never ratified the 1929 Geneva Convention on treatment of prisoners of war, the Allies still found them derelict in their treatment of POW's and thus guilty of crimes against humanity.

Similarly, even though there had been no Geneva Convention prior to the Civil War, the treatment of Union soldiers in the Confederate POW camp at Andersonville was considered barbarous at the time.[13] After the war, Capt. Henry Wirz, the Confederate commandant, was charged, among other things, with "murder in violation of the laws and customs of war." Wirz was subsequently found guilty and hanged.

Giving no quarter in battle may be tolerated in many instances, and soldiers as warriors may, on occasion, indulge themselves in wanton ruthlessness and cruelty in the name of fighting spirit and the heat of battle. The POW, however, is no longer a warrior, and his mistreatment is universally viewed by civilized and honorable peoples as inhumane.

Some atrocities against opposing military personnel are monstrous in the enormity of the number of victims involved as well as the inhumanity of the act itself. Such an offense was Katyn (see FitzGibbon 1971). In 1939 Germany attacked Poland using Blitzkrieg warfare. Just as the Poles had managed to halt the German advance, Soviet Russia attacked Poland from the east. Poland collapsed and, with the signing of the Ribbentrop Molotov Treaty, Poland was divided almost equally between Germany and

---

[13] McKinley Kantor's novel *Andersonville*, (1955) which painted a graphic picture of the agonies of life in that infamous camp, became a best seller.

Russia. The Russians, wishing to destroy the existing social structure, undertook to eliminate persons in positions of leadership. In
this connection, some 15,000 Polish officers from the armed forces,
the police, and the frontier guard were arrested and sent in groups
of 4,000 to 6,000 to three special camps. For a time the prisoners
existed in appalling conditions at the camp, but by March 1940 the
Russians determined to empty the camps and exterminate most of
the officers, thereby permanently crippling Poland's military
capability. After that date nothing else was heard of any of the
15,000 men, with the exception of about 400 that the Russians took
out of the camps to be used by them for various purposes. The exact fate of the men from two of the camps is not known, although
it is assumed that they were killed. In the case of the third camp at
Kozielsk, the fate of the inmates was revealed when the Germans
later attacked Russia and came to occupy the former Russian portion of Poland. The Germans heard rumors about murdered Polish
officers from members of the local population and began to dig in
the Katyn Forest near the site of the former prisoner camp. They
ultimately uncovered 4,250 corpses, the remains of the Polish officers. Most of the Polish officers had been shot in the back of the
head, many had their hands tied behind their back, and some had
bayonet wounds. The Germans attempted to draw world-wide attention to the slaughter, but many people thought that this might
simply be another of Dr. Goebbels's propaganda efforts. The Germans, however, did bring in an international medical commission,
which concluded that the Russians had committed the crime.
Toward the end of World War II the Russians recaptured the area
and had a commission (composed entirely of persons from the communist world) investigate the bodies and attempt to blame the
murders on the Germans. Curiously, the American military was
reported to have suppressed information about the crime, and a
number of high-ranking American officials, including President
Roosevelt, apparently clung to the belief that the Russians were not
guilty. There was even an attempt to pin the guilt for the Katyn
massacre on Hermann Goering, and this was included in his indict-
ment. The total facts about Katyn have never been revealed, no information about the prisoners at the other two camps has ever appeared, and no one has ever been punished for the massacre. The
preponderance of evidence, however, suggests that the Russians
were guilty of this monstrous military crime against person—a
military crime of this variety without parallel in modern times.

DESECRATION OF THE DEAD

Although the dead feel no pain, practically all societies place great emphasis on treatment of the dead. Desecration of the dead is often viewed as a more heinous offense than assaulting or even killing the individual (especially if it is done in "honorable" combat). To desecrate the dead is symbolically to attack the very fabric of society itself; it is a contravention of the component value system, and is the very embodiment of inhumanity. The military, perhaps more than any other group in society, places enormous importance on proper respect for the dead and the appropriate ceremonial disposition of the dead—i.e., burial with full military honors.[14] For the soldier, death is omnipresent, and the anxiety generated by this fearsome exigency is further exacerbated by the prospect of an ill-attended body, an unmarked grave, an unnoted death, and the lack of symbolic presence in the social entity.[15] Concern with the care of the body is as great as with any other of the death anxieties. In combat, defilement of the body, inadvertently or deliberately, is often inevitable. The dead are completely helpless. To defile the corpse is to defile the memory and accomplishments of the deceased, and the affection and respect in which they were held. It is an attack on the sacred theology and philosophical ideology of the society itself. To desecrate or defile the dead in war is viewed as the mark of moral depravity and inhumanity, and is theoretically abhorred by civilized peoples everywhere.

In spite of such sentiments, desecration and defilement of dead military personnel has been endemic to most armed forces, both civilized and barbarous, albeit considered an extremely serious military normative offense and subject to severe punishment by the parent military unit or the enemy, if the perpetrator is captured.

Perhaps the classic form of defilement of an enemy's body is to eat it. Historically primitive societies that have practiced can-

---

[14] Concern with the proper ceremonial care of their remains is not just a characteristic of the modern-day soldier. Even among the Roman legionnaires of ancient times, a small sum was deducted from their pay for dues to a burial club that would arrange for their funeral (Robinson 1971:18, 31). During the Civil War, soldiers on both sides often arranged with local undertakers to take care of their remains if they were killed in battle. For a fuller exposition on this ceremonial configuration, see Bryant (1978).

[15] As illustrated by the practice among some folk and preliterate societies of reciting the deeds of the dead. (In our own society we do much the same in the process of bragging about the exploits of deceased ancestors).

nibalism have seen fit to eat captured or killed enemies, as much for symbolic and ceremonial purposes as for food value. To be eaten would be a disgrace and would prevent the body from being appropriately processed by his own people in terms of ceremony and burial. Knowing this, cannibal societies might go to great lengths to enhance the defilement and to prevent recovery of even parts of the body. The Maoris, for example, were not content merely to eat the flesh of the enemy, but would save the bones and use them for purposes that they thought degrading, making such items as flutes, the barbs of fishhooks, needles for sewing dogskin mats, and rings for the legs of captive parrots (Vayda 1967:373). The skulls might be used for carrying water for the oven or as a canoe bailer.[16] In lieu of such utility, the bones of the enemy victim might simply be broken up and burned. In any event, the kinsmen of the dead victim could not gather up the bones and deposit them in the sacred places of the tribe. The Maoris also collected the tattooed heads of detested enemy chiefs, which were taken home, cured, processed for preservation, and kept where they could be "reviled and insulted," or impaled on a stick on top of the village stockade.

A number of preliterate groups, while not performing cannibalism, have practiced headhunting. So, too, have more civilized people.[17] In medieval Japan the Samurai thought it militarily appropriate to collect the heads of vanquished enemies (Turnbull 1977:22). The Samurai wished to avoid such disgrace and defilement themselves, however, and if faced with defeat or capture would commit hara-kiri. In addition, a trusted friend would decapitate them at the same moment and, by fastening stones to the head, sink it in the river, thereby preventing it from falling into the hands of enemies who might defile it by keeping it on display as a trophy.

Not unlike headhunting was the practice of scalping by the American Indians. Actually, scalping at the time of the American

---

[16] In a matter perhaps illustrative of his barbarous nature, Stalin is supposed to have had a portion of Hitler's skull recovered from the command bunker where he committed suicide, and is said to have used the skull fragment as an ashtray on his desk.

[17] Cannibalism is not unknown even in modern armies. Some isolated instances were reported of cannibalism of dead bodies among starving German soldiers at Stalingrad. In the Vietnamese conflict there were also some reports of Cambodian soldiers eating prisoners, and, in one case, eating a paymaster when he did not have money to pay them.

Revolution was encouraged by the British, French, and American policy of paying their Indian allies for enemy scalps—a kind of bounty-hunting arrangement (Ward 1952:856).[18] Large numbers of persons suffered the fate of scalping during the skirmishes and battles of the war, sometimes several hundred in a single battle. The Indians were prone to capture prisoners and torture and decapitate them if they did not scalp them. The Americans were not infrequently just as savage as their Indian enemies. In 1779 the U.S. Continental Congress dispatched a punitive expedition led by Maj. Gen. John Sullivan against the Indians of the Six Nations (Ward 1952:638–45). The expedition was to destroy villages and crops, and to capture as many prisoners as possible for use as hostages to insure the Indians' good behavior in the future. The Indians had been a military annoyance to the Americans by raiding and killing along the frontier to assist the British and their Tory allies. The expedition did manage to destroy many Indian villages and fields, although the Indians fell back fighting, along with some British regulars and some Tory troops. The dead left behind were immediately scalped by the Americans. Two Indian bodies were found and skinned from their hips down, to make boot legs for Colonial officers. In mopping up, the American expedetionary forces found an Indian squaw and a crippled Indian boy, whom they put in a remaining hut as a practical joke and then fired the hut, burning the two Indians alive in it. Even though the Americans were frequently guilty of scalping and mutilating their dead enemies, there is no question that it was viewed as an inhumane and

---

[18] Paying for scalps sometimes backfired on those who did. The Tories and British were paying the Indians for scalps but were themselves victimized (Ward 1952:496). One Jane McCrea was engaged to marry David Jones, a Tory officer on the march with Burgoyne. Hoping to greet her fiance when he arrived, she went to Fort Edward and stayed with Mrs. McNeil, a cousin of British General Fraser, who lived in a cabin near the fort. On July 27, 1877, two days before Burgoyne and his British army arrived at the deserted fort, some of his Indian forerunners came to the cabin, seized Jane McCrea and Mrs. McNeil, and started back toward the British army at Fort Ann. The Indians got into a dispute over who should guard Jane McCrea and she was subsequently shot, scalped, and the clothes stripped from her body. When the Indians took the scalp and Mrs. McNeil back to the British, David Jones recognized his fiancee's hair. General Burgoyne was outraged and wanted to execute the guilty Indian, but was dissuaded from it because if he did so, all the Indians would desert the army. The Colonials were equally outraged and the American Maj. Gen. Horatio Gates wrote Burgoyne and took him to task for this "horrid" and barbarous deed.

detestable practice. When Col. George Rogers Clark of the Colonial army surrounded the British Lieutenant General Hamilton in Fort Sackville in Vincennes, he demanded unconditional and immediate surrender. Ward (1952:860) describes his military resolve in this regard:

> To punctuate this demand Clark dealt sternly with five Indians who had been surprised and captured as they entered Vincennes carrying American scalps. They were tomahawked in sight of the garrison.

Scalping continued to be an Indian practice for more than the next hundred years, and it was not unknown among the white men, since "Indian fighters" needed trophies as well as Indians. Whether committed by Indian or white, scalping was always considered to be an inhumane and despicable act of defiling the dead, and a gross violation of the norms of civilized combat.

In addition to eating, decapitating, skinning, and scalping the dead, not to mention retaining the head or other parts of the anatomy, or scattering the bones, there have been other patterns of desecrating and defiling the dead in warfare. One such brutal practice has been that of castrating or otherwise mutilating dead enemy bodies. This was a common act on the part of Moroccan troops in the Spanish Civil War. Thomas comments on this and observes (1961:247):

> [General] Yagüe certainly did not intervene to prevent bloodshed. But on Franco's orders he did restrain the Moors from castrating corpses of their victims—an established Moorist battlerite. Even so, German officers testified to Robert Brasillach that they saw many bodies so treated—several with crucifixes laid on their breast.

The practice occurred from time to time in the Italo-Ethiopian War of 1935–1936. The Italian soldiers were told that if they were captured by the Ethiopian tribesmen, they would be tortured and castrated (Dugan and Lafore 1973:245). This did occur, although some of the tribes were hostile to the Ethiopian regime and perpetrated such offenses against their own Ethiopian soldiers. In one battle at Mount Aradam, the Ethiopian troops retreated in the face of a fierce Italian aerial attack, and were then attacked by Galla tribesmen, who had been fighting on their own side. According to Dugan and Lafore (1973:254):

For now, in defeat, the Ethiopians faced another enemy, not less terrible, whose weapons were not bombs and gas but hatred and atavism. The Gallas fell upon the survivors. They robbed, castrated and killed all of the soldiers of the imperial army they could find.

Even the bodies of the Ethiopian Prince Mulugeta and of a British officer who was head of a small medical unit were stripped and castrated.

Castrating or otherwise mutilating the bodies of dead enemies occurred occasionally in World War II and in Korea, where sometimes American soldiers would be found dead, having been shot with their hands tied behind their backs, and also castrated, with the severed penis stuffed in the mouth. The practice did not abate in Vietnam. The Vietcong would kill and castrate American servicemen from time to time. In some instances one act of defiling the dead would bring, as retaliation, other similar acts. Parks (1968:18), in his diary of combat in Vietnam, recalls:

Just found out our company is being deadlined for a couple of days. It comes as no surprise. We rode through some towns with five dead VC's tied to our tracks. This, I suppose, was revenge for our guys who were killed and castrated yesterday. The Vietnamese people were horrified. And you couldn't blame them. It was a bad scene, those bloody corpses turning gray from the heat and paddy mud. Then some of the guys have been mutilating the VC bodies like they claim Charlie does. I've seen Sergeant Young wearing a pair of dried-out VC ears around his neck on a string. I've heard others were cutting off privates. I've never seen this, thank God.

The collecting of enemy ears was relatively common in Vietnam, and there are reports of armored personnel carriers moving about with a string of Vietcong ears tied to the radio aerial. Similarly, in World War II, there was a significant incidence of U.S. servicemen cutting the ears from the bodies of dead enemy soldiers as souvenirs. This practice seems largely confined to the Pacific theatre and to the Japanese as victims of such defilement. Robert Leckie (1957:129), in his autobiographical account of war in the Pacific theatre in World War II, recounts that a sailor asked:

"Did the marines really cut off their [the Japanese] ears?" "Oh, hell yes! I knew one fellow had a collection of them. Got most of them at the Battle of Hell's Point—the Tenaru, y'know. He hung them out on a line to dry out, the dope, and the rain rotted them all away. It rained like hell one night and ruined the whole bunch."

The taking of enemy ears is certainly nothing new. It has been reported that it occurred during the American Revolution, and that it was Americans who took the ears of British and Tory soldiers. Ward (1952:436), however, asserts that some of these accounts were distorted and exaggerated.

Defilement of the body sometimes has had an economic motive. Just as the Nazis systematically removed gold from the teeth of the Jewish victims of their death camps, soldiers have sometimes desecrated the dead for the gold in their teeth. Leckie (1957:128, 238) tells of a marine in World War II, cited earlier, who had had the forethought to purchase dentist's pliars and a dentist's flashlight before he went into combat, and would collect gold from the teeth of dead Japanese soldiers. According to Leckie:

> One of the marines went methodically among the dead armed with a pair of pliers. He had observed that the Japanese have a penchant for gold fillings in their teeth, often for solid gold teeth. He was looting their very mouths. He would kick their jaws agape, peer into the mouth with all the solicitude of a Park Avenue dentist—careful, always careful not to contaminate himself by touch—and yank out all that glittered. He kept the gold teeth in an empty Bull Durham tobacco sack, which he wore around his neck in the manner of an amulet. Souvenirs, we called him.

Whether the defilement and desecration of the dead is prompted by economic motives, a desire to acquire symbolically the manhood and courage of the fallen enemy, or simply the ultimate insult or revilement of the opponent, any offense against the dead military opponent is almost universally recognized as an offense of repugnant and abhorrent quality, at least from the standpoint of the victim and his side. In many instances the offender would be sanctioned even by his fellow soldiers, who would probably see such behavior as pathologically inappropriate, if not inhumane. Such an offender would also likely be formally sanctioned by his superiors if observed or reported. Certainly if captured by the enemy, a soldier who was known to be a defiler of the dead would likely be tortured or killed on the spot by enemy troops, who would view such a crime against person as a detestable and barbaric form of military deviancy.

Chivalrous Norms in Combat Behavior

Almost all societies that engage in war or combat, from the most rudimentary to the most technologically advanced, contain a warrior segment. This may be a full-time social role, such as that of the Samurai of feudal Japan, the iKhehla of nineteenth-century Zululand, or the professional soldier from West Point. It may also be a part-time role, the adult male turning from his traditional pursuits of farming or hunting to the exercise of war and combat, perhaps with the metamorphosis facilitated by some fraternal or group mechanism; examples include the Cheyenne Dog Soldier Society, the U.S. Army Reserve, or the Cossack tribal alliance. In any event, where there is a warrior category or caste, there is frequently a special code of conduct bearing on the behavior of the warrior. The role specificity of the warrior is usually much more rigid than that of other societal roles. Elaborate proscriptions and prescriptions may dictate dress, dietary habits, appropriate sexual activity, living arrangements, and relationship with nonwarrior segments of the population.[19] Most important, these normative dictates will address the required and appropriate behavior in regard to war and combat, and especially the proper relationship toward and interaction with the enemy. How the enemy is to be fought, the respect or disdain to which he is entitled, and how he is to be treated if captured are concerns constituent to the warrior's role or code. Such concerns frequently involve the appropriate manner of death of an enemy, or even his treatment after death. All such matters are subject to normative specification and enforcement. Violation of the norms, whether formal or informal, represents a vagrancy from expected military behavior, and thus deviancy and crime.

Not infrequently, the norm imposing on the warrior his treatment of the live or dead enemy might run counter to those values held by the enemy, who might have a totally different conceptualization of what is the appropriate treatment of an enemy, dead or alive. According to Clive (1973:18), among the iKhehla warriors

[19] As mentioned in an earlier chapter, a number of African tribes, such as the Zulu and the Masai of Kenya, traditionally required their young warriors to live apart from other members of the tribe and remain celibate during the period of their military service. In the case of the Masai, sexual mutilation of the penis insured celibacy during this period.

of the Zulu, "a slain warrior must be disembowelled by his slayer so that his spirit was released, and the victor then return to his kraal for the rituals of cleansing."

The professional warriors or knights of Japan, the Samurai, for centuries adhered to an elaborate code of military loyalty and obedience, bravery, duty, and honor. The Samurai code of norms was known as Bushido—the "way of the warrior" (Nitobe 1968). This code embraced both ethical and philosophical rationale for his allegiance to his master, his combat bravery, and his relationship to his enemy. Bushido emphasizes seven distinctive virtues, including justice, courage, benevolence, politeness, veracity, honor, and loyalty. Although the Samurai were the epitome of knightly chivalry and displayed all respect for "worthy opponents," they also adhered to the practice of collecting the heads of vanquished enemies. Turnbull (1977:22) relates that, "this was the form of trophy which, throughout samurai history, was to furnish the best proof of a task successfully accomplished." The Samurai's bravery, similar to that of many other soldiers or warriors of traditional chivalrous bent, was not without dysfunction, as Turnbull (1977:90) explains it:

> The samurai's bravery, which was in some ways his greatest strength, proved now to be a weakness. The tradition of being first into battle, collecting heads and particularly of challenging a worthy opponent to individual combat, proved to be completely irrelevant against a foreign enemy. As we saw during the Gempei War, the actual practice of formal combat played a relatively small part in the overall conduct of battles, but it was an enduring myth in which every samurai believed.

The Samurai were quite formal in their solitary combat with "worthy opponents." Turnbull (1977:19) relates that for a Samurai, "When challenging an opponent to individual combat it became the custom to proclaim one's pedigree and the history of one's house." The enemies that the Samurai fought, such as the Mongols, tended to fight more as a disciplined mass and were less concerned with individual bravery, especially if foolhardy. By many standards the Samurai practice of taking heads would hardly seem chivalrous or honorable, but the Samurai saw no dishonor in it, especially since all other warriors viewed it the same way—as a duty as well as a privilege of the winner of combat. Certainly the taking of heads in no way diluted the many manifestations of chivalry and honor that the Samurai did display toward their opponents. As one example, in a battle in 1587 the army of one Samurai, Shimazu Iehisa, defeated the army of his opponent, Chōsokabe Motochika, and killed his son. Chōsokabe fled to the coast in an attempt to escape. Unfortunately, the tide was out and he could not reach his boats out in the harbor, because an area of quicksand, uncovered by the tide, lay in his way. In despair he was about to commit suicide when he received a message from the pursuing Shimazu, delivered by a soldier. The message read (Turnbull 1977:182):

> We regret exceedingly to have killed your son in yesterday's engagement. Meanwhile we perceive how difficult it is to get to your boats over that quicksand. Wait tranquilly till the tide comes in. I wish you a safe return.

Under the warrior's code, bravery and honor are sacred duties; any dereliction in this regard constitutes a serious form of military deviancy, and appropriate sanctions must attend the offense. The sanctions in some instances may be self-inflicted, such as suicide to avoid the shame of cowardice, or surrender, or defeat.

With the advent of mass machine warfare, and death and destruction in a massive, impersonal, and indiscriminate fashion, the warrior-knight became obsolete and irrelevant to the demands of modern combat. The ideology of bravery, honor, and even respect for one's opponents became something of an anachronism in the face of trench warfare, gas, flame throwers, and the artillery barrage. The aviator, perhaps more than any category of military personnel, retained the legacy of the warrior—the Samurai, the knight, or the gentleman officer. The sky still offered the opportunity for the single combat of champions, and the demonstration of chivalry along with bravery. Illusion or not, the aviator and the public, in a sense, bought the illusion and the legacy. The aviator became the new warrior of the skies, replete with implicit code of norms and etiquette. As Jablonski (1971:xv) has described the warrior mystique of the aviator:

> Courage in war is not a rare or exclusive commodity: all people have it and draw upon it when they must. What makes the heroism of airmen so much more romantically fascinating is the otherworldly element in which they perform: The cloud-laden, cerulean, vasty skies. And when the airmen "bought it," his going was spectacular to witness; experiencing it was another matter.

Still there seemed something so clean and pure about falling five miles before ramming into the earth in a splash of flame. . . .

The camaraderie of the air in World War I made aviators of both sides share an ideology of worthy opponent and honorable combat to which those fighting on the ground were not privy. There were many acts of humaneness, courtesy, respect, and even affection demonstrated by aviators of both the Allied and Axis forces during World War I. The sense of respect of one's airborne enemies and the feeling of mutual perspective fostered by their unique mode of fighting transferred easily to the context of World War II, at least initially.

Jablonski (1971:163–66) illustrates this point with an interesting account of airwar. In 1941 Wing Commander Douglas Bader of the RAF was piloting his Spitfire over France, leading a formation of planes, when his planes were attacked by a group of German Messerschmitts. In the dogfight that followed, Bader collided with an enemy plane. He bailed out, but one of his legs was artificial and remained caught in the cockpit. As he floated down to earth, a German plane flew at him but did not fire (at this point in the war such behavior would still have been thought a violation of the code of the warrior). Bader was captured and imprisoned by the Germans when he landed. Adolf Galland, a noted German ace, undertook to contact the British and have them deliver a replacement leg to Bader. The British did so, but were less sporting than the Germans in that they dropped a box containing the new leg just after a bombing raid. The original leg in the crashed Spitfire was found and carefully repaired by the Germans, who then presented it to Bader. Bader and Galland may have been enemies in the skies, but even as a prisoner Bader was a worthy opponent, and, as a fellow aviator warrior who had demonstrated his skill and bravery in shooting down his share of German planes, was entitled to courtesy, honor, and respect, even by his captors.

As time moved on, the code of the aviator became eroded by the direction and nature of the war. There are instances from both sides of inappropriate combat techniques and behavior toward enemy fliers.[20] An incident occurred during the air war over Ger-

[20] Although the incidence of fliers shooting at enemy pilots who had to bail out while they were still dangling from a parachute was perhaps not frequent, it did occur. The Germans apparently were strong adherents of chivalry in the skies and there were fewer such occurrences in the European theater than in the pacific; the Japanese had strafed parachuting pilots from the very beginning of

many, however, that may stand as a classic recent example of a violation of the informal and implicit norms of the warrior. On August 14, 1943, the 100th Bombardment Group sent its B-17's as part of an attack over Regensberg and Schweinfurt, Germany. The planes of the 100th were in the rear and were therefore especially vulnerable to attack by German fighter planes. One of the B-17's, flown by Captain R. Knox, was damaged by the fighter attacks, and first one and then a second engine went out. The plane was now flying at a very slow rate of speed and would soon be destroyed by the fighters. According to an observer flying in another plane of the 100th, the wheels of Knox's plane were lowered, which was a recognized signal that the plane had surrendered. Jablonski (1971:179) says that, "according to the Code of the Air, once this was done attacks upon the bomber would cease." At this point several German fighters flew alongside the American plane to guide Knox to a German airdrome. Suddenly, the gunners on the B-17 opened up on the accompanying German fighters, "blasting" them "out of the sky." The pilot put the wheels up and tried to make a dash for England. It is believed that perhaps the two dead engines may have started running again and the pilot felt that he had a chance to make it. Whatever the reason, according to Jablonski (1965:180):

> Within fifty seconds the maddened fighters tore the plane to pieces and it too went down.
>   After this *flagrant violation of the Code of the Air* [italics added], so the legend went, the 100th Bombardment Group was marked for extinction by the *Luftwaffe*. The Me–109s and FW–190s would ignore all other planes in the bomber formation concentrating upon the 100th; it had become a personal grudge; the Luftwaffe against the Bloody 100th.

The pilot and crew of the offending B-17 had violated no international treaty, no military proscription, nor had they acted in a necessarily inhumane fashion. They had, however, failed to act in the fashion of honorable warriors and had not given appropriate

---

the war. In the memoirs of Col. Gregory "Pappy" Boyington, he recounts the story of Sam Logan, an American pilot shot down during the Guadalcanal campaign. Logan said that after he bailed out of his flaming plane, a Japanese pilot in a flaming Zero had repeatedly attacked him with his machine guns. When his ammunition was gone, the pilot then dove into the American, cutting his ankle so badly that his foot had to be amputated (Boyington 1959:130).

respect and consideration to their enemy, the *Luftwaffe*. The *Luft-waffe* accordingly treated them as military criminals, and gave them no quarter. Thereafter, assignment to the 100th Bombard-ment Group was tantamount to a death sentence, as comments of some airmen reveal. When one pilot from the 100th tried to tell some American pilots from other units that he had made 40 mis-sions (enough to get reassigned), they didn't believe him (Jablonski 1971:197). One of them said, "Nobody lives long enough in the 100th to get in 40 deals." An air force sergeant confided to another NCO, "I'm not going to make it. They just put me in the 100th Group. I haven't got a chance." The unsportsmanlike action of the B-17 was apparently viewed not only by the *Luftwaffe* as a deviant offense. A young first lieutenant, Stanley Russel, recently assigned to the 100th, met an attractive WAC officer at a service club (Jablonski 1965:171). They danced and were becoming acquainted when she asked about his unit. When he told her where his unit was stationed, she stopped dancing with the lieutenant and walked away with the explanation, "I'm not going to dance with you. I don't want to have anything to do with you. Not after what you men did." Presumably the WAC was only reflecting the attitudes she had experienced where she worked, in one of the air force headquarters. This stigmatized and ill-fated unit was to become known as the "Bloody 100th."

The Spontaneous Informal Norms of War

Above and beyond all treaties and laws, ideological convic-tions, rules and codes of combat, and treatment of the enemy, there also tend to exist in war situations that precipitate another set of norms, usually spontaneous and ephemeral. These norms are in-formal, but unlike a warrior's code of chivalry, which grows out of custom and tradition and only serves to refine the process of killing the enemy, the spontaneous informal norms usually have mutual survival as a motive, based on the concept of reciprocity.

Regardless of the ideological or political strength of conviction at the societal level, or even on the part of the military high com-mand, the common soldier who is called upon to do the fighting and dying may be less convinced. In this sense, if no other, there is a commonly shared characteristic among soldiers of all armies in all times—a desire to survive. As one German sergeant captured by the Americans during World War II phrased it (Shils and Janowitz 1948:284):

> When you asked such a question, I realize well that you have no idea of what makes a soldier fight. The soldiers lie in their holes and are happy if they live through the next day. If we think at all, it's about the end of the war and then home.

When ordered by their superiors, soldiers have charged, captured, killed, and been killed. When left to their own devices, soldiers sometimes have acted in a less aggressive fashion when confronted by the enemy—and this behavior has often been mutual. Throughout history there have been instances of individual soldiers encountering enemy soldiers and interacting in a friendly fashion, or simply walking away from each other, rather than attacking. Small groups of soldiers have sometimes walked silently past groups of enemy soldiers without firing a shot. Soldiers have, on their own, declared all sorts of "informal" truces with the enemy, in the interest of survival. Kay (1971:177–78), for example, in his composite account of life in the Confederate army in the Civil War, speaks of picket duty:

> Holding a river line, when both armies were in winter quarters, was not a dangerous occupation, and there was little need to take cover. The men simply did not shoot at each other, unless their opponents tried to force the river. On quiet days pickets even traded tobacco—plentiful in the South—for coffee—which wasn't. Small boats made from pieces of board would be sailed across to the enemy's bank; the freight of tobacco would be removed, and the toy sent back with a cargo of coffee.

In the interest of survival and creature comfort, both sides cooperated in not fighting to enjoy a respite and economic reciprocity. To have violated such an idyllic, albeit informal, truce would have represented deviancy of truly despicable proportions. Similar instances of informal interaction and trading of items have occurred in many of our wars. The pattern of trench warfare in World War I, however, provided a particularly fertile context for such informal dereliction of the combat dictate (Ashworth 1968). For the soldiers in the trenches, there was a formal norm of offensiveness, while at an informal level there was observance of "the live and let live" principle or norm. This norm is described by Ashworth (1968:411):

> The Live and Let Live principal was an informal and collective agreement between front-line soldiers of opposing armies to inhibit offensive activities to a level mutually defined as tolerable. This understanding was tacit and covert; it was expressed in activity or nonactivity rather than in verbal terms. The norm was supported by a system of sanctions. In the positive sense it constituted a system of mutual service, each side rewarded the other by refraining from offensive activity on the condition, of course, that this nonactivity was reciprocated. Negatively, violations of the norm were sanctioned. . . .

The troops would go about their business, ignoring the enemy, cutting grass in front of their trenches, delivering front-line rations, occasionally retrieving game that had been shot in no-man's-land, all without interference. Occasionally a shell would come too close and, in retaliation, a round would be fired so as to make the shell fall close to the enemy, to let them know that sort of thing would not be tolerated. Even offensive action would be regulated and thus moderated, such as mutually agreeing to throw bombs to the left or right of the trench, rather than in it. Firing or shelling was mutually routinized as a predictable activity, and such periods of hostility were labeled as "morning hate" or the "evening strafe." Violation of such norms of institutionalized offensive action was "negatively sanctioned by raising offensiveness to the formally prescribed and maximum level." Such an antimilitary posture is explained by the fact of enemy and Allied soldiers having "a vested interest of a biological sort in the perpetuation of such a situation." By normatively moderating offensive activity, both combatants enjoyed "a greater chance of survival and a diminution of discomfort, whereas to gear offensive activity to the institutionally prescribed level would be to maximize the probability of death and discomfort" (Ashworth 1968:420).

Individuals and small groups in the military everywhere have acted on occasion on a relatively spontaneous basis to establish systems of informal combat expectations, not infrequently involving temporary cessation of hostilities. Such respites, although ephemeral, may serve to enhance the possibility of survival and the quality of military existence. These informal normative systems are mutually developed and established and maintained by reci-

procity. Violation of the norms would bring retaliation in the form
of escalation of aggression and violence. In one sense those involved
in such informal behavior are in violation of the formal military
posture toward the enemy, but in doing so are subscribing and conforming to the more universal norm of survival and humanity, and
presumably are more fearful of the sanctions attendant to the proscriptions involved.

Summary

Combat between honorable men is subject to a variety of
treaties, codes, and traditions. Various weapons have at one time
or another been formally outlawed—dum-dum or expanding
bullets, for example, or chemical weapons. The Italians used gas in
limited quantities during the Ethiopian campaign, inasmuch as
they were not fighting "civilized" opponents. The rule has been
bent to some extent in Vietnam, with the U.S. military employing
tear gas and other nonlethal chemical agents. In both Korea and
Vietnam some servicemen were alleged to have borrowed shotguns
from MP units or Special Services stockrooms and utilized them in
combat.

In the World War I era there was a residue of chivalrous
camaraderie between aviators on both sides, but by World War II
there were incidents of fliers being shot in their parachutes by both
Axis and allied pilots. Accepted military practice today calls for
shooting paratroops before they touch ground, where possible.

Prisoners of war are in theory entitled to humane and dignified
treatment according to treaty. In actual practice it sometimes
becomes necessary or efficacious to kill prisoners in the interest of
"military expediency," such as when there is no practical means of
transporting them to a rear area (the Malmédy massacre, for example). All armies, including the U.S. Army, have had occasion to
take such drastic action, although some unit commanders and individual soldiers have been more prone than others to do so. There
have been occasions when prisoners of war have been systematically mistreated, deprived of the essentials of life, or tortured in order
to obtain intelligence information.

The nature of the guerilla-type fighting in Vietnam has been
such that combat servicemen have been prone to violate regula-

tions concerning captured enemy soldiers, in some instances with the tacit (or open) approval of their superiors. The factor of survival apparently is such that traditional humane values are often eroded in face of the exigencies of combat necessity, and there is sometimes minimal reluctance to perpetrate crimes of violence against prisoners of war.

CHAPTER TEN

Crimes Against Performance

The common soldier must fear his officer more than the enemy.

Frederick the Great, quoted in John Keegan, *The Face of Battle*

The nature of the military mission is such that the organization must operate with speed and precision. Timing and coordination are critical factors in effecting decisive maneuvers and mounting successful attacks. To achieve the necessary degree of operational precision and efficiency, it is imperative, at least in theory, that orders, implicit or explicit, be carried out immediately, and to the letter. A hesitation on the part of one individual in the organization may imperil the success of a unit action. The failure of one person to comply with his orders may disrupt an entire military operation. A serviceman's overriding responsibility is to aquit himself honorably in his performance in combat with the enemy. He should obey orders and, if necessary, close with the enemy, killing or being killed in the process, if his orders so dictate. One individual running in the face of the enemy may precipitate a general rout of whole units. Surrender without good reason, failure to comply with a combat order, or display of cowardice in the face of the enemy may prove disastrous to the larger military entity and its mission. Nor does the responsibility for loyalty incumbent upon military personnel cease with capture and imprisonment. Even the POW is still at war with the enemy, and his attendant behavior may have a direct bearing on the outcome of the conflict.

Accordingly, perhaps the most serious and rigorously sanctioned norms within the military context are those that circumscribe the behavior and performance of individuals vis-à-vis the enemy. There is a high degree of specificity in such norms, and they are stringently enforced and severely sanctioned, sometimes to the point of ruthlessness.

Because of the ramifications for the military unit and for its members, official sanctions for violations of norms specifying appropriate performance in regard to the enemy are sometimes reinforced or displaced by unofficial sanctions. War and combat produce a traumatic, if not terrifying, experience for even the most stoic and courageous of warriors, however, and since time immemorial members of the military have violated such norms and become guilty of the most serious of all military deviancies—crimes against performace in regard to the enemy.

Unauthorized Maneuvers

Battle plans involve large numbers of military units, and their movements and maneuvers must be carefully articulated and coordinated. Units must follow their assigned orders, since to make an unauthorized movement might destroy the integrity of the overall tactical plan. For this reason all military personnel, and especially commanders, are constrained to proceed exactly according to plans and orders, and not to exercise prerogatives that are not assigned. Such norms have serious impact and, if violated, may invoke severe sanctions. Military expediency and the situational demands may, however, necessitate breaking such rules and moving independently. Battles have been won by commanders who disregarded orders from higher authority and exercised their own best judgment. By the same token, wars have been lost because orders have not been followed, and overall strategy disrupted. In the face of the possible sanctions for not following orders, a decision to disregard a directive from above is not taken lightly.

An example of such a situation might be the plight of German Col. Jochen Peiper in the Ardennes campaign in World War II

(Whiting 1971:38–39). Peiper was leading a Panzer battle group in the breakthrough of Allied lines and was running low on fuel. He learned that there was an Allied fuel dump not too far from his line of advance. Unfortunately, it was on the route assigned to another German unit. In this instance Hitler had ordered the commanders of all units to stay on their assigned routes. Peiper also "knew that anyone who disobeyed the order to stick on his own road could expect to suffer the death penalty." Realizing that without fuel his unit could not continue and would ultimately be captured or destroyed by Allied troops, he chose to disobey orders. He diverted to the other route, found and captured the Allied fuel dump, refueled his tanks, and returned to his original route before the other German unit came along. Had the other unit come sooner and both units collided, the confusion would have been chaotic and any further advance for either would have been impossible. As it turned out, the other German unit was held up by an American infantry regiment, and Peiper's decision had proved expeditious and appropriate. Inasmuch as it succeeded, he was not subsequently sanctioned.

Later in the same battle, Colonel Peiper and the remnants of his battle group were surrounded by U.S. forces and were being shelled by heavy artillery. Peiper realized that he might be able to break out of the encirclement, but only if his men were on foot. The tanks and equipment and all the wounded would have to be left behind. Unfortunately, his superiors would not authorize such a move, and gave the direct order that "You may break out but only if you bring all wounded and vehicles" (Whiting 1971:172). Again Peiper chose to disobey orders and attempt the breakout on foot. Peiper succeeded in reaching German lines with some of his men, but because of the confusion of the situation again managed to escape punishment for having disobeyed orders.

An almost parallel situation on the U.S. side in the same battle took a diferent twist (Toland 1959:240, 248, 252–53, 269, 270). An American major was commanding some infantry troops at a roadblock at Belle Haie, not far from Bastogne. He managed to hold the roadblock against the German advance for some time. Because of his action, his immediate commander intended to recommend him for a Silver Star. The commander had also told the major to "walk out the best you can, you've done enough," when it was apparent that the major and his men were surrounded by German troops. Unfortunately, his divisional commander had earlier ordered that everyone was to "hold at all cost." When the major did decide to break out, he was down to a few vehicles, and further resistance would have been hopeless. He burned his remaining vehicles and managed to filter through enemy lines on foot back to U.S. lines, and to save every one of his men. When he returned to his division and reported to the divisional commander, the general asked him, "Why did you destroy government equipment?" The major explained that he felt that it was most important that he bring his men back to safety, and that they could not have gotten out with the vehicles. The general replied, "Major, I call that misbehavior." Later the general wanted to have the major court-martialed for cowardice, and only the refusal of his regimental commander and his divisional combat commander to endorse the court-martial charges saved the major from trial and serious sanction.

Sometimes unauthorized maneuvers have the effect of desertion, but the individual involved is of such a towering military stature that cowardice or desertion is an inappropriate charge. Such an instance was the rather odd case of Bvt. Maj. Gen. George Armstrong Custer and the occasion when he, in effect, went AWOL in the face of the enemy (DiMona 1972:91). After the Civil War, General Custer volunteered for cavalry duty in the Indian campaign. Ordered West, he left his bride at Fort Riley, Kansas, and assumed command of the Seventh Cavalry. He was to "hunt out and chastise the Cheyennes." In May 1867 he was at Fort Hayes, Kansas, and was to wait for further orders. He became impatient, and also heard that a cholera epidemic was raging in the area around Fort Riley, where he had left his wife. He was "impulsive in love" and so, disregarding orders, set out for Fort Riley, 275 miles away, to see his wife. He took 76 men, several officers, and fresh horses with him. The expedition cost two dead and six wounded, and General Custer was court-martialed on a number of charges, including absenting himself from his command without proper authority at a time when he was supposed to be fighting Indians. He was also charged with expropriating mules and ambulances for his own use, and overworking government horses. The counts also included abandoning a detachment under attack, not sending help to the beleaguered detachment, failing to pursue the attackers, and failing to recover and bury the bodies of two of his men supposedly killed in the fight. Finally, he was charged with having three of his own men shot down as deserters and refusing them medical treatment; one subsequently died. The crimes against performance with which Custer was charged were staggering in their enormity, and the possible consequences fearsome to contemplate.

The testimony at the trial would seem to confirm all of the charges. He testified in his own behalf and, in spite of his "awesome" reputation as a military hero, the members of the court seemed to think that the testimony and evidence supported the charges. They found him guilty of all charges except denying medical attention to the wounded deserters. He was subsequently suspended from rank and command for one year and forfeited his pay for that same period. Later the judge advocate general reviewed the case and reported (DiMona, 1972:91):

> The conclusion unavoidably reached under this branch of the inquiry is that General Custer's anxiety to see his family at Fort Riley overcame his appreciation of the paramount necessity to obey orders which is incumbent on every military officer; and thus the excuse he offers for his acts of unsubordination are afterthoughts.

Indian fighters were still needed, General Custer was an enormously popular military hero, and General Sheridan, his supervisor, immediately began petitioning for Custer's return to active duty. Withing ten months he was reinstated to duty and for the next nine years was involved in the campaigns against the Indian tribes. On June 24, 1876, Custer again impulsively disregarded his orders, attacked an Indian army of 6,000 with his force of 224 men, and died with his men at the Little Big Horn as a result of his deviancy. It is interesting to note that, because of his military accomplishments in the Civil War and in the Indian campaigns, most people today think of him as a colorful hero, unaware that he was also a convicted military criminal.

Negligence and Dereliction of Duty

Somtimes even an act of omission, prompted by strain, trauma, or even physical exhaustion, may prevent the individual from discharging his responsibilities appropriately, and may thus be viewed as dereliction of duty, and accordingly a crime against performance. Because of the pressures and exigencies of battle, such behavior may have to be accorded the urgency and dispatch that informal sanctions can afford. Matthews (1947:125, 182), in his autobiographical account of combat on Iwo Jima as a marine rifleman during World War II, tells of an incident in which he and two comrades fell asleep in a gun enplacement. A counterattack by the Japanese was expected and the three men were supposed to serve as the crew for a light machine gun. Had the attack caught them while still asleep, they would likely have been overrun and killed, and their entire unit wiped out. Their sergeant found them asleep, however, and woke them with the warning:

> And let me tell you something: the next time I find all three of you asleep again I'm going to throw a grenade in that hole myself. And don't think I won't.

In some instances noncommissioned officers and officers have actually thrown grenades in a foxhole or shot sleeping sentries to serve as examples to their troops. In World War II, Russian officers routinely shot soldiers who were derelict in their duty. Some of the Cossack officers in units serving with the Germans would make their rounds of senties at night and shoot any they found asleep. In Vietnam there was a well-publicized case of a soldier who refused to get in a helicopter to be flown out into combat. His exasperated sergeant pulled out his .45 pistol and shot the soldier dead on the spot (and was subsequently court-martialed).

On a formal level, members of the military have traditionally been severely punished for acts comprising negligence or dereliction of duty. Examples might include sleeping on duty, quitting a guard post, failing to perform some critical duty, not being properly prepared for an attack, permitting weapons or equipment to become lost, destroyed, or damaged, and failing to provide necessary leadership or direction. Any such acts that compromise one's behvior or the unit's performance vis-à-vis the enemy represent military deviancy of the highest order.

Although remembered by few Americans and seldom mentioned in most history books, there was an earlier historical incident that in many ways tended to parallel the details of the more recent Pueblo affair (DiMona 1972:21–42). On June 22, 1807, the 36-gun U.S. frigate *Chesapeake* sailed out of Hampton Roads carrying Commodore James Barron to take command of the U.S. Naval Forces in the Mediterranean. Commodore Barron sailed on board the *Chesapeake* as fleet commander, with that vessel designated to be his flagship in the Mediterranean. The actual captain of the ship was Commandant Charles Gordon.

According to DiMona, a few miles at sea the *Chesapeake* encountered a British squadron at anchor, no doubt waiting for
French shipping (the British were then at war with Napoleon).
One of the British vessels, the 50-gun frigate HMS *Leopard*, hauled
up its anchor and moved out ahead of the *Chesapeake*. For most of
the day the British ship stayed ahead of and parallel with the
American ship, tacking whenever it did. On board the *Leopard*,
the ship was being cleared for action. DiMona relates that in the
afternoon the British ship turned around and hailed the American
ship, requesting permission for an officer to come aboard. The
British officer gave a dispatch from Adm. George Cranfield
Berkeley to Commodore Barron. The British listed several of their
ships from which British sailors had deserted and joined the crew of
the *Chesapeake*. They wanted to search the American warship.
Barron had investigated all of the crewmen before coming aboard
and believed all to be American citizens, and so responded to the
British. Unknown to the commodore, there was one British
deserter on board the *Chesapeake*, and the British knew he was
there. The British officer returned to his ship, and the Americans
realized that the *Leopard* was ready for battle. Barron now told
Captain Gordon to prepare the *Chesapeake* for battle. Unfortunately, it was too late. The British guns smashed the hull and
masts of the *Chesapeake* and raked her decks with cannon fire. According to DiMona (1972:26) Barron ordered that the guns of the
American ship be fired, but they were not ready, powder horns
were not filled, matches were not primed, and there were no hot
coals. Barron realized that resistance was hopeless and struck his
colors just as one cannon on the *Chesapeake* managed to fire. Barron offered to surrender his ship to the British as booty of war, but
they refused. They searched the ship, found the British deserter,
"John Wilson," took him back to the *Leopard*, and sailed away.
The honor of the U.S. Navy, and even of the country, had been
tarnished, and Commodore Barron was court-martialed. He had
many enemies in the navy and public sentiment was strongly
against him.

On January 4, 1908, fittingly enough on the deck of the
Chesapeake anchored in Norfolk harbor, his trial convened. Barron
was charged with "negligently performing the duty assigned him,"
"neglecting, on the probability of an engagement, to clear his ship
for action," "failing to encourage in his own person his inferior officers and men to fight courageously," and "not doing his utmost to

take or destroy the *Leopard*, which vessel it was his duty to encounter" (DiMona, 1972:27). The testimony and evidence against him was damaging, but Barron's own testimony was impassioned and sincere. The court found him innocent on charges one, three, and four but guilty on charge two, failing to clear his ship for action. He was sentenced to be suspended from the navy for five years. Commondore Barron should not have given up the ship.

Approximately 150 years, later, the *Pueblo* incident was a reflection of many of the same circumstances of the *Chesapeake* debacle (Murphy 1971). The *Pueblo* was a converted World War II army supply ship orginally named FS-344, reclassified as an AKL (auxiliary light-cargo ship) and given its new name. The *Pueblo* was ostensibly to be engaged in peaceful oceanographic research, but in reality had an intelligence-gathering mission. It was a "spy ship," as it were. The ship was armed only with .45 pistols, a few submachine guns, one .30 carbine, and two .50-caliber machine guns. The *Pueblo* was sent to the waters off the North Korean coast just below the 42nd parallel and southward. On January 23, 1968, 15.8 miles off the island of Ung Do, clearly in international waters, a Soviet-type SO-1 subchaser flying the North Korean ensign intercepted the *Pueblo*, and circled it. The North Korean ship signaled the *Pueblo* to "Heave to or I will fire." Three North Korean P-4 motor torpedo boats then approached the *Pueblo*, at the same time as MIG jets made a pass over the ship. The cannon of the subchaser began firing at the *Pueblo*, as did the machine guns of the torpedo boats. Although the *Pueblo* tried to steam away, the North Korean ships were faster and surrounded the American vessel. Commander Bucher, the captain, did not order the crew to fire back at the North Korean ships, whose gunfire wounded some of the crew of the *Pueblo*, several seriously. The North Korean ships signaled the *Pueblo* to follow them, which it did; then it stopped, and the enemy vessels fired again. At this point, Commander Bucher waved a white stocking cap, surrendering the *Pueblo*. The North Koreans sent a boarding party aboard the *Pueblo* and took it into Wonsan harbor. The *Pueblo* was now the prize of the North Koreans and the crew were their prisoners. Commander Bucher had lost an American vessel without a fight.

Ultimately Bucher and his crew were returned to the United States. The navy established an official court of inquiry. The major issues were whether or not the *Pueblo* had actually "intruded" into North Korean territorial waters, whether Bucher had a viable alternative to surrendering the ship, and whether there had been negligence in the loss of classified documents. The court returned a series of recommendations shocking to the principals of the case. They recommended that Commander Bucher be tried by general court-martial for five offenses. These included (Murphy 1971:399):

> Permitting his ship to be searched while he had the power to resist; failing to take immediate and aggressive protective measures when his ship was attacked by the North Korean forces; complying with the orders of the North Korean forces to follow them into port; negligently failing to complete destruction of classified material aboard USS *Pueblo* and permitting such material to fall into the hands of the North Koreans; and negligently failing to ensure, before departure for sea, that his officers and crew were properly organized, stationed, and trained in preparation for emergency destruction of classified material.

The court of inquiry went on to recommend trial by general court-martial against Lt. Stephen Harris, officer in charge of the *Pueblo's* research detachment, for dereliction of duty in connection with the failure to destroy classified material. The court recommended non-judicial punishment, in the form of a letter of admonition, against the *Pueblo's* executive officer, Lt. Edward R. Murphy, Jr., for "alleged dereliction of duty in the performance of his duties as executive officer." Finally, the court recommended letters of reprimand be issued to Rear Adm. Frank L. Johnson, Commander of Naval Forces, Japan, at the time of the seizure of the *Pueblo*, and Capt. Everett B. Gladding. According to the court of inquiry, Admiral Johnson (Murphy 1971:400)

> was derelict in the performance of duty in negligently failing to plan properly for effective emergency support forces for contingencies such as occurred during the execution of the *Pueblo's* mission, and negligently failing to verify effectively the feasibility of rapid emergency destruction of classified equipment and documents carried by the *Pueblo* research detachment.

Captain Gladding was director of naval Security Group, Pacific, during the outfitting of *Pueblo*. The court alleged (Murphy 1971:401) that Gladding was

> derelict in the performance of duty in negligently failing to develop procedure to ensure the readiness of *Pueblo's* research detachment for the mission assigned, and to coordinate other services and agencies to provide intelligence support to *Pueblo* during the mission.

The U.S. Navy, as represented by the official court of inquiry, apparently viewed the entire *Pueblo* incident and the performance of everyone involved as an extremely grave violation of the appropriate norms of military performance. The publicity surrounding the entire affair, however, mandated that the case be closed as quickly as possible. In this connection Admiral Hyland, commander in chief of the U.S. Pacific Fleet, reviewed the recommendations of the court of inquiry and subsequently recommended that Bucher and Harris receive letters of reprimand rather than court-martial. The letter of reprimand to Johnson and the letter of admonition to Murphy he sustained, and Admiral Hyland further recommended that Captain Gladding be completely exonerated. At about the same time, however, Secretary of the Navy Chafee, announced that all charges were being dropped, because "they have suffered enough, and further punishment would not be justified." From the standpoint of the U.S. Navy, the case was closed. However, the careers of all the naval officers involved had been clouded by the shadow of crimes against performance.

The attack on the *Chesapeake* and then the loss of the *Pueblo* 150 years later demanded that guilt be assigned, and both incidents attracted their share of public furor. But for the sheer magnitude of hostility precipitated by an omission in performance, few military cases in history equal Pearl Harbor. The Japanese attack on Pearl Harbor on December 7, 1941, stunned the nation, shocked military leaders around the world, and did devastating but, fortunately, temporary damage to the military capability of the United States. When a military disaster of this magnitude occurs, it is in the nature of the military process to attach guilt and blame—to identify a military criminal, as it were. In the aftermath of Pearl Harbor, there were repeated efforts to attach a significant amount of the blame for the destruction caused by the Japanese attack on Adm. Husband E. Kimmel, then commander-in-chief of the Pacific Fleet. Shortly after the December 7 attack, there were demands from the public and on the floor of Congress that Admiral Kimmel be court-martialed. "On April 6, 1942, at Pikeville, Kentucky, Mr. Andrew J. May, Chairman of the military affairs committee of the House of Representatives, suggested in a speech that Admiral Kimmel and General Short, the army commander on Hawaii, should be shot!" (Kimmel 1955:170). Admiral Kimmel received letters of support from former subordinates, naval colleagues, and well-wishers. There were also many letters of vitriolic denunciation.

Shortly after the Pearl Harbor attack, an investigating commission, the Roberts Commission, was dispatched by presidential order to Hawaii to examine the facts in the situation. Admiral Kimmel was the unofficial "defendant," but this commission was conducted by a special set of rules (Kimmel 1955:147,148). Admiral Kimmel was denied any knowledge of what any witness testified, he never found out what testimony was *not* recorded, and it was only two years later that he managed to find out what *was* recorded. He was not permitted to confront witnesses or submit evidence on subjects they discussed. He was not permitted to have counsel. He even had difficulty in obtaining permission to read and verify the transcript of his own testimony. It turned out that the transcript was garbled and distorted. Admiral Kimmel felt that the purpose of the commission was to find a scapegoat to "save the administration," and, as he saw it (1955:149):

> Apparently Short and I were elected before the commission left Washington. How a justice of the U.S. Supreme Court, two generals and two admirals could lend themselves to such an undertaking is past understanding.

Although the Roberts Commission was only a "fact-finding tribunal," it was in reality an unofficial trial in which Admiral Kimmel and General Short were the defendants and were, for all practical purposes, found guilty without being able to defend themselves effectively. Admiral Kimmel (and General Short) subsequently applied for retirement. He was put on an extended leave status for a time and, not too much later, his retirement was approved.

In 1944 the rumblings about the irregularities of the activities of the Roberts Commission led to an official investigation of the Pearl Harbor disaster—the Hart Investigation. Admiral Hart gathered a substantial amount of insightful information. In June 1944 Congress, by resolution, demanded an investigation of the Pearl Harbor disaster by the executive branch of the government. The army subsequently convened a board of investigation and the Navy convened a court of inquiry. Admiral Kimmel enjoyed the usual rights in these hearings. After the conclusion of the investigation, the naval court cleared Kimmel by making, in effect, a positive finding of "no blame or mistakes in judgment" on his part, and concluding that he did everything possible under the circumstances (Kimmel 1955:160). The findings of the naval court were transmitted up through channels. Admiral King, as ranking naval officer, added an endorsement to the report *reversing* the findings of the court of inquiry, and sent it on to the secretary of the navy. The secretary of the navy was displeased with the findings of the court of inquiry and ordered another investigation—the Hewitt Investigation. The Secretary of War, displeased with the findings of the army board, also called for another investigation. Ultimately, Congress undertook its own investigation, but the congressional investigation became mired in partisan politics, with the Democrats essentially controlling its direction. As Admiral Kimmel (1955:169) viewed it, "In the main the views of the administration prevailed," the findings were inconclusive, and Admiral Kimmel never received the exoneration he sought. While never formally charged with dereliction of duty or even errors of command judgment, he was essentially found guilty—by the public, the navy, and the Democratic administration—of crimes against performance, and informally sanctioned accordingly.

Failure and Defeat

In battle and war, there can never be two winners. It is true, of course, that there are sometimes negotiated cease-fires or surrenders that are conditional. Similarly, there are battles where both sides are badly mauled, and the contest is essentially a draw. But there are no instances of both sides winning, and in most battles one side is the decisive looser. Inasmuch as the role of the warrior is to conquer the enemy, failure to do so is technically a crime against performance. Failure or defeat is traditionally the basis for shame and dishonor. In ancient times, the kings and generals of defeated armies might fall on their swords or have an aide kill them. Defeated generals might be taken prisoner by their conquerors and paraded through the streets of the capital of the winning nation. If they succeeded in returning to their own country, they might likely have been stripped of their rank and honors, and possibly even imprisoned or executed for their failure. Although in recent times the U.S. military has not gone so far as to execute commanding officers who do not win the battle, there are innumerable instances in World War II, and some more recent, of commanding officers of all levels from company to corps being relieved of command and replaced by someone of more forceful and aggressive leadership. This was essentially why Lincoln chose Grant, and why General Bernard Montgomery assumed command of British forces in North Africa. In such instances, being relieved from command is essentially a public rebuke for crimes against performance, and the stigma attached to the action tends to follow one throughout a military career.

Because failure is tantamount to dishonor and disgrace throughout history, members of the military have often tended to elect self-punishment in the form of suicide rather than public and official sanction. The custom of "going down with one's ship" is, for all practical purposes, suicide because of having lost the ship. Although it has tended sometimes to be rationalized differently, officers of the British Navy clung to their custom until contemporary times. In World War II, in the Pacific, Japanese torpedo planes attacked the British battleships *Prince of Wales* and *Repulse*. Both were sunk. On board the *Prince of Wales*, Captain Leach ordered all hands to abandon ship. Then he and the flag fleet commander, Admiral Phillips, "stood together on the bridge and waved to their departing men" (Toland 1971:277). The ship sank beneath the waves, taking the two men with it.

Sanctions for failure and defeat may then, in some instances, be self-inflicted, such as suicide being committed in order to avoid the attendant shame and stigma. Again the Samurai warrior and the code of Bushido provide an excellent example of suicide resulting from military defeat. In this instance, hara-kiri was originally intended as an extremely painful type of suicide. The individual would stab himself in the abdomen and literally slash himself open, thus effectively disemboweling himself. In earlier times, a friend, servant, or other Samurai would decapitate the hara-kiri victim and perhaps fasten stones to his head and sink it in the river, thereby preventing it from falling into the hands of enemies. Hara-kiri has continued up until the present, although the mechanics have been modified somewhat, especially to minimize the physical pain. In this regard, Turnbull (1977:47) has commented that "so horrible was the idea of hara-kiri that even the Samurai modified it in later years to a purely nominal stabbing, while a friendly second cut off the victim's head."

Hara-kiri was relatively common among members of the Japanese armed forces during World War II. Sometimes large numbers of soldiers would permit themselves to be led (or charge spontaneously) in "banzai charges," in effect committing suicide.

In other instances, facing defeat or capture, they would take their own lives by various means. In Toland's (1971:585–88) account of Japanese-American fighting during World War II, he tells of several Japanese military suicides in the Saipan campaign: several wounded Japanese soldiers on a beach detonate a grenade and kill themselves; a Japanese chief surgeon shoots himself in the throat, and his assistant, a lieutenant, slashes his own throat; a nurse in the same field hospital tries to kill herself with a grenade, but fails; many thousands of civilians on Saipan (and on other islands as well) commit suicide by leaping off cliffs into the sea. The suicides of many of the civilians and some of the military were prompted more by fear of capture than by need to atone for military defeat. Thanks to distorted Japanese propaganda, both civilian and military personnel thought that if captured by the Americans, they would be tortured and killed. They had been led to believe, for example, that the American "devils" had Japanese prisoners torn apart with tanks.

There were instances during World War II of some Japanese military personnel, mostly officers, committing hara-kiri in the traditional manner, by slashing open their abdomens. These suicides were prompted mostly by the disgrace of defeat and possible capture. In Toland's book (1971:586) mention is made of a naval lieutenant on Saipan who had intended to commit hara-kiri, but failed to do so because of injuries that made him pass out. When he came to, he was relieved to be alive, but "was so exhausted that it didn't occur to him until later that he, an officer, *had disgraced himself by surviving the last assault*" [italics added]. For the Japanese reared in the ideology of Bushido, defeat or capture was disgrace and dishonor—and a violation of the norms of the warrior. This was particularly true among the higher-ranking officers in the Japanese military, most of whom viewed themselves as true Samurai in the traditional sense. In the Okinawan campaign during World War II, suicide was endemic among Japanese troops, and even civilians, on the island. When American troops were about to overrun the Japanese naval base force in a cave, the commanding officer, Rear Adm. Minoru Ota, radioed his superior the following message (Belote 1970:293):

> Enemy tank groups are now attacking our base headquarters. The Naval Base Force is dying gloriously at this moment. . . . We are grateful for your past kindnesses and pray for the success of the Army.

Later in the battle, when Lt. Gen. Mitsuru Ushijima, the commanding general of all Japanese forces on the island, was faced with surrender and capture, he ordered the remaining officers and men of his staff to make a final charge on hill 95, then held by American forces (Belote 1970:317–18). He and his chief of staff, Lt. Gen. Isamu Cho, donned their full dress uniforms, replete with sword and medals, went out on a rock ledge overlooking the sea, knelt on a white sheet laid over a heavy comforter, and opened their tunics, bearing their abdomens. Then, one at a time, each took a knife handed him by his adjutants and stabbed himself, committing hara-kiri. Simultaneously, their adjutants slashed their necks with a saber, severing their spinal columns. General Cho's epitaph, which he had written on his white silk mattress cover, was buried with him. It read, "I depart without regret, shame, or obligations." As true Samurais, these Japanese officers had atoned for deviancy from the code of the warrior. For military failure, they had, as Belote phrased it, "fulfilled in the ancient way their ritual propitiation."

Japanese officers (and enlisted men) were not the only military personnel in World War II with a sense of adherence to a warrior's code that included the self-inflicted sanction of suicide for the offense of military defeat. A number of individuals, especially of high rank, took their own lives when faced with the exigency of defeat and capture. It is to be granted that some German officers committed suicide rather than face the alternative—the wrath of Hitler. General Rommel, for example, when confronted with the possibility of military trial, disgrace, and possible execution, as well as the loss of benefits and pension to his widow, voluntarily elected suicide, and subsequent burial with full military honors. There were sufficient examples of officers freely electing suicide over surrender and disgrace in the classic Prussian tradition. Perhaps the outstanding instance of an individual in the military *violating* the implicit code of the warrior, however, and in effect committing a crime against tradition, was that of General von Paulus, commander of the beleaguered German Sixth Army at Stalingrad. Hitler wanted the surrounded army to stand fast and fight to the last man. To insure that this would occur, Hitler promoted von Paulus to field marshal. In all of history, no German field marshal had ever, of his own volition, suffered the ignominy of defeat and capture. Hitler therefore anticipated that von Paulus would have his men fight to the end, and then honorably take his own life. As things turned out, von Paulus surrendered himself and his men to the Russians and committed an offense against the expectations of the code of the traditional soldier.

Cowardice and Desertion

Even the most battle hardened of elite shock troops will sometimes retreat without orders, or run away from combat—"bug out," as it were, if the combat situation is hopeless enough, or enemy fire is totally devastating. Because of this eventuality, all militaries have explicit norms and rules regulating the stance of their troops in the face of the enemy. The attendant sanctions are usually the most severe of any that punish violations of military law. In some instances an offender will be severely punished as a lesson to the other troops, and/or as a means of "stiffening" their resolve. Only in unusual situations is the punishment less than the most severe of sanctions.

During the Spanish civil war, many of the foreign volunteers to the Republican side became disillusioned after a time and wanted to return home, which they were not permitted to do. As a result, they tended to attempt desertion, especially before impending battles. According to Thomas (1961:390):

> The punishment for attempting desertion or escape was at least confinement in a "re-education camp," for whose cruel rigours many idealistic but easily disgusted young men from Anglo-Saxon or Scandinavian countries were not prepared.

Deserters, if caught, might be executed. The British Foreign Office in London, however, managed to negotiate a settlement with the Republican government that exempted British volunteers from the death penalty. Lack of discipline and aggressiveness in combat was a problem that plagued the Republican forces throughout the war. One commander "staged a mock execution of deserters to prevent weakness in the trenches" (Thomas 1961:349). A major factor in the lack of military discipline and fighting spirit was the fact that the Republican army, particularly in the foreign volunteer brigades, was operated on extremely democratic principles. As Thomas (1961:203) described it: "It was not easy for an officer of the Spanish Army to lead a body of men who sometimes insisted on a show of hands before an attack."

Discipline was somewhat stiffer in the Nationalist forces, and the German Condor Legion and the various Spanish Moorish and Foreign Legion units were all superb combat organizations. The volunteer Italian troops were a different story. In numerous instances they developed an early dissaffection with the war, and many gave themselves self-inflicted wounds, or bandaged themselves when there was nothing wrong with them. Those that were detected in their malingering were usually shot as cowards (Thomas 1961:387).

Unpopular wars and unwilling recruits have historically made for high desertion rates. Where the conditions of combat are particularly severe and the enemy and their firepower especially fearsome, cowardice in the face of the enemy has not been an infrequent occurrence. In the American Revolution the problem of desertion was serious because of its frequency. Death was often the punishment for desertion by enlisted men. "Cowardice was charged against not a few officers; most of them were acquitted, a few cashiered" (Ward 1952:379). Sometimes there were more curious sanctions for desertion in the face of the enemy. In the Battle of Guilford some entire Colonial units, and a number of individuals in various militia units, had broken and run in the face of British fire. Ward (1952:798) reports that subsequently:

> By a resolution of the "Council Extraordinary" of North Carolina it was provided after Guilford that "every man who abandoned his post in the late action should be enrolled in the Continental army for 12 months."

Several hundred such men were rounded up and placed in the command of Gen. Nathanael Greene, where they are said to have behaved well. The British army, while much better trained and disciplined, also had an endemic problem of desertion. As an illustration of the magnitude of the problem, when the British forces moved from Philadelphia to the Battle of Monmouth, they lost 136 men by desertion while on the march, and the Hessian troops accompanying them lost 440 in the same manner (Ward 1952:585).

In the American Civil War, the troops on both sides experienced mass warfare, almost unbelievable physical deprivation, and exposure to devastating gunfire in near-suicidal charges in the battles. It is therefore not surprising that large numbers of men from both the Union and Confederate forces deserted, or ran away under fire in battle. Punishment for desertion was severe, and during the war 141 Union men were executed for this offense. Many others were tried, found guilty, and sentenced to die for desertion, but were granted a pardon by President Lincoln, who preferred, he said, to "take the risk on the side of mercy" (*American Heritage* 1960:381). Some soldiers compounded the crime of desertion by profiting from it. Some unscrupulous individuals who had no intention of rendering any real military service would enlist, collect their bounty money, desert at the first chance, reenlist under another name, collect another bounty, desert again, and continue repeating the process. These "bounty jumpers" were universally detested (*American Heritage* 1960:485). Sometimes deserters would leave their units but, rather than return home, would simply tag along on the fringe of the army, occupying themselves with marauding and looting. Deserters from the other side might even join them and combine efforts. These groups of drifters, under no military control, were known as "bummers." In his march through Georgia, Sherman had the problem of "bummers" but made little effort to control their robbing and pilfering, inasmuch as they were accomplishing what he had set out to do (*American Heritage* 1960:547). In some instances desertion was prompted more by reasons of altruism than selfish fear. When Sherman invaded North Carolina, "hundreds of North Carolinians deserted Lee's army to protect their homesteads" (*American Heritage* 1960:599).

Cowardice and desertion have sometimes been the isolated behavior of a single individual, and sometimes the collective impulse of whole units. It is reported that in some armies in the past there was such a tendency for soldiers in battle to run before the enemy that noncommissioned officers had to force the men forward physically in an attack. Keegan (1976:183) suggests that this was essentially the function of the halberds, issued to sergeants along with swords in the Napoleonic era. He observes that:

> In one of General Lejeune's paintings of a Napoleonic battle in which he fought, he has actually portrayed a French sergeant pushing against the back of one of the French ranks, using his halberd horizontally in both hands to hold the men in place. It is not improbable to think of British sergeants having done the same at Waterloo.

At Waterloo the Belgium officers were reputed to have been particularly brutal with their own soldiers who attempted to flee the battle. In some British units officers and noncommissioned officers were forced to push and "thump" men into gaps in the attacking rank. Keegan (1976:183) even views the famed British square as a "disciplinary device" designed to prevent soldiers from running away in battle, by making it easier to exercise control over them, while at the same time giving the soldiers more of a sense of safety, security, and solidarity, even though it was actually a highly vulnerable formation. Akin to this desire to be close to one's comrades was the curious phenomenon of "piles" of French soldiers at Waterloo. When the battle turned against them, many French units disintegrated, with the men fleeing in all directions. If they came across enemy troops they tried to surrender, often throwing themselves on the ground. Sometimes they would crowd together on the ground, actually forming human piles in their search for safety and security.

It was apparently not unusual for an officer to have to force a soldier back into the line of attack, either at saber point or by striking the soldier with the flat of a sword. Some of the more experienced or more dependable units were used to prevent other, less aggressive units from running away in the face of the enemy. In the Battle of Waterloo such a practice was widespread. Keegan (1976:182) indicates:

> Much more positive, in the case of those soldiers who wanted or tried to run, was the simple mechanism of coercion. Most of the reports we have are of British soldiers, particularly British cavalry, acting to prevent the non-British contingents leaving position. The 10th Hussars stood behind some Brunswickers during the French cavalry attacks and "kept their files closed" to prevent them leaving the field; the 11th Hussars did likewise, and the 16th Light Dragoons; Vivian stood his hussars "10 yards behind infantry which were running away."

In World War I, as in the Napoleonic wars, the problem of desertion and fleeing in the face of the enemy was a serious one to the military. Just before the Battle of the Somme, in many British units there were "a number of soldiers [who] inflicted wounds on themselves to avoid having to 'jump the parapet' [go over the top]" (Keegan 1976:270–71).[1] Desertion, self-inflicted wounds, and sim-

---

[1] In nineteenth-century Russia some serfs are reported to have avoided military conscription in the czar's army by the simple expedient of knocking out their front teeth. In those days it was necessary for soldiers to be able to bite the musket cartridge in the process of loading the weapon. Without front teeth, of course, the serfs could not handily accomplich this (Keegan 1976:270).

ple refusal to go into combat[2] all tended to snowball as the war went on. Keegan (1976:271) reports the remarks of a medical officer of the Second Royal Welch Fusiliers, who wrote on October 15, 1917:

> Two or three score mean fellows are encouraged to slip away every time there is risk to their skins, so more and more average men learn to shirk with impunity, attacks fail, and losses run into untold thousands, because the most dutiful of our men are not backed up.

The situation grew so bad in the French army that by May 1917 "collective indiscipline" occurred in 54 of the 110 divisions on the western front. The French army was forced to take Draconian measures to stop the spread of the mutiny. Representative soldiers from various units were executed as an example to the rest of the men.[3] On both Allied and Axis sides desertion and running away from the enemy was a persistent problem. There were courts-martial aplenty and severe punishments were meted out, but the effect was minimal.[4] In some cases officers simply dispensed justice on the spot. Again Keegan (1976:277) quotes an observer:

> Another more formidable party of stragglers cut across. . . . They are damned if they are going to stay. . . . . A young sprinting subaltern heads them off. He draws his revolver. . . . They take no notice. He fires. Down drops a British soldier at his feet. The effect is instantaneous. They turn back. . . .

British units, like those of all the combatants, had to establish "battle police" to grab deserters, round up stragglers, and send them back into the lines.[5]

---

[2] There have been isolated instances of individuals refusing to go into combat in all of our wars. In the Vietnamese conflict, a particularly unusual case of this was a Strategic Air Command officer, the pilot of a B52 bomber, who reportedly refused to fly a combat mission over North Vietnam during the massive raids against the Hanoi area in 1973 (Associated press 1973bb). The Air Force claimed that he was the "first and only" B52 crew member to fail to obey an order to fly a combat mission, although there were unconfirmed reports that other B52 crew members had been "quietly" returned to the United States when they balked at flying missions over the heavily defended Hanoi area.

[3] This process was vividly portrayed in the movie *Paths of Glory*, which starred Kirk Douglas.

[4] Desertion under fire in World War I was the subject of another classic film. In *The Fighting 69th* James Cagney played the part of a young private who talks tough but, when confronted with the terror of battle, runs away. He is caught and sentenced to be executed, but in good Hollywood style he escapes and voluntarily goes into a battle, where he is killed while performing an act of heroism.

[5] Very few persons realize that one of the functions of the Military Police corps in the U.S. army is patrol on a line somewhat to the rear of the front lines.

In more recent wars, such as World War II, some armies (e.g., the Russian) would prevent the problem of running in the face of the enemy by the simple expedient of placing machine guns at the rear of their own charging troops with orders to shoot any man that tried to run or retreat. In World War II the German army was one of the best trained, best disciplined, and most effective of any to take the field. Toward the end of the war, however, the German army on the eastern front began to disintegrate. The Russians were advancing with enormous numbers of troops and employing an almost incredible amount of artillery. The German army was being pulverized but was retreating in generally good order. As might be expected, there was an inordinate amount of straggling as whole units were decimated, as well as a number of both officers and enlisted men deserting in an attempt to escape the Russian onslaught. In a number of instances, dazed and hungry German soldiers who may have run in the face of the enemy were simply wandering about aimlessly.

In order to keep the retreat orderly, to patch together replacement units out of stragglers and remnants of units, and to minimize desertion and cowardice in the face of the enemy, the German army set up field police stations along the retreat routes. They would arrest stragglers and deserters, prevent the plundering of army stocks, and in some cases try to form scratch units from remnants of other units essentially destroyed in battle. In numerous cases, however, drumhead courts were set up in tents and deserters and stragglers were simply found guilty and shot on the spot, or hanged by the side of the road so the retreating troops could observe the punishment of cowardice. The various Waffen SS units, because of their political and military reliability, were used for such duty. Neumann (1958:243–45) relates how, toward the end of the war, he and his SS unit were ordered to "arrest all deserters and shoot them immediately, in case of resistance." The SS troops set up a roadblock on the Mohilev-Minsk road in White Russia, and all military trucks and cars heading west were checked. Those officers and men who could not produce written orders were "ruthlessly" shot. In one incident a Mercedes,

---

Ostensibly they are to protect the troops in the front lines from attack from the rear, and rear-echelon troops from ambush from guerrilla forces, partisans, and infiltrating enemy units, but one of the obvious latent functions is to catch deserters from the front lines and round up stragglers.

camouflaged with branches, stopped at the roadblock. Inside were a captain and two other officers. Neumann approached the car and asked for their movement orders, but all they produced was their front-line identification permit. As he describes the three officers:

> Abject fear is written all over the faces of the three men. They are obviously Staff Officers who, having no effective command, must have decided to head for Minsk off their own bats. But at a time when all of our resources should be mustered to try and hold the Bolsheviks, it is nothing more or less than treason to run away without fighting.

The officers were ordered out of the car and their papers scrutinized, verifying Neumann's supposition about their status. They were led to a field off the road and shot to death with machine pistols.

Neumann (1958:250–251) also relates how 30 German deserters were hanged from the arches of the bridge over the Hungarian Repse River at Gyor. They had received no form of trial. Hanging on the chest of each body was a wooden board with one word written on it—*Feigling* (coward), indicating why they had been executed. As Neumann phrased it, "they died because they were afraid, afraid to die." Thousands more deserters were shot or hanged along all of the retreat routes out of Russia. The German army was shattered, and fighting against overwhelming odds. Neumann states (1958:260):

> The men are completely whacked. An uninterrupted week's fighting has brought them to the limit of human endurance. Morale could not be lower. Discipline has suffered as a result. An Unterscharfuhrer of the 3rd Anti-tank Battalion yesterday refused to obey an order to go out on patrol. He was immediately shot.

As the Russian troops rumbled through Austria toward Vienna, some municipal officials expressed a desire to have Vienna declared an "open city." The Germans saw this as cowardice, and according to Neumann (1958:261), "Sepp Dietrich, who is commander-in-chief in Vienna, immediately dealt with them. They will never cause us any trouble again."

Along other parts of Russia the German army had set up roadblocks, military police posts, and field interrogation units that could sentence a straggler to death or assign him to a penal battalion without benefit of court-martial. Sajer (1972:332) relates how he and a number of other stragglers were caught at a roadblock and interrogated. A lieutenant in the line in front of him was the only survivor of his unit, which had been annihilated in combat. The interrogator was prejudiced by the fact that the lieutenant was the only survivor, and was suspicious that he might have fled in the face of the enemy. The interrogator also, however, was concerned about the fact that the lieutenant was missing some of his issued equipment, included his Zeiss fieldglasses, his map case, and the section telephone for which he was responsible. To lose equipment is as much a crime against performance as a crime against property. A German officer was not supposed to lose equipment, and the lieutenant had obviously failed in his duty. This, coupled with the suspicion about his straggling, caused the interrogator to sentence the lieutenant to a penal battalion, and to have three grades stripped from his rank. Sajer thought the lieutenant lucky at that. Sajer himself, an enlisted man, barely escaped being sent to a penal battalion, because he also was missing several items of equipment, including his gas mask, and because he had apparently been retreating with his unit.

The German soldier was generally excellent in combat and would stand firm in the face of an attack, but the Russian advance was of such a magnitude that even the most battle-hardened German troops would frequently break and run. As Sajer (1972:335) depicts it:

> The lookouts in the shallow trenches scratched into the hills overlooking the river, who were supposed to provide an illusion of protection, watched the shouting hordes of Russian infantry flood down to the river. These soldiers quickly realized they would never be able to stop that irresistible tide, and succumbed to a moment of absolute panic. Some ran, through the deafening explosions of Soviet rockets which drowned out our spandaus and light mortars. The Russsians, driven by expectations of victory, and by the exhortations of the people's commissars, pushed forward regardless of the cost.

Toward the end of the war the German army had run out of manpower and, as an expedient means of creating reserve units, rounded up the remaining scraps of the male population—old men of 65 and boys of 13. These wretched individuals were organized into *Volksturm* units, given the most perfunctory training, equipped poorly, and sent into combat to defend the cities against the advancing Russians hordes. They were extremely ill prepared to perform in a militarily satisfactory fashion in combat. As Neuman (1958:266) comments:

None of these old men, who were enlisted voluntarily or otherwise in their quasi-military units, has ever possessed the morale to give him even a minimum of confidence in the orders he has received.

Inasmuch as the members of the *Volksturm* units had such minimal potential as combat soldiers, they tended to perform poorly and not infrequently deserted and ran from the enemy in battle. Since these units were the last defense against the Russian armies, military justice had to be extremely severe if there was to be any hope of insuring that the members of the *Volksturm* would stand and fight to the last man and the last bullet. In spite of the serious consequences, many of the individuals in such units did give way under fire and deserted. Neumann (1958:266) tells of an incident in Vienna where ten Austrian members of the *Volksturm* were accused of desertion in the face of the enemy. A special court-martial was convened within two hours. They were all found guilty, lined up against a half-ruined wall, and executed by SS troops.

The problem of desertion in combat and fleeing in the face of the enemy in battle has been exacerbated in recent times not only by the traumatizing savagery of modern weaponry and other forms of military technology, but also by the erosion of the traditional concept of the "right to flight." Historically, if the enemy attack became too devastating, the soldier had the implicit "right" to seek temporary shelter or respite, or leave the battlefield. Battles were not fought to the last man and the last round. Keegan (1976:309) discusses this concept and points out that in the Battle of Agincourt, when the French cavalry force begin to receive the rain of arrows from the English archers, they veered off to safety in some woods near the battlefield. Similarly, at Waterloo, a large number of Belgian troops took refuge in some woods near the place of fighting and waited till the battle was almost over. As Keegan explains it:

> This right to flight is naturally not one which generals are willing to concede. But its availability is one of the things which in the past have made battle bearable, by allowing the soldier to believe that his presence on the battlefield was ultimately voluntary, and it has been frequently exercised by armies of all nations, not always with results fatal either to individuals or the greater cause; first Bull Run, the Second Battle of the Somme, and Kasserine provide the most obvious modern verifications of the half-truth that he who fights and runs away lives to fight another day.

As he points out, "indeed for an army to run away can be to inflict a very serious frustration on its enemy's plans." Nevertheless, in recent times, the tendency has been to demand that the soldier stand his ground in battle, regardless of ferocity of the attack and the consequences to him. Any vagrancy from strick conformity to this norm is viewed as a serious offense against performance and severely sanctioned.

It should be noted, however, that there is a certain element of altruism in the rigidity of the norm proscribing flight in the face of the enemy, and the severity of sanction attendant to any violation of the norm. Ardant du Picq, the nineteenth-century French military analyst, observed (Keegan 1976:71):

> that soldiers die in largest numbers when they run, because it is when they turn their backs to the enemy that they are least able to defend themselves. It is their rational acceptance of the danger of running that makes civilized soldiers so formidable, he says, that and discipline which has them in its bonds and by discipline he does not mean the operation of an abstract principle but the example and sanctions exercised by the officers of an organized force. Men fight, he says in short, from fear: fear of the consequences first of not fighting (i.e. punishment), then of not fighting well (i.e. slaughter).

Desertion from combat does not always involve a panic-stricken aimless flight from the enemy or his gunfire. Desertion may take the form of "internal desertion" (Keegan 1976:310). In times of siege warfare, individuals might "desert" by the simple expedient of hiding in the fortress. To combat this, the commandant would concentrate all food supplies in a central place that he could monitor and hold secure. In more recent times, the size of the battlefield has enlarged considerably and the debris of war, including preserved foodstuffs, is usually littered widely about the area. It has therefore not been difficult even in modern times for individuals to engage in "internal desertion" and simply hide somewhere on the battlefield. Static warfare, such as the trench warfare of World War I, has tended to facilitate such behavior. As an incidence of such desertion, Keegan (1976:311) relates:

> The wastes of the "old Somme battlefield," pitted with dugouts and trenches over many square miles, were, during 1917, colonized by a freebooting gang of Australians, who lived by raiding military dumps and eluded the search of the military police for many months, some say until the end of the war.

Keegan also points out that during the siege of DienBienPhu, a large number of the non-French garrison "deserted" by burrowing holes for themselves in the banks of the little river that meandered through the fortress. They managed to survive by pilfering what they needed from the loads of supplies dropped by parachute each night into the perimeter of the fort. Sometimes they would even fight the combatants for their share of the supplies. When the garrison capitulated, it is believed that the number of "internal deserters" actually outnumbered the size of the active garrison.[6] As previously mentioned in this chapter, there were "internal deserters" (known as "bummers") in the Civil War who followed along at the edge of the advancing army.

Perhaps the most widely publicized case of cowardice and desertion in modern times is that of Pvt. Eddie D. Slovik of the 28th Infantry in France during World War II (Huie 1954; DiMona, 1972). Slovik's official offense was a relatively simple, albeit terribly serious, crime against performance. He was charged with violating the 58th article of war—desertion to avoid hazardous duty. He was court-martialed in a brief trial on November 11, 1944. Inasmuch as Slovik had written and signed a confession of having deserted, there was relatively little testimony or evidence to be introduced, and thus little complexity to the trial. The members of the court readily found him guilty of the charge and gave him the maximum sentence (DiMona 1972:122): "To be dishonorably discharged from the service, to forfeit all pay and allowances due or to become due, and to be shot to death with musketry."

The case is exemplary in its pathos as well as its simplicity. Slovik was an individual of Polish extraction, from an impecunious

---

[6] The magnitude of this incident of "internal" desertion is much overshadowed by the situation in France during World War II. It was estimated that there were almost 19,000 Americans who had gone AWOL; most of them congregated in and around Paris, constituting something of an underworld. Gangs of these deserters would highjack trucks and even whole trainloads of supplies such as food, soap, and cigarettes. They were highjacking an average of 1,000 gallons of gasoline a day. Most of these supplies were sold on the French black market. The deserters in turn were corrupting individuals in regular units to aid them in their illegal activities. One whole railway battalion was reported to have been involved. In one Paris detention barracks there were 1,308 Americans under arrest, more than half of whom were charged with "misappropriation." The deserters were guilty of crimes against property because of their theft, but they were also guilty of crimes against performance because of the fact that their thefts and misappropriations deprived their comrades in combat of desperately needed supplies. This made them "saboteurs" as well as deserters (Toland 1959:222; Giles 1965:111–12).

family. He was a person of moderate intelligence but limited ability, ambition, and sophistication. In growing up he was a petty delinquent. He quit school when he was 15, interacted with unsavory associates, stayed out late, drank, and stole. He was arrested on several occasions, put on probation, and ultimately sent to the reform school at Ionia, Michigan, for the crime of embezzling $59.60 worth of candy, chewing gum, and cigarettes, which he took home from his job at a drugstore without paying for them, as well as pocketing change received over the counter. In the time he was at the reform school, no one ever visited him. He was paroled after about a year, but subsequently went on a drinking spree, stole a car for a joyride, and wrecked it. He was sentenced to prison and transferred back to the reform school a few months later. Three years later, at 22, he was released from prison and got a job as a plumber's helper. He fell in love with the bookkeeper at the plumbing shop, a woman five years older than he, and they ultimately married. He now had a job, a wife, an apartment, a 4-F draft rating, and, in his opinion, a future. In November 1943 his draft classification was changed from 4-F to 1-A. Inducted, trained, and shipped to Europe, he was poorly equipped psychologically, intellectually, or emotionally for military life, and even less for combat. In letters he called his wife "mommy." He landed on Omaha Beach in France several months after the invasion and was assigned as a replacement rifleman to G Company, 109th Infantry, 28th Division. Trucks took him and other replacements toward his unit at the front. In the French town of Albuff they came under fire and dug in. When the shelling ceased, the other replacements moved out to join their units, but Slovik stayed in his foxhole, too frightened to move. Later he joined up with a Canadian unit and stayed with them for 45 days. The Canadian unit saw no combat during this period. In time he reported to the commanding officer of his assigned unit and told him that if he had to go into combat again he would run away. The officer said there was nothing he could do, and Slovik walked away from him. The next morning he appeared with a signed confession that ended with the remark, *"and I'll run away again if I have to go their [sic]"* [italics in original]. Clearly Slovik expected and wished to be court-martialed, sentenced to the stockade, where he would be safe for the duration of the war, and then probably released shortly after the end of the war. He apparently did not expect to be shot.

The sentence of the court-martial was upheld by his divisional commander, later by General Eisenhower, and finally by the office of the judge advocate.

On January 31, 1945, Pvt. Eddie D. Slovik, #36896415, was shot and killed by a firing squad of 12 soldiers in a snowy field in the Vosges mountains. Several observations concerning the entire case are worthy of review. Slovik himself finally accepted his fate philosophically and died quietly and stoically (Huie 1954:138–146), but as he was being tied up to be led to the place of execution he commented:

> I'm okay. They're not shooting me for deserting the United States Army. Thousands of guys have done that. They just need to make an example out of somebody and I'm it because I'm an ex-con. I use to steal things when I was a kid, and that's what they are shooting me for. They're shooting me for bread and chewing gum I stole when I was twelve years old.

The divisional judge advocate reviewed the case and indicated that if a test case was desired, Slovik, with his criminal record, should be it (DiMona 1972:123). General Coda, the divisional commander who approved the sentence, said (Huie, 1954:110–11):

> Given the situation as I knew it in November, 1944, I thought it was my duty to this country to approve that sentence. If I hadn't approved it—if I had let Slovik accomplish his purport, then I don't know how I could have gone up to the line and looked a good soldier in the face.

Finally, the remarks of Maj. Frederick J. Bertolet, the reviewing officer in the office of the theater judge advocate, are instructive. Bertolet reflected (Huie 1954:117–18):

> There can be no doubt that he deliberately sought the safety and comparative comfort of the guardhouse. To him, and to those soldiers who may follow his example, if he achieves his end, confinement is neither deterrent nor punishment. He has directly challenged the authority of the government, and future discipline depends on a resolute reply to this challenge. If the death penalty is ever to be imposed for desertion it should be imposed in this case, not as a punitive measure nor as retribution, but to maintain that discipline upon which alone an army can succeed against the enemy. There was no recommendation for clemency in this case and *none here is recommended.*

It should be recalled that there was thousands of cases of desertion in the military during World War II. It was an endemic prob-

lem. Some 2,864 men were actually tried for this offense, and 49
death sentences were approved but later commuted. Thus in the
interest of maintaining military discipline and reinforcing the
system of military norms and sanctions, Private Slovik became the
only American serviceman executed for cowardice since 1864, and
the only American executed for this crime against performance
during World War II.

Aiding the Enemy

Giving aid or comfort to the enemy is tantamount to treason,
and is therefore a most serious form of military crime against performance. There have been defectors and "turncoats" in the armed
services in practically all nations throughout history. Sometimes
whole armies, or at least the population equivalent of whole armies, have gone over to the other side. During World War II, for
example, when German forces moved into Byelorussia and the
Ukraine, they were at first received as liberators and conquerors.
Large numbers of Russians were recruited into the ranks of the
Germany army, including Russian civilians and Russian POW's.
Sometimes such individuals were integrated into regular German
units, and in other cases special units were created with nothing
but Russians, such as the very effective Kaminsky Brigade (Dallin
1952). There were a number of Russian Cossack units that fought
on the German side, some even being shipped to France. In all
cases, had they been recaptured by Russian forces they would have
been treated as treasonous members of their own military who had
betrayed their cause and aided the enemy, and punished severely,
probably by death.

Just as civilian American citizens such as Tokyo Rose and Ezra
Pound aided and collaborated with the enemy and were punished
accordingly, individuals in the military who aid the enemy side are
viewed as criminal offenders and sanctioned in the most severe
fashion. The classic instance of a member of the military aiding the
enemy is that of Maj. Gen. Benedict Arnold and his treasonous
behavior in the American Revolution (DiMona 1972:1–20). Arnold
had been an excellent officer in the Continental army. He had
demonstrated his outstanding abilities as a tactician in various battles, and had also shown his bravery in combat. He had been

wounded in the Battle of Quebec and was respected as a national hero. However, he kept poor accounts of the money he had been advanced by the Continental Congress for the salaries and expenses of his military unit. He was criticized for this, and there was suspicion that he might be misappropriating funds. Because of their dispute with Arnold about his finances, the Continental Congress withheld his salary and tied up his accounts.

General Arnold, as military commander of the Philadelphia area, became involved in some questionable activities that suggested personal profit as a motive. He had given permission for a private ship to sail through the American lines. He also closed the shops and stores in Philadelphia while allegedly making considerable private purchases for his own benefit. He had additionally commandeered some wagons belonging to the state of Pennsylvania and used them to transport private property. He was subsequently court-martialed for these activities (and for another charge) and, in spite of his vigorous and elaborate defense, the court found him guilty in regard to the matters of the ship and the wagons, and sentenced him to receive a reprimand from General Washington. Arnold, already angry at the Continental Congress about his funds, and annoyed that his military services were not recognized and appreciated as he thought they should be, found Washington's angry reprimand too much to take. Embittered, Arnold made contact with the British and conspired to deliver the post at West Point to them. He then asked General Washington for command of the post, which he subsequently received. Later he met with a British officer to arrange the details of his treachery, but the British officer was captured on his way back to New York and incriminating papers were found on him. Word reached Arnold of the capture of the officer and the discovery of the papers while he was having breakfast with General Washington. He hastily excused himself and fled, ultimately escaping to England, where he lived until his death. The British, liking traitors no better than the Americans, treated him with "scorn and neglect," while the Americans made the name Benedict Arnold synonymous with treason and betrayal. Had he been caught, he would have been tried and formally punished. As it was, he was punished informally by having his name represent the historical epitome of military crime against performance.

There is another almost equally well-known historical case of an individual in the military being accused and punished for aiding the enemy. This is the famous Dreyfus affair (Lewis 1973). It differs from the Arnold case, however, in that Dreyfus was innocent and was unjustly convicted and punished. All of the facts in the case are involved and convoluted, but the gist is simple. Captain Alfred Dreyfus was a brilliant staff officer in the French army. He was also Jewish, and there was considerable anti-semitism in France at that time. An important, handwritten *bordereau* (outline) listing various classified military items, purportedly communicated to the Germans by a French officer, fell into the hands of French military counterintelligence. For various complicated reasons, Captain Dreyfus was tentatively identified as the French officer. Captain Dreyfus was arrested, court-martialed, and convicted on the basis of extremely flimsy and obviously conspiratorial evidence. He was sentenced to public dishonor and life imprisonment in a fortified place, the maximum penalties. The public dishonor was accomplished in the form of the military ceremony of public degradation. Some 5,000 soldiers and officers of the French army were assembled, in front of whom Captain Dreyfus was brought out to be degraded. The commanding officer of the troops, Gen. Paul Darras, uttered the sentence, "Dreyfus, you are unworthy to bear arms. In the name of the people of France we degrade you" (Lewis 1973:57). At this point a sergeant of the Garde Republicaine stepped in front of Dreyfus and tore off his buttons, medals, braid, epaulettes, and sleeve and trouser stripes. Dreyfus then offered his sword, which the sergeant broke over his knee. Dreyfus was then marched past the troops in shame. He was now a civilian and a criminal. Dreyfus was transported to the French penal colony in Guiana and later transferred to Devil's Island, where he was imprisoned. After several years, innumerable inquiries and investigations, charges and countercharges, and the intervention of many influential people, such as Emile Zola, who published the essay "J'Accuse," Dreyfus was cleared and pardoned. Ultimately Dreyfus was ceremonially reintegrated into the army and inducted into the Legion of Honor. He retired a year later, in 1907, but returned to active duty during World War II. Although Dreyfus was innocent and wrongly convicted and punished, the example of crime against performance by reason of aiding the enemy is classic in its format, and the ceremonial aspects of the attendant sanctions are illuminating. Until he was cleared, Cap. Alfred Dreyfus was one of the most publicized military criminals in history.

Misconduct as a Prisoner of War

The responsibilities incumbent on a member of the military for loyalty to his cause, his society, and his superiors; for bravery and resoluteness in the face of danger and adversity; and above all for obedience to orders and command, do not cease upon capture and imprisonment by the enemy. In the U.S. military, POW servicemen are bound to obey the highest-ranking Allied POW in their camps and to attempt escape where possible (as a means of returning to the fight, or at least making the enemy devote the maximum manpower effort toward keeping the prisoners confined). The American POW is also duty bound to avoid cooperating with the enemy beyond what is required by treaty (such as necessary work details for camp maintenance). Captured military personnel should not behave in such a way as to cause harm to their fellow POW's or refuse to render such aid as they can. Traditionally, the captured military member was constrained from providing his captors with any information other than his name, rank, and serial number (and of course his branch of service). In recent wars this prescription has proved to be ineffective and unworkable. In World War II and earlier wars, the captors could usually induce their POW captives to reveal more information than that officially required and permitted. In most instances coercion, such has physical deprivations, threats, and even torture, was not usually necessary or even frequent. In both World Wars, POW's were, in general, treated relatively well. The Allied forces were usually quite circumspect in their posture toward POW's, and the Germans also attempted to be correct in their treatment of military prisoners. The Japanese tended to be somewhat more harsh toward POW's, but this was often not so much an instance of deliberate brutality as it was simply a reflection of the Japanese military attitude toward those who surrender in war.

By the time of the Korean War, however, American POW's were systematically and deliberately mistreated and abused. Physical deprivation, torture, and brainwashing were used by the North Koreans to induce captured American servicemen to reveal critical military information, to neglect or commit offenses against fellow prisoners, to denounce the U.S. publicly, or to admit to war crimes or atrocities. Such treatment of American prisoners led to the creation and articulation of a new Cold of Conduct for American POW's that specifically proscribed and prescribed appropriate behavior for captured servicemen. Violation of the various provisions of the Code could result in court-martial and attendant punishment. Some of the most severely sanctioned offenses would be those involving crimes against fellow POW's (such as neglect, theft of food, or actual physical violence), or betraying the United States through collaboration with the enemy.

During World War II, in the European theater, the Allied POW's in German camps and prisons were generally well organized and disciplined, supportive and helpful of each other, and, most important involved in constant efforts to escape, often with success. Some of the these escape activities have been well documented (see, for example, Reid 1953), and have provided the inspiration for numerous fictional accounts in books, articles, movies, and television. In Korea, however American POW escapes from North Korean prison camps were nonexistent, and even attempts were rare. For almost the first time, American POW's did not routinely obey the orders of their superiors. They stole from each other, and in some instances killed their comrades, either deliberately or through neglect. In many cases they gave valuable information to the enemy, and collaborated to the extent of making peace statements and condemning the United States. Several American POW's in Korea even elected not to accept repatriation. Out of those POW's who were ultimately returned to the United States after the prisoner exchange at Panmunjon, some were subsequently court-martialed and punished. In the Vietnamese conflict the enemy was perhaps even more harsh and deliberately and systematically cruel in its treatment of captured Americans. Such treatment included all manner of physical deprivation, severe beatings, tying prisoner's arms and legs so tightly that they actually suffered permanent damage to their limbs, and a variety of tortures. The long period of imprisonment and the treatment and conditions of confinement in Vietnam may have precipitated and encouraged some violations of the Code and other military regulations as well. There were many instances of providing information to the North Vietnamese, signing various "admissions" of war guilt, and even more serious forms of collaboration with the enemy.

One of the most publicized instances of inappropriate behavior on the part of American military personnel captured by the enemy was that of the crew of the *Pueblo,* whose capture off shore of North Korea in 1968 has been described in detail earlier in this chapter.

Although theoretically prohibited from giving other than the barest amount of information to captors, officers and crew of the *Pueblo* provided a voluminous amount of information from the earliest hours of their capture. When first questioned, Captain Bucher gave the size and composition of the crew, and a false statement of the ship's mission. His executive officer was shocked by the captain's behavior and later revealed (Murphy 1971:160):

> There was a very empty feeling in the pit of my stomach. What Bucher was saying was of course gibberish; from what I could hear, he was betraying nothing classified. But that he was saying anything more than name, rank, and serial number— meant that he had abandoned the Code!

Subsequently, officers and crew would respond to questions by the North Koreans, and in some cases signed "confessions" that the *Pueblo* had violated Korea's territorial waters. The men of the *Pueblo* also posed for "propaganda" photographs and spoke at propaganda press conferences. It is to be admitted that the North Koreans did mistreat and beat the men of the *Pueblo,* but the military Code of Conduct does not accept this as mitigating circumstances. Nevertheless, because of all the publicity and controversy about the *Pueblo* incident, the navy saw fit to address itself primarily to the surrender of the ship and the compromising of classified documents, and relatively to ignore the crew's misconduct as POW's.

An interesting recent report of extreme misconduct as a POW is the case of Marine Pfc. Robert R. Garwood, who had been listed as a prisoner of war in Vietnam for 13 and a half years, although it was generally believed that he was dead. Garwood turned up alive in Hanoi and sent word to the U.S. State Department that he wished to return to the United States. It has been alleged that he defected to the enemy, switched allegiance, "as a matter of conscience," and even served as an armed guard in Vietcong prison camps, informing on the U.S. prisoners that he guarded (*New York Times* 1979). When the other U.S. prisoners were released after the American withdrawal in 1973, it is said that he remained behind. The investigation is not complete at this date, but Pfc. Garwood could conceivably be tried for teason as well as desertion as a result of his behavior.

Misconduct as a POW can assume forms other than violating the expectations of their own military. Prisoners are also expected to obey the rules and regulations imposed by their captors. Unruliness, insubordination, or attempting escape, for example, might elicit punative sanctions. More serious offenses such as harming or killing a guard or another prisoner might well call for severe punishment, probably death, In 1945 in a POW compound at Fort Leavenworth, some German prisoners of war murdered a fellow prisoner when they discovered that he was an informant, and was therefore by their standards a traitor. They were subsequently tried by court martial and seven of those involved were hanged (for a detailed account of this case see Whittingham 1971).

Summary

A serviceman's overriding responsibility is to acquit himself honorably in his performance vis-à-vis the enemy. He should obey orders and, if necessary, close with the enemy, killing or being killed in the process, if his orders so dictate. To fail in the discharge of this responsibility represents perhaps the most serious violation of military norms that he can commit. To surrender without good reason, to fail to comply with a combat order, or to display cowardice in the face of the enemy may result in severe sanction, including imprisonment, dishonorable discharge, or even death. In World War II, Pvt. Eddie D. Slovik deserted in the face of the enemy, was court-martialed, and subsequently "shot to death by musketry" at the hands of an American firing squad, finally being buried in an unmarked grave (Huie 1954). In some armies such behavior may result in execution on the spot by the commanding officer or field police.

Nor does the responsibility for obedience, loyalty, and bravery incumbent upon military personnel cease upon capture and imprisonment. In the U.S. army, POW servicemen are duty bound to obey the highest-ranking Allied POW in camp, to attempt escape where possible, to avoid cooperating with the enemy beyond what is required by treaty (such as necessary work details for camp maintenance), and to refrain from giving information to the enemy that would be helpful in pursuing the war. (In theory, the only allowable information a U.S. serviceman may give is his name, rank, and serial number.) Captured military personnel should not behave in such a way as to cause harm to their fellow POW's or refuse to render such aid as they can. Since the Korean conflict, the U.S. military has articulated a Code of Conduct for American POW's that specifically proscribes and prescribes appropriate behavior for captured servicemen. Breach of the Code would constitute a serious violation of military norm. The most severely sanctioned offenses committed while a POW are those involving crimes against fellow POW's (such as neglect, theft of food, or actual physical violence), or betraying the United States through collaboration with the enemy.

In Korea, POW escapes were nonexistent and attempts were rare. For almost the first time U.S. POW's did not obey orders, stole from each other, killed each other, and in many cases gave valuable information to the enemy, and collaborated to the extent of making peace statements and condemning the United States. In Vietnam, the long period of imprisonment and the conditions of privation may have motivated some violations of the Code and other military regulations as well.

Epilogue

This book has posited a comprehensive system of deviancy and criminality—that associated with the military institution. Every institutional context tends to engender a normative structure, but the inherent, and often singularly unique, opportunity structure for deviancy, the stresses and disaffections characteristic of that particular institutional context, and the rationalizing milieu of the institutional culture, all frequently combine to promote an endemic pattern of norm violation. The military is no exception. There has been a persistent literature addressing war as uncivilized and military behavior, either collective or idiosyncratic, in combat situations as often inhumane and thus criminal. This literature has largely concerned itself with atrocities and "war crimes" involving the treatment of enemy civilians or members of the enemy military. But the broader context of illegal military behavior has been largely ignored, although some of the deviant parameters of such behavior have been noted in sources ranging from the poetry of Kipling to contemporary situation-comedy television series such as M*A*S*H. Similarly, behavioral scientists of various disciplinary persuasions, have in recent years taken increased interest in selected manifestations of military norm violations such as homosexuality, violence directed toward supervisors and peers, and mutiny.

This study, however, has sought to conceptualize military norm violation in a more inclusive fashion by defining a more complete and systematic set of deviant-behavior categories in the military context. In addition to the traditional bifurcation of crimes against property and crimes against person, the conceptual paradigm has also introduced a third category of proscribed behavior: crimes against performance—a dereliction of expectation in regard to role behavior.

Military operations do not occur within a social vacuum. Unlike some institutional contexts, the military interfaces with several other social systems, and thus military behavior is subject to controls attendant to these interfaces as well as subject to its own internal constraints. The military, not infrequently encounters civilian populations, both friendly and enemy, and the consequent interaction is often subject to social control, both internal and external to the military institution. Similarly, in their confrontations with an enemy armed service, members of the military are contrained by norms originating both within the parent military and the enemy military, as well as even external to both, in some instances. There are, in effect, three separate contextual loci of normative control and deviancy, and the paradigm and discussion accordingly, treats intra-, extra-, and inter-occupational systems of military norms and subsequent violations. This book attempts to conceptualize military criminality, to articulate the typological components of the system, to document the existence of each categorical modality of deviancy, and to afford insights into the social causation of military criminality.

The military institution is essentially universal, historically as well as cross-culturally, and so too, are the social controls that affect it. Violation of these norms of social control are also universal. Some forms of military crime are as old as the pyramids and the campaigns of Alexander. Others are as recent as yesterday's news. Warriors in preliterate societies were subject to normative restraints on their behavior in training and combat just as are members of the military of modern industrial societies. Because military order and discipline are universal, as is military deviancy, this study has randomly drawn on illustrations, examples, and anecdotal accounts from many periods of history and from many different societies. The intent was to document the existence of many component similarities, historically and cross-culturally, within the military context of illegal and deviant behavior. The preponderance of examples, however, are taken from accounts, both historical and personal, in the American armed services.

Recent trends and events in the U.S. military may tend to alter or qualify some of the material contained in this discussion. The all-volunteer armed services of recent years may well introduce a new dimension to the military context for illegal behavior. While it is true that the pre–World War II military—the military about which James Jones wrote, for example—was an all-volunteer military, today's military differs considerably. The military of the 1930s was a depression military, and many young men who otherwise would have sought civilian careers joined the army or navy as an economic expedient when other jobs were unavailable. In many ways, such young men probably did not differ that much from their peers who had been fortunate enough to find civilian employment. Today's volunteer military, however, stands in considerable contrast to that of the pre–World War II era.

The volunteer U.S. military of today is experiencing considerable difficulty in recruiting an adequate number of qualified persons to fill its ranks, and there is widespread concern in some military circles about the problem of declining standards in attracting volunteers. Because the military cannot find sufficient numbers of volunteers who meet its educational and physical requirements, there is now a very vocal advocacy of reinstating the draft. The implications of the present-day and future population composition of the military, in terms of socioeconomic and intellectual abilities, for the occurrence of deviant behavior is difficult to predict, but it seems safe to assume that culturally deprived or intellectually substandard individuals make inept soldiers, and inept soldiers may have more difficulty in complying with the complexity of modern-day military normative order.

The contemporary volunteer military, especially the enlisted ranks, also contains a much higher proportion of blacks than in the 1930s and previously, and the percentage appears to be rising. For many blacks, the military affords career opportunities not previously or otherwise available, and in time both officer's and non-commissioned ranks will be filled with larger numbers of blacks. Exactly how this change in the racial composition of the

U.S. military will affect military culture and values remains to be seen. Similarly, what it may portend for discipline, racial rivalries, and conformity to traditional, largely white-oriented norms can only be inferred vaguely from the present situation. The Vietnam war experience saw considerable inter-racial hostility and conflict in the military, and this in turn was a contributing factor to the general erosion of discipline. Any military with prominent racial divisions has inherent potential problems of conflict and disorder, which could be dysfunctional to the military mission.

The introduction of an increasing number of women into the military is another unpredictable factor in the area of khaki-collar crime. How women, especially if their proportion in the armed services reaches a significant level, will react to military order and discipline, particularly in combat situations, is a question that has yet to be answered. Women police officers have proved to be very effective, even in situations involving dangerous or violent offenders. Their presence in previously all-male military units, however, could precipitate sexual rivalries and attendant conflict, as well as promote potentially disruptive flirtations, romances, or sexual affairs. However, a number of foreign military establishments have had sexually integrated units even in combat situations, and it would appear that these countries have experienced minimal disciplinary problems or disorder as a result. Likewise, the U.S. military has long had female nurses in medical units with no significant difficulty in maintaining order and efficiency. This may have been partly the result of the fact that nurses are officers, which effects sufficient social distance between them and male enlisted men. There are, however, accounts of enterprising servicemen sneaking into off-limits nurses' quarters, or vice versa, and otherwise accomplishing to interact socially or sexually with the nurses, often in violation of military proscription to the contrary.[1] The large number of WACs, Waves, and other women involved in clerical and logistical activities in the U.S. military during World War II, did not seem to foster organizational disequilibrium to a significant degree. Women are, however, now being utilized in positions in the U.S. military where only men were used before; the

---

[1] The U.S. Navy recently assigned both female officers and enlisted women to sea duty aboard the USS *Vulcan*, a 530-foot repair ship. This is the first and only ship with enlisted females. Already, however, it has been reported (Associated Press 1979) that there has been a "raid" of the enlisted women's quarters by some "rowdy sailors."

results are yet to be seen. At least one woman Coast Guard officer now commands a ship and an all-male crew. Women are flying planes in the Air Force, and presumeably will eventually be integrated into combat flight groups. Women may well prove to be more amenable to military order and discipline, and may be more circumspect in their adherence to military norms than men. It would seem reasonable to assume that women who have joined the volunteer armed services would have a military orientation. Also, as any new group will, the women will probably prove to be keener converts. Furthermore, the very presence of women in military units may well foster better conduct among the men. There have been experimental programs to intergrate male and female prisoners in some correctional institutions, and indications are that they are extremely successful in promoting good behavior. Inmates of both sexes apparently tend to try and be on their best behavior and exhibit the maximum decorum and conformity when in the presence of persons of the opposite sex. The sexual integration of military units may well promote a similar attitudal posture on the part of both service men and service women. Still, combat involving sexually integrated units may well introduce a whole new dimension to the situation, and how members of the military of both sexes will react will have significant import for possible deviant acts.

The increasing technological development of military weaponry and equipment may also have significance for the future of khaki-collar crime. With many of the emerging weapons systems, it is only necessary to push a button to destroy entire units or whole villages. In such a situation, it is far easier to assume an attitude of detachment from the act of destruction. "Smart-bombs" and rockets can find their targets with minimal help from an individual, and the massive firepower of many automatic weapons makes possible a more indiscriminate slaughter than the individual infantryman could accomplish in the past. In Vietnam, where the enemy was seldom seen by servicemen, destruction was often accomplished by saturation fire rather than aimed shots. The combat of the future may well involve an even more massive use of automated or otherwise technologically sophisticated weapons that, in effect, reduce the serviceman to little more than a technician servicing a machine. Operating an automatic weapon system in a heliocopter or a remote-controlled rocket becomes a game not unlike operating a pinball machine. Inasmuch as future

wars or "police actions" will likely be waged in Third World countries, where the indiginous population will stand in sharp cultural
contrast to our own military, it will probably be relatively easy to
conceptualize the enemy and the local civilian population as inferior, backward, or even subhuman. Thus, a combination of
technological detachment and cultural ethnocentrism may well
combine to facilitate military attrocities in the future.

Advancing technology may contribute to military crime in
other respects. Today there are machine systems that replace
human control, but in some instances the technological sophistication of some military equipment may exceed the ability of certain
individuals to effectively operate it. In spite of much more
elaborate training, some ships, planes, or other equipment may be
so complex that in certain emergencies the individual in charge
may not be able to control it properly. Human error could thus increase, and the individual accountable for the equipment may be
sanctioned for the results of his error. Even a slight lapse of attention or miniscule failure in judgment might well imperil a nuclear
carrier or cause irreparable damage to a multi-million dollar
equipment installation. If an infantry private can be held liable for
damage done to his rifle as a result of unintentional negligence, he
could more likely find himself guilty of negligence or misuse of
some far more sophisticated weaponry whose care and operation
he did not fully understand.

Criminal skills have a way of keeping pace with, if not exceeding, technological development. In today's business world,
white-collar criminals have emerged who are fully capable of ex-
ploiting corporate computer analysis and bookkeeping systems.
Similarly, larcenous employees have developed sufficient imagina-
tion to subvert the most convoluted organizational procedures to
their own benefit, and convert even the most esoteric company
property to their own profit. Military equipment and supplies have
become increasingly more expensive and accordingly are often
more tempting to persons of criminal bent than in the past. Also,
the military hardware of today is somewhat more convertible to a
civilian market than in the past. Electronic components or portable
X-ray equipment are far more salable and profitable than used
cavalry saddles or stale hardtack.

The younger generation of today, thanks in part to mass communications and a considerably more permissive cultural climate
since World War II, is far more independent minded, more preoc-

cupied with individual prerogatives, less militaristic, and much less ameneable to authoritative control and discipline than their ancestors. As we saw in Vietnam, American GI's (and this is true in other militaries as well) simply do not always react well to traditional military discipline, nor are they always prone to support the military mission enthusiastically. In the event of a reinstatement of the draft, the ranks of the army will be filled with large numbers of young men who have little penchant or toleration for military regimentation and authoritarianism, and who had not anticipated being in the military. Insubordination, hostility, violence directed toward superiors, and refusal to obey repugnant or hazardous orders may well increase in the future.

In the final analysis, individuals will probably be less inured to the stresses and dissaffections of military life in the future. The routine and regimentation of military life will fare less well in comparison to the freedom and material affluence of civilian life. Young men and women (and older as well) will likely be less attracted by the Hollywood image of the glory and glamour of war. In Vietnam and on television news they have seen the genuine nature of battle, the carnage and terror of real war, and what they have seen may well dilute their enthusiasm for combat. There is more escapism with drugs and alcohol today than in the past, and this trend will likely continue. Valorous performance in the face of the enemy and stoicism in captivity may become less frequent in future conflicts.

The military population of today (especially of the U.S.) is significantly different in social origin, ideology, and preoccupation, and the general response to the military milieu of its members, from the past. Military norms and order persist, but so too do violations of those norms. Given the changes that are occurring in military population and in military context, there is strong indication that military deviancy will, if anything, increase, and that the armed forces of this and other nations will continue to be confronted with the endemic malaise of khaki-collar crime.

References

ADAMS, JIM
1970   "G.I. Black Market Deals Confirmed." *Bowling Green–Park City* (Kentucky) *Daily News*, November 2.

ADLEMAN, ROBERT H., AND WALTON, GEORGE, COL.
1966   *The Devil's Brigade*. Radnor, Penna.: Chilton.

The Advocate
1975   "Second Sergeant Comes Out" and " 'Unfit' WACS Going to Court." August 13.

AMERICAN ANTHROPOLOGICAL ASSOCIATION
1967   "War: The Anthropology of Armed Conflict and Aggression." Plenary Session of the 66th Annual Meeting, later published as a collection of articles in a special supplement of *Natural History*, December 1.

American Heritage (Richard M. Ketchum, ed. in charge)
1960   *American Heritage Picture History of the Civil War*. 2 vols. New York: American Heritage.

ANDELMAN, DAVID A.
1974   "Married Cadet Is Found Guilty of Violating Code at West Point." *New York Times*, July 7.

ANDERSON, JACK
   1970   "Veterans Do Bustling Business Pushing Dope at Reed Hospital." Syndicated column, appearing in many newspapers across the country, August 13.

ANONYMOUS
   1945–46   "Informal Social Organization in the Army." *American Journal of Sociology* 51:365–70.

ASHWORTH, A.E.
   1968   "The Sociology of Trench Warfare, 1914–1918." *British Journal of Sociology* 19 (December):407–23.

ASSOCIATED PRESS
   1972a   "Statue Sales Irking NASA." *Roanoke Times*, July 22, p. 4.
   1972b   "Honor Withheld from Spacemen." *Roanoke Times*, July 23, p. A-2.
   1972c   "Astronaut Transferred." *Roanoke Times*, September 1.
   1972d   "Astronauts Sell Autographs." *Roanoke Times*, September 16.
   1972e   "Defense Rests Case in Fragging." *Roanoke Times*, November 12.
   1973a   "Pilot Allegedly Refuses to Fly B52 Bomb Mission." *Roanoke Times & World News*, January 11.
   1973b   "Naval Reservist Bucks Order to Have Hair Cut." *Roanoke Times*, March 24, p. 3.
   1974a   "Sailor Acquitted of Cursing Charge." *Roanoke Times*, June 26.
   1974b   "Army Rejected Bid for Justice Inquiry into an Ad Contract." *New York Times*, August 25.
   1974c   "Criminal Inquiry Kept in Army Circle." *Roanoke Times*, August 25.
   1974d   "His Beard Approved." *Roanoke Times*, December 19.
   1975a   "Self-styled Bisexual Sues to Stay in Naval Reserves." *New York Times*, July 6.
   1975b   "Sailor Shorn of Secret." *Roanoke Times*, October 4.
   1975c   "Woman Marine Officer Resigns." *Roanoke Times*, November 8, p. 12.
   1976a   "Navy Sets Court-martial Aboard Tied Destroyer." *Roanoke Times*, March 18, p. 41.
   1976b   "Four Charged by Marines in Death." *Roanoke Times*, April 29.
   1976c   "Army Meat Switch Detailed." *Roanoke Times*, May 11.
   1976d   "Gay Ensign Checks Out of Navy." *Roanoke Times*, June 4.
   1976e   "Ex-Belknap Officer Explains Failure to Ask Ship Direction." *Roanoke Times*, June 22.
   1976f   "Officer of Belknap Guilty in Collision." *Roanoke Times*, June 23.

1976g "Navy Places Curbs on Hairstyle Freedom." *Roanoke Times,* June 24, p. 2.

1976h "Homosexual Tries to Rejoin Navy: Claims Case Mishandled." *Roanoke Times,* June 28.

1976i "Marine DI Acquitted in Death of Recruit." *Roanoke Times,* June 29.

1977a "Army Woman Near Expulsion." *Roanoke Times and World News,* June 25.

1977b "Marine Gets 30 Years in Slaying." *Roanoke Times and World News,* July 29.

1978 "General Agrees to Retire." *Roanoke Times and World News,* April 29, p. A–3.

ATWELL, LESTER
1958 *Private.* New York: Popular Library.

AUBERT, VILHELM
1952 "White-collar Crime and Social Structure." *American Journal of Sociology* 58 (November):263–71.

BALDWIN, HANSON
1974 "Troubled Waters in the Navy: The U.S. Navy in Crisis," *The Saturday Evening Post* 246 (May):52–57.

BAREA, ARTURO
1972 *The Forging of a Rebel.* New York: Viking Press (A Richard Seaver Book).

BARNES, PETER
1972 *Pawns: The Plight of the Citizen-Soldier.* New York: Knopf.

BEACH, EDWARD L.
1966 *The Wreck of the Memphis.* New York: Holt, Rinehart and Winston.

BEDNAR, RICHARD J., CAPT.
1962 "Discharge and Dismissal as Punishment in the Armed Forces." *Military Law Review* 16 (April):1–42.

BELOTE, JAMES, AND BELOTE, WILLIAM
1970 *Typhoon of Steel: The Battle For Okinawa.* New York: Harper & Row.

BENSMAN, JOSEPH, AND GERVER, ISRAEL
1963 "Crime and Punishment in the Factory: The Function of Deviancy in Maintaining the Social System." *American Sociological Review* 28 (August):588–98.

BERGER, MORRAE
1946 "Law and Custom in the Army." *Social Forces* 25 (October):82–87.

BEVERIDGE, N. E.
1968 *Cups of Valor.* Harrisburg (Pa.): Stackpole Books.

BISHOP, JOSEPH W., JR.
1970   "The Quality of Military Justice." *New York Times Magazine*, February 22, pp. 32–40; see also *Justice Under Fire*. New York: Charterhouse, 1970.

BLACKMAN, N.
1947   "The Problem of Military Delinquency: A Statistical Study of 2,142 General Prisoners." *Journal of Clinical Psychopathology* 8 (July–October):849–61.

BLAKE, JOSEPH A.
1970   "The Organization as Instrument of Violence: The Military Case." *Sociological Quarterly* 11 (Summer):331–50.
1973   "The Anti-war Movement in the U.S. Military." Unpublished manuscript, University of New Mexico.

BLANKENSHIP, WILLIAM D.
1974   *The Leavenworth Irregulars*. Indianapolis: Bobbs-Merrill.

BLAU, ELEANOR
1974   "American Sikh Faces Court-martial for Failing to Remove His Beard and Turban." *New York Times*, January 6.

BLOEM, WALTER, CAPT.
1976   *The Advance from Mons*. New York: Award Books.

BOHANNAN, PAUL, ED.
1967   *Law and Warfare: Studies in the Anthropology of Conflict*. Garden City, N.Y.: Natural History Press.

BORUS, J.F.
1973   "Reentry: I. Adjustment Issues Facing the Vietnam Returnee." *Archives of General Psychiatry* 28 (April):501–506.

BOSHES, LOUIS D., AND HERMANN, PHILLIP J.
1947   "Study of Naval Delinquency by Questionnaire," *Journal of Criminal Law, Criminology and Police Science* 38 (September): 218–19.

BOWERS, FAUBIAN
1970   "How Japan Won the War." *New York Times Magazine*, August 30, pp. 5–7, 35–39, 42–44.

BOYINGTON, GREGORY "PAPPY," COL. (USMC, RET.)
1959   *Baa Baa Black Sheep*. New York: Dell.

BRAHAM, J.R.D.
1961   *Night Fighter*. New York: Norton.

BROTZ, H., AND WILSON, E.
1946   "Characteristics of Military Society." *American Journal of Sociology* 51 (March):372–74.

BROWN, DEE
1970   *Bury My Heart at Wounded Knee: An Indian History of the American West*. New York: Holt, Rinehart & Winston.

BROWN, KENNETH H.
1964   "The Brig," *Tulane Drama Review* 8 (Spring):222–59.

BROWNMILLER, SUSAN
1975   *Against Our Will.* New York: Simon & Schuster.

BRYANT, CLIFTON D.
1972   "Khaki-collar Crime: A Neglected Form of Occupational Deviance." Paper delivered at Annual Meeting of the Southern Sociological Society, New Orleans, Louisiana, April.
1973   *Deviant Behavior: Occupational and Organizational Bases.* Chicago: Rand McNally.
1978   "Full Military Honors: Ceremonial Interment in the Military." Unpublished paper.

CAFFREY, KATE
1973   *Out in the Midday Sun.* New York: Stein & Day.

CHAPPELL, RICHARD A.
1945   "Naval Offenders and Their Treatment," *Federal Probation* 4 (April):3–7.

CLIVE, WILLIAM
1973   *The Tune That They Play.* New York: Simon & Schuster.

COHEN, ALBERT K.
1966   *Deviance and Control.* Englewood Cliffs, N.J.: Prentice-Hall.

COLLINS, ORVIS; DALTON, MELVILLE; AND ROY, DONALD
1946   "Restriction of Output and Social Cleavage in Industry." *Applied Anthropology* 5 (Summer):1–14.

COLLINS, WHIT
1971   "Patton: Guns Made Him Great." *Guns and Ammo* 15 (August): 30–34, 80–81.

COOMBS, FRAN
1976   "Some Still Trying Enlistment to Avoid Local Prosecution," *Roanoke Times & World News*, March 28.

CORNSWEET, A.C., AND LOCKE, B.
1949   "Alcohol as a Factor in Naval Delinquencies." *Naval Medical Bulletin* 46 (November):1690–95.

CRAIN, WILLIAM
1964   "The Chronic 'Mess-up' and His Changing Character." *Federal Probation* 28 (June):50–56.

CROMLEY, RAY
1971a "Army Takes Practical and Humane Approach to Drugs." *Bowling Green–Park City Daily News* (a nationally syndicated newspaper column), January 26.
1971b "Drugs-for-GI's Traffic Booms." *Bowling Green-Park City Daily News* (a nationally syndicated newspaper column), July 11.

CROWDER, ENOCH A.
1919–1920 "Courts-martial Sentences During the War," *Journal of Criminal Law, Criminology and Police Science* 10 (May):16–41.

Daily Oklahoman
1973 "Tinker Theft Trial Witness Short on Detail." April 4, p. 16.

DALLIN, ALEXANDER
1952 *The Kaminsky Brigade 1941–1944: A Case Study of German Military Exploitation of Soviet Disaffection.* Cambridge, Mass.: Harvard University Press (Russian Research Center).

DALTON, MELVILLE
1948 "The Industrial 'Rate-buster': A Characterization." *Applied Anthropology* 7 (Winter):5–18.

DANIELS, ARLENE K., AND DANIELS, RICHARD R.
1964 "The Social Function of the Career Fool." *Psychiatry* 27 (August):219–29.

DEPARTMENT OF THE ARMY (HEADQUARTERS)
1963 *Military Law and Boards of Office.* ROTCM 148–85. Washington: Government Printing Office.
1967 *Military Training Management.* Department of the Army Field Manual FM–21–5. Washington: Government Printing Office.
1969 *Manual for Courts-Martial United States 1969.* Rev. ed. Washington: Government Printing Office.

DiMONA, JOSEPH
1972 *Great Court-Martial Cases.* New York: Grosset & Dunlap.

DORNBUCH, SANFORD M.
1955 "The Military Academy as an Assimilating Institution." *Social Forces* 33 (May):316–21.

DOUGHERTY, CLIFTON A., COL., AND LYNCH, NORMAN B., LT. COMMANDER
1968 "Administrative Discharge: Loophole in Military Justice?" *Trial* 4 (February/March):19–21.

DRUSS, RICHARD G.
1967 "Cases of Suspected Homosexuality Seen at an Army Mental Hygiene Consultation Service." *Psychiatric Quarterly* 41 (January):62–70.

DUBERMAN, MARTIN
1975 "The Case of the Gay Sergeant." *New York Times Magazine,* November 9, pp. 16–17, 58–71.

DUGAN, JAMES, AND LAFORE, LAURENCE
1973 *Days of Emperor and Clown: Italo-Ethiopian War, 1935–1936.* Garden City, N.Y.: Doubleday.

DUNCAN, DONALD
1967 *The New Legions.* New York: Random House.

EDWARDS, MICHAEL
1973   *A Season in Hell.* New York: Taplinger.

EINSTADTER, WERNER J.
1969   "The Social Organization of Armed Robbery." *Social Problems*
17 (Summer):64–83.

ELKIN, HENRY
1946   "Aggressive and Erotic Tendencies in Army Life." *American
Journal of Sociology* 51 (March):408–13.

ELLACOTT, S.E.
1970   *The Seaman.* 2 vols. London: Abelard-Schuman.

EMERSON, GLORIA
1971   "A Major in Vietnam Gives All He's Got to the War on Heroin."
New York Times, September 12, p. 2.
1972   *Winners and Losers.* New York: Random House.

ERIKSON, KAI F., AND MARLOWE, DAVID H.
1959   "The Schizophrenic in Basic Training." Pp. 99–133 in Lt. Col.
Kenneth L. Artiss, ed., *The Symptom as Communication in
Schizophrenia.* New York: Grune & Stratton.

EVERETT, ROBINSON O.
1972   "Some Comments on the Role of Discretion in Military Justice."
Law and Contemporary Problems 39 (Winter):173–215.

FALK, RICHARD Q.; KOLKO, GABRIEL; AND LIFTON, ROBERT JAY, EDS.
1971   *Crimes of War.* New York: Random House.

FISCHER, K.
1932   *Das militar.* Zurich: Steinmetz Verlag.

FITZGIBBON, LOUIS
1971   *Katyn.* London: Stacey.

FORT, JOHN P., JR.
1966   "Heroin Addiction Among Young Men." Pp. 76–91 in John A.
O'Donnell and John C. Ball, eds., *Narcotic Addiction.* New
York: Harper & Row.

FRIEDMAN, LEON, ED.
1972   *The Law of War: A Documentary History.* 2 vols. New York:
Random House.

GALE, LESLIE G.
1970   "The Civilianization of Crime in the U.S. Military: An
unlooked-for Corollary of the Civilanization Hypothesis in
Military Sociology." Paper read at the Sixty-fifth Annual
Meeting of the American Sociological Association, Washington,
D.C., September 1.

GARDNER, FRED
1970   *The Unlawful Concert.* New York: Viking.

GAULT, WILLIAM BARRY
  1971 "Some Remarks on Slaughter." *American Journal of Psychiatry* 128 (October): 82–86.

GEIS, GILBERT
  1962 "Toward a Delineation of White-collar Offenses." *Sociological Inquiry* 32 (Spring):160–71.
  1968 *White-Collar Ciminal: The Offender in Business and the Professions.* New York: Atherton.

GELLER, ALLEN, AND BOAS, MAXWELL
  1969 *The Drug Beat.* New York: McGraw-Hill.

GIBBS, D. N.
  1957 "The National Serviceman and Military Delinquency." *The Sociological Review* 5 (December): 255–263.

GILBERT, ARTHUR N.
  1974 "The *Africaine* Courts-martial: A Study of Buggery and the Royal Navy." *Journal of Homosexuality* 1 (1):111–22.

GILES, JANICE HOLT
  1965 *The GI Diary of Sergeant Giles.* Boston: Houghton-Mifflin.

GLOVER, MICHAEL
  1973 *An Assemblage of Indian Army Soldiers and Uniforms.* London: Perpetua.

GOFFMAN, ERVING
  1961 *Asylums.* Garden City, N.Y.: Doubleday.

GROVE, MICHAEL L.
  1977 "The Summary Court-martial in Constitutional Perspective." *Houston Law Review* 14 (January):449–73.

HAKEEM, MICHAEL
  1946 "Service in the Armed Forces and Criminality." *Journal of Criminal Law and Criminality* 37 (May-June): 120–131.

HALEY, JAMES L.
  1976 *The Buffalo War: The History of the Red River Indian Uprising of 1874.* Garden City, N.Y.: Doubleday.

HAMMER, RICHARD
  1971 *The Court-Martial of Lt. Calley.* New York: Coward, McCann & Geoghegan.

HARE, JOHN S.
  1940 "Military Punishments in the War of 1812." *Journal of the American Military Institute* 4 (Winter):225–39.

HARRINGTON, FRED HARVEY
  1942 "The Fort Jackson Mutiny." *Journal of Negro History* 27 (October):420–31.

HARRIS, DAVID
1979 "War Made Easy by Conscription," *Roanoke Times & World News*, March 4, p. F–3.

HART, ROLAND J.
1978 "Crime and Punishment in the Army," *Journal of Personality and Social Psychology* 36 (December):1456–71.

HARTUNG, FRANK E.
1950 "White-collar Offenders in the Wholesale Meat Industry in Detroit." *American Journal of Sociology* 56 (July):25–34.

HEADRICK, RITA
1978 "African Soldiers in World War II." *Armed Forces and Society* 4 (Spring):501–26.

HEBERLE, RUDOLF
1936 "Structure and Texture of Combat Troops." Unpublished manuscript translated from a German version that originally appeared in *Soldatentum* (a journal published by the psychological testing and morale branch of the German Reichswehr) in 1936.

HEMINGWAY, ERNEST
1968 "Introduction." Pp. 5–20 in Ernest Hemingway, ed. *Men at War*. New York: Berkeley.

HERSEY, JOHN
1947 *The War Lover*. New York: Knopf.

HERSH, SEYMOUR
1970 "My-Lai 4: A Report on the Massacre and Its Aftermath." *Harper's* 240 (May):53–84.
1972 *Cover-Up*. New York: Random House.

HODGES, H. EUGENE
1974 "A Sociological Analysis of Dud Behavior in the United States Army." Pp. 27–43 in Clifton D. Bryant, ed., *Deviant Behavior: Occupational and Organizational Bases*. Chicago: Rand McNally.

HOLLES, EVERETT
1971 "Navy Drug Center on Coast Is Vexed." *New York Times*, November 14.

HOLLINGSHEAD, AUGUST
1946 "Adjustments to Military Life." *American Journal of Sociology* 51 (March):440.

HOOK, JUDITH
1972 *The Sack of Rome*. London: Macmillan.

HORNING, DONALD N.M.
1970 "Blue-collar Theft: Conceptions of Property, Attitudes Toward

Pilfering, and Work Group Norms in a Modern Industrial Plant." Pp. 46–64 in Erwin O. Smigel and H. Laurence Ross, eds., *Crimes Against Bureaucracy*. New York: Van Nostrand Reinhold.

HOUGH, RICHARD
1973   *Captain Bligh and Mr. Christian: The Men and the Mutiny*. New York: Dutton.

HUIE, WILLIAM BRADFORD
1954   *The Execution of Private Slovik*. New York: New American Library (A Signet Book).

JABLONSKI, EDWARD
1965   *Flying Fortress*. Garden City, N.Y.: Doubleday.

JANIS, IRVING L.
1945   "Psychodynamics of Adjustment to Army Life." *Psychiatry* 8 (May):159.

JANOWITZ, MORRIS
1960   *The Professional Soldier*. New York: Free Press.

JEFFERS, H. PAUL, AND LEVITAN, DICK
1971   *See Paris and Die*. New York: Hawthorn Books, Inc.

JOHNSON, HAYNES, AND WILSON, GEORGE C.
1972   *Army in Anguish*. New York: Pocket Books.

JOHNSON, PAUL
1979   "Also Known as Bertie" (a review of Edward VII: Prince and King). *The New York Times Book Review*, February 25, pp. 7, 34.

JONES, JAMES
1953   *From Here to Eternity*. New York: The New American Library.

JOSEPH, NATHAN, AND ALEX, NICHOLAS
1972   "The Uniform: A Sociological Perspective." *American Journal of Sociology* 77 (January):719–30.

Journal of Criminal Law, Criminology, and Police Science
1970   "O'Callahan v. Parker, 395 U.S. 258 (1969): New Limitation on Court-martial Jurisdiction." 61 (June):195–206.

KANTOR, MACKINLAY
1955   *Andersonville*. Cleveland and New York: World.

KARSTEN, PETER
1978   *Law, Soldiers and Combat*. Westport, Conn.: Greenwood.

KATZ, ROBERT
1973   *Massacre in Rome*. New York: Ballantine Books.

KAY, MAJOR WILLIAM K.
1971   "Isham Randolph Harrison." Pp. 168–84 in Martin Windrow and Frederick Wilkinson, eds., *The Universal Soldier: Fourteen*

Studies in Campaign Life, A.D. *43–1944*. Garden City, N.Y.: Doubleday.

KECSKEMETI, PAUL
1957 *Strategic Surrender: The Politics of Victory and Defeat*. Santa Monica: Rand Corporation.

KEEGAN, JOHN
1976 *The Face of Battle*. New York: Viking.

KIMMEL, HUSBAND E.
1955 *Admiral Kimmel's Story*. Chicago: Henry Regnery.

KIPLING, RUDYARD
1940 *Rudyard Kipling's Verse*. Garden City, N.Y.: Doubleday.

KIRKPATRICK, CLIFFORD, AND KANIN, EUGENE
1957 "Male Sex Aggression on a University Campus." *American Sociological Review* 22 (February):52–58.

KLAPP, ORRIN E.
1962 *Heroes, Villains and Fools* (esp. chap. 3, "Fools," pp. 69–91). Englewood Cliffs, N.J.: Prentice-Hall.

KNOLL, ERWIN, AND McFADDEN, JUDITH NIES, EDS.
1970 *War Crimes and the American Conscience*. New York: Holt, Rinehart and Winston.

KNOPF, RICHARD C.
1956 "Crime and Punishment in the Legion, 1792–1793." *Historical and Philosophical Society of Ohio Bulletin* 14 (July):232–38.

KNUDTEN, RICHARD D.
1970 "The System of Military Justice." Chapter 19 of *Crime in a Complex Society: An Introduction to Criminology*. Homewood, Ill.: Dorsey Press.

KROLL, JEROME
1976 "Racial Patterns of Military Crimes in Vietnam." *Psychiatry* 39 (February):51–64.

LAFFIN, JOHN
1973 *Americans in Battle*. New York: Crown.

LAMMERS, CORNELIS J.
1969 "Strikes and Mutinies: A Comparative Study of Organizational Conflicts Between Rules and Ruled." *Administrative Science Quarterly* 14 (December):558–72.

LANE, MARK
1970 *Conversations with Americans*. New York: Simon & Schuster.

LANG, DANIEL
1969 *Casualties of War*. New York: McGraw-Hill.

LECKIE, ROBERT
1957 *Helmet for My Pillow*. New York: Random House.

LEE, ALTON
  1966   "The Army 'Mutiny' of 1946." *Journal of American History* 53 (December):555–71.

LENGEL, JOHN
  1971   "Army Drug Problem Unique, Stoned Soldiers Do Dull and Dangerous." *Bowling Green-Park City Daily News*, April 7, p. 9.

LEVY, CHARLES
  1971   "ARVN as Faggots: Inverted Warfare in Vietnam." *Transaction* 8 (October):18–27.

LEWIN, LEONARD C.
  1967   Introductory material to *Report From Iron Mountain on the Possibility and Desirability of Peace*. New York: Dell.

LEWALLEN, JOHN
  1971   *Ecology of Devastation: Indochina*. Baltimore: Penguin.

LEWIS, DAVID L.
  1973   *Prisoners of Honor: The Dreyfus Affair*. New York: Morrow.

Life
  1956   "The Trial of the Corps." *Life* (July 30):29–32.

LIFTON, R.J.
  1973   *Home from the War*. New York: Simon & Schuster.

LINDEN, EUGENE
  1972   "Fragging and Other Withdrawal Symptoms: The Demoralization of an Army." *Saturaday Review* 55 (January 8):12–17, 55.

LITTLE, ROGER W.
  1956   "The 'Sick Soldier' and the Medical Ward Officer." *Human Organization* 15 (Spring):22–24.

Los Angeles Times
  1972   "Astronaut Attempted to Stop the Sale of 100 Postal Covers." *Roanoke Times*, September 4, p. 1.

LOWRY, ROBERT
  1971   *Casualty*. Westport, Conn.: Greenwood.

LYNCH, NORMAN B.
  1970   "The Administrative Discharge: Changes Needed?" *University of Maine Law Review* 22 (1):141–69.

LYON, WALDO B.
  1969   "Military Service and American Youth: Some Reflections After 17 Years of Psychological Evaluation of Navy and Marine Corps Recruits." *American Journal of Orthopsychiatry* 39 (March):223–24.

  1972   "Military Service and American Youth: Some Reflections After Seven Years of Psychological Evaluation of Marine Corps Recruits." *Psychiatric Opinion* 9 (December):22–27.

MacCormick, Austin H.
1946 "Statistical Study of 24,000 Military Prisoners," *Federal Probation* 10 (April):6–11.

MacDonald, Charles B.
1947 *Company Commander.* Washington: Infantry Journal Press.

Malinowski, Bronislaw
1961 *Argonauts of the Western Pacific.* New York: Dutton.

Mannheim, Hermann
1940 *War and Crime.* London: Watts & Co.

Marcovitz, Eli, Capt., and Myers, Henry J., Capt.
1944 "The Marijuana Addict in the Army." *War Medicine* 6 (December):382–91.

Mares, William
1971 *The Marine Machine.* Garden City, N.Y.: Doubleday.

Marjot, D. H.
1977 "Delirium Tremens in the Royal Navy and British Army in the 19th Century." *Journal of Studies of Alcohol* 38 (Spetember): 1613–23.

Marshall, S.L.A.
1947 *Men Under Fire.* New York: Morrow.

Marszalek, John F., Jr.
1972 *Court-Martial: A Black Man in America.* New York: Charles Scribner's Sons.

Mathews, Jay
1975 "Homosexual GI Fights Release from Service." *Washington Post*, May 28.

Matthews, Allen R.
1947 *The Assault.* New York: Simon & Schuster.

Mattick, Hans W.
1954 "Parolees in the Army During World War II." *Federal Probation* 24 (September):49–55.

Maurer, Maurer
1964 "Military Justice under General Washington." *Military Affairs* 28 (Spring):8–16.
1965 "The Court-martialing of Camp Followers, World War I." *American Journal of Legal History* 9 (July):203–15.

McCallum, Malcolm
1946 "The Study of the Delinquent in the Army." *American Journal of Sociology* 51 (March):479–82.

McDonagh, Edward C.
1945 "Military Social Controls," *Sociology and Social Research* 29 (January–February):197–205.

McGRADY, MIKE
1968   *A Dove in Vietnam.* New York: Funk & Wagnalls.

McGRORY, MARY
1976   "Brutality Continues: Tell It to the Marines." *Roanoke Times,* May 1.

McKEAN, WILLIAM BAGGARLEY
1958   *Ribbon Creek.* New York: Dial.

McKEE, CHRISTOPHER
1978   "Fantasies of Mutiny and Murder: A Suggested Psychohistory of the Seaman in the United States Navy, 1798–1815." *Armed Forces and Society* 4 (February):293–304.

MELVILLE, HERMAN
n.d.   *White Jacket.* New York: Grove Press.
1962   *Billy Bud, Sailor (An Inside Narrative).* Chicago: University of Chicago Press (Phoenix Books).

MILLER, STUART C.
1970   "Our My Lai of 1900: Americans in the Philippine Insurrection." *Transaction* 7 (September):19–28.

MOORE, ROBIN, AND COLLINS, JUNE
1971   *The Khaki Mafia.* New York: Crown.

MORGAN, SAMUEL
1946   "Army Courts-martial: The Double Standard." *Atlantic* 178 (December):97–102.

MORRIS, ERIC
1973   *Blockade: Berlin and the Cold War.* New York: Stein & Day.

MOSCOS, CHARLES C.
1970   *The American Enlisted Man: The Rank and File in Today's Military.* New York: Russell Sage Foundation.
1973   "Studies on the American Soldier: Continuities and Discontinuities in Social Research." Paper read at the Annual Meeting of the American Sociological Association, New York.

MURPHY, EDWARD R., JR.
1971   *Second in Command.* New York: Holt, Rinehart and Winston.

NATIONAL SCIENCE FOUNDATION
1978   "Computer Security." *Mosic* 9 (July/August):2–10.

NEUMANN, PETER
1958   *The Black March.* New York: Bantam Books
1960   *Other Men's Graves.* London: Weidenfeld and Nicolson.

Newsweek
1970a   "Court-martial: The Trial of One G.I. for Murder." 76, August 31:21.
1970b   "U.S. Military Justice on Trial." 76 (August 31):18–23.

1971   "The Troubled U.S. Army in Vietnam." 77 (January 11):29–37.
1974a "Attention! (Please)." 84 (November 4):45.
1974b "The Dumdum Debate," 84 (September 9):53–54.
1975   "The Cat's Meow." 86 (September 22):33.

New York Times
1971   "Navy Reports Rise in Drug Discharges." October 10, p. 35.
1974   "Seabee Louie Makes History." December 1.
1979a "Beating a Tattoo," March 4, p. E–9.
1979b "Marine in Hanoi is Facing Inquiry in Return to U.S." March 4:26.

New York Times NEWS SERVICE
1972   "Navy Schedules Hearings on Bias Charges," *Roanoke Times*, November 12.

NITOBE, INAZO
1968   *Bushido, The Soul of Japan.* Los Angeles: O'Hara.

O'CONNOR, RICHARD
1973   *The Spirit Soldiers.* New York: Putnam.

PABEL, REINHOLD
1955   *Enemies Are Human.* New York: Holt, Rinehart and Winston.

PACIFICA TAPE LIBRARY
1973   "The Kitty Hawk Trials." Pacifica Tape Library Program, BC1150.

Parade
1973   "Hippie Army." October 7.

PARKS, DAVID
1968   *GI Diary.* New York: Harper & Row.

PEACOCK, JERE
1962   *Valhalla.* New York: Dell.

PETERSON, DAVID M.
1971   "Informal Norms and Police Practice: The Case of the Quota System." *Sociology and Social Research* 55 (April):354–62.

PIRTLE, CALEB, III
1974   "A Haitian Diary." *Southern Living* 9 (November):96–99, 106–109.

QUINNEY, RICHARD
1963   "Occupational Structure and Criminal Behavior." *Social Problems* II (Fall):180–85.

RADINE, LAWRENCE B.
1977   *The Taming of The Troops: Social Control in the United States Army.* Westport, Conn.: Greenwood Press, p. xi.

Ramparts
1971   *Two, Three . . . Many Vietnams.* San Francisco: Canfield.

RANDAL, JONATHAN C.
1972   "The Girls They Left Behind," *The Washington Post*, September 24, p. B-4.

REID, P. R.
1953   *Escape From Colditz.* Philadelphia: J. B. Lippincott Company.

REVIE, ALASTAIR
1974   *The Bomber Command.* New York: Ballantine Books.

Roanoke Times
1976   "Vice Scandal." August 8.

ROBINSON, H. RUSSELL
1971   "Caius Largennius" Pp. 17–31 in Martin Windrow and Frederick Wilkinson, eds., *The Universal Soldier.* Garden City, N.Y.: Doubleday.

ROY, DONALD
1952   "Quota Restriction and Goldbricking in a Machine Shop." *American Journal of Sociology* 57 (March):427–42.
1953   "Work Satisfaction and Social Reward in Quota Achievement: An Analysis of Piecework Incentive." *American Sociological Review* 18 (October):507–14.
1954   "Efficiency and the 'Fix': Informal Intergroup Relations in a Piecework Machine Shop." *American Journal of Sociology* 60 (November):255–66.
1959   "Banana Time: Job Satisfaction and Informal Interaction." *Human Organization* 18 (Winter):158–68.

RUGABER, WALTER
1971   "PX's: Hands in the Till at the 'Big Store'." *New York Times*, November 7, sec. E, p. 6.

RYAN, CORNELIUS
1966   *The Last Battle.* New York: Simon & Schuster.
1974   *The Bridge Too Far.* New York: Simon & Schuster.

SAJER, GUY
1972   *The Forgotten Soldier.* Translated by Lily Emmet. New York: Ballantine Books.

SCHELL, JONATHAN
1967   *The Village of Ben Suc.* New York: Knopf.

SCHNEIDER, ALEXANDER, J. N. AND CYRUS W. LAGRONE, JR.
1945   "Delinquents in the Army: A Statistical Study of 500 Rehabilitation Center Prisoners." *American Journal of Psychiatry* 102 (July): 82–91.

SCHREIBER, E. M., AND WOELFEL, JOHN C.
1977   "Women in Men's Boots: Performance and Adjustment of Women in the Coed American Army of the 1970's." Paper

presented at the 72nd Annual Meeting of the American Sociological Association in Chicago, Illinois, September 9.

SECRETARY OF WAR
1892 *Annual Report of the Secretary of War for the Year 1891.* Volume 1. Washington: Government Printing Office.

SEGAL, DAVID R.
1977 "Illicit Drug Use in the U.S. Army." *Sociological Symposium* (Spring):66–83.

SHAINBERG, DAVID
1967 "Motivations of Adolescent Military Offenders." *Adolescence* 2 (Summer): 243–254.

SHATON, C. F.
1973 "The Grief of Soldiers: Vietnam Combat Veterans' Self-help Movement." *American Journal of Orthopsychiatry* 43 (July):640–53.

SHEEHAN, NEIL
1971 *The Arnheiter Affair.* New York: Dell.

SHERMAN, EDWARD T.
1970 "The Civilization of Military Law." *University of Maine Law Review* 22 (1): 3–103.

SHERRILL, ROBERT
1970 *Military Justice Is to Justice as Military Music Is to Music.* (esp. chap. 2, "The Presidio 'Mutiny' ") New York: Harper & Row.

SHILS, EDWARD A., AND JANOWITZ, MORRIS
1948 "Cohesion and Disintegration in the Wehrmacht in World War II." *Public Opinion Quarterly* 12 (Summer):280–315.

SINGER, J. DAVID, AND SMALL, MELVIN
1972 *The Wages of War, 1816–1965: A Statistical Handbook.* New York: Wiley.

SIPE, WARREN
1959 "Deutsche Drillinge." Pp. 136–140 in John T. Amber, ed., *Gun Digest.* 13th edition. Chicago: Gun Digest Company.

SLATER, PHILIP
1970 *The Pursuit of Loneliness: American Culture at the Breaking Point.* Boston: Beacon Press.

STACK, RICHARD
1975 *Warriors: A Parris Island Photo Journal.* New York: Harper & Row.

STANTON, M. DUNCAN
1973 "The Soldier." Pp. 407–502 in D. Spiegel and P. Keith-Spiegel, eds., *Outsiders USA.* San Francisco: Rinehart Press.

STODDARD, ELLWYN
    1968   "The Informal 'Code' of Police Deviancy: A Group Approach to 'Blue-coat' Crime." *Journal of Criminal Law, Criminology, and Police Science* 59 (June):201–13.

STOUFFER, SAMUEL, ET. AL.
    1949   *The American Soldier.* vol. 1, pp. 411–12. Princeton, N.J.: Princeton University Press.

STRENGHOLT, ROY D.
    1962   "The Bably Nambu." Pp. 158–60 in *Gun Digest.* 17th ed. Chicago: Follett.

SUSKIND, JEROME A.
    1965   "Military Administration Discharge Boards: The Right to Confrontation and Cross Examination." *Michigan State Bar Journal* 44 (January):25–32.

SUTHERLAND, EDWIN H.
    1940   "White-collar Criminality." *American Sociological Review* 5 (February):1–12.

SWEET, LOUISE
    1965   "Camel Raiding of North Arabian Bedouin: A Mechanism of Ecological Adaptation." *American Anthropologist* 67 (October):1132–50.

SWIFT, PAMELA
    1975   "Hair Again" in "Keeping Up With Youth" column, *Roanoke Times,* March 2.
          "Army of Hippies" in "Keeping Up With Youth" column, *Roanoke Times,* July 6.

SZASZ, THOMAS S.
    1972   "Scapegoating 'Military Addicts': The Helping Hand Strikes Again." *Transaction* 9 (January):4–6.

TAUBER, PETER
    1971   *The Sunshine Soldiers.* New York: Ballantine.

TAYLOR, TELFORD
    1971   *Nuremberg and Vietnam: An American Tragedy.* New York: Bantam Books.
    1972   "Foreword." Pp. xiii–xxv in Leon Friedman, ed., *The Law of War: A Documentary History.* 2 vols. New York: Random House.

THOMAS HUGH
    1961   *The Spanish Civil War.* New York: Harper & Row.

Time
    1956   "The Trial of Sergeant McKeon." *Time* (July 30):12–14.
    1968   "Russia: Power Play on the Oceans." 91 (February 23):23–28.

TIMES WIRE DISPATCHES
1975 "Church Takes Justice Stance." *Roanoke Times*, July 5.

TOLAND, JOHN
1959 *Battle: The Story of The Bulge*. New York: New American Library.
1971 *The Rising Sun: The Decline and Fall of the Japanese Empire, 1936–1945*. New York: Bantam Books.

TOMPKINS, DOROTHY CAMPBELL
1967 *White Collar Crime: A Bibliography*. Berkeley: Institute of Governmental Studies, University of California.

TRENAMAN, JOSEPH
1952 *Out of Step*. London: Methuen & Co.

TRIP, C. A.
1975 *The Homosexual Matrix*. New York: McGraw-Hill.

TURNBULL, S. R.
1977 *The Samurai: A Military History*. New York: Macmillan.

UJEVICH, ROBERT M.
1969 *Military Justice: A Summary of Its Legislative and Judicial Development*. Washington: Library of Congress (American Law Division).

U.S. DEPARTMENT OF ARMY
1952 *The Army Correctional System*. Washington, D.C.: Office of the Adjutant General, U.S. Department of Army.

UNITED STATES SENATE COMMITTEE ON GOVERNMENT OPERATIONS (PERMANANT SUBCOMMITTEE ON INVESTIGATIONS)
1971 *Report on Fraud and Corruption in Management of Military Club Systems: Illegal Currency Manipulation Affecting South Vietnam*. Report No. 92–418. Washington: Government Printing Office.

UNITED STATES GOVERNMENT
1969 *Manual for Court-Martial United States 1969*. Rev. ed. Washington: Government Printing Office.

VATH, RAYMOND EUGENE
1965 *The Influence of Military Service on Rates of Alcoholism in the General Population*. Medical thesis, University of Washington School of Medicine, Seattle.

VAYDA, ANDREW P.
1967 "Maori Warfare." Pp. 359–80 in Paul Bohannan, ed., *Law and Warfare: Studies in the Anthropology of Conflict*. Garden City, N.Y.: Natural History Press.

VIDICH, ARTHUR J., AND STEIN, MAURICE R.
1960 "The Dissolved Identity in Military Life." Pp. 493–506 in

Maurice R. Stein, Arthur J. Vidich, and David Manning White, eds., *Identity and Anxiety: Survival of the Person in Mass Society*. New York: Free Press.

VIETNAMESE VETERANS AGAINST THE WAR
The Winter Soldier Investigation: An Inquiry into American War Crimes. Boston: Beacon Press.

WALLINGA, J. B.
1956 "Severe Alcoholism in Career Military Personnel." *U.S. Armed Forces Medical Journal* 7 (April):551–61.

WAR DEPARTMENT
1940 *Rules of Land Warfare*. FM 27–10. Washington: Government Printing Office.

WARD, CHRISTOPHER
1952 *The War of the Revolution*, edited by John Richard Alden. 2 vols. New York: Macmillan.

WARE, EUGENE F., CAPT.
1960 *The Indian War of 1864*. New York: St. Martin's Press.

Washington Star-News
1973 "Army General Sentenced." *Roanoke Times*, February 10, p. 26.

WEINBERG, S. KIRSON
1945 "Problems of Adjustment in an Army Unit." *American Journal of Sociology* 50 (January):272.

WEINRAUB, BERNARD
1977 "Carter Disciplines General Singlaub, Who Attacked His Policy on Korea." *New York Times*, May 22, p. 1.

WEISS, MELFORD
1967 "Rebirth in the Airborne." *Transaction* 4 (May):23–26.

WELTNER, GEORGE A.
1947 "Millions of Guilty Men." *Harper's* 194 (January):81–84.

WEST, LOUIS JOLYON, MAJ., AND SWEGAN, WILLIAM H., M. SGT.
1956 "An Approach to Alcoholism in the Military Service." *American Journal of Psychiatry* 112 (June):1004–1009.

WESTLEY, WILLIAM A.
1953 "Violence and the Police." *American Journal of Sociology* 59 (July):34–41.

WHITING, CHARLES
1971 *Massacre at Malmédy*. New York: Stein & Day.

WHITNEY, CRAIG R.
1974 "Army Feuds with Officer on Haircut." *New York Times*, September 8.

WHITTINGHAM, RICHARD
  1971 *Martial Justice: The Last Mass Execution in the United States.*
        Chicago: Henry Regnery Company.

WILKINSON, FREDERICK
  1971 "Roger de Dinan." Pp. 32–46 in Martin Windrow and Freder-
        ick Wilkinson, eds., *The Universal Soldier.* Garden City, N.Y.:
        Doubleday & Company, Inc.

WILLIAMS, COLLIN J., AND WEINBERG, MARTIN S.
  1971 "The Military: Its Processing of Accused Homosexuals."
        American Behavioral Scientist 14 (November/December):
        203–17; for fuller exposition, see *Homosexuals and the Military:
        A Study of Less Than Honorable Discharge.* New York: Harper
        & Row.

WILTSEY, NORMAN B.
  1961 "Spencer's Great 7-shooter." Pp. 4–13 in John T. Amber, ed.,
        Gun Digest. 16th ed. Chicago: Follett Publishing Company.

WINCOTT, LEN
  1974 *Invergordon Mutineer.* London: Weidenfeld and Nicolson.

WINICK, CHARLES, AND KINSIE, PAUL M.
  1971 *The Lively Commerce: Prostitution in the United States.* New
        York: New American Library.

WOOD, S. M.
  1966 "Uniform—Its Significance as a Factor in Role-relationships."
        Sociological Review 14 (July):139–51.

WOUK, HERMAN
  1951 *The Caine Mutiny.* Garden City, N.Y.: Doubleday.

ZURCHER, LOUIS A., JR.
  1965 "The Sailor Aboard Ship: A Study of Role Behavior in a Total
        Institution." *Social Forces* 43 (March):389–400.
  1967 "The Naval Recruit Training Center: A Study of Role Assimila-
        tion in a Total Institution." *Sociological Inquiry* 37 (Winter):
        85–98.

Name Index

379

Subject Index

384